GW00853508

The
Great Golf Hotel
2000 Guide

A Big Publishing Publication

Welcome to

Fore!word

When I'm asked the question, "Peter, what exactly do you do?", my reply, at the end of the day, is that I travel, play golf and write about it. Reactions to that answer tend to fall into two categories. One is that this is not a real 'go to the office' grown up job and that they know someone who could maybe help me when my summer holiday is over. Fine, but I am 38! The other raises a rather interesting issue – is going on lots of golf holidays really travelling?

My feeling is that, just as our holiday habits have progressed from bucket-and-spade trips to a beach near a charter airport, golf travel will do the same. I don't mean that our children will go off with rucksac replaced by golf bag, trekking for days to find a 100 Baht room with views over the sixth green on one side and the Gulf of Thailand on the other – sadly, those rooms will never exist. I mean you and I enjoying the world's great golf courses and the world's most beautiful places in the same journey.

The long-haul golf market is small at the moment, but it is the fastest growing sector and in many ways it is what this book is all about. Look beyond the simple packages and let golf take you closer to the flora, fauna and culture of the destinations covered here.

The experiences that I have had this year – trying to organise a tee-time in Kenya, hunting for size 11 golf shoes in Greece, going head to head with the local boy wonder in Thailand and playing on a course cut out of jungle in Malaysia – actually took me closer to the local cultures than I have achieved in any of my travels, 100 Baht rooms and all. You see, golfers have something special in common, and although each country has its own fascinating twists on the Royal and Ancient traditions there is a camaraderie on and around the golf course that can open more than just conversations.

Regular readers will notice many new features in this edition. Within the pages that follow you will find the most comprehensive and international selection of luxury accommodation and quality golf courses ever put together. We are delighted to showcase nearly 150 Great Golf Hotels (plus more than 200 others that we can recommend) in the 2000 edition of the Guide, which is now firmly established as the world's leading golf travel resource.

At the heart of the Guide are three key components: choice of destination, where to stay and where to play when you are there. You will find some additional pointers on the après golf and cultural offerings for each region, these should help you fine-tune your selection.

As in past years the Guide has expanded to cover new destinations. This time's newcomers include the established destinations of Australia, New England and Arizona, plus emerging spots such as The Indian Ocean, Egypt, South America and China where golf is finding its feet. We have also introduced a section at the back of the Guide that offers additional recommended resorts and golf courses for many of the 35 areas covered.

For the increasing number of you who like to use the web to make travel arrangements you will find our sister site www.golftravel4u.com invaluable. And, while you are there, please take a minute to vote in the 2001 Hertz International Golf Travel Awards and you could win a dream Malaysian golf holiday.

Our research tells me that just over half of you get to take a golf trip each year. That means that just under half need a little more encouragement or some new ideas. Either way you are in the right place.

Pick up your clubs and head for sunny fairways. In a world full of stress and pressures, golf and travel frees the spirit like nothing else.

Peter Gould
Managing Director
Great Golf Hotels

our world of golf

PETER BURRINGTON
A former staffer at the *Daily Mirror*, Peter now runs his own editorial and design consultancy and writes regularly on golfing matters for a range of publications.

NIGEL COOMBES
Former editor of *Travel Trade Gazette*, Nigel is now a prolific freelance writer and broadcaster, working regularly for the BBC.

JACQUES DELGADE
A Frenchman who has lived and worked extensively in the USA, Jacques combines food writing with his love of golf.

MICHAEL GEDYE
Having criss-crossed the world in his quest for the perfect game, Michael is a golfing enthusiast whose words and pictures have appeared in a range of specialist and general interest titles.

PETER JOLLY
A British Guild of Travel Writers executive member, Peter combines his interest in travel with a deep-rooted passion for golf. He contributes to a number of publications and looks at courses worldwide from the perspective of a higher handicapped golfer.

ROBERT KLAMMER
Based in Chicago, Robert covers the US golf scene for a broad range of European and Asian publications.

ROGER ST. PIERRE
Co-editor of *The Great Golf Hotel Guide*, Roger has visited 88 countries and walked courses in most of them. A former editor of *Golf Buyer* magazine, he now edits *Holiday & Leisure World* magazine.

PAUL TROW
A managing editor at Hayters Press Agency, in London, Paul is a full-time sports writer with a penchant for playing golf around the world as well as commenting on it.

Contents

How to use your Guide

Price guide €

180 Euros or less	
180 to 250	
250 to 320	
320 or more	

Accommodation price guide

For each member hotel, we give a broad indication of the price for a standard double/twin room in high season.

As this is an international publication, covering different and fluctuating currencies, we use Euro equivalents, the Euro and the US dollar are roughly on a par, as we go to print.

Carefully selected for inclusion in *The Great Golf Hotel Guide*, our member hotels and resorts offer high quality accommodations, superlative food and wines, attentive service and superb locations. Each member hotel's entry gives full details of its offer, along with information on nearest courses, other local attractions and, in simple-to-understand icon form, a table of the hotel's own amenities.

AMERICAN EXPRESS OFFER

For advance booking on American Express Card you receive a **10% discount on rack rate**.

Many of our member hotels and resorts offer you a little extra for making an advance booking with American Express. It could be a free round of golf, a room upgrade or a tempting discount on the price of accommodation. Just quote 'Great Golf Hotels offer' when you use your American Express card to make your reservation.

All offers are strictly subject to availability.

Key symbols for maps

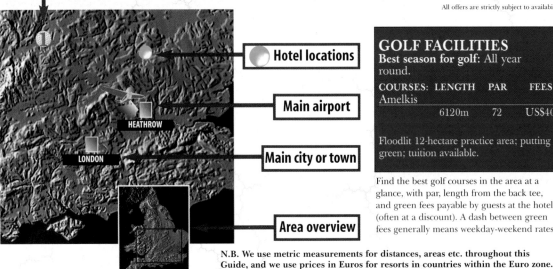

① **FAVOURITE FAIRWAYS**

Hotel locations

Main airport

HEATHROW

LONDON

Main city or town

Area overview

GOLF FACILITIES
Best season for golf: All year round.

COURSES:	LENGTH	PAR	FEES
Amelkis			
	6120m	72	US$40

Floodlit 12-hectare practice area; putting green; tuition available.

Find the best golf courses in the area at a glance, with par, length from the back tee, and green fees payable by guests at the hotel (often at a discount). A dash between green fees generally means weekday-weekend rates.

N.B. We use metric measurements for distances, areas etc. throughout this Guide, and we use prices in Euros for resorts in countries within the Euro zone.

Key symbols for hotels

Total number of rooms and/or suites/villas — Meeting/conference facilities, showing maximum number of delegates — Caters for families — Cable/satellite in all bedrooms — Golf course on site — Practice facilities on site — Coaching available — Tennis court on site — Fitness gym on site — Riding available locally — Fishing available locally — Shooting available locally — Outdoor swimming pool — Indoor swimming pool

167   **300**

This colour denotes facility not available at this hotel

Bernard Gallacher, Ryder Cup Captain 1991 - 1995.

BURBERRY
GOLF

IRELAND WINS
GOLF DESTINATION OF THE YEAR
1999 HERTZ INTERNATIONAL GOLF TRAVEL AWARDS

Formal confirmation of Ireland's growing international reputation as 'Europe's Golf Mecca' has come with the recent accolade 1999 Golf Destination of the Year conferred by the prestigious Hertz International Golf Travel Awards at the World Travel Market in London. After over a century of growth Irish golf has now taken centre stage for the international tournament circuit and its global television audience, the latest scheduled fixture being the Ryder Cup in 2005.

This island destination boasts at least one golf course for every mile of its 300-mile length - 375 courses in all, including an amazing 30 per cent of the world's links courses. Every challenge is catered for, from enjoyably modest tests for the weekend social golfer to formidable hazzard-laden confrontations that only a world-class arena can offer. The whole competitive spectrum is here - and it's here in abundance. For all their individuality the golf courses of Ireland share one feature in common - the warmth of their welcome for the visitor. In Ireland friendship, like golf, just comes naturally.

IRELAND HOSTS RYDER CUP IN 2005

Ireland

Bord Fáilte Irish Tourist Board, Baggot Street Bridge, Dublin 2.
Information: 1850 230330. Reservation: 1800 668 669 E-mail: user@irishtouristboard.ie

The Hertz
International Golf Travel Awards
2000

Nominees and winners of the 2000 awards

Global Golf Resort of the Year

Winner: Pinehurst Resort   North Carolina

Global Golf Course of the Year

Winner: Pebble Beach   California

European Golf Resort of the Year

Winner: Gleneagles   Scotland

Hyatt Regency La Manga	Spain
Penha Longa Golf Resort	Portugal
Gloria Golf Resort	Turkey
La Cala Resort	Spain
Quinta do Lago	Portugal

European Golf Course of the Year

Winner: Druid's Glen   Ireland

Wentworth West	England
San Lorenzo GC	Portugal
Turnberry Ailsa	Scotland
Barseback	Sweden
Valderrama	Spain

Asian/Pacific Golf Resort of the Year

Winner: Blue Canyon CC   Thailand

Mines Resort	Malaysia
Datai Langkawi	Malaysia
Millbrook Resort	New Zealand
Le Meridien Nirwana Golf & Spa Resort	Bali
Puerto Azul Beach Hotel	Philippines

Asian/Pacific Golf Course of the Year

Winner: New South Wales GC   Australia

Laem Chabang Int. CC	Thailand
Blue Canyon CC	Thailand
Damai Indah G&CC	Indonesia
Datai Bay	Malaysia
Mauna Kea	Hawaii

Africa/Middle East Golf Resort of the Year

Winner: Palace of the Lost City   South Africa

Fancourt Hotel and CC	South Africa
The Selborne Country Lodge & GC	South Africa
Palmeraie Golf Palace	Morocco
Le Paradis	Mauritius
Leopard Rock	Zimbabwe

Africa/Middle East Golf Course of the Year

Winner: Leopard Rock   Zimbabwe

Lost City	South Africa
The Emirates Majlis	Dubai
Dubai Creek GC	Dubai
Royal Dar Es Salam	Morocco
Les Dunes	Morocco

Americas Golf Resort of the Year

Winner: Turnberry Isle Resort & Club   Florida

Pinehurst Resort	North Carolina
The Greenbrier Hotel	West Virginia
Casa de Campo	Dominican Republic
The Boulders	Arizona
The Villas of Grand Cypress	Florida

Americas Golf Course of the Year

Winner: Troon North Monument   Arizona

Harbour Town	South Carolina
Caledonia Golf Fish Club	South Carolina
Pinehurst No. 2	North Carolina
Pebble Beach	California
Teeth of the Dog	Dominican Republic

Small Golf Hotel of the Year

Winner: Adare Manor   Ireland

Main Street Inn	South Carolina
Balbirnie House	Scotland
Estalagem Senhora da Guia	Portugal
Château de Vaugouard	France
Mas de Torrent	Spain

Golf Tour Operator of the Year

Winner: BA Golf Holidays   United Kingdom

Perry Golf	USA
Golf Pac	USA
Lotus Supertravel Golf	United Kingdom
Airtours Germany	Germany

Golf Destination of the Year

Winner: Portugal: Algarve

Nominated destinations:	South Carolina
	Arizona
	Ireland
	Scotland
	Andalucia

Emerging Golf Destination of the Year

Winner: South Africa

Nominated destinations:	Thailand
	Indonesia
	Turkey
	Dubai
	Morocco

VALDERRAMA

Your earthly paradise...

Close to the shimmering Mediterranean and with magnificent mountains as its backdrop, Valderrama is the golfer's paradise on earth.

Set on the world-renowned Costa del Sol, just 40 kilometres from fashionable Marbella and convenient to the airports, the Robert Trent Jones Senior designed course - rated by many as Europe's finest - is set within the delightful 2,000 hectare Sotogrande residential complex, with its marina, comprehensive sporting facilities and several golf courses. Now you can own your own piece of this wonderland.

Valderrama Estates has acquired part of the land surrounding Valderrama's fourth and fifth holes and within this privileged enclave is creating Los Altos de Valderrama - the most exclusive urbanisation in Spain.

Some 95 plots, each with a minimum size of 2,000 square metres, are available, set in beautifully preserved natural surroundings and providing stunning views over the golf course.

Access-controlled cobbled roads bordered with Bermuda grass, electronic security systems and a gatehouse manned 24 hours a day ensure privacy.

Valderrama Estates offers a complete turn-key management service to clients wishing to build their own houses in this magnificent location.

A complete team of skilled lawyers, town planners, architects, quality surveyors and builders guarantees best advice and the highest quality product, finished according to your wishes and delivered on time. Alternatively, if you merely wish to seek advice or wish us to supervise the building under your own direction, we are here to help.

Valderrama: Built in 1985 and rated since 1991 as Continental Europe's Number One course and now confirmed for 2000 and 2001. Host to the 1997 Ryder Cup.

VALDERRAMA ESTATES, S.A.

The Ryder Cup 1997 Real Estate Agency
La Inmobiliaria de la Ryder Cup 1.997

**Club de Golf Valderrama, 11310 Sotogrande, San Roque (Cádiz), España
Tel:+34 (9)56 791 206 - 791 209 Fax:+34 (9)56 794 507
E-mail valdestates@mx3.redestb.es**

SOTHEBY'S
INTERNATIONAL REALTY

The *Americas*

FLORIDA The Sunshine State's driving force

Millions now flock across the great herring pond every year to Florida, irresistably drawn by wonderful beaches and the world's greatest concentration of theme parks.

Orlando is the strongest magnet of all – Disney, Universal Studios, Sea World, Wet 'n' Wild, Church Street Station and the outlet shops, restaurants and bars strung along International Drive providing more than enough to fill a couple of weeks holiday.

The Tampa Bay area, taking in St. Petersburg and Clearwater, also has a myriad of things to do, with Busch Gardens as the biggest draw, while, on the other coast there's a whole string of beach resorts – from Daytona Beach down through Palm Beach, Fort Lauderdale, Miami's trendy South Beach and on down through the causeway-linked islands of the Florida Keys.

Less well-known elements to Florida's holiday offer include air-boating through wilderness Everglades swamps or canoeing along deserted creeks and rivers to admire the teeming wildlife.

GETTING THERE Direct flights from a number of European cities to Miami, Fort Lauderdale, Orlando or Tampa, with a wide choice of scheduled or charter flights – and some bargain prices – make getting there easy. Florida has an efficient network of freeways and turnpikes.

APRÈS GOLF The major resorts all feature extensive theatre, concert and sporting programmes – and are more sophisticated in their offer than you might expect. The state has several symphony orchestras and the world's largest Salvador Dalí museum and artwork collection. Food portions are huge and sweet — waffles, bacon and maple syrup for breakfast! — many Europeans will find a single course sufficient.

OFF THE COURSE The theme parks can prove very expensive, especially if you have several children in tow – so watch out for special ticket offers. Florida is home to several major league professional sports teams as well as the famous Daytona Speedway, with its banked oval track car racing, and also has unsurpassed facilities for participant sports, both land and water-based.

NOT TO BE MISSED Alligators, bald eagles, turtles, manatees and other wildlife; the amazing rocket displays at Space Coast; the art deco charms of South Beach.

FACTS & FIGURES

- Florida claims that it is America's premier golf state
- Grand Cypress Resort has more courses exclusively designed by Jack Nicklaus than any other location in the world.
- Tom Fazio is Florida's favourite golf architect, having designed 15 of the top ranked 100 courses.
- Diamondback Golf Club in Haines City has been carved from 100 hectares of virgin Florida forest.
- Orlando regards itself as the fun capital of the world, with an unrivalled volume and variety of theme parks.
- Readers of *Florida Golf News* voted Worlds Woods Pine Barrens in Hernando County as the state's top course.

Florida is the ultimate paradise for those who like their golf played in sunshine on beautifully manicured fairways and immaculately tended greens surrounded by silver sand bunkers and man-made lakes. From Amelia Island to Miami, the state can't be faulted for its quantity or quality of golf. Visitors from Europe have the added attraction of knowing that, in the winter season, conditions for the sport are ideal. Mid-summer is possibly the only time to avoid, when humidity and the threat of storms and hurricanes loom.

There's a proliferation of challenging and scenic courses – around 1200 at the latest count – far more than in any other state, nearly always traversed in a golf cart, which is often compulsory, because few want to walk the course in the tropical climate.

The sport is vital to the state's economy, worth some $5billion a year, and it is estimated an incredible 60 million rounds are played annually. With low, low prices, the Sunshine State is also a great place to stock up on equipment. For the retired or those lucky enough to have a second home, golf communities are scattered everywhere, with luxury homes surrounding courses and country clubs that combine fine living and the highest quality sporting facilities.

Golfers who prefer to try an area yet untested by Euro tourists may like a visit to Daytona Beach. This stretch of coast is lined with some excellent courses, and the lively nightlife is a bonus. Slightly further north on the Palm Coast, the courses offer some of the cheapest green fees in Florida. Similarly undiscovered is the Panhandle, a narrow strip of land that stretches westward from the Florida peninsula, bordered by the Georgia state line to the north Louisiana to the west and the waters of the Gulf to the south.

NEW DEVELOPMENTS

- A new development at Poinciana, opened in January 2000, comprises an 18-hole par 72 course designed by Ron Garl, with 6500 new homes nearby.
- A $900,000 remodelling and landscaping has been completed at the Winter Springs Golf Club, where fees are around $35, while Boca Resort and Country Club is celebrating the redevelopment of its main 18-hole championship course.
- Florida is now home to more than 20 professional golf tournaments every year
- The Barefoot Resort and Golf Club in North Myrtle Beach is one of the most impressive golfing developments currently under construction anywhere. This $812 million resort will feature residential communities, two exclusive resort hotels, conference and leisure facilities and four world-class courses, built by an illustrious quartet: Greg Norman, Tom Fazio, Pete Dye and Davis Love III.

Hotels

⬤ **The Breakers**
Page 16

⬤ **Turnberry Isle Resort**
Page 17

◯ **The Villas of Grand Cypress**
Page 18

Favourite fairways

1 BOCA RATON RESORT AND CLUB

A dramatic mixture of architectural styles, this lavish golf resort around 30 kilometres from Palm Beach combines modern luxury and elegant links with the past. The improved championship course at the hotel is the ultimate in Florida perfection, with thousands of tonnes of earth moved to make an undulating course on the flat Florida land, requiring considerable finesse. The resort has great facilities for all sports along with its own beach.
Par 72   Length 6021m (Country Club Course)
501 East Camino Real, Boca Raton Fl 33431
Tel:+1 407 447 3076 Fax:+1 407 391 3183

2 TURNBERRY ISLE RESORT AND CLUB

An elegant tropical oasis between Miami and Fort Lauderdale, this stunning Mediterranean style hotel offers two Robert Trent Jones championship courses. The whole resort with its sport and beach facilities, nestles in 120 hectares of tropical gardens and has a selection of award-winning eateries.
Par 70   Length 5782m (North Course)
Par 72   Length 6404m (South Course)
19999 West Country Club Drive, Aventura Fl 33180
Tel: +1 305 932 6200 Fax: +1 305 933 6560

3 PGA NATIONAL RESORT AND SPA

Host of the Ryder Cup in 1993, this is the headquarters of the PGA of America, and its five courses are always kept in tournament condition. Whatever your ability, there is a course to suit your game, including beginners. The courses are designed by Jack Nicklaus, Tom and George Fazio, Arnold Palmer and Karl Litten. If the golfing is exhausting, the spa offers more than 100 treatments.
Par 72   Length 6421m
400 Avenue of the Champions, Palm Beach Gardens Fl 33418
Tel: +1 407 627 1800 Fax: +1 407 627 1800

4 THE BREAKERS

The only oceanfront resort found in the heart of Palm Beach, and one of the oldest established resorts on the coast, The Breakers completed a $75million renovation several years ago. The Ocean Course was designed by Alexander J Gindlay and revamped by Joe Lee in 1992. A few miles inland lies The Breakers West, a 6314-metre par 71 designed by William Byrd.
Par 70, Length 5502m (Ocean course); Par 71, 6314m (Breakers West)
One South County Road, Palm Beach Fl 33480
Tel: +1 561 655 6611 Fax: +1 561 659 8403

5 THE LEGACY

Recently voted in the top ten of Florida's favourite courses, this excellent 5142-metre par 72 course was designed by Arnold Palmer and opened two years ago. Lakes and wetlands are prominent hazards and the greens are challenging.
Par 72   Length 5141m
8255 Legacy Boulevard, Bradenton, Fl 34202
Tel: +1 941 907 7067 Fax: +1 941 907 7012

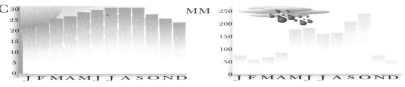

The most up-to-date golf travel information is always at www.golftravel4u.com

CLIMATE

The 'Snowbirds' – visitors from Canada and the Northern USA – flock to enjoy Florida's lovely mild winters. Summers can be very hot and humid. Rainy season is from July to September when there can also be a risk of hurricanes.

°C
30
25
20
15
10
5
0
J F M A M J J A S O N D

MM
250
200
150
100
50
0
J F M A M J J A S O N D

Sample point: Miami

Price guide

€

Round of golf		Golf balls	
Small beer		4/5 star hotel room	

CONTACT

Visit Florida, 661 East Jefferson Street, Suite 300, Tallahassee, Florida 32301
Tel: +1 850 488 5607   Fax: +1 850 224 9589

THE BREAKERS

Hotel information

One South County Road
Palm Beach
Florida
FL 33480

Tel: +1 561 655 6611
Fax: +1 561 659 8403
Web: www.thebreakers.com

Accolades

☆☆☆☆☆ Mobil Travel Guide
AAA Five Diamond

Airport

Palm Beach (PBI): 15 mins
Fort Lauderdale: 50 mins
Miami International: 1 hr 20 mins

Accommodation price guide

€

Accepted credit cards
AE DC MC V

Preferred tour operator

From UK
British Airways
Holidays   Tel: +44 (0) 870 242 4245
North America Travel
Service   Tel: +44 (0) 113 246 1466
From Germany
Airtours
International – contact your Travel Agent

Palm Beach County has truly become a golfer's paradise, with close to 150 championship golf courses. Set amid 56 hectares of oceanfront property resides the timeless Breakers Palm Beach, which recently completed a $100-million revitalisation and expansion programme. It now features the new oceanfront spa and beach club and offers an extraordinary getaway for travellers who share the passions of golf and well-being.

Select from an array of recreational activities that satisfy your every playful whim. There's fine golf at either of the two championship golf courses. The Ocean, located at the resort, was designed by Alexander J Findlay, re-designed by Donald Ross in 1926 and extensively renovated in 1992. The spectacular Breakers West course was designed by Willard Byrd and situated a few miles inland at the Breakers West Club. Or you may simply want to be pampered and indulge at the new luxury spa.

The resort, which is known as an oceanfront playground, exhilarates the senses with a vast number of recreational activities for land and sea.

When it comes to wining and dining, take pleasure in any of the seven new restaurants at the hotel, which include The Seafood Bar and Flagler's Steakhouse, enjoy a drink at the Italian-style piazza, or simply stroll into Palm Beach itself.

Recreational facilities

Tennis, The Spa at The Breakers, two fitness centres, four swimming pools, Jacuzzi; private beach, jogging trail; aerobics, bicycling, scuba diving, snorkelling, watersports, deep sea fishing; family and children's programmes; shopping arcade on site.

Meeting/business facilities

25 rooms, for up to 1400 delegates; business centre.

Local attractions

Yacht cruises, Kravis Centre for the Performing Horse and greyhound tracks, airboat Everglades tours, Palm Beach Polo Club, and the famous shopping and entertainment districts of Worth Avenue and Clematis.

GOLF FACILITIES
Best season for golf: All year round.

COURSES:	LENGTH	PAR	FEES
Breakers Ocean			
	5502m	70	$110
Breakers West			
	6314m	71	$135

20 courses in easy driving distance; two driving ranges; packages available; Todd Anderson Golf Academy.

Facilities key

572 **1400**

TURNBERRY ISLE RESORT & CLUB

The Mediterranean-style Turnberry Isle Resort & Club has two Robert Trent Jones Snr golf courses at the centre of 120 hectares of lushly landscaped grounds, each having been refurbished in the past few years. These Jones designs, a combination of sprawling greens and water hazards, have 18 holes apiece and together are rated as one of the top golf courses in the United States.

Off the course, Turnberry Isle combines old-world elegance with a modern resort. The new 2300m² European Spa and Fitness Center is scheduled for completion in June 2000. This state-of-the-art facility, created by famous spa designer Tag Galyean, will be a shining jewel in Turnberry's royal crown. The Spa's three floors are connected through a grand spiral staircase which showcases cascading waterfalls and fountains, all accented by a glass dome skylight. There are 26 treatment rooms in total, a 340m² fitness centre, complete with aerobics, studio, weight and cardio rooms.

The hotel's 395 guest rooms and suites were voted "the best rooms in the South" in a recent Zagat Survey. Each room has a separate seating area, private balcony, bar, three dual-line telephones, two cable televisions and a marble bathroom with a Jacuzzi tub and a separate glass shower.

Culinary experiences range from the eye-opening breakfast spread to the gourmet 'Floribbean' cuisine and extensive wine list in the Veranda.

Hotel information

19999 West Country Club Drive
Aventura
Florida 33180

Tel: +1 305 932 6200
Fax: +1 305 933 3811
Email: turnbres@aol.com
Web: www.turnberryisle.com

Accolades

☆☆☆☆☆
Member The Leading Hotels of the World

Airport

Miami: 30 mins
Fort Lauderdale: 20 mins

Accommodation price guide

Accepted credit cards
AE MC V DC

Recreational facilities

Two on-site 18-hole championship golf courses; two lit tennis clubs with clay and hard courts; 117-slip marina; deep sea fishing; watersports at Ocean Club.

Meeting/business facilities

21 rooms, for up to 1500 delegates; conference centre.

Local attractions

Near South Beach nightlife, across from the Aventura Mall and near Bal Harbour shops; nearby sports include Dolphin Football, Marlin Baseball, Florida Panthers Hockey and Miami Heat Basketball.

GOLF FACILITIES
Best season for golf: All year round.

COURSES:	LENGTH	PAR	FEES
Turnberry North			
	5835m	70	$60-100
Turnberry South			
	6270m	72	$60-100

Driving range, putting green, pro shop, club rentals, clubhouse, golf lessons, cart rental.

Facilities key

395   1500

THE VILLAS OF GRAND CYPRESS

Hotel information

One North Jacaranda
Orlando
Florida
FL 32836

Tel: +1 407 239 4700
Fax: +1 407 239 7219
Email: resortinfo@grandcypress.com
Web: www.grandcypress.com

Accolades

☆☆☆☆ Mobil
Four Diamonds (AAA)

Airport

Orlando International: 20 mins

Accommodation price guide

Accepted credit cards
AE MC V DC

Preferred tour operator

From UK
Foxtons
Worldwide   Tel: +44 (0) 171 911 3911
From Germany
F&B Golfreiesien
International Tel: +49 (0) 6233 31880

Recreational facilities

45 holes of Nicklaus-designed golf; golf academy; swimming, tennis, horseback riding, biking.

Meeting/business facilities

Three rooms, for up to 300 delegates.

Local attractions

Walt Disney World, Universal Studios, Sea World; Florida Mall, shopping at International Drive.

In the heart of Central Florida you will discover a distinctive retreat – close to Orlando's renowned attractions, yet worlds apart. 600 pristine hectares of lush greenery, surrounded by some of the world's finest golf courses, will greet you at Grand Cypress.

Every Mediterranean-style club suite and one, two, three or four-bedroom villa features elegant and thoughtfully designed decor and superb in-room amenities. Club suites provide extra room, with a separate sitting area, while most villas offer a variety of sophisticated appointments – from full kitchens, fireplaces and private terraces to whirlpool tubs and spectacular views of the waterways and fairways of the North Course.

Golf at Grand Cypress is phenomenal, with 45 holes of Jack Nicklaus signature designed golf, featuring the Grand Cypress North/South Tournament Course and East nine, plus the New Course – whose 18 holes are reminiscent of the legendary Old Course at St. Andrews. *Golf* magazine has awarded the resort a gold medal as one of the finest golf resorts in America.

The Grand Cypress Golf Pro Shop, ranked among the country's top 100, offers an impressive array of sportswear, equipment and speciality items, while the Grand Cypress Academy of Golf combines state-of-the-art technology with expert instruction to offer the ultimate learning experience for golfers.

GOLF FACILITIES
Best season for golf: October to April.

COURSES:	LENGTH	PAR	FEES
Grand Cypress North			
	3521m	36	$165
Grand Cypress South			
	3472m	36	S$165
Grand Cypress New			
	6773m	72	$165

45 holes of golf on site, golf academy; tuition available.

Facilities key

146   300

Avoid the rough.

Daily flights to Miami and Orlando.

Contact 01293 747 747 or www.virgin-atlantic.com

virgin atlantic *Virgin*

SOUTH CAROLINA The New World's cradle of golf

Live oaks adorned with Spanish moss, gracious ante-bellum mansions, sultry weather and the locals' good manners, warm welcomes and charming drawl will let you know that this is the heart of the Old South, a fascinating state redolent with memories of the Civil War and the Confederacy.

It was at For Sumnter, standing offshore of the genteel old city of Charleston that the first shots were fired in anger between the Rebs and the besieged Yankee garrison. The bay is also today the home of a US Navy museum centred on a mighty World War Two aircraft carrier.

Charleston – site of America's first golf course – is arguably the nations most picturesque city, and a haven from neon lights and brash commercialism. Myrtle Beach, the USA's answer to Blackpool, stands in stark contrast. Brash, lively, full of family fun, it is renowned for its lavish shows and busy shopping centres. To north and south stretch the 40 carefully tended kilometres of beaches renowned as 'The Grand Strand'.

Just north of the Georgia border, Kiawah Island and Hilton Head are upscale resorts, while gracious Savannah, Georgia, setting for *Bonfire Of The Vanities* is but a short drive away.

GETTING THERE While South Carolina has no direct air links to Europe, its modern and recently expanded airports network with major international hubs like Atlanta, Minneapolis/St. Paul and Newark.

APRÈS GOLF Happy hour means bargain priced cocktails, including the Southern speciality, mint julep. People eat early here – dinner at 5pm is not unusual. Seafood is the big treat, with soft-shell crab, snow crabs, huge shrimps and all manner of fish on the menu. Lively discos and bars cater for the party people.

OFF THE COURSE South Carolina justly claims some of America's finest beaches. It's northerly enough to have four distinct seasons but is rarely very cold in winter. Outlet malls offer designer goods – and lots of golf equipment too – at way below European prices. The gentle terrain makes bicycling a pleasure while the wildlife is also a great attraction.

NOT TO BE MISSED Stroll past the splendidly ornate townhouse mansions of Charleston — and visit the more modest but equally charming Jamestown.

FACTS & FIGURES

- South Carolina has 384 golf courses, a third of which have been built in the last ten years. Five of these are ranked in *Golf Digest*'s US top 100.
- Last year's estimated golf spend was $1.2 billion.
- 2.3 million golfing tourists came here in 1998, accounting for half of the 14 million rounds played.
- Most come down from the northeast USA and Canada. Almost half the international visitors are from the UK.
- The DuPont World Amateur Championship – the world's largest golf tournament – sees over 5,000 golfers take over Myrtle Beach each Autumn.
- Professional tournaments include events on the Seniors Tour, the Ladies Tour and the MCI Heritage Classic on the full USPGA Tour.

Myrtle Beach has well over 100 good courses

Golf in America originated in 1786, when the South Carolina Golf Club was founded at Harlesden Green. Today, thanks to 200 years of golfing pedigree, visitors to South Carolina will enjoy one of the finest golf Meccas in the world. Tourism is concentrated in three main coastal regions. Each offers fantastic golf and warm hospitality, but each also has a very different ambience.

Hilton Head Island is located at the southernmost point of South Carolina. As it is 27 kilometres long, it is hard to imagine how 28 high quality golf courses can exist side by side here without the slightest feeling of overcrowding. Yet they do, and when combined with the impressive selection of hotels, restaurants, entertainment facilities and stunning beaches, they make Hilton Head undoubtedly one of the most enjoyable venues for a golf holiday anywhere in the USA.

Two hours north, no fewer than 22 championship golf courses surround the charming old town of Charleston, with spectacular opportunities for golf being offered on the nearby barrier islands. The most notable is Kiawah Island Resort, famous for staging the 1991 Ryder Cup. Equally good golfing experiences can be found at the nearby Wild Dunes and Seabrook Island resorts.

A further 90 minutes north is Myrtle Beach. Nowhere on earth will you find such a concentration of golf courses. Attempts to quantify them prove futile, as the figure is usually outdated by the time it leaves your lips. The only thing to match the seemingly exponential growth of fairways is the provision of hotels and lively entertainment.

Golf among the pine

NEW DEVELOPMENTS

- One of the most exciting courses to open this year has been the Tournament Players Club (TPC) of Myrtle Beach. Tom Fazio and Lanny Wadkins collaborated to design this 16th facility of the TPC network. Open for public play now, the course will host the Seniors Tour Championship in the year 2000.
- True Blue is another great new golf course recently opened by designer Mike Strantz. The ex-associate of Tom Fazio, he has already designed one of the area's most beautiful golf courses – the Caledonia. For details call: +1 843 235 0900.
- Barefoot Resort and Golf Club, under construction in North Myrtle Beach, is one of the most impressive developments anywhere in the world. This $812m resort will feature 12 residential communities, two resort hotels, full conference and leisure facilities and, most importantly, four new world-class courses, designed by the illustrious quartet of Greg Norman, Tom Fazio, Pete Dye and Davis Love III.

Hotels

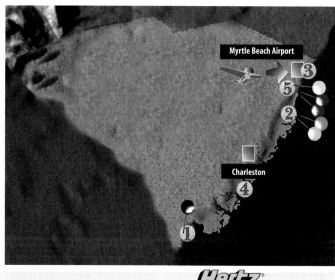

RECOMMENDED CAR HIRE *Hertz®*

UK: +44 (0) 870 848 4848 Germany: +49 (0) 180 533 3535
Website: www.hertz.com

The most up-to-date golf travel information is always at www.golftravel4u.com

Favourite fairways

① HARBOUR TOWN

Host each year to the MCI Classic, Harbour Town is regularly rated as one of world's finest courses. Designers Pete Dye and Jack Nicklaus, have created some of the smallest greens in championship golf to ensure that the secret to good scoring rests on accuracy and finesse rather than brute strength.
Par 71   Length 6321m
**Sea Pines Resort, Hilton Head Island, South Carolina 29938
Tel: +1 843 363 4485   Fax: +1 843 363 4501**

② CALEDONIA GOLF & FISH CLUB

Built on a former rice plantation, Caledonia was opened in 1994 to huge critical acclaim. America's 'hottest' new designer Mike Strantz has created a work of art that incorporates as much of the natural landscape as possible. Located 24 kilometres south of Myrtle Beach, Caledonia Golf Club ensures the visitor gets a true taste of Southern hospitality.
Par 70   Length 5965m
**369 Caledonia Drive, Pawleys Island, South Carolina 29585
Tel: +1 843 237 3675   Fax: + 1 843 237 4762**

③ TIDEWATER GOLF CLUB

Moulded around the salt-water marshes of Cherry Grove Beach Inlet, Tidewater offers dramatic views of the Intracoastal Waterway and the Atlantic Ocean. Architect, Ken Tomlinson has designed 18 holes of outstanding character and natural beauty that visitors never fail to find enchanting.

Par 72   Length 6535m
**Tidewater Golf Club & Plantation, North Myrtle Beach, SC
Tel: +1 843 249 3829   Fax: +1 843 249 5281**

④ KIAWAH ISLAND (OCEAN COURSE)

Site of the dramatic 1991 Ryder Cup matches, this Pete Dye masterpiece is undoubtedly one of the finest coastal courses in the world. Played from the back tees the course is no less terrifying than it is spectacular. However, much kinder teeing grounds ensure that every golfer will enjoy the experience and have an opportunity to make 'the Bernard Langer putt' on the 18th green.
Par 72   Length 6737m
**12 Kiawah Beach Drive, Kiawah Island, South Carolina 29455.
Tel: +1 843 768 2121   Fax: +1 843 768 6099**

⑤ TOURNAMENT PLAYERS CLUB AT MYRTLE BEACH

One of the most exciting recent developments in Myrtle Beach was the building of the area's 100th course. The TPC is a modern classic that provides tournament playing conditions throughout the year. Tom Fazio and Lanny Wadkins collaborated to create a fine course that is already scheduled to host the US Senior Tour Championship in November 2000.
Par 72   Length 6352m
**Murrells Inlet, Myrtle Beach, South Carolina 29576
Tel: +1 843 357 3399   Fax: +1 843 357 0123
Web: www.tpc-mb.com**

CLIMATE

South Carolina weather is...*great!* The summers may be hot, but, winters are very mild. Spring and fall offer beautiful weather for the many festivals held here.

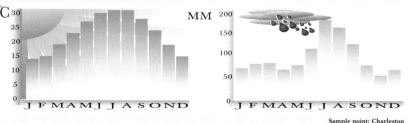

Sample point: Charleston

Price guide   €

| Round of golf | 🏌🏌🏌🏌 | Golf balls | 🏌🏌🏌 |
| Small beer | 🏌🏌 | 4/5 star hotel room | 🏌🏌🏌🏌 |

CONTACT

South Carolina Office of Tourism, 1205 Pendleton Street, Columbia, South Carolina 29201, USA
Tel: +1 803 734 0129   Fax: +1 803 734 1163

CROWN REEF AT SOUTH BEACH RESORT

Hotel information

2913 South Ocean Blvd.
Myrtle Beach
SC 29577

Tel: +1 843 626 8077
Fax: +1 843 626 2928
Email: crownreef@aol.com
Web: www.crownreef.com

Airport

Myrtle Beach International: 5 mins

Accommodation price guide

Accepted credit cards
AE DC MC V

Recreational facilities

Lazy river, ocean-front pool, indoor pools, fitness centre, massage therapy; arcade and video game room; Breezes Beach Club; gift shop; miniature golf, sail boating, Hobie Cat rentals available.

Meeting/business facilities

Eight rooms, for up to 1200 delegates. Business centre located in Crown Reef Conference Centre.

Local attractions

Myrtle Beach Grand Prix motor racing; par 3 floodlit driving range across street.

One of the world's great golfing capitals, greater Myrtle Beach offers more than 100 fine courses to play. This ever popular beach resort has a new crowning glory with the opening of the upscale The Crown Reef at South Beach Resort, a truly splendid property offering a variety of rooms and suites – all oceanfront with private balconies.

Amenities on-site include four delightful restaurants, a beach club, no fewer than 21 spacious indoor and outdoor pools and Jacuzzis, Myrtle Beach's longest "lazy river", Breezes Beach Club and a superbly equipped weight room.

Located in the hotel's conference centre, Tradewinds Restaurant provides an elegant atmosphere and a sumptuous dining experience. Casual dining is at its best in the full-service Crown Café restaurant, while the Treasure Chest Express Café provides prompt service and tasty food.

Oceanfront dining is offered both inside and outside on the elevated decks overlooking the sparkling pools and the beautiful Atlantic Ocean.

The resort's desirable location provides easy access to all the local showcase theatres, shopping malls and other attractions. Check-in and registration are made easy at the highly efficient guest services desk, located in the lobby of the conference centre.

GOLF FACILITIES

Best season for golf: February to May, September to December.

COURSES:	LENGTH	PAR	FEES
TPC of Myrtle Beach			
	6900m	72	$72-135
Myrtlewood			
	6600m	72	$20-55
Caledonia			
	6500m	72	$55-120
Kings North			
	6800m	72	$45-100
Wild Wing			
	6900m	72	$30-90
Prestwick			
	7000m	72	$30-85

A choice of package plans is available to suit all budgets while in-house golf staff are available to facilitate the perfect golfing break.

Facilities key

514 1200

FOUR POINTS SHERATON

Hotel information

2701 South Ocean Boulevard
Myrtle Beach
SC 29577

Tel: +1 843 448 2518
Fax: +1 843 448 1506
Email: sheraton@sccoast.net
Web: www.sheratonresort.com

Airport

Myrtle Beach International: 5 mins

Accommodation price guide

Accepted credit cards
AE MC V DC

Recreational facilities

Indoor and outdoor pools, ocean-front deck, whirlpool, health club with sauna; game room, volleyball, tennis privileges; gift shop; minaiture golf, sail boating; Hobie Cat rentals available locally; Myrtle Beach Grand Prix motor racing.

Meeting/business facilities

12 meeting rooms.

Local attractions

Miles of beautiful sands; shopping malls and showcase theatres.

Four Points Sheraton, Myrtle Beach, located in the middle of all the excitement, offers beach fun, excellent golf and outstanding amenities. This luxuriously appointed hotel is dedicated to providing vacation enjoyment and a high level of services and comfort.

The hotel consists of 223 bright, spacious, and tastefully decorated rooms, efficiencies and suites –– most with their own private balcony. All the guest rooms have refrigerators, coffee makers, cable TV and other amenities.

Facilities include Kokomo's Restaurant and Lounge, famous for delicious cuisine, fun outdoor deck buffets, tropical drinks, and live entertainment – plus a casual and relaxed oceanfront atmosphere.

The hotel also offers a weight room, a gift shop and both indoor and outdoor pools.

Natural beauty, a mild year-round climate, and an endless variety of activities have made Myrtle Beach a family vacation paradise, a golfer's dream and a superb meeting destination – and Four Points Sheraton encapsulates the very best of what's on offer in this ever popular South Carolina resort.

Convenient to a majority of the best local courses and only minutes from the Myrtle Beach International Jetport, the hotel has available a variety of packages and seasonal specials.

GOLF FACILITIES
Best season for golf: February to May and September to December.

COURSES:	LENGTH	PAR	FEES
Prestwick	7000m	72	$30-85
Belle Terre	7100m	72	$50-80
Legends	6900m	72	$35-85
TPC of Myrtle Beach	6900m	72	$72-135
Myrtle Beach National	6850m	72	$20-50
True Blue Plantation	7000m	72	$45-120

More than 100 quality courses in locality; driving range and par 3 course within walking distance.

Facilities key

LEGENDS RESORTS

Hotel information

1500 Legends Drive
Myrtle Beach
South Carolina
SC 29508

Tel: +1 843 236 9318
Fax: +1 843 236 0516
Email: reservations@legendsgolf.com
Web: www.legendsgolf.com

Accolades

☆☆☆ One Star Relais du Golf
PGA of Europe award winner.

Airport

Myrtle Beach International: 10 mins

Accommodation price guide

Accepted credit cards
AE MC V

Preferred tour operator

From UK
Destination
Golf   Tel: +44 (0) 208 891 5151
From Germany
Fairtime
Touristik   Tel: +49 (0) 89 81 12 041
Nova Reisen Tel: +49 (0) 89 615 66 621

Legends Resorts is a stylish 525-hectare golf resort offering superb villa accommodations, with a choice of two- and three-bedroomed villas, each with two bathrooms, living room, dining room and kitchen. The resort houses two great restaurants, tennis courts, hot tub and bike trails.

Legends is at the heart of popular Myrtle Beach, set 13 kilometres from the airport, ten kilometres from the ocean. Directly across the street are the Myrtle Beach Factory Stores, with other popular shopping, eating, theatres or clubs within easy reach.

Reminiscent of the great Scottish clubhouses, the distinctive Legends clubhouse greets guests upon arrival and stays with them as a visual landmark while they are playing the delightful courses.

Cited by several golf writers as the best 54-hole golf destination anywhere, Legends offers nationally rated courses – three on site: Heathland, Parkland, Moorland; with a further three courses off-site: Oyster Bay, Marsh Harbour, Heritage. All provide a distinctive and provocative golfing experience, playing with their unique undulations, strategically placed bunkers and lush deep rough.

Recreational facilities

Two outdoor pools, hot tub; two tennis courts, walking and biking trails; beach and watersports 10km.

Meeting/business facilities

Two rooms, for up to 80 delegates.

Local attractions

Factory stores directly opposite Legends Drive; NASCAR speedway, aquarium; Barefoot Landing and Broadway at the Beach, for shops, dining, clubs, theatres; Brookgreen Gardens.

GOLF FACILITIES

Best season for golf: Spring and Autumn.

COURSES:	LENGTH	PAR	FEES
Heathland	6204m	71	inclusive
Moorland	6217m	72	inclusive
Parkland	6556m	72	inclusive
Heritage	6387m	72	inclusive
Oyster Bay	6113m	72	inclusive
Marsh Harbour	6108m	72	inclusive

Flood-lit 12-hectare practice area, open 6am-11pm; putting green; tuition available; tournaments open to guests, including Father & Sons tournament.

Facilities key

225   80

LITCHFIELD BEACH & GOLF RESORT

Hotel information

Post Office Drawer 320
14276 Ocean Highway 17
Pawleys Island
South Carolina
SC 29585

Tel: +1 843 237 3000
Fax: +1 843 237 4282
Email: info@litchfieldbeach.com
Web: www.litchfieldbeach.com

Accolades

AAA Three-diamond
American Express Golf Annual "Top 75 Golf Resorts"

Airport

Myrtle Beach: 30 mins
Charleston: 1 hr 20 mins

Accommodation price guide

Accepted credit cards
AE MC V DC

Preferred tour operator

From UK
Destinations
Golf   Tel: +44 (0) 208 891 5151
British Airways
Holidays   Tel: +44 (0) 870 2424249
3-D Golf   Freephone: 0800 333 323

Litchfield Beach & Golf Resort is a spacious resort plantation, extending from the scenic Intracoastal Waterway to the shores of the blue Atlantic Ocean, tucked among giant oaks, sparkling lakes, and beautiful gardens. Set along Litchfield Beach, just north of Pawleys Island, the resort offers its guests an unparalleled selection of amenities in a truly glorious setting.

Accommodations at Litchfield include an all-suite hotel featuring 96 spacious one-bedroom suites; one, two, three, and four-bedroom condominiums and villas which overlook the ocean and natural marshes, or alongside the golf course fairways.

There is a great choice of on-site restaurants, from Webster's Lowcountry Grill & Tavern to the Calypso Beach Bar & Grill, located oceanfront at the Litchfield Inn. Litchfield Country Club dining is available to Litchfield resort guests, who are granted temporary membership while in residence at the resort. Finally, Willbrook Plantation Golf Club and River Club also features grills.

Surrounding the resort is an area abounding with history, mystery and romance, from historic Brookgreen Gardens, with America's largest display of outdoor sculpture to the nearby great plantation homes and other landmarks, Litchfield Beach & Golf Resort offers its visitors a natural choice for an unforgettable escape from the ordinary.

Recreational facilities

Three championship golf courses: Litchfield Country Club, River Club and Willbrook Plantation; Litchfield Racquet Club, ranked number seven in the USA by Tennis Magazine, with discounts available to resort guests; cycling; basketball, raquetball; health club, with steam room, sauna, indoor pool, and beauty salon.

Meeting/business facilities

10 rooms, for up to 250 delegates; business resource centre.

Local attractions

Shopping at Hammock Shops, Island Shops; Brookgreen Gardens Sculpture Park; historical tours of nearby Georgetown and Charleston; Myrtle Beach, with attractions like Planet Hollywood, Hard Rock Cafe and Ripley's Sea Aquarium.

GOLF FACILITIES

Best season for golf: April to October.

COURSES:	LENGTH	PAR	FEES
Litchfield Country Club			
	6145m	72	$14-55
River Club			
	6085m	72	$14-55
Willbrook Plantation			
	6110m	72	$14-55
King's North			
	6395m	72	$60-120
Long Bay			
	6398m	72	$19-85
Blackmoor			
	6027m	72	$20-95

Practice facilities, including putting greens and chipping areas; driving range; tuition available.

Facilities key

520   250

PAWLEYS PLANTATION

Hotel information

70 Tanglewood Drive
Pawleys Island
South Carolina
SC 29585

Tel: +1 843 237 6009
Fax: +1 843 237 0418
Email: pawleys@sccoast.net
Web: www.pawleysplantation.com

Accolades

Ranked by *Golf For Women* as one of USA's top ten women friendly courses.

Airport

Myrtle Beach: 30 mins
Charleston: 1 hr 30 mins

Accommodation price guide

Accepted credit cards
AE MC V

Recreational facilities

Outdoor pools, floodlit HydroCourt tennis courts; golf pro shop.

Meeting/business facilities

Seven rooms, for up to 300 delegates.

Local attractions

Minutes from Pawleys Island beaches; Brookgreen Gardens, Huntington Beach State Park, Atalaya Castle; deep sea fishing, waterway cruises; Myrtle Beach entertainments, historic Charleston.

Cleverly planned around an outstanding Jack Nicklaus designed signature course at the heart of South Carolina's low country, Pawleys Plantation Golf & Country Club is a world-class golf and resort community skillfully designed to foster the natural splendour of the landscape.

With subtle greens guarded by sand bunkers, challenging fairways dotted with water, and with tricky obstacles evident on every hole, this is a player's course which demands strategy, ingenuity and concentration. Guests also have privileged access to more than 100 other courses in the region.

Set amid 235 hectares of natural wetlands, salt marshes, stands of centuries-old live oaks and magnolias and open countryside, a variety of recreational and leisure activities are available for guests to enjoy.

Casual elegance flourishes in the gracious antebellum style clubhouse, which provides the heart of this wonderful community with its pro shop, grill and dining rooms and conference centre.

Lively Myrtle Beach and the Grand Strand are just 40 kilometres to the north while the gracious southern city of Charleston with its wealth of picturesque buildings and historic sites is an easy drive away in the other direction.

GOLF FACILITIES

Best season for golf: All year round – Spring and Autumn ideal.

COURSES:	LENGTH	PAR	FEES
Pawleys Plantation	6424m	72	$76

Over 100 courses in locality; driving range, practice putting green; Phil Ritson/Mel Sole golf school – rated among top 25 in US – on-site; special golf packages.

Facilities key

180 300

SEA PINES

Hotel information

32 Greenwood Drive
Hilton Head Island
South Carolina
SC 29928

Tel: +1 843 785 3333
Fax: +1 843 842 1475
Email: rentals@seapines.com
Web: www.seapines.com

Accolades

Ranked among the top 100 courses of the world by Golf Magazine and The Golfer.

Airport

Savannah International: 1 hr 15 mins
Hilton Head: 15 mins

Accommodation price guide

Accepted credit cards
AE MC V DC

Recreational facilities

Eight kilometres of Atlantic Ocean shoreline; three golf courses, 23 tennis courts; two marinas; equestrian centre; fitness centre; 245-hectare forest preserve; range of restaurants featuring specialities of southern cuisine.

Meeting/business facilities

Five facilities, for up to 400 delegates.

Local attractions

Beaches, historic Savannah (72km) and Charleston (152km) with Civil War heritage; theatres, shops and restaurants; nature preserve.

Sea Pines is a glorious 2000-hectare oceanfront resort community on Hilton Head Island, South Carolina, blending world-class vacation amenities with a setting of stunning natural beauty.

There are more than 500 one- to six-bedroomed luxury villas and homes, providing ocean, fairway, marsh or Harbour Town views. Many have their own pools, while complimentary tennis, preferred tee times, discounted green fees, a bike rental programme and exclusive pool and charge privileges are all part of the visitor offer.

Sea Pines provides resort dining at its very finest. Heritage Grill, in the famed Harbour Town Clubhouse, is an upscale yet casual Southern grill. Fun open-air dining and oceanfront cook-outs can be enjoyed at the Sea Pines Beach Club, while bountiful breakfasts, the island's best bagels, overstuffed sandwiches, soups and salads are served at the Harbour Town Bakery & Café. Catering choices range from specialised shopping service for your villa to lavish banquets.

Three championship golf courses, Sea Pines Racquet Club, two marina villages, eight kilometres of beach, 24 kilometres of leisure trail, and equestrian centre, 245 hectares of forest preserve, a fitness centre and two pools are all part of the potent mix.

GOLF FACILITIES
Best season for golf: All year round.

COURSES:	LENGTH	PAR	FEES
Ocean			
	5644m	72	$87
Sea Marsh			
	5640m	72	$78
Harbour Town Golf Links*			
	6324m	71	$150

Driving ranges, putting greens, practice bunkers; golf academy.
*Closed for restoration May 2000 – January 2001.

Facilities key

530+   400

BECAUSE YOU CAN NEVER HAVE ENOUGH POWER.

A philosophy at Bentley, one which has led to the development of the Arnage Red Label.

Housing a turbocharged, 6.75 litre V8 engine, it produces 400bhp and almost 50% more torque than its nearest rival – a phenomenal 619lb.ft.

0 – 60mph is reached in under 6 seconds, and 30 – 70mph in an effortless 5.5 seconds;

performance figures that would make impressive reading for a car half its stature.

Such performance is contained, when needed, by four huge ventilated anti – lock disc brakes; powerful enough to bring the motor car from 60 – 0mph in a mere 2.85 seconds.

The Bentley Arnage Red Label. Appealing to the megalomaniac in all of us.

Bentley Motors Limited,
Crewe, Cheshire, CW1 3PL, UK.
Telephone: +44 (0) 808 100 5200 for further information,
or visit our website at www.bentleymotors.co.uk

NORTH CAROLINA Seriously good golf

Flatlands near the coast of North Carolina give way to the rolling country further inland, which in turn gives way to the mystical Great Smoky Mountains and the neighbouring Blue Ridge Mountains where hillbilly life still thrives.

Downtown Wilmington is a classic of the Old South, there's Civil War history to discover at Greenboro and elsewhere, while golfing enthusiasts will surely be drawn by the fascinating PGA Golf Hall of Fame at Pinehurst.

GETTING THERE Raleigh is one of America's busiest regional airports. Explore beyond the freeways to discover the real essence of the Southern States.

APRÈS GOLF Life is unhurried in these parts; try to take in a country fair – and a visit to one of the numerous flea markets. Discover some real home cooking, Southern-style. Try some grits (like porridge) for breakfast. Rib shacks are an experience, with their mammoth servings.

OFF THE COURSE If you like the outdoor life there's so much to do here. North Carolina has some good white-sand beaches and offshore islands to explore, while the mountain regions abound with beautiful lakes and vast woods.

NOT TO BE MISSED Tour a tobacco plantation; visit the huge North Carolina Aquarium, the USS North Carolina Battleship Memorial and not least, the cottonfields.

FACTS AND FIGURES
- **Until 1935, when course irrigation was introduced, Pinehurst was played with sand greens.**
- **Now there are 42 courses in its immediate area, and more than 350 in the state which you can visit.**
- **Black Mountain, near Ashville, has one of the world's longest holes – an 683 metres par six.**

Think of North Carolina, think of Pinehurst. It has become a focal point for visiting players, with more courses than you will ever play. Closely linked to the early history of golf in the States, it was almost certainly the first purpose-built holiday golf resort in the New World when a nine-hole course was created there more than a hundred years ago.

There is, however, far more to the state than Pinehurst alone. The varied terrain allows golfing visitors to choose between courses in mountain country in the west, the Blue Ridge and Smokies; what is charmingly termed 'the heartland' in the pine-carpeted centre; or the shallows and dunes of the Atlantic coastline.

Its mild climate makes North Carolina popular for off-season golf holidays. A great destination for families, couples and small groups.

NEW DEVELOPMENTS
- **The ultimate accolade finally arrived at Donald Ross's revered masterpiece, Pinehurst No.2, when the US Open was held there in 1999.**

CLIMATE
Generally, the climate is mild, with four distinct seasons giving vibrant colours in spring and autumn, skiing in North Carolina's mountains in winter and warm to sweltering summer days.

Sample point: Charlotte

RECOMMENDED CAR HIRE *Hertz*
UK: +44 (0) 870 848 4848
Germany: +49 (0) 180 533 3535
Website: www.hertz.com

Price guide
Round of golf / Golf balls
Small beer / 4/5 star hotel room

CONTACT
North Carolina Division of Tourism, Department of Commerce, 301 North Wilmington Street, Raleigh, North Carolina 27601 – 2825 USA
Tel: +1 919 733 4171   Fax: +1 919 733 8582

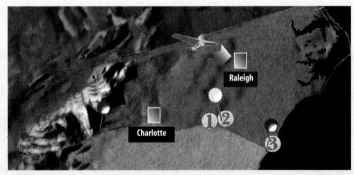

Favourite fairways

① PINEHURST
The world's largest golf resort has eight 18-hole courses. The most famous, No. 2, was created by Scotsman Donald Ross, and is generallly acknowledged as a supreme test of accuracy and approach play. The course undulates past ranks of mature pine over ideal sandy land.
Par 72   Length 6419m (No. 2 Course)
1 Carolina Vista, P.O. Box 4000, Village of Pinehurst, NC 28374
Tel: +1 910 295 8141
Fax: +1 910 295 8503

Hotels

◗ **Sea Trail Golf Resort**	Page 30
◖ **Springdale Country Club**	Page 31
○ **Talamore Golf & Country Club**	Page 32

② TALAMORE AT PINEHURST
Highly ranked since its inception, this Rees-Jones designed course has gentle slopes, subtle mounding and large sculpted sand traps. All the hazards are visible, as are the many mature pines bordering each fairway.   *Par 71   Length 6419m*
48 Talamore Drive, Southern Pines, NC 28387
Tel: +1 910 692 5884   Fax: +1 910 692 4421

③ BALD HEAD ISLAND
Tucked away on a car-less island reached only by passenger ferry, this is a fine example of George Cobb's philosophy of letting nature have its way. The holes wind past 15 freshwater lagoons, through maritime forest and across Atlantic dunes.
Par 72   Length 6268m   **South Bald Head Wynd., 28461**
Tel: +1 910 457 7310   Fax: +1 910 457 7395

SEA TRAIL GOLF RESORT & CONFERENCE CENTRE

Hotel information

211 Clubhouse Road
Sunset Beach
North Carolina 28468

Tel: +1 910 287 1100
Fax: +1 910 287 1104
Email: seatrail@infoave.net
Web: www.seatrail.com

Accolades

AAA Three Diamonds

Airport

Myrtle Beach Int (S. Carolina): 45 mins
Wilmington (N. Carolina): 55 mins

Accommodation price guide

Accepted credit cards
AE MC V DC

Preferred tour operator

From UK
Eagle
Golf Tours   Tel: +44 (0) 1273 749661
Destination
Golf   Tel: +44 (0) 20 8891 5151
From Germany
Blue
Ridge Tours Tel: +49 (0) 5137 122600

Recreational facilities

Golf, tennis, badminton, volleyball, indoor and outdoor swimming pools, whirlpools, fitness classes; sauna and spa, massage therapist; group activities such as paintball and team building exercises; children's activities (seasonal and holiday); biking, jogging, walking.

Meeting/business facilities

24 rooms, for up to 2000 delegates; secretarial services available.

Local attractions

Fort Fisher historical site, the Palace Theatre; unspoilt barrier island beach within five minutes.

Gloriously located on 54 holes of golf, just five minutes from the barrier island oceanfront of Sunset Beach, the wonderful Sea Trail Resort promises beautiful scenery and great golf without the slightest chance of a traffic jam.

Guests stay in efficiencies, mini-suites or one- to four-bedroom luxury fairway villas. Efficiencies offer bed and bath only; mini-suites include a kitchenette with microwave and refrigerator; villas have a fully-equipped kitchen with a dishwasher, washer and dryer, living room and open or screened porch.

The PGAS-sanctioned golf school, floodlit driving range, putting greens and two clubhouses – with full-service pro shops, snack bars, restaurants and lounges – round out the golfing experience. In addition to the resort's own three fine courses, there are more than 100 other courses to play in the area.

The Village Activity Center offers complimentary membership to resort guests, with indoor and outdoor pools and whirlpools, an exercise centre, sauna, licenced massage therapist, fitness classes and children's activities in high season.

The state-of-art 2800m^2 Carolina Conference Center is ideal for meetings of from 10 to 2000.

Special rates are available for groups, extended stays, holidays and off-season bookings.

GOLF FACILITIES

Best season for golf: March to May and September to December.

COURSES:	LENGTH	PAR	FEES
Sea Trail Rees Jones			
	6146m	72	$70
Sea Trail Willard Byrd			
	6136m	72	$65
Sea Trail Don Maples			
	6137m	72	$65

Putting green, floodlit driving range, golf clinics, large range of tournaments open to guests.

Facilities key

531   2000

SPRINGDALE COUNTRY CLUB

Recreational facilities

On-site restaurants: The Dining Room, The Sourwood Grille; golf, golf shop, lounge, gardens, golf practice facility.

Meeting/business facilities

Four rooms, for up to 100 delegates.

Local attractions

Baltimore Estate, Pisgah National Forest, Cherokee Indian Reservation; fishing, biking, hiking.

Hotel information

200 Golfwatch Road
Canton
North Carolina
28716

Tel: +1 828 235 8451
Toll free in the USA: 800-553-3027
Fax: +1 828 648 5502
Email: info@springdalegolf.com
Web: www.springdalegolf.com

Airport

Asheville: 45 mins

Accommodation price guide

Accepted credit cards
AE   MC   V

Located in the Great Smoky Mountains of western North Carolina, Springdale combines the challenge of a championship, 5560-metre, par 72 mountain golf course with the serenity of a classic mountain retreat.

Unlimited golf awaits you on one of Carolina's most scenic courses. The front nine features tree-lined mountain fairways leading to large bent grass greens. Among these holes is the notorious 'Springdale Spasm', an uphill, 391-metre par four with a dog-leg to the right and a mountain stream from tee to green. Once you have mastered the Spasm, the back nine leads you through a scenic valley for more mountain vistas. Spend a little extra time on the 17th tee to take in the grandeur of the Great Smoky Mountains.

Your complete golfing package includes unlimited play, lodgings in your own mountain cottage, breakfast every morning, and authentic Southern dining each evening. After a round or two, you may wish to explore the beautiful landscape and many famous attractions nearby, or you can just settle into a rocker on your own private deck and watch the sun set as you plan tomorrow's assault on the Springdale Spasm.

GOLF FACILITIES
Best season for golf: All year round.

COURSES:	LENGTH	PAR	FEES
Springdale	6218m	72	included

Full length driving range, putting greens, chipping greens, practice bunker, personal golf cart provided for entire length of stay.

Facilities key

6   100

TALAMORE VILLAS

Hotel information

48 Talamore Drive
Southern Pines
North Carolina
28387

Tel: +1 910 692 1070
Fax: +1 910 693 0111
Email: travel@talamore.com
Web: www.talamore.com

Accolades

☆☆☆☆ Championship golf course

Airport

Southern Pines/Pinehurst: 5 mins
Raleigh/Durham: 1 hr 15mins
Greensboro: 1 hr 10 mins

Accommodation price guide

Accepted credit cards
MC V

Talamore's New Villas offer privacy and spectacular views of Reservoir Park and Talamore's four-star Rees Jones golf course.

From its very beginning, Talamore has been much more than the ordinary. This 125-hectare tract of rolling pines features a dramatic 50-metre elevation change from the entrance to the glistening pond which challenges tee shots across the dramatic 18th fairway. Since its opening in 1991, Talamore has drawn praise from both players and reviewers.

Each fully-equipped villa features a complete kitchen, washer/dryer, two bedrooms, two en-suite baths, three TVs and a VCR as well as a spacious living room and dining area. Daily maid service, cable TV, free local calls and use of the new swimming pool and cabana are inclusive, all adding up to the offer of a true home away from home.

Conveniently located on Midland Road, in the Village of Pinehurst area, Talamore's luxurious villas are minutes away from all the Championship golf courses, restaurants and shopping. Reservoir Park is also immediately adjacent, with its many miles of nature trails and scenic overlooks.

Talamore features a full-service property management company and a golf and travel service whose attentive staff will attend to all the details of your golf, business, lodging and ownership needs.

Whether you stay for a night or a year, Talamore provides superior service at all levels.

Recreational facilities

Outdoor swimming pool, cabana, walking and nature trail; equestrian facilities, tennis, spa treatments all available locally.

Meeting/business facilities

One room, for up to 40 delegates.

Local attractions

Village shopping, pottery, Sandhills Community College Horticultural Gardens.

GOLF FACILTIES
Best season for golf: Mid-February to mid-November.

COURSES:	LENGTH	PAR	FEES
Talamore			
	6214m	71	$49-99
The Legacy Golf Links			
	6478m	72	$39-99
The Carolina			
	6395m	72	$49-89
Tobacco Road			
	6050m	71	$49-89
Plantation Golf Club			
	6575m	72	$59-109

18-hole Rees Jones four-star rated golf course, driving range, practice putting green, a number of tournaments open to guests.

Facilities key

60
100

NEW ENGLAND
Where heritage is a way of life

The English explorer Captain John Smith, while cruising the coast of North America in 1614, christened it New England. This heavily forested region is scattered with picturesque villages and towns, small farms, granite mountain ranges and lakes and ponds, with a dramatic coast 10,000 kilometres long.

Here you can find quaint clapboard houses by the harbour and vast cities exuding culture and excitement, 'Ivy League' college towns and idyllic mountain wilderness.

It is quite simply the most beautiful, historic and dignified area of America. Not suprisingly, therefore, tourism is big business, and golf, though not often a priority for visitors, is well catered for.

NEW DEVELOPMENTS
● Steve Durkee has designed an extra nine holes at the Brattleboro Country Club.
● Okemo Valley Resort in Ludlow opens in the summer of 2000 and is expected to be one of the finest courses in New England.

CLIMATE
Expect changeable weather and rain at any time of year. Both summer and winter conditions can be extreme. Temperatures can vary from day to day.

RECOMMENDED CAR HIRE — Hertz
UK: +44 (0) 870 848 4848
Germany: +49 (0) 180 533 3535
Website: www.hertz.com

Price guide €
Round of golf	🍺🍺🍺	Golf balls	🍺🍺
Small beer	🍺🍺🍺	4/5 star hotel room	🍺🍺🍺

CONTACT
Boston Convention & Visitors Bureau, Greater Boston CVB, 2 Copley Place, Suite 105 Boston, MA 02116
Tel: +1 617 867 8259   Fax: +1 617 424 7664

The most European of all the USA's major cities, Boston manages at the same time to be very Irish, German, British, Italian and, well, American.

This is the heartland of the American establishment. They study at Harvard and go to play on Cape Cod and the exclusive offshore islands of Nantucket and Martha's Vineyard.

Massachusetts is brim-full of place names recalling colonial days – including Plymouth, where the Pilgrim Fathers stepped ashore to found their pioneering settlement.

GETTING THERE Boston's airport is one of the USA's very busiest, with a wide range of scheduled services.

APRÈS GOLF New England clam chowder is outstanding. Boston and other towns offer international cuisine as well as succulent lobsters and steaming shellfish.

OFF THE COURSE With superb galleries and outstanding street entertainment, you don't have to spend heaps of money to have fun. When the snow falls, winter sports supplant the golf which is pure joy at other times.

NOT TO BE MISSED The bustling student town of Cambridge; whale and dolphin watching; the pretty neighbouring states of Vermont and New Hampshire.

FACTS AND FIGURES
● The Ryder Cup returned to the place of its birth in 1999 when the 33rd staging of the event was played at the Brookline Country Club.
● Lyman Orchards is based on one of America's oldest working farms, established since 1741, and offers 36 holes of championship golf.

Favourite fairways

1 THE COUNTRY CLUB OF VERMONT
The course, designed by Canadian Graham Cooke, was opened in the spring of 1999 to rave reviews. A links style course, be prepared to hit from countless, uphill, downhill and sidehill lies – simply walking the course can be a challenge. And so can the extensive bunkers, particularly on the fairways. The back nine venture in the woods where the views are spectacular and the atmosphere is completely different, with less of a 'Scottish' feel. Green fees are high, but worth it; and there is quite an air of exclusivity about the club.
Par 72   Length 6222m
2800 Country Club Road, Waterbury, Vermont
Tel: +1 802 244 1800

2 SAGAMORE SPRINGS
Despite its 'main street' address, this charming 1926 course seems remote and untouched, protected as it is by the unspoilt woods and meadows of the Lynnfield conservation area. Built by the Luff brothers, and still run by their family, its bent grass layout – from the dead straight, big-hitting 425-metre par five opening hole, through the devilish ninth, to the steep uphill

165-metre par three final challenge – will flatter and torment in equal measure. A stone's throw from Boston, open year-round, with week day green fees as low as $30 and and no mandatory carts this is a treat not to be missed. Rounds vary from £55 to £100.
Par 70   Length 5428m
1287 Main Street, Lynnfield, Massachussetts 01940
Tel: +1 781 334 3151

3 RICHTER PARK GOLF CLUB
One of *Golf Digest*'s 'Top 25 Municipal Courses in America' this scenic and beautifully manicured 18-hole championship course offers something for everyone. Families will enjoy the welcome given to children (they run a 'junior program' for eight- to 17-year-olds throughout the summer), and the serious player will relish some of Connecticut's trickiest holes (the par four 12th is particularly unforgiving of over-enthusiastic putting). Relaxed and informal, this is holiday golf at its best.
Par 72   Length 5786m
Richter Park Golf Course, 100 Aunt Hack Road, Danbury Connecticut 06811 .
Tel: +1 203 792 2550

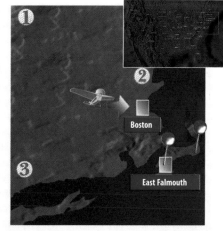

Hotels
● **New Seabury Resort**
Page 34

● **Wequassett Inn Resort & Golf Club**
Page 35

NEW SEABURY
RESORT & CONFERENCE CENTER

Recreational facilities

Cabana and two outdoor pools, 16 all-weather tennis courts, bicycle rentals, jogging trails; marketplace with shops and eateries.

Meeting/business facilities

16 rooms, for up to 200 delegates.

Local attractions

Organised excursions to Martha's Vineyard, Nantucket; antique shopping.

Hotel information

PO Box 549
New Seabury
Massachusetts
MA 02649

Tel: +1 800 999 9033
Fax: +1 508 477 9790
Email: info@newseabury.com
Web: www.newseabury.com

Airport

Barnstable-Hyannis: 30 mins
Boston (Logan): 1 hr 30 mins
Providence (T.F.Green): 1 hr 30 mins

Accommodation price guide

Accepted credit cards
AE DC MC V

Mention Cape Cod and people immediately think: "Holidays!" But, with its solitary stretches of sandy beaches, drifting dunes and sparkling waters, the Cape is also the perfect place for business groups. You'll find an abundance of the Cape's natural resources at New Seabury, one of the most ambitious projects in resort planning in the USA's northeast.

Cape Cod's largest resort extends over 800 lush hectares. Everywhere you look, from winding roads to hidden ponds to major golf courses, you will be aware of the efforts made to enhance man's relationship with nature.

Originally billed as "The Pebble Beach of the East", with the ocean visible on seven holes, New Seabury's Blue Course is the big brother to the Green Course and is of true championship calibre.

Howling winds, lengthy par fours framed by sea and sand and the occasional sight of the bluefish jumping in the waters of Nantucket Sound will make this a round to remember.

Designed by William Mitchell and opened in 1964, the opening holes run along the oceanfront, with the spectacular third perhaps the most photographed hole in New England. The back nine is wooded and tight, and the holes challenge even the low handicappers.

GOLF FACILITIES
Best season for golf: Spring, Summer, Autumn.

COURSES:	LENGTH	PAR	FEES
Blue Championship	6584m	72	$115
Green Challenger	5518m	70	$75

Two great 18-hole golf courses on site.

Facilities key

157 200

WEQUASSETT INN RESORT & GOLF CLUB

Hotel information

Pleasant Bay
Chatham
Cape Cod
Massachusets 02633

Tel: +1 508 432 5400
Fax: +1 508 432 5032
Web: www.wequassett.com

Accolades

★★★☆ Mobil

Airport

Logan International: 90 mins
Barnstable Municipal: 20 mins

Accommodation price guide

Accepted credit cards
AE DC MC V

Recreational facilities

Four tennis courts, heated outdoor swimming pool; private beach; sailing; croquet, shuffleboard, volleyball; fitness centre; country store; tours of Pleasant Bay; horse riding, whale watching, fly fishing school all available locally.

Meeting/business facilities

Eleven rooms for up to 250 delegates; business centre.

Local attractions

Cape Cod Museum of Fine Arts, Museum of Natural History; antique shopping; Nantucket and Martha's Vineyard.

Wequassett Inn is distinguished as Cape Cod's only Mobil Four Star resort and a member of Preferred Hotels, an association of independent luxury hotels located around the world.

The property encompasses nine beautifully landscaped waterfront hectares, 20 buildings, including Cape Cod-style cottages and colonial structures, house the facility's 104 luxurious guest rooms and public space.

Wequassett Inn also offers 1100 square metres of function space, suitable for hosting groups of from 10 to 250 people. Many settings include patios and decks offering spectacular views of Pleasant Bay and Round Cove.

An abundance of recreational activities are available on-site, including four tennis courts, a heated swimming pool, private beach, fitness centre, sailing and croquet.

Guests have exclusive non-membership privileges at the new private golf club adjacent to the property. Designed by Cornish, Silva and Mungeam, Cape Cod National sits on 60 hectares of sandy loam. At 6273 metres, it offers heavily-wooded slopes and kettle holes with dramatic elevation changes and outstanding views of the bay and the ocean.

GOLF FACILITIES

Best season for golf: April to November.

COURSES: LENGTH	PAR	FEES
Cape Cod National		
6273m	72	$120
Captain's Course		
6212m	72	$60
Cranberry Valley		
6168m	72	$60

Facilities key

104   250

ARIZONA Discover the old West

Arizona is redolent of classic Westerns and contains some of the USA's most spectacular scenery, from the cavernous depths of the Grand Canyon to the desert-like scenery outside Phoenix and its leisure resort offspring Scottsdale. Here you can discover native American culture and folklore, in the tribal lands of the Hopi, Navajo and Apache.

GETTING THERE Phoenix has direct flights from Europe. Arizona's superbly engineered and well-surfaced backroads reveal fresh delights at every twist and turn.

APRÈS GOLF Phoenix – America's fastest growing city – has all the entertainments and culture you would expect, while Scottsdale has an abundance of gourmet food havens. The South West also has its own distinctive cuisine – anyone for rattlesnake and super hot chillies?

OFF THE COURSE With a water table lying just beneath the surface, the Arizona desert produces a veritable carpet of flowers at springtime. Venture out of your air-conditioned room to mountain bike, horse ride, hike or take a 4x4 off-roader safari hosted by a genuine Apache.

NOT TO BE MISSED Indian craft centres, restored cow towns and mining settlements and an aircraft or helicopter ride through the Grand Canyon.

FACTS & FIGURES

- Arizona has 242 golf courses – 4896 holes in total – mostly concentrated in the area around Phoenix.
- Arizona provided three out of the 1999 US Ryder Cup team: Phil Mickelson, Jim Furyk and Tom Lehman.
- The two courses at the London Bridge Golf Club on the shores of Lake Havasu lie in the shadow of the former London Bridge, sold to the US and transported brick by brick in the early '70s.

Arizona golf, always popular in the States, is attracting more and more foreign visitors. Ease of access, superb locations, diversity of top quality courses and the ability to play year-round are key factors. Desert temperatures make October to April the prime season, but the north is cooler and bargains can be had in high summer.

The 'Valley of the Sun' – the Phoenix/Scottsdale area offers more five-star accommodation than any other city in the US. Native American arts and crafts – Arizona is the site of the Navajo nation – and silverware, the wildlife of the Sonoran desert and the mythic lifestyle of the Old West make Arizona an ideal destination for non-golfing partners and families too.

NEW DEVELOPMENTS

- Verde Santa Fe is Arizona's newest course. Its location in the foothills 1200 metres above Phoenix means comfortable temperatures all year.
- Group deals are common across Arizona. The Raven at Sabino Springs offers a ten-play pass for $350 which can be used for consecutive plays by two or more together.
- The Golfing Holiday Company's Arizona-specific brochure features over 120 courses.

CLIMATE

Clean, dry, desert air and many long hours of sunshine makes for pleasant golf. Winter days are sunny and mild but cold at night and it snows in the high country.

Sample point: Phoenix

RECOMMENDED CAR HIRE *Hertz*
UK: +44 (0) 870 848 4848
Germany: +49 (0) 180 533 3535
Website: www.hertz.com

Price guide

Round of golf	🍺🍺🍺🍺	Golf balls	🍺🍺🍺
Small beer	🍺🍺	4/5 star hotel room	🍺🍺🍺🍺

CONTACT
Arizona Tourist Bureau, Phoenix, Arizona Tel: +1 602 952-2106

Favourite fairways

① RIO RICO

"I really felt I had a classic on my hands." So said Robert Trent Jones of his Rio Rico design, and once you have experienced its tight landing areas and speedy, slippery greens you will be forced to agree. The ability to hit accurate straight shots is what counts here, with dense clusters of trees and the ever-present lakes.
Par 72   6114m
1069 Camino Caralampi, Rio Rico, Arizona 85648 Tel: +1 520 281 8567

② GRAYHAWK

Scene of Greg Norman's $1m victory in the 1999 Anderson Consulting World Championship. Greyhawk's two courses, designed by David Graham and Gary Panks – feature a number of memorable holes.

The Talon offers the 'Three Sisters', a set of bunkers to the right of the green on the par 5 third so deep they require wooden planking to support the walls, while the Raptor is a less dramatic round – but it has more hazards (an extra 22 bunkers).
Par 72, 5849m (Talon); Par 72, 6053m (Raptor)
19600 North Pima Road, 85255 Scottsdale
Tel: +1 602 502 1800 Web: www.grayhawk.com

RAVEN AT SOUTH MOUNTAIN

Renowned for the quality of its service and amenities, this David Graham/Gary Panks designed course is eminently playable.

The par 4 third is a 436-metre uphill test of strength, while the heavily-bunkered 296-metre fifth really needs a long iron or a three wood from the tee. The 18th is a fabulous finish – a delicate second shot to the green must avoid the water to the right and the bunkers to the left.
Par 72   6008m **3636 East Baseline Road, Phoenix 85040 Tel: +1 602 243 3636**

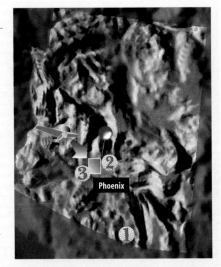

Hotels

 Scottsdale Princess

Page 37

THE FAIRMONT SCOTTSDALE PRINCESS

Hotel information

7575 East Princess Drive
Scottsdale
Arizona 85255

Tel: +1 480 585 4848
Fax: +1 480 585 0086
Web: www.scottsdaleprincess.com

Accolades

AAA   Five Diamonds
Conde Nast Traveler's Top Ten
Travel and Leisure's Top 100 Resorts

Airport

Phoenix Sky Harbour Int'l: 30 mins

Accommodation price guide

Accepted credit cards
AE MC V DC

Preferred tour operator

From UK
British Airways Golf
Holidays   Tel: +44 (0) 1293 722 745

Recreational facilities

Tennis, spa, golf, basketball, squash, racquetball, volleyball, badminton, table tennis, fishing; the Princess Shop, fashion boutiques, country & western shop, Southwestern specialty shop, swim shop, tennis pro shop, golf pro shop, spa shop; horseback riding, desert jeep tours, Hummer tours, river rafting, balloon rides and mountain biking all available locally.

Meeting/business facilities

28 rooms, for up to 2000 delegates; business centre.

Local attractions

Rawhide western town, Sedona, Old Town Scottsdale, Taliesin, Heard Museum, botanical gardens, Bank One ball park.

The Fairmont Scottsdale Princess, located where the mountains meet the desert, is a celebrated year-round resort offering superb accommodations, fitness facilities, dining, and entertainment. There are 450 guest rooms in the main building, 125 casitas, and 75 villas all with living and working areas, walk-in closets, and terraces.

With more than 156 golf courses to boast of, Scottsdale is home to many of the world's finest and most challenging golf courses. At the resort's dedicated golf reservations centre, where it's par for the course for every golfer to be treated like a pro, the Fairmont Scottsdale Princess's expert agents can book tee-times for guests at more than 40 fine courses in the area or provide all the assistance needed in planning the perfect golf vacation.

Restaurants on site include La Hacienda, a AAA four diamond award winner and Mobil Guide's only four-star Mexican restaurant in North America. Traditional American and Southwestern cuisine, including club sandwiches, hearty salads, fajitas, and new rotisserie and wood-burning specialties are offered at Las Ventanas. A contemporary steak and seafood venue, The Grill features prime and dry-aged prime steaks, fresh seafood, and lobster. One of two AAA five diamond restaurants in Arizona, Marquesa features a blend of Catalan and Mediterranean cuisines.

GOLF FACILTIES
Best season for golf: January to April.

COURSES:	LENGTH	PAR	FEES
TPC			
	6393m	71	$181
Grayhawk			
	6973m	72	$200
Suridge Canyon			
	6238m	71	$150

Scottsdale district boasts more than 156 courses; hotel's dedicated golf reservations centre is able to book tee-times at 40 courses; two 18-hole tournament players' courses adjacent to hotel; practice facilities; guest tournaments.

Facilities key

 650 **2000**

THE CARIBBEAN   Islands of individual character

Most people have their dream island in the sun – and in most cases the location is somewhere in the sunny Caribbean sea.

It's the nature of island groups that however close they might be, each individual island has its own unique nature – and that's certainly true in these parts.

It's partly a matter of topography: the Dominican Republic's lofty peaks, almost Alpine in stature, contrasting with the low, rolling hills of Barbados and its also a matter of differing cultures.

The British, French, Dutch, Danes, Spanish and, yes, the Americans too, have left their imprint here; so too have the Africans who came as slaves and the native Indian tribes, the Caribs and the Arawaks, who were squeezed off the islands. The result is an amazing cacophony of colour, sights and sounds – from the rhumba of Cuba to the reggae of Jamaica.

Cuba in itself is one of the great melting pots, a fascinating opening out for tourism once again.

GETTING THERE There are a host of scheduled and charter flights from North America and Europe into the islands (either direct or via Miami) and a busy network of inter-island services too.

APRÈS GOLF Chilling out is a pre-occupation in an environment where haste is the last word on anyone's mind. Relax with a rum punch and you're king of the world, or at least this little piece of it. Food ranges from bland and boring to magnificent. Try the lobster, the ubiquitous conch (as fritters or chowder) and dolphin (no, not Flipper, but a type of fish!). Curried goat, plantain, salt fish and ackee, the choice is wide.

OFF THE COURSE Catching the sun and spending time either on, in or under the water is high on most people's list. Enjoy the vestiges of a colonial past and maybe take in a game of cricket. Driving is easy and rewarding in the Dominican Republic, difficult in Cuba where car hire is not easy for visitors, though there are numerous coach tour options.

NOT TO BE MISSED A jaunt from the Dominican Republic into Haiti, with which nation it shares the island of Hispaniola; the faded colonial glories of old Havana; lively Bridgetown with its marina and bars.

FACTS & FIGURES

- Water for irrigation is scarce throughout the region. Frequently the primary water supply is rain water captured from elaborately designed roof systems.
- The Manchester Country Club is Jamaica's oldest course, having been built over 100 years ago.
- Despite an enormous growth of interest in recent years, Antigua has only three courses – Cedar Valley, Jolly Harbour and the private, members-only nine-hole Mill Reef Club.
- St George's Golf Club in Bermuda is only five minutes from Penno's Wharf, a major docking point for Caribbean cruise ships.

Jamaica's Half Moon features four top-class courses

As if a tropical climate and clear blue warm waters were not enough, the Caribbean can boast some of the world's most beautiful and challenging golf courses, host to many major and local tournaments.

Jamaica, Barbados and Bermuda are the premier golfing destinations for Europeans but enthusiasts should not ignore Puerto Rico where no fewer than four Robert Trent Jones Senior courses are to be found at Cerromar Beach.

Bermuda has some claim to be the golfing capital of the region, with eight high-quality courses. Be warned, though, that booking tee-time before travel is not possible on most courses, and times can only be requested on arrival in the resort.

Jamaica may be more readily associated with rum-punch and reggae, but golfing on this historical island shows it in a different light. Here you can find some of the finest courses in the world, and the addition of the David Leadbetter Golf Academy offers the possibility of improvement to players of all standards. The Sandals resort at Ochos Rios has a tricky course with some of the finest scenery in the Caribbean.

Barbados is home to the legendary Sandy Lane, which sprawls over the site of a former sugar plantation, but the hotel is now undergoing considerable refurbishment.

Most courses have in-season and off-season prices, as well as guest and non-guest, member and non-member prices. Many courses are are also part of resorts or hotels, and the most prestigious require carts and a mandatory caddy.

NEW DEVELOPMENTS

- A few kilometres from Mustique, the eight square kilometre Canouan Island is home to the newly-opened exclusive Carenage Bay Club: 178 villas set in 320 hectares of tropical beauty. A high point is the 26-hectare golf course.
- Port Lucaya Marketplace, 25000 square metres of waterfront shopping and restaurants, now rivals Freeport as a tourist Mecca.
- The opening of the San-San Golf Club in Port Antonio, Jamaica, brings the number of courses on the island to 12.
- The David Leadbetter Academy is based at the Half moon Club, Jamaica.

Hotels

- ◐ **Casa de Campo**
  Page 40
- ◑ **Melia Caribe**
  Page 41
- ◯ **Melia Las Americas**
  Page 42
- ◑ **Royal Westmoreland**
  Page 43
- ◯ **The Tryall Club**
  Page 44
- ◑ **The Westin Rio Mar**
  Beach Resort Page 45

Favourite fairways

RECOMMENDED CAR HIRE *Hertz*
UK: +44 (0) 870 848 4848
Germany: +49 (0) 180 533 3535
Website: www.hertz.com

① CEDAR VALLEY

This exhilarating, undulating course has hosted the Eastern Caribbean Golf Championships and is home to the Antigua Open. With green fees as low as US$35 and US$20 for a buggy, this is a course everyone should play. There is a wide variety of holes, from the par 4 fifth, its lofty tee affording spectacular views, to the par 3 11th across the lake (which has been known to dry up!), and the par 5 ninth where a massive drive seems like such a good idea and lost balls are almost inevitable.
Par 69   Length 5424m
Cedar Valley Golf Club, St John's, Antigua
Tel: +1 268 462 0161

② LUCAYA GOLF & COUNTRY CLUB

Designed by Dick Wilson in 1963, the Lucaya is the number-one course in the Bahamas and is rated in the top three for the Caribbean. Beautifully maintained, it features more than 70 bunkers and a rough composed of that really tricky, wiry Bermuda grass. Water comes into play around the halfway mark, with the 355-metre par 4 ninth demanding a long iron second shot to avoid the lake. The view from the tenth tee of the clubhouse amid the jungle is stunning, and the trip back involves some big hitting.
Par 72   Length 6218m
Lucaya Golf & Country Club, Port Lucaya, Bahamas
Tel: +1 242 373 1066

③ HALF MOON

This fabulous resort boasts access to Montego Bay's four par 72 courses, but the jewel in the crown is its own Robert Trent Jones-designed championship course which is an unforgettable challenge

for even the most seasoned golfer. The spacious course, with its David Leadbetter Golf Academy, is set in a 160-hectare estate alongside some of Jamaica's most beautiful beaches. Repeated play will reap rewards in scoring terms, as many of the holes contain traps for the unwary.
Par 72   Length 6510m
Half Moon Golf, Tennis & Beach Club, PO Box 80, Rose Hall, Montego Bay, Jamaica Tel: +1 876 953 2211 Fax: +1 876 953 2731

④ RIDDELL'S BAY GOLF & COUNTRY CLUB

Designed as a links course by Devereux Emmett (architect of Washington's Congressional course, site of the 1997 US Open) and opened in 1922, Riddell's Bay is Bermuda's oldest club. It winds along a peninsula which measures only 550 metres at its widest point. Recent improvements (under the direction of American designer Ed Beidel) have maintained the course's reputation as a shot-maker's delight while modernising the overall look.
Par 70   Length 5182m
PO Box WK 236, Warwick, Bermuda
Tel: +1 441 238 1060   Fax: +1 441 238 8785

⑤ JOLLY HARBOUR GOLF CLUB

Next to the thriving Jolly Harbour marina's super-yacht terminal, this newly reconstructed championship course is set around seven treacherous lakes in luxurious tropical parkland. The wide, open fairways and absence of trees reassure, but the greens are subtle (especially on the back nine), and the easterly wind can catch out even the most experienced. Designed by Florida's Karl Litton.
Par 71   Length 5424m
Jolly Harbour, Antigua   Tel: +1 268 480 6950

CLIMATE

Almost everywhere the wettest months are from May-October while winter is relatively dry. The climate is warm to hot and usually humid.

Sample point: Santo Domingo

Price guide   €

Round of golf	🪙🪙🪙	Golf balls	🪙🪙🪙🪙
Small beer	🪙🪙🪙	4/5 star hotel room	🪙🪙🪙

CONTACT

Each of the myriad islands in the region has its own tourist board – they're too numerous to mention here. Check with your local travel agent.

CASA DE CAMPO

Hotel information

PO Box 140
La Romana

Tel: +1 809 523 8171
Fax: +1 809 523 8547
Email: sales@ccampo.com.do
Web: www.casadecampo.cc

Accolades

Caribbean's Golf Resort of the Year –
Caribbean World Magazine
Pinnacle Award winner – Successful
Meetings

Airport

La Romana/Casa de Campo: 5 mins
Las Americas/Santo Domingo: 1 hr 30 mins
Punta Cana: 1 hr 30 mins

Accommodation price guide

Accepted credit cards
AE MC V

Recreational facilities

La Terraza Tennis Centre has 13 courts;
private beach with watersports; horse
riding and polo; gym; shooting centre
offers trap, skeet and sporting clays;
deep sea and river fishing; 'Kids'n'Casa'
supervised programme.

Meeting/business facilities

Nine rooms, for up to 500 people.

Local attractions

Altos de Chavon artists' village, with craft
shops, galleries and open-air theatre.

Designer Pete Dye said he actually only created
11 holes of the Teeth of the Dog course – God
created the seven skirting the ocean. Be that as it
may, it was Dye who directed 300 Dominican
labourers to sculpt the course, down to lining each
fairway with the native coral rock known as *diente del
perro* – 'teeth of the dog'.

Casa de Campo is sited on the Dominican
Republic's south-eastern coast, the tropical
atmosphere accentuated by palm trees,
bougainvillea and ocean views. In addition to the
new and luxury hotel rooms, families can take over
an entire villa with a special maid and the
supervised 'Kidz 'n' Casa' children's programme,
while the Excel Club villas offer, among other
luxuries, a pool or Jacuzzi, concierge, and private
maid or butler. A variety of international and *à la
carte* restaurants, bars and lounges are also on site.

Nearby is Altos de Chavon, an artists' colony and
home to a school of design affiliated with New
York's Parsons School. At the heart of the village is
the church of St. Stanislaus, art galleries showcasing
works of Dominican and international artists, and
the Museum of Archaeology, with its collection of
indigenous Taino artefacts. There is also a
spectacular 5000-seat Greek-style open-air theatre,
which has seen performances by such stars as Julio
Inglesias and the late Frank Sinatra.

Other sports at Casa de Campo include a clay-
pigeon shooting centre, polo and showjumping.

GOLF FACILITIES
Best season for golf: All year
round.

COURSES:	LENGTH	PAR	FEES
Teeth of the Dog			
	6298m	72	US$162
Links			
	5908m	71	US$108

Practice range, practice green; tuition
available; golf carts mandatory and
caddies available.

Facilities key

450   500

MELIÁ CARIBE

Hotel information

Playa Bávaro
Higuey
Dominican Republic

Tel: +1 809 686 7499
Fax: +1 809 686 7699
Email: melia.caribe@codetel.net.do

Accolades

★★★★

Airport

Punta Cana International: 30 mins

Accommodation price guide

Accepted credit cards
AE MC V DC

COCOTAL
GOLF & COUNTRY CLUB

Recreational facilities

Cocotal Golf & Country Club, fitness centre, four tennis courts, volleyball, aerobics, beach soccer, watersports, vast lake-sized swimming pool, scuba diving; entertainment theatre; casino.

Meeting/business facilities

Nine rooms, for up to 1,000 delegates.

Local attractions

Extensive beaches, colonial attractions of the island's capital city, Santo Domingo (195 km).

The latest addition to the Sol Meliá group's distinguished portfolio of hotels in the Caribbean, the luxurious Meliá Caribe has been specially designed for couples – especially honeymooners – as well as incentives groups, while an especial welcome is accorded to visiting golfers.

As Meliá Tropical and Cocotal Golf & Country Club, this development is part of the outstanding Palma Real complex. The Meliá Caribe is in complete harmony with its luxuriant surroundings, with a mangrove dividing the main building from the first seven bungalows and the swimming pool and beach area. There are some 22 bungalow blocks in all, between them providing some 522 air-conditioned superior rooms, all decorated in an elegant and colourful Caribbean style.

Within the 'all-inclusive' plan, guests may choose from a range of six on-site restaurants or opt to dine at the sister Meliá Tropical or Meliá Bávaro hotels, without extra charge. Superlative sporting and leisure facilities include a full range of non-motor watersports, tennis, beach games and what is probably the largest swimming pool in the entire Caribbean.

GOLF FACILITIES
Best season for golf: All year round.

COURSES: LENGTH	PAR	FEES
Cocotal		
6568m	72	US$85

Two free rounds of 18 holes per seven-day stay; one per four- to six-day stay (cart not included); on-site Sol Meliá Golf Academy run by PGA professionals.

Facilities key

522   1000

MELIÁ LAS AMERICAS

Sited alongside the new Varadero Golf Course and adjacent to the beach, this five-star deluxe resort has 220 standard rooms in the main hotel and 81 junior suites located in the bungalow section of the 340 room beachfront complex, adjacent to Plaza Americas Commercial Centre, and in walking distance of the clubhouse of the 18-hole golf course.

Inclusive features include a vast range of non-motorised watersports, four outdoor pools and a selection of restaurants and bars – as well as both daytime and night-time entertainment. The pool and children's care service offer an ideal option for enjoying family vacations.

Book the breakfast & dinner meal plan and you can take your choice of eating at any of the 12 restaurants of Sol Club Palmeras, Meliá Varadero, or Meliá Las Americas. You will receive a US$20 voucher for each dinner you purchase, redeemable in the Sol Meliá restaurant of your choice.

The optional golf programme – priced at US$50 per person per round of 18 holes; storage and lockers available. This price does not include caddy service, clubs, balls, and mandatory golf cart – enables guests to book their tee times at the hotel and save 20% at the course.

Facilities key

340   150

ROYAL WESTMORELAND

Hotel information

St. James
Barbados
West Indies

Tel: +1 246 422 4653
Fax: +1 246 422 7633
Email: villas@royal-westmoreland.com
Web: www.royal-westmoreland.com

Accolades

★★★★☆

Airport

Bridgetown Barbados: 40 mins

Accommodation price guide

€

Accepted credit cards
AE MC V

Recreational facilities

Two floodlit Har-Tru clay tennis courts, croquet; two swimming pools, whirlpool, children's pool; Sanctuary health spa, fitness centre, beauty salon, massage, aerobics, aromatherapy; golf driving range and putting green; golf pro shop.

Meeting/business facilities

In-villa meeting space for up to 20 delegates per villa.

Local attractions

Nearby fine dining and nightlife of Holetown; duty-free shopping in Bridgetown; colonial plantation heritage.

Offering the very personification of 'the good life', Royal Westmoreland features palatial and spectacular villas set around an exclusive golf course designed by the redoubtable Robert Trent Jones Jnr.

Each villa has been individually designed by leading internationally renowned architects and interior designers to provide guests with a superlative 'home from home' providing the ultimate in space and comfort.

A private housekeeper staffs every villa in the resort, while the larger villas – with up to four or more bedrooms each – have the added luxury of a cook and a butler. The larger villas also have private pools while the smaller villas have access to one of the resort's two main swimming pools.

Breakfast is available daily at the Clubhouse restaurant, which also offers fine dining and international cuisine throughout the day. On the fine, white sandy beaches of the Platinum Coast, five minutes' drive away, there is an array of watersports and calm, azure waters ideal for swimming.

The resort's unique Platinum Plan affords five 18-hole rounds of golf with an electric cart, plus a complimentary golf lesson. In addition, the seven-night package includes limousine transfers, car hire, a stocked fridge, a free massage and full membership of the Pelican Club for children.

GOLF FACILITIES

Best season for golf: All year round.

COURSES:	LENGTH	PAR	FEES
Royal Westmoreland			
	6282m	72	US$90-120
Sandy Lane			
	6004m	72	US$100

Fully equipped eight-hectare double-ended grass-only practice range; tuition by arrangement.

Facilities key

100   400

THE TRYALL CLUB

Hotel information

PO Box 1206
Montego Bay

Tel: +1 876 956 5660
Fax: +1 876 956 5673
Email: tryallclub@cwjamaica.com
Web: www.thetryallclub.co.uk

Accolades

★★★★☆

Airport

Montego Bay: 30 mins

Accommodation price guide

Accepted credit cards
AE MC V

Recreational facilities

18-hole golf course, tennis, watersports; beauty salon.

Meeting/business facilities

One free room for every 20 rooms booked; green fee discounts for groups.

Local attractions

Scuba diving, horseback riding, Dunn's River Falls, Rafting, etc.

Golfers in search of the ultimate thrill need seek no further: Tryall's beautiful course is considered one of the world's best, attracting the game's leading players to such prestigious events as the Johnnie Walker World Championships, Mazda Champions, The Jamaica Classic and Shell's Wonderful World of Golf.

Designed by Ralph Plumber, the sculpted fairways and manicured greens meander through forest-clad green hills, passing stands of coconut palms and fruit trees, round lily-padded ponds and down a two-kilometre stretch beside the sparkling blue Caribbean Sea.

The resort spreads over a lush 880-hectare property on a quiet, pristine stretch of Jamaica's north coast. 56 luxurious Estate Villas have private pools, well tended gardens and full-time staff – typically cook, maid, laundress, gardener and even a butler – to anticipate every need.

Annexed to the graceful Georgian Great House are 13 Great House Villas, with views across the golf course to the sea. Besides golf, facilities include nine cushioned Laykold tennis courts, the Almond Tree Bar, Beach Café and Restaurant and The Great House Terrace Restaurant and Cocktail Bar.

GOLF FACILITIES

Best season for golf: All year round.

COURSES:	LENGTH	PAR	FEES
Tryall Club	5688m	72	US$40-80*

Driving range, putting green; tuition packages available.

*Fees given are applicable to guests staying in villas.

Facilities key

THE WESTIN RIO MAR BEACH RESORT, COUNTRY CLUB & OCEAN VILLAS

Hotel information

6000 Rio Mar Boulevard
Rio Grande
Puerto Rico
00745-6100

Tel: +11 787 888 6200
From USA: 1-800 WESTIN-1
Fax: +11 787 888 6320
Web: www.westinriomar.com

Accolades

AAA Four Diamond
Gold Tee Award – Meetings & Conventions

Airport

San Juan International: 45 mins

Accommodation price guide

Accepted credit cards
AE MC V DC

Recreational facilities

Beachfront pools with separate adult and activity pools; watersports centre with wave-runners, sailing, kayaking, parasailing; tennis centre with 13 Har-Tru courts; dive shop; full-service spa and compete fitness centre; casino; game room; bicycle hire.

Meeting/business facilities

24 rooms, for up to 2200 delegates; oceanfront conference centre

Local attractions

El Yunque Caribbean National Forest tour; Camuy Cave tour; eco-kayaking; historic Old San Juan; PADI certified dive trips; snorkelling.

Incomparable beauty, unparalleled luxury, endless recreation opportunities and pampering hospitality are the hallmarks of this premier destination – a true golfer's paradise, designed to provide unforgettable vacations.

Atlantic panoramas, ocean breezes and iguanas play along the entire length of Tom and George Fazio's Ocean Course, a classic lay-out featuring four sets of tees, numerous bunkers and elevated greens. The signature 16th, an oceanside par three, rates among the Caribbean's best. Then there's the delightful Greg Norman designed River Course to enjoy as it rolls along lush fairways beside the Mamayes River, with vistas of mountains and sea.

Add to this, full sports and leisure facilities, 695 luxurious guest rooms, suites and oceanfront villas and you have a magic format for an ultimate sports destination. Guests enjoy 12 superb restaurants and lounges, a casino and award-winning service.

In Autumn 2000, The Ocean Villas will open as the Caribbean's newest luxury beachfront villas. The Westin Rio Mar Beach Resort, Country Club & Ocean Villas resort is truly the essence of a golfer's paradise.

GOLF FACILITIES

Best season for golf: All year round.

COURSES:	LENGTH	PAR	FEES
River Course			
	7414 m	72	US$60-150
Ocean Course			
	6371m	72	US$60-150

Practice facility; tournaments open to guests.

Facilities key

695   2200

SOUTH AMERICA The great adventure starts here

Golf and South America are not words you would automatically put together. Those who travel to Brazil, Argentina or Chile usually do so for reasons other than practising their swings. But for the more adventurous golfer, heading south offers an unbeatable combination of relaxation and play.

There is the chance to play on the many courses which make up the newly inaugurated Tour de las Americas. Admittedly the tour is very much in its infancy compared to the professional circuits in the United States or Europe, but what the golf may lack in organisation or prize money it more than makes up for in charm.

NEW DEVELOPMENTS
- Brazil will for the first time play host to a European Tour event at the São Paulo Resort in 2000.
- The Brazil 500 Years Open runs from 30th March to 2nd April 2000 and is worth a total of US$750,000 in prize money.

CLIMATE

Most of this region lies within the tropics and has a hot steamy climate, although to the south it can be quite chilly. Rainy seasons vary from region to region.

Sample point: Rio de Janerio

RECOMMENDED CAR HIRE — *Hertz*
UK: +44 (0) 870 848 4848
Germany: +49 (0) 180 533 3535
Website: www.hertz.com

CONTACT
Brazil Tourist Office, 32 Green St, London, W1Y 4AT
Tel: +44 (0) 207 499 0877

Price guide €
Round of golf	Golf balls
Small beer	4/5 star hotel room

Relative newcomers to the golf vacation scene, Brazil and Argentina are the very essence of Latin America, offering everything from rain forests and dense jungle to lonely pampas and the towering white-capped Andes.

Rio de Janeiro's towering Sugar Loaf Mountain must be one of the world's most photographed sights, and there's plenty more to set cameras clicking. Those in the right frame of mind can make carnival last all year.

Brazil and Argentina meet at the mighty Iguassu Falls, which dwarf Niagara with their sheer flow of water. Here golf can be savoured with a backdrop of tropical flowers, screeching parakeets and glorious butterflies in a true Eden.

GETTING THERE It isn't cheap to fly to South America but once there you'll live at bargain prices.

APRÈS GOLF Latin Americans know how to strut their stuff – leading to a vibrant street life. These countries have a strong sense of national identity, and there's still a rich heritage of native cultures to be found.

OFF THE COURSE Good regional airline networks in Brazil and Argentina make it easy to explore – but don't try to cram too much in between your rounds.

NOT TO BE MISSED Eat meat! (it's what Brazil and Argentina are renowned for – though there's an abundance of fresh fruit and veg for vegetarians); take all the excursions – there's so much to see.

FACTS AND FIGURES
- Golf is a rapidly growing sport throughout the continent and the courses are still relatively cheap and uncrowded to play on.

Favourite fairways

1 IGUASSU
With its formidable 18th, Iguassu boasts what is claimed to be the world's only legitimate par 6 hole but while purists continue to insist that par is possible on this 866-metre challenge, realists scoff and point out that even the greatest golfers of all time have to a man found nothing but frustration here, though several bogey sevens have been scored during the latter part of the dry season. Less ambitious players will content themselves with the course's glorious setting close by the vast and dramatic falls which mark the Argentine/Brazil border.
Par 72   Length 6983m
Av Das Cataraatas 6845, Foz Do Iguagu, Parana, CEP 85853-000, Brazil
Tel: +55 (0) 45 523 4749
Fax: +55 (0) 45 523 5737

2 BÚZIOS
One of Latin America's greatest. This idyllically cited course takes full advantage of the topography, featuring the dramatic shaping of the fairways and greens which is such a typical feature of courses designed by the Colorado, USA, based Pete and Perry Dye design team. Set amid tropical trees and shrubs, the course winds through hills and valleys bordering picturesque lakes.
Par 72   Length 6949m
Tel: +55 (0) 24 629 1240
Email: buziosgolf@openlink.com.br

3 GAVEA
Founded in 1923, this club on the outskirts of Rio de Janeiro is the second oldest in Brazil and has been the venue for numerous national championships. In the 1974 Brazilian Open, Gary Player had a second round of 59 on his way to winning the title for the second time. The course, which has several hilly holes in its attractive valley setting, was laid out by Scotsman Arthur Davidson.
Atlantico Course.   *Par 68   Length 5400m*
Estrada da Gávea 800, Rio de Janeiro, Brazil
Tel: +55 (0) 21 322-4141

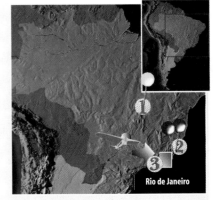

Rio de Janeiro

Hotels
- **Hotel Vila Boa Vida**
- **Fazendinha Blancpain**
- **Iguassu Golf Club & Resort**

HOTEL VILA BOA VIDA

Hotel information

Rua "Q" – Lote 12
Praia Da Ferradura
Armaçáo Dos Búzios
RJ 28925-000

Tel: +55 (0) 24 6236767
Fax: +55 (0) 24 6236727
Email: hotelvbv@mar.com.br
Web: www.buziosonline.com.br/vilaboavida

Accolades

✰✰✰ Quatro Rodas guide

Airport

Rio de Janiero: 2 hrs

Accommodation price guide

Accepted credit cards
AE DC MC V

Preferred tour operator

From Germany
DER   Tel: +49 (0) 699588 00
From Canada
A & TIC   Tel: +1 905 943 9763
From Argentina
PUB   Tel: +54 (0) 11 4723 8081

Visitors to this picture postcard Brazilian coastal resort are able to enjoy the exotic tropical beaches, meet fascinating people and sample an exciting night-life in a town filled with delight. To make the experience truly unforgettable, the charming and intimate Vila Boa Vida Hotel offers a warm welcome and exceptional comfort in delightful colonial style apartments, with floral gardens and spectacular views overlooking Ferradura beach.

All these outstanding features combine with the attractions of what is one of South America's very finest 18-hole golf courses – the Búzios Golf Club, designed by Pete and Perry Dye, of Dye Designs. Just 15 minutes from the hotel, this outstanding par 72 course makes the most of its lush tropical setting.

At night, the peaceful by day street of Rua das Pedras, right at the heart of the traditional fishermen's village, becomes a lively meeting place for those who wish to sample the picturesque local bars, restaurants and night clubs. Reserve your own place in Paradise!

Recreational facilities

Equestrian centre; tropical gardens; free transport to town and beaches; tennis, diving, windsurfing, schooner trips, scooter and bicycle hire all available locally.

Meeting/business facilities

One conference room, plus support rooms, for up to 200 delegates.

Local attractions

World-famous nightlife with unique bars and restaurants.

GOLF FACILITIES
Best season for golf: April to November.

COURSES:	LENGTH	PAR	FEES
Búzios Golf Club			
	6949m	72	US$23

Facilities key

  35 200

FAZENDINHA BLANCPAIN BEACH & GOLF HOTEL

Hotel information

PO Box 112 333
28950-970
Buzios
Rio de Janiero

Tel: +55 (0) 24 623 6490
Fax: +55 (0) 24 623 6420
Email: fazendinha@mar.com.br
Web: www.buziosonline.com.br/blancpain

Accolades

☆☆☆☆
Member – Roteiros de Charme

Airport

Buzios: 10 mins
Cabo Frio: 25 mins
Rio de Janiero: 2 hrs

Accommodation price guide

Local attractions

22 local beaches, Brazil's unique colour and culture.

A member of the exclusive Roteiros de Charme group, the delightful Hotel Fazendinha Blancpain is a small and charming sophisticated country inn, owned and run by Paul and Philippa Blancpain, an Anglo-Swiss couple who make a point of receiving their guests personally and making any stay the most pleasurable possible experience.

Fazendinha – which means 'little farm' – is just a few kilometres from Buzios, the well-known seaside village paradise, and close to a superb golf course which hosts the Tartaruga Open. Many other activities are available on site or nearby, including riding, sailing, swimming. The Fazendinha is renowned for its good cuisine, using products from the property itself. All rooms have individual safes.

Recreational facilities

Swimming pool, horse riding; sailing, surfing, fishing, scuba diving all available locally.

GOLF FACILITIES

Best season: All year round

COURSES:	LENGTH	PAR	FEES
Buzios	6200m	72	US$15/20

Host course for the Tartaruga Open Tournament.

Facilities key

6

IGUASSU GOLF CLUB & RESORT

Hotel information

Av Das Cataraatas 6845
Foz Do Iguagu
Parana
CEP 85853-000

Tel: +55 (0) 45 523 4749
Fax: +55 (0) 45 523 5737
Email: iguassu.golf@frn.net
Web: www.iguassugolf.com.br

Airport

Iguassu International: 10 mins
Puerto Iguazu: 30 mins
Ciudad dell Este: 45 mins

Accommodation price guide

Accepted credit cards
AE DC MC V

Local attractions

The mighty Iguassu Falls and gigantic Itaipu hydro-electric dam; bird park, Acqua Mania water park, Macuco safari.

Set amid irresistible tropical scenery, surrounded by the beauty of a national park and the stunning Iguassu Falls, you will find Iguassu Golf Club & Resort – a very special place offering excellent golf and the most modern refinements, in ecological harmony with the region's natural beauty.

After a game of golf at the hotel's magnificent 18-hole course or a friendly game of tennis, volleyball or basketball, guests can relax in the sauna, Jacuzzi or the pool, with its breathtaking waterfalls. If you are hungry or thirsty you can enjoy a simple snack or you can appreciate the finest of delicious Chinese and French cuisine, accompanied with fine wines.

Come and take part in this enchantment. You will truly discover the secret of the good life.

Meeting/business facilities

One room, for up to 100 delegates.

Recreational facilities

Playground, Jacuzzi, outdoor swimming pool, football field, sauna, tennis course, jogging trails, basketball court.

GOLF FACILITIES

Best season: All year round

COURSES:	LENGTH	PAR	FEES
Iguassu	6985m	72	US$30

18 hole golf course, club house with all the modern conveniences: saunas, locker rooms, pro shop and rental for clubs, shoes and carts.

Facilities key

70   100

Asia
and the
Pacific

THAILAND The dream destination

Gentle, friendly, enchanting, Thailand has, without exaggeration, been labelled 'The Land Of Smiles'.

Still ruled over by a King – who happens to be a golf enthusiast – it's a stable constitutional monarchy set in what has been one of the more turbulent regions of the world. Indeed, for the very definition of peace you don't have to look much further than the delightful, uncrowded and totally unspoilt beaches of the island paradise of Phuket, set in the azure blue Andaman Sea.

Bangkok is one of the world's noisiest, most congested cities but is not only located in easy reach of lush, green countryside but has its own charms, thanks to the wealth of majestic Buddhist temples and royal palaces, reflecting the heritage of a Kingdom which has endured for 700 years.

GETTING THERE Bangkok and others airports are today served from around the world.

APRÈS GOLF Thai cuisine is quite simply exquisite, with its subtle flavours of lemon grass and coriander hiding the inner fire of garlic, chilli and ginger. The beer's good too.

Night life is lively and exotic, with karaoke, lavish cabaret and peep-shows all having their place.

OFF THE COURSE Sightseeing runs the gamut, from temple visits to trawling for bargains in the teeming street markets. Watersports facilities match the best, with snorkelling and scuba diving presenting endless underwater glories.

NOT TO BE MISSED — Watch the elephants at work; buy locally produced silks and jewellery; visit Bangkok's floating markets.

FACTS AND FIGURES

● Although the earliest golf was played within a Bangkok horse racing circuit, the first 18-hole course was built at Hua Hin in 1924 by a Scottish railway engineer, AO Robins, at the behest of the Thai royal family, who regularly holidayed there. Best season for golf runs from November to March.

● It is not uncommon to see a six-ball (or more) teeing off, particularly around Bangkok, known locally as a 'Thai crocodile'.

● Uniformed lady caddies are a singular feature of Thai golf. A club may have 300-400 of them on call. At an average rate of 160 Baht for 18 holes (US$4.20), it is not uncommon for a player to employ three at a time – one for the bag, one for his sun-shielding umbrella and one to carry a folding chair.

● Some courses have 'long boys' to wait by main water hazards to retrieve errant balls for a tip.

No shortage of caddies here!

If there is anywhere in the world that currently fulfills every holiday golfers dream, it has to be Thailand. With guaranteed winter sunshine at midsummer temperatures, it has three times as many golf courses as the whole of the Costa del Sol and the Algarve put together. Most of these venues were built to the highest levels of modern construction and design in the last 15 years by such great international names as Jack Nicklaus, Arnold Palmer, Peter Thomson, Ronald Fream, Pete Dye and Greg Norman.

Helped by favourable exchange rates, green fees equate to the cost of a round of drinks. Young smiling lady caddies will charm you for 18 holes for the price of a golf ball. Elegant clubhouses built like marble palaces offer exotic menus for a song.

You can buy a fortnight's golfing holiday in a five-star hotel for the cost of a week in Europe. Thailand is the great undiscovered bargain in holiday golf and has some of the best courses, equal to many found in Spain, Florida, Myrtle Beach or Palm Springs.

Access has improved enormously with direct flights from major cities reducing travel time. You can fly from London non-stop in around eleven hours, the same time as California. Suddenly it is a case of the 'not-so-Far-East', opening up one of the world's most interesting and exotic destinations.

This ancient kingdom with a fascinating culture is now established in world holiday golf. Ideal for small groups and golfing couples.

NEW DEVELOPMENTS

● The rise of current US superstar Tiger Woods, who has a Thai mother, has had an important influence on the growth of the local game.

● There are now around 300,000 domestic players, and the country has more than 200 golf courses, spread throughout the Kingdom.

● Tourist golfers tend to favour six areas: Chonburi/Pattaya, Khao Yai, Chiang Mai/Chiang Rai, Kanchanaburi, Cha-Am/Hua Hin and Phuket.

Hotels

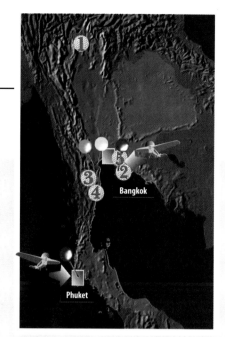

Blue Canyon Resort	Page 52
Palm Hills Golf Resort	Page 53
Springfield Beach Resort	Page 54
Laem Chabang International Country Club	Page 56

Favourite fairways

① SANTIBURI COUNTRY CLUB

Probably the best conditioned course to be found in the country. On a gently undulating site, Robert Trent Jones Jr. has created a very fair course, where large areas of water and no little sand have to negotiated. Delightful off the normal tees, demanding off the back, here is golf to be enjoyed as much for the myriad flowers and sheltering mountain views as the course itself.
Par 72   Length 5793m
12 Moo 3, Huadoi-Sobpao Rd., T.Wiang-Chai, Wiang Chai District, Chiang Rai 57210
Tel: +66 (0) 53 662 828   Fax: +66 (0) 53 717 377

② LAEM CHABANG INTERNATIONAL COUNTRY CLUB

Three distinctly different nines – Mountain, Lake and Valley – by legend Jack Nicklaus give plenty of choice. Whether negotiating the slopes and hillside ravines of holes nestling in the surrounding wooded hills or the acres of strategic water below, this is golf with real class as well as much beauty and fine conditioning.
Mountain 2800m, Lake 2762m, Valley 2965m, all par 36
106/8 Moo 4, Beung, Sriracha, Chonburi 20230
Tel: +66 (0) 38 372 273   Fax: +66 (0) 38 372 346

③ NICHIGO RESORT & COUNTRY CLUB

27 holes by Japanese architect Mitsuaki Kobayashi has produced some highly-rated golf in a dramatic setting of limestone crags and escarpments. Laid out beside the Kwai Yai river, the relatively level holes wind past numerous white sand traps, trees and strategic water, plus a profusion of colourful flowers. There are excellent facilities to be found in this complete resort.
Lake Course 2847m, River Course 2827m, Mountain Course 2935m, all par 36
106 Moo 4, Tambol Wangdong, Amphur Muang, Kanchanaburi 71000   Tel: +66 (0) 34 513 304   Fax: +66 (0) 34 513 334

④ SPRINGFIELD ROYAL COUNTRY CLUB OF CHA-AM

A fine championship-level course in a magnificent setting backed by low, wooded hills. It bears all the hallmarks of its designer, Jack Nicklaus, with much penal water, waste sand areas, small greens and mounded rough. A real challenge, especially from the back tees. Young palms and other trees will feature as they mature on what is the western seaboard's top layout. A further 18 are planned.
Par 72   Length 5743m
825/5 Jumnong-Poomivej Rd., Km.210 Petchkasem Highway, Cha-Am, Petchburi 76120
Tel: +66 (0) 32 471 303   Fax: +66 (0) 32 471 324

⑤ NATURAL PARK HILL GOLF COURSE

Sweeping down from a wooded mountain backdrop, the course has a wealth of mature mango and palm trees shaping each hole. A fine effort by American Ronald Fream, whose skill as a strategist still leaves room for his eye for scenic beauty with tumbled rocks and a riot of flowers. Much punishing water along the lower holes of a course where careful thought and ball placement wil pay dividends.
Par 72   Length 5808m
159/1 Moo 2, Saensuk, Bangphra Road, Muang Chonburi 20130
Tel: +66 (0) 38 393 001   Fax: +66 (0) 38 393 019

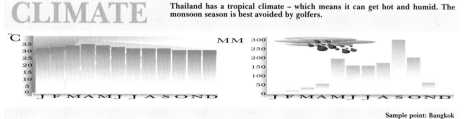

The most up-to-date golf travel information is always at
www.golftravel4u.com

CLIMATE

Thailand has a tropical climate – which means it can get hot and humid. The monsoon season is best avoided by golfers.

Sample point: Bangkok

Price guide   €

Round of golf		Golf balls	
Small beer		4/5 star hotel room	

CONTACT

Tourism Authority of Thailand
202 Le Concorde Plaza, Ratchapadapisek Rd, Bangkok 10320
Tel: +66 (0) 2 94 1222 Fax: +66 (0) 2 94 1220

BLUE CANYON COUNTRY CLUB

Hotel information

165 Moo 1 Thepkasattri Road
Thalang
Phuket 83140

Tel: +66 (0) 76 327440
Fax: +66 (0) 76 327449
Email: reservation@bluecanyonclub.com
Web: www.bluecanyonclub.com

Accolades

Asian & Pacific Golf Course of the Year
1999 – Hertz International Golf Travel
Awards London
Finest Golf Clubs of the World

Airport

Phuket: 10 mins

Accommodation price guide

Accepted credit cards
AE MC V DC

Recreational facilities

Outdoor swimming pool, tennis courts,
fitness/health centre, massage, Jacuzzi,
sauna; horse riding, fishing, shooting,
watersports.

Meeting/business facilities

On-site meeting and conference
facilities.

Local attractions

On-site conference facilities; canoeing,
scuba diving, snorkelling available
locally; shopping for local handicrafts;
Wat Chalong; Phuket Fantasea.

Cradled in a secluded, verdant valley, the Blue Canyon Country Club basks in Phuket's tropical sunshine. This fabulous golfing venue lies within ten minutes of Phuket International Airport and is 29 kilometres from Phuket Town.

Carved into lush landscape surrounded by freshwater lakes, the Canyon Course – named Asian & Pacific Golf Course of the Year in the 1999 Hertz International Golf Travel Awards London – brilliantly features natural hazards, towering trees, multiple tees, rolling fairways, narrow landing areas and well guarded slick Bermuda Tiffdwarf greens.

The recently opened Lakes Course is a mixture of water-filled canyons, created by open-cast mining and rubber plantations, combined with a number of natural water hazards. With a north-to-south layout, the course is wide enough that only holes 17 and 18 flow consecutively in the same direction.

Blue Canyon Country Club has staged two Johnnie Walker Classics (in 1994 and 1998), as well as other major tournaments. The two 18-hole championship golf courses – designed by Yoshikazu Kato – have been expertly planned to offer well-appointed amenities for the discerning golfer.

GOLF FACILITIES

Best season for golf: All year round.

COURSES:	LENGTH	PAR	FEES
Canyon Course			
	6507m	72	US$86
The Lakes Course			
	6516m	72	US$86

Host to the Johnnie Walker Classic 1994 and 1998 and Honda Invitational 1996; driving range, BCGA (Blue Canyon Golf School), pro shop.

Facilities key

50 60

PALM HILLS GOLF RESORT

Hotel information

259 Sukhumvit Road
Wattana
Bangkok 10110

Tel: +66 (0) 2 651 1000
Fax: +66 (0) 2 255 2441
Email: rsvn@grandpacifichotel.com
Web: www.grandpacifichotel.com

Accolades

★★★★☆

Airport

Bangkok Int'l (Don Muang): 30 mins

Accommodation price guide

Accepted credit cards
AE MC V DC

Preferred tour operator

From Worldwide
Hua Hin
Golf Tours   Tel: +66 (0) 32 530 119
From Sweden
Winburgs Resebyrai
Esloy   Tel: +46 (0) 413 60 2248

Recreational facilities

Outdoor swimming pool, massage, barber and beauty salon, fully equipped fitness centre; Robinson's department store, in hotel building.

Meeting/business facilities

Eight rooms, for up to 1000 delegates; business centre; full secretarial service.

Local attractions

Emporium Shopping Centre, Brewhouse pub, Queen Sirikit National Convention Centre.

The splendid Palm Hills Golf Resort, opened in December 1991, offers full service to members and guests alike, with luxurious rooms and choice of international, Japanese, Thai and Chinese restaurants. The 18-hole par 72 course, arranged in two distinctive nine-hole sections divided by the clubhouse and a rock outcrop extending from the mountain range, was skilfully designed by American golf architect Max Waxler.

Palm Hills was the tournament base for the inaugural Thailand World Pro Am, in January 1993, receiving acclaim as "an outstanding success" by the British PGA officials, who have granted their full approval for future events.

The first hole sets the precedent for the next 17. The rolling and undulating fairways provide Palm Hills with a distinctive identity which marks it out from all the other courses in the area. Water comes into play on the short signature hole par three where the green is some 80 metres above sea level, providing a breathtaking view of the town of Hua Hin and the Gulf of Thailand.

The country club is a separated building, offering a wide variety of sports, including tennis, squash, and badminton. Facilities include an outdoor pool, fitness room, sauna and children's playground.

GOLF FACILITIES

Best season for golf: October to end of March.

COURSES:	LENGTH	PAR	FEES
Palm Hills Golf Resort			
	6281m	72	1200-1800 Baht

30 per cent green fee discount to groups of 16 and over; putting green, chipping green and bunker practice, driving range and club rental; Palm Hills has hosted Thai PGA Singha Challenge tournament every year since inception.

Facilities key

400

1000

SPRINGFIELD BEACH RESORT

Hotel information

825/5 Jumnong-Poomivej Road
Cha-Am
Petchburi 76120

Tel: +66 32 451 181
Fax: +66 32 451 194
Email: sfield@ksc.th.com
Alternative email: kelly@loxinfo.co.th
Web: www.frangipani.com/springfield

Accolades

☆☆☆☆☆

Airport

Hua Hin: 10 mins

Accommodation price guide

Accepted credit cards
AE MC V DC

Preferred tour operator

From UK
Tradewinds   Tel: +44 (0) 1254 220277
From Germany
TUI   Tel: +49 (0) 511 5670
From Sweden
Always, Saga
& Tjaerborg   Tel: +46 (0) 8 5551 3200

Recreational facilities

Beach, swimming pool, fitness centre; mini-mart and souvenir shop; tennis and children's playground locally.

Meeting/business facilities

Eight rooms, for up to 200 delegates.

Local attractions

King's palace; Pala-u waterfalls.

To the uninitiated, playing golf in the Kingdom of Thailand is a new and truly rewarding experience, which the expert and the family golfer can both enjoy equally. The Hua Hin area, in which the Springfield Beach Resort and the Royal Golf Club have become landmarks, enjoys a pleasant climate due to mild sea breezes wafting in from the Gulf of Thailand. With its secluded beaches and quiet Thai charm, it has been the favoured holiday resort of royalty since the 1920s.

The Beach Resort is set in spacious grounds, looking directly onto the beautiful beach, with the mountains behind it. All rooms feature views over the Gulf. Famous Thai cuisine and seafood dominate the hotel's catering, which is widely recognised as the best in the region.

Now well established, the Jack Nicklaus designed Springfield Royal Country Club is generally considered to be one of the premier golfing resorts in Thailand. The magnificent clubhouse commands views over a panorama of golf holes, streams, lakes and trees, while, away in the distance, wide valleys allow unrestricted views of the Gulf of Thailand. Professional expertise provides the nucleus of the complex, which is now a Mecca for enthusiasts and a memorable holiday venue.

GOLF FACILITIES

Best season for golf: November to March.

COURSES:	LENGTH	PAR	FEES
Springfield Royal	6437m	72	Bt.1200-1800
Lakeview	6302m	72	Bt.1200-1800
Palm Hills	6302m	72	Bt.1200-1800
Majestic Creek	6492m	72	Bt.1200-1800

Complete driving range, year-round golf academy (two PGA pros); buggies for hire; four annual member tournaments; host to 1995 Omega Tour School and 1998 Asia Junior Pacific Championship.

Facilities key

80   200

SPOIL YOUR GAME

Experience the dream golf destination
equipped with premier courses
and hospitable caddies, luxurious
spa treatment, exquisite banquets
and traditional Thai massage.
Where else can you be pampered
with such a wondrous accommodation.

amazing THAILAND
EXPERIENCE The SPLENDOURS Of A KINGDOM

Contact: Tourism Authority of Thailand, Le Concorde Building, 202 Ratchadaphisek Rd., Huai Khwang, Bangkok 10310, Thailand
Tel. (66-2) 694-1222 (80 lines) Fax. (66-2) 694-1220, 694-1221 E-mail: center@tat.or.th Internet: www.tourismthailand.org, www.amazingthailand.th

LAEM CHABANG GOLF LODGE

Hotel information

106/8 M.4 Beung
Sriracha
Chonburi 20230

Tel: +66 (0) 38 372273
Fax: +66 (0) 38 372275, 372318
Email: lcic1997@chonburi.ksc.co.th
Web: www.pattaya.com/laemchabang

Accolades

☆☆☆☆☆
The most beautiful golf course in
Thailand1995 - Bangkok Golf Service

Airport

Bangkok (Don Muang): 2 hrs

Accommodation price guide

€

Accepted credit cards
AE DC MC V

Local attractions

Tiger zoo, elephant village, Nong Nooch
tropical gardens.

"Truly world class in every respect" – that's how course designer Jack Nicklaus describes Laem Chabang's fine championship golf course.

Challenging and visually inspiring, the 27 holes are arranged in mountain, lake and valley settings. Situated amid this profusion of natural beauty, The Laem Chabang Golf Lodge provides 42 luxurious accommodations to suit the requirements of the most demanding golf traveller.

The resort boasts a superb two-storey club house: serving Thai, Chinese, Japanese and European Cuisine, the main restaurant has a panoramic view of the golf course, while complete facilities are provided for business meetings. A wide range of other leisure facilities is provided.

Facilities key

42   80

Meeting/business facilities

Four rooms, for up to 80 delegates.

Recreational facilities

Golf on-site, swimming pool, snooker; diving, karting, sailing, bowling locally.

GOLF FACILITIES
Best season for golf: All year round.

COURSES:	LENGTH	PAR	FEES
Laem Chabang	9326m	36x3	US$35
Natural Pk. Resort	9720m	36x3	US$50
Natural Pk. Hill	6807m	72	US$50

Putting green, driving range; tuition packages; pro shop.

Sol Meliá Golf. The ultimate golfing challenge has never been easier.

Who can resist the lure of exotic Asia? The perfect climate, the exotic scenery, and some of the finest golf courses in the world, designed by luminaries such as Jack Nicklaus and Greg Norman. Now, Sol Meliá, the world's largest resort management company,

Meliá Bali —
A Utopia of pure enchantment

has brought together a collection of first class golf challenges in Asia under the banner of Sol Meliá Golf. These championship standard courses offer new experiences in golf, backed by Sol Meliá's legendary expertise in hospitality. Ensuring the perfect Asian golfing holiday, with everything arranged for you from the tee off to the 19th hole. So all you have to do is relax and play the Asian way.

Meliá Hua Hin —
The jewel of Thai Resorts

SMG
Sol Meliá **Golf**

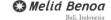

MALAYSIA Lush green and plush greens

The much vaunted tiger economy might have lost some of its roar but Malaysia remains a magnetic destination – a strident, modern young country but with a proud and ancient heritage.

Here you'll find the world's current tallest building – Kuala Lumpur's twin towers – and state of art resort complexes with every modern amenity for a comfortable stay amid pampered luxury.

GETTING THERE Kuala Lumpur has global direct air links, or fly in via Singapore. Malaysia is a regular port of call for cruise ships, enabling cruising / golfing holidays.

APRÈS GOLF Though redolent with Chinese and other influences, Malaysia has its own tasty national cuisine and also brews the popular Tiger beer. Most entertainment is offered on-site at the tourist resorts.

OFF THE COURSE Sightseeing runs the gamut, from temple visits to trawling for bargains in the teeming street markets. Snorkelling and scuba diving present endless underwater glories.

NOT TO BE MISSED — Watch the elephants at work; buy locally produced silks and jewellery; visit Bangkok's floating markets.

FACTS AND FIGURES

● The oldest club in the country is the Royal Selangor Golf Club, formed in 1893 at Petaling Hill, Kuala Lumpur. By 1931, it had 36 holes and remains the premier club, despite damage due to Japanese occupation during WWII, with 2700 members, 45 holes, 20 tennis courts and two swimming pools.
● There are almost 200 courses in Malaysia and an estimated 100,000 domestic golfers.

Golf has been around in Malaya (as it was when it formed part of the British Empire) for a long time. A group of coffee planters established a nine-hole course more than a hundred years ago and formed the Selangor Club. At first, the game spread slowly but, over the last 20 years, has exploded in all directions.

The country is now one of Asia's leading lights, with courses up in the cool highlands, in lush green valleys and along the coastline of the South China Sea, in the distant provinces of Sabah and Sarawak and on offshore islands such as Langkawai and Penang. An exciting nation, with a racial mix of Malay, Indian and Chinese. Recommended for small groups (not short stay) and mature golfing couples.

NEW DEVELOPMENTS

● The World Cup came to the new Mines Golf Resort just south of Kuala Lumpur in November 1999. As with the World Cup at Bangkok's Navatanee in 1975 and Indonesia's Pondok Indah in 1983, the course designer was Robert Trent Jones Jr.
● Recent new courses include the Clearwater Sanctuary Resort (Ipoh), Serendah Golf Links (Selangor), Golden Valley Golf & Country Club (Malacca), Tanjung Puteri Golf & Country Club (Johor) and Awana Kijal Beach & Golf Resort (Trengganu).

CLIMATE Being in the tropics, the region has an equatorial climate, with the temperature averaging 22–32 degrees. The monsoon season is between Sept and November to the west, and October to February in the east.

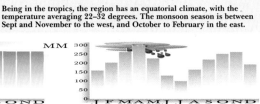

Sample point: Kuala Lumpur

RECOMMENDED CAR HIRE **Hertz**
UK: +44 (0) 870 848 4848
Germany: +49 (0) 180 533 3535
Website: www.hertz.com

Price guide €

Round of golf		Golf balls	
Small beer		4/5 star hotel room	

CONTACT

Tourism Malaysia 109 jalan Ampang, 50450 Kuala Lumpur
Tel: +60 (0) 03 264 3929 Fax: +60 (0) 03 262 1149

Favourite fairways

① THE MINES
Just south of Kuala Lumpur, and centrepiece of a fantasy resort, Robert Trent Jones Jr.'s 1999 World Cup course makes good use of palms, indigenous trees, strategic water and natural wetlands.
Par 71   Length 6224m
**Off Jalan Sungai Besi, 43300 Seri Kembangan, Selangor Darul Ehsan
Tel: +60 (0) 3 943 4176
Fax: +60 (0) 3 943 9212**

② SAUJANA GOLF & COUNTRY CLUB
Located near the airport on a former oil palm plantation, this 36-hole complex by Ronald Fream is a visual delight and provides testing golf. Good use is made of the fairly demanding contours, with natural vegetation, palms, lakes, waterfalls and colourful flowers adding to the the quality of this well-kept resort location.
Par 72   Length 6400m

Batu Tiga, off Jln. Lapangan Terbang Antara Subang, PO Box 8148, Kelana Jaya
**Tel: +60 (0) 3 746 1466
Fax: +60 (0) 3 746 2316**

③ KELAB GOLF NEGARA SUBANG
The original 18 holes, by SI Inouye, have more than 30 years' maturity, and trees on this former rubber estate provide good definition to an excellent course. Bunkers are a prime feature, especially the 'seven widows' at the seventh.
A further 18 holes have been added as well as many other recreational facilities.
Par 72   Length 6586m
**Jalan SS7/2, 47301 Petaling Jaya
Tel: +60 (0) 3 776 0388
Fax: +60 (0) 3 775 5267**

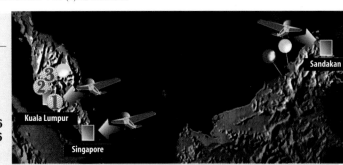

Hotels

Pan Pacific Glenmarie
Shangri-La's Rasa Ria Resort
Shangri-La's Tanjung Resort

THE PAN PACIFIC GLENMARIE

Hotel information

I.Jalan Usahawan U1/8
Section U1
40250 Shah Alam
Selangor Darul Ehsan

Tel: +60 (0) 3 703 1000
Fax: +60 (0) 3 704 1000
Email: general@ppgr.com.my
Web: www.panpac.com

Accolades

★★★☆
"Excellence in hotel services", first class category – Tourism Malaysia Awards

Airport

Kuala Lumpur International Airport: 30 mins
Sultan Abdul Aziz Shah Airport: 7 mins

Accommodation price guide

Accepted credit cards
AE   MC   V   DC

Preferred tour operator

From UK
Gold Medal Travel
Group   Tel: +44 (0) 645 757 767
Northenden
Travel Group Tel: +44 (0) 161 945 4321
Jebsens
Travel   Tel: +44 (0) 20 7932 0998

Recreational facilities

Free-form swimming pool plus Olympic size pool, indoor and outdoor tennis, squash, gym, sauna, steam room, massage, Jacuzzi, convenience kiosk, children's playground.

Meeting/business facilities

Eight rooms, for up to 500 delegates.

Local attractions

Water theme parks; Genting Highlands (recreation and casino); country tours; Kuala Lumpur city; major shopping complexes; Chinatown, Central Market, KL Tower.

Set amidst 180 hectares of lush greenery, overlooking two of the finest 18-hole golf courses in Malaysia, The Pan Pacific Glenmarie Kuala Lumpur forms an integral part of the Glenmarie Golf & Country Club. Just 30 minutes away from the Kuala Lumpur International Airport and 25 minutes from the city centre, the resort is ideal for business or pleasure.

The moment you step into the resort a warm welcome awaits. A grand open air lobby, cooled by the swaying punkah fans, gently lulls you into a relaxed frame of mind and onto the threshold of another world.

The resort offers 291 luxuriously appointed guest rooms and suites, of which 237 offer stunning panoramic views of the golf courses, while the rest overlook the landscaped gardens. An unforgettable choice of dining is available, including Japanese, Chinese and international cuisine. Meetings and conferences could not be set in a more relaxed and efficient atmosphere, with a full range of facilities and equipment at the disposal of organisers.

In 1999, the Glenmarie golf course, designed by Max Wexler, hosted the Kosaido Malaysian Ladies' Tournament for the third time, while the resort's sister course, the Kota Permai, was last year's venue for the Volvo Masters.

GOLF FACILITIES

Best season for golf: All year round.

COURSES:	LENGTH	PAR	FEES
Glenmarie	5997m	72	RM120-160
Kota Permai	5865m	72	RM105-189
Seri Selangor	6195m	72	RM50-80
Saujana	5815m	72	RM178-305

33-bay driving range, practice greens and chipping area; tuition packages; buggies for hire.

Facilities key

291   500

SHANGRI-LA'S TANJUNG ARU RESORT

Located within easy access of five idyllic islands, amidst ten hectares of landscaped gardens overlooking the South China Sea, Shangri-La's Tanjung Aru Resort is only ten minutes from Kota Kinabalu city centre and its international airport.

The award-winning 500 room resort, ranked amongst the 100 finest in the world, offers every modern amenity for recreation and business. The resort treats its guests like family, offering the warmest welcome and the most impeccable service. Five restaurants and bars within the resort serve Asian, local and Continental cuisine.

Borneo is a golfing paradise. The courses are designed to take advantage of the natural facades of this beautiful land, rich in flora and fauna.

Hotel information

Locked Bag 174
88744 Kota Kinabalu
Sabah, Borneo

Tel: +6 (0) 88 225 800
Fax: +6 (0) 88 217 155
Email: tah@shangri-la.com
Web: www.shangri-la.com

Accolades

★★★★☆
Gold List Of The World's Best Hotels – Conde Naste Traveller (USA)
Best Of The Best Hotels In Malaysia 1999 – Tourism Asia

Airport

Kota Kinabalu International: 10 mins

Accommodation price guide

Accepted credit cards
AE DC MC V JCB

Local attractions

Mount Kinabalu, coral islands, scuba diving, orangutan sanctuary, turtle islands.

Meeting/business facilities

Eight rooms, for up to 1200 delegates

Recreational facilities

Health club, gym, watersports, games rooms, tennis, in-house tour operators.

GOLF FACILITIES
Best season for golf: All year.

COURSES:	LENGTH	PAR	FEES
Dalit Bay	6310m	72	RM184.00

Dalit Bay open daily; pro shop; driving range; separate pitching and putting greens; wet driving range; nine-hole pitch and putt within the Tanjung Aru Resort.

Facilities key

500 1200

SHANGRI-LA'S RASA RIA RESORT

Shangri-La's Rasa Ria Resort nestles in 160 hectares of grounds on the magnificent stretch of Pantai Dalit beach, some 40 minutes away from Kota Kinabulu. Within the resort lies the Dalit Bay Golf and Country Club facility, a challenging and primarily water hazard 18-hole championship golf course. Play often runs alongside lush and dense tropical forest, providing thrills to challenge even the most seasoned player.

Exquisitely appointed, most rooms overlook a stunning vista of white sands – a great setting for spectacular sunset views and romantic walks.

Verdant gardens and excellent recreational facilities compliment the resort's own golf course and nature reserve.

Hotel information

Pantai Dalit
PO Box 600
89208 Tuaran, Sabah

Tel: +6 (0) 88 792888
Fax: +6 (0) 88 792777
Email: rrr@shangri-la.com
Web: www.shangri-la.com

Accolades

★★★★☆
Best of the Best Resorts '99 – Travel Asia
Best Theme Venue Resort '99 Gold Award – M&C, Asia Pacific

Airport

Kota Kinabalu International: 40 mins

Accommodation price guide

Accepted credit cards
AE DC MC V JCB

Local attractions

Mengkabong (sea gypsies) water village; Tuaran Sunday Tamu (local market); pottery factories; Kinabalu Park.

Meeting/business facilities

Eight rooms for up to 800 delegates.

Recreational facilities

3km beach; watersports centre; fitness centre with gym, steam bath, Jacuzzi, massage; horse riding; children's club.

GOLF FACILITIES
Best season for golf: All year.

COURSES:	LENGTH	PAR	FEES
Dalit Bay	6310m	72	RM184.00

Dalit Bay open daily; pro shop; driving range; separate pitching and putting greens; wet driving range

Facilities key

330 800

INDONESIA & CHINA

Golf in Indonesia is something of a paradox. In a vast country of 13,000 islands, the game is localised to two of the biggest, Java and Sumatra, plus the holiday resort of Bali, Kalimantan (formerly Borneo) and, most recently, on the Riau archipeligo just off Singapore, a destination catering primarily to golf-mad, land-starved Singaporeans.

Golf has been played longer here than in any other part of Asia but remains a preserve of the privileged. For the visitor, it means an opportunity to play some really great courses, laid out in lush tropical surroundings by some of the world's leading golf architects, with excellent service at reasonable prices.

Chinese interest in the game is centred just south of Hong Kong, providing the opportunity for a two centre rural/big city holiday.

NEW DEVELOPMENTS

● Recently the game has mushroomed but mostly in the same areas. In 1986, there were five courses in Jakarta and two just south near Bogor. Now there are more than 40, nearly half the national total, with more planned.
● Visiting golfers should call ahead for tee reservations and avoid weekends.

CLIMATE Indonesia's larger islands are mountainous with cold, rainy conditions. The lowlands are equatorial. Rainfall intensity depends on monsoon conditions. In parts it is the most thundery place on earth.

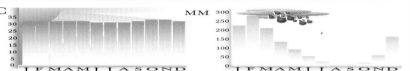

Sample point: Bali

RECOMMENDED CAR HIRE *Hertz*
UK: +44 (0) 870 848 4848
Germany: +49 (0) 180 533 3535
Website: www.hertz.com

Price guide €

Round of golf	Golf balls
Small beer	4/5 star hotel room

CONTACT

Indonesian Tourist Board, Merdeka Barbarat 16-19, Jakarta Indonesia
Tel: +62 (0) 21 3103117 Fax: +62 (0) 21 421 8110
Hong Kong Tourist Board, 9th-11th Floor, City Core Centre, 18 Whitfield Rd, North Point, Hong Kong
Tel: +852 (0) 2807 6543 Fax: +852 (0) 2806 0303

Two of golfing's newer destinations, Indonesia and China, are two of the world's biggest countries, both in population terms (200 million in Indonesia, a whopping 1.2 billion in China) and sheer size.

GETTING THERE You can reach Indonesia's golfing destinations via the bustling capital city of Jakarta or by direct flight. China now has a very modern airway network and comfortable high-speed trains too. Hong Kong and Guandong are key international airports.

APRÈS GOLF Indonesian food is spicy, highly varied and intriguingly different – with the famed *rijstaffel* (invented by the Dutch colonialists) a good way of sampling the varied tastes. Chinese food – from the fiery hot tastes of Szechuan to the subtle flavours of Canton – is one of the world's great cuisines.

OFF THE COURSE Indonesia is a bustling melting pot spread across countless islands; China is modernising at amazing pace – one-fifth of all the world's construction cranes are said to be currently working in Shanghai.

NOT TO BE MISSED Meet the locals, sample the local arts and crafts; silks and inexpensive suits, bronze and carved wood artefacts; visit the temples and holy places.

FACTS AND FIGURES

● The British (as always) built the first course, in 1872, which changed its name to Jakarta Golf Club in 1932. On a compact site, it remains a short but thoughtful test with subtle greens.
● When China's late President became addicted to golf, many of the fast-rising new middle-class promptly followed suit.

Favourite fairways

① BALI HANDARA KOSAIDO COUNTRY CLUB

As near as most of us will get to heaven on this earth, an amazing floral delight laid out in the lush green bowl of an ancient volcano. Designers Thomson, Wolveridge and Associates created a superb course, often cool at 1076 metres above tropical Bali – as much an equatorial garden as it is a genuine test of golf. Not to be missed.
Par 72   Length 6423m
Pancasari, Bedugul, Bali
Tel: +62 (0) 361 22646
Fax: +62 (0)361 23048

② PONDOK INDAH GOLF & COUNTRY CLUB

A superb course by Robert Trent Jones Jr., now reaching maturity. Two loops of holes surround a central hill, with the Grogol River as an ever-present hazard. Site of the 1983 World Cup, the course presents playable golf off the member's

tees and a genuine test off the back.
Par 72   Length 6401m
Jalan Metro Pondok Indah, Kebayoran Baru, Jakarta Selatan
Tel: +62 (0) 21 769 4906
Fax: +62 (0) 21 750 2602

③ CIKARANG GOLF & COUNTRY CLUB

Part of a green infrastructure in a new commercial and residential city growing 35km. east of Jakarta, this is a first effort by master golfer Nick Faldo. Gentle shaping, a multitude of strategically-placed bunkers and acres of lakes ensure a genuine challenge on a relatively level layout. Many exotic tropical shrubs and trees grace a well-planned leisure complex.
Par 73   Length 6556m
Jalan Raya Lemahabang, Cikarang Baru, Bekasi, Jawa Barat   Tel: +62 (0) 21 689 4336
Fax: +62 (0) 62 21 893 4571

Hotels

● **Meridien Nirwana**   Page 62
● **Mission Hills Resort** Page 63

LE MERIDIEN NIRWANA GOLF & SPA RESORT

Hotel information

P O Box 158
Tabanan 82171
Bali

Tel: +62 (0) 361 815 900
Fax: +62 (0) 361 815 902
E-mail: sales@balimeridien.com
Web: www.balimeridien.com

Accolades

★★★★☆
Best New Resort 1998 - Asia Pacific Pata Travel Award
Asia/Pacific Golf Resort of the Year 1999 - Hertz International Golf Travel Awards

Airport

Ngurah Rai: 45 mins

Accommodation price guide

Accepted credit cards
AE   DC   MC   V

Recreational facilities

Golf, spa, tennis, squash, fitness club, village cycling, water polo, volleyball, badminton, water aerobics, Balinese dance practice.

Meeting/business facilities

Five rooms, for up to 600 delegates.

Local attractions

Jetskiing, waterskiing, parasailing, rafting, excursions, diving and snorkelling, trekking, cycling.

Voted the top Asian-Pacific golf resort in last year's Hertz International Golf Travel Awards, the superb Le Meridien Nirwana Golf & Spa Resort is the crowning glory of what is one of the most spectacular golf courses on the planet, with many of the fairways nestled among picturesque rice paddies and surrounded by creeks and rivers.

Overlooking the beautiful sunset point of Tanah Lot temple, the 278-room resort is located in the Kingdom of Tabanan regency. It is surrounded by breathtaking views of cascading rice fields, natural creeks, the Indian Ocean, the mountain background and pretty Balinese villages, yet only 40 minutes away from Bali International Airport and 20 minutes from the shopping precinct of Kuta.

Le Meridien Nirwana combines its 18-hole signature golf course and all the usual services expected of a great hotel with extensive recreational facilities, exclusive residential villas and resort homes.

The par 72 championship golf course, designed by Greg Norman, is one of Asia's most sensational courses, with holes carved through those rice paddies, over creeks and with three holes played along the cliffs overlooking the ocean, giving truly breathtaking views. Each hole presents a different challenge for the player.

GOLF FACILITIES

Best season for golf: March to November.

COURSES: LENGTH PAR   FEES
Nirwana Bali Golf Club

      6002m   72   US$72-102

This is one of the world's most unusually spectacular courses with many of the fairways nestled among rice paddies and surrounded by creeks and rivers; three of the holes are ocean facing and command breathtaking views of the Indian Ocean; without doubt this is one of the finest courses you can play in the world; practice facilities include putting greens and driving nets.

Facilities key

278 600

MISSION HILLS RESORT

Hotel information

Mission Hills Road
Guanlan Town
518110 Shenzhen

Tel: +86 (0) 755 802 0888
Fax: +86 (0) 755 801 0713
Web: www.missionhillsgroup.com

Accolades

★★★★☆

Airport

Shenzhen Airport: 25 mins

Accommodation price guide

Accepted credit cards
AE MC V DC

Adjacent to Mission Hills Golf Club, the most famous golf club in China, Mission Hills Resort nestles the within rolling hills and lakes of four championship courses.

All 228 rooms of the resort, including 21 superb suites and the Imperial Suite, have private balconies and provide a panoramic view across the courses, lakes and mountains.

Mission Hills Golf Club is the only 72-hole golf club in China, and the only club in Asia (outside Japan) to host the World Cup of Golf. The four championship courses have been designed by three of the world's greatest golfers: Jack Nicklaus, Nick Faldo and Jumbo Ozaki. The new courses at Mission Hills are being developed by Landmark Golf Company of California, USA – the world's most experienced golf course development and management company.

A truly opulent resort, Mission Hills caters for the needs of both golfer and family. Youngsters can enjoy the Kingdom of Fun Play Castle with childcare, children's play area with ball pit, games and toys; while parents enjoy the peace.

The Mountain Cafe's extensive *à la carte* menu, along with mouth-watering seasonal specialities, offers tempting western options. In the Chinese Restaurant the Master Chef enjoys an enviable reputation.

Recreational facilities

51 world class tennis courts with 3000-seat stadium court; swimming pool in tropical garden; 64-bay floodlit driving range; squash, badminton and basketball courts; table tennis and billiard tables; fully equipped health spa with sauna, steam, Jacuzzi, and massage and beauty suite.

Meeting/business facilities

Function rooms with full conference facilities, to accommodate up to 200.

Local attractions

'Window of the world'; Chinese folk culture village; the splendour of China.

GOLF FACILITIES
Best season for golf: October to May.

COURSES:	LENGTH	PAR	FEES
World Cup	6438m	72	on request
Valley	6417m	72	on request
Stadium	6409m	72	on request
Canyon	6411m	72	on request

Features long bunkers and many water hazards; terraced natural turf practice range, 64-bay floodlit driving range, night golf, Mission Hills Golf Academy.

Facilities key

228 200

AUSTRALIA In the swing down under

Not merely a country, Australia is an entire continent – with all the diversity which that implies. For golfers, the prime interest centres on Western Australia, around Perth, and, near to 2,000 miles away on the opposite coast, the states of Victoria and New South Wales.

Both regions offer favourable climates and some of the world's best beaches, with surfing a national passion – along with the ubiquitous 'barbie', or barbecue, which is never better enjoyed than within the sight, sound and smell of the crashing ocean breakers.

GETTING THERE Qantas, Australia's flagship carrier has plentiful services from Europe and the USA while many other major airlines serve the country and, given the huge distances, it's no surprise that there's a complete web of domestic routes criss-crossing the country using everything from Jumbos to tiny six-seaters.

APRÈS GOLF The Aussies like their beer ice-cold. Their wines are now among the world's best, especially the Chardonnays. As for the food, forget the bland meat pies of the past – there's a whole generation of new, young chefs exploring the Pacific Rim idiom.

OFF THE COURSE Australia is in love with the great outdoors, and nobody is more fixated on sport – whether participating or spectating. The big cities have renowned orchestras, good theatre and lots more.

NOT TO BE MISSED Cuddle a koala; snorkel the Great Barrier Reef; explore old mining camps and early settlements; eat out under the stars.

FACTS AND FIGURES

- Melbourne is already home to a huge variety of courses ranging from sandbelt, like the par 73 Commonwealth Golf Club, to coastal venues like the par 71 Dunes Golf Links and the par 71 National Club in Victoria.

Course names such as Sandringham, Brighton and Kingston would make English golfers feel instantly at home. But there is virtually nowhere better to go to get away from it all.

The Melbourne area is rich in clubs for all standards of player. The Commonwealth, Huntingdale and Yarra Yarra combine rugged terrain with breathtaking scenery, while Royal Melbourne has been ranked the top course in Australia and sixth in the world.

For those who do not care for the challenge of some of the most testing championship courses, there really is something for everyone.

Southern Australia's coastal circuits offer many spectacular views of the Pacific Ocean and are surprisingly similar to some British links.

NEW DEVELOPMENTS

- **Golf Australia Ltd will shortly begin to develop the five-star Moonah Links resort, situated on the Mornington Peninsula, 70km south-east of Melbourne. From 2002 the Australian Open will be held at the resort at least once every two years.**

CLIMATE

Melbourne rarely experiences cold weather but it can be wet at any time of year. Perth has a Mediterranean-type climate, but cyclones occasionally blow. Summer brings bouts of extremely hot weather.

Sample point: Melbourne

RECOMMENDED CAR HIRE *Hertz*®

UK: +44 (0) 870 848 4848
Germany: +49 (0) 180 533 3535
Website: www.hertz.com

Price guide

Round of golf	🏌🏌	Golf balls	🏌🏌🏌
Small beer	🏌🏌🏌	4/5 star hotel room	🏌🏌🏌

CONTACT

Bureau of Tourism Research GPO Box 1545, Canberra ACT 2601, Australia
Tel: +61 (0) 2 6213 7124 Fax: +61 (0) 2 6213 6983

Favourite fairway

① ROYAL MELBOURNE GOLF CLUB

Reckoned to be the best course in Australia, it owes much to the great Dr Alister Mackenzie, of Augusta National and Cypress Point fame, whose collaboration with Alex Russell produced the West Course in 1927. Built by horse and hand from natural linksland near the coast, its superb holes and fast greens have tested the best in the World Cup and Australian Open.

Par 72   Length 6009m
Cheltenham Rd, Black Rock 3193, Melbourne
Tel: +61 (0) 2 598 6755

Hotels

◐ **Crown Towers**	Page 65
◑ **Joondalup Resort**	Page 66

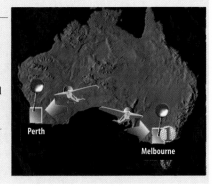

Perth

Melbourne

CROWN TOWERS HOTEL

Hotel information

8 Whiteman Street
Southbank
Victoria 3006
Melbourne

Tel: +61 (0) 3 9292 6666
Fax: +61 (0) 3 9292 6600
Email: hotelreservations@crownltd.com.au
Web: www.crownltd.com.au

Accolades

★☆☆☆☆

Airport

Melbourne International: 30 mins
Essendon: 20 mins

Accommodation price guide

Accepted credit cards
AE DC MC V

Preferred tour operator

From Australia
May Chow Sales
& Marketing Tel: +61 (0) 3 9292 5055
Unlimited
Golf   Tel: +61 (0) 3 9509 5955

AMERICAN EXPRESS OFFER

For advance booking on American
Express Card you receive a
complimentary bottle of Champagne.

Quote 'Great Golf Hotels offer' at time of
reservation. All offers are strictly subject to
availability.

Crown Towers Hotel is the premier five star hotel located within the Crown Entertainment Complex, the largest entertainment resort of its kind in the world, and one of Victoria's most popular tourist attractions. The extraordinary quality, standard of customer service and attention to detail at Crown Towers set it apart as a world-class international tourism icon; setting the standard for the 21st Century.

Crown Towers covers more than 75,000 square metres and features 484 beautifully appointed guest rooms, including 88 suites and 33 villas. All the guest rooms have panoramic views over the city, the Yarra River or Port Phillip Bay and feature oversized marble bathrooms with spa, separate dressing room and personal safe.

Hotel guests have exclusive use of the Crown Spa, one of the finest such facilities in the world, with the latest and best in hair and body care, health and therapeutic treatments and a complete range of Eastern and Western tactile therapies.

The hotel also features five signature restaurants for an unprecedented choice of dining options. Crown Towers have formed a close association with Jo Breadmore and his team at Unlimited Golf, who assist hotel guests with access to some of the most prestigious courses in an area world-renowned for great golf.

Recreational facilities

Spa resort: swimming, sauna, massage, gym; kids' club activities; tennis court hire; 24-hour Crown Casino, featuring 350 tables and 2500 gaming machines; 900-seat showroom featuring live entertainment; Australia's largest hotel convention and banquet facilities including Australia's largest hotel ballroom; world-class shopping promenade; more than 50 restaurants and bars; 14-cinema complex.

Meeting/business facilities

26 rooms, for up to 3000 delegates; business centre.

Local attractions

Melbourne Zoo; Royal Botanical Gardens; National Gallery of Victoria; Victorian Arts Centre.

GOLF FACILITIES

Best season for golf: All year round.

COURSES:	LENGTH	PAR	FEES
Royal Melbourne Golf Course			
	6341m	72	Aus$360
Huntingdale Golf Course			
	6360m	73	Aus$260
Metropolitan Golf Course			
	6400m	72	Aus$310

Prices include green fees, booking fees and limousine transfer. Group prices on application. Courses subject to availability at time of booking.

Through Unlimited Golf, Crown Towers is able to arrange golf days for guests at a range of golf courses located within five minutes from the hotel or at a number of world renowned sandbelt and coastal courses.

Facilities key

484   **3000**

JOONDALUP RESORT

Hotel information

Country Club Boulevard
Joondalup
WA 6027

Tel: +61 8 9400 8888
Fax: +61 8 9400 8889
Email: hotel@joondalupresort.com.au
Web: www.joondalupresort.com.au

Accolades

★★★★☆

Airport

Perth International: 40 mins

Accommodation price guide

Accepted credit cards
AE DC MC V JCB

The moment you arrive at Joondalup Resort you're treated to the highest standards of hospitality, with the first class service being refreshingly relaxed. The resort hotel has been designed in harmony with its natural setting, and is very much part of the golfing experience. The accommodation is superb, and every room enjoys views of the magnificent 27-hole International Championship golf course or the picturesque natural bushland. Described by Robert Trent Jones Jr. as "one of the world's great golfing experiences" you would find it hard to beat this experience anywhere.

With free-roaming kangaroos and bright native birds all abundant in this natural setting, you would think you were miles from anywhere, but there are many other excellent activities close by this picturesque Australian bush setting. Being only five minutes from the white sandy beaches, which are the boundary to the bright blue Indian Ocean and just 25 minutes, drive north of Perth's central business district. So although our hotel offers a number of restaurants and bars to ensure that your stay is as comfortable as possible, there is very easy access to alternative restaurants and activities for those who want to explore.

Recreational facilities

Lagoon-style swimming pool, Jacuzzi; gym; volleyball, day/night tennis; jogging track.

Meeting/business facilities

Nine rooms, for up to 250 delegates. Business centre with internet access, scanner, colour printer, copying and conference call facilities.

Local attractions

Sports stadium; international casino; sandy beaches, nature-based attractions such as 'The Pinnacles', free-roaming kangaroos, native birds, whale watching; Marina shopping centre at Sorrento Quay with restaurants; diving and snorkelling centre.

GOLF FACILITIES

Best season for golf: All year round.

COURSES:	LENGTH	PAR	FEES
Joondalup Resort Quary	3168m	36	$28.50
Joondalup Resort Lakes	3120m	36	$28.50
Joondalup Resort Quary	3065m	36	$28.50

Flood-lit driving range, practice fairway and two putting greens.

Facilities key

70   250

Africa *and the* Middle East

DUBAI & QUATAR International class relaxation

Dubai Creek's clubhouse

Blue skies and warm blue seas are year-round conditions in the United Arab Emirates. Hot but desert-dry, it's perfect for golf, and for lazing by the pool or at the beach, too.

These pearls of the Middle East offer unique adventure in an Arabian desert setting – with majestic sunsets and thrilling 4x4 safaris – but it is also about tax-free shopping, historic sights, and a glimpse of another culture.

GETTING THERE British citizens do not need to arrange a visa in advance to enter the UAE (it is issued on the spot when arriving) but other nationalities do. As a refuelling and stop-over point for a vast array of Europe-Asia flights, the airport one of the world's busiest.

APRÈS GOLF You will find classic Arabic food out on the street and in local restaurants while the hotels present a cornucopia of first-rate cuisine from around the world. Shopping is a passion, with jewellery, gold and handicrafts especially sought after.

OFF THE COURSE The city has many parks and playgrounds to keep the children amused, and everyone enjoys the clean white sandy beaches. World-class scuba diving and watersports attract the active, while there's also some of the best horse racing in the world, top-level soccer and numerous major golfing tournaments to enjoy.

NOT TO BE MISSED With 700,000 inhabitants, Dubai is a kaleidoscope of contrasts – a distinctive blend of modern city and timeless desert, east and west, old and new. Take in the traditional souks, including the famed gold market; sail the Gulf in a statuesque Arab *dhow*.

FACTS AND FIGURES

● The game may still be establishing itself as a viable pastime among the Qataris, but Qatar is rapidly developing its own style – best seen in the Doha Golf Club, home to a European Tour event, the Qatar Open.

For a holiday combining year-round sunshine and outstanding sandy beaches with first-class golfing facilities, look no further than Dubai. The principality built its first championship layout on grass in 1988 and now has three golf courses supporting a lucrative leisure industry in addition to two professional tour events. The three clubs (Dubai Creek Golf & Yacht Club, Emirates Golf Club and the Dubai Golf & Racing Club) have a total of four 18-hole courses.

Each course offers a different, international-standard challenge. And adding to the relaxed atmosphere of Dubai is the calm which results from the relatively uncluttered state of the courses. You can work on improving your game without having to crawl your way to each green.

Qatar may currently lag behind Dubai in the golfing stakes, but indigenous interest is significantly growing. Indeed, a holiday in Qatar offers luxury and solitude in equal measure and the chance to practise your swing in peace on an outstanding course.

NEW DEVELOPMENTS

● Colin Montgomerie and Greg Norman have each designed courses at the new Emirate Hills development and the £160 million project will open early in 2000.

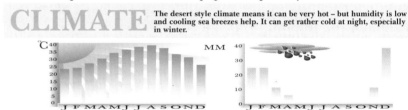

CLIMATE The desert style climate means it can be very hot – but humidity is low and cooling sea breezes help. It can get rather cold at night, especially in winter.

Sample point: Dubai

RECOMMENDED CAR HIRE *Hertz*

UK: +44 (0) 870 848 4848
Germany: +49 (0) 180 533 3535
Website: www.hertz.com

Price guide

Round of golf	Golf balls
Small beer	4/5 star hotel room

CONTACT

Dubai Tourism & Commerce Marketing, PO Box 594 Dubai UAE
Tel: +971 (0) 423 00 00 Fax: +971 (0) 451 17 11

Hotels

Favourite fairways

① EMIRATES GOLF

The first course to be built in the Middle East, the Emirates Golf Club opened in 1988 and the Majilis Course was until recently the venue for the annual Dubai Desert Classic. It is an American-style course featuring raised greens, straight fairways and six lakes. Two further courses, designed by Greg Norman and Colin Montgomerie respectively, will open in early 2000.
Majilis Course: Par 72 Length 6493m
Wadi Course: Par 72 Length 5998m
PO Box 24040 Dubai
Tel: +971 (0) 4 480 222
Fax: +971 (0) 4 481 888

② DUBAI CREEK

Built in 1993, this recent addition to the Dubai golfing panoply is a stunning oasis in the heart of the city. The par 72 Championship Course rolls along undulating fairways lined with coconut and date trees. The most famous feature of the course is its clubhouse designed in the shape of an Arab *dhow*, but the deceptively simple looking course itself is well worth a long visit.
Par 72   Length 6380 m
PO Box 6302 Dubai
Tel: +971 (0) 4 821 000
Fax: +971 (0) 4 820 921

③ DOHA

Home of the Qatar Open, Doha Golf Course opened in 1998 and has already drawn considerable praise from the professionals who have taken part in that competition. The championship course measures slightly over 6400 metres and, while demanding, offers an enjoyable test with a number of birdie opportunities.
Par 72   Length 6450m
Doha Golf Club, PO Box 13530, West Bay, Doha, Qatar
Tel: +974 (0) 832338
Fax: +974 (0) 834790

CITY CENTRE HOTEL & RESIDENCE

Hotel information

PO Box 61871
Dubai
United Arab Emirates

Tel: +971 (0) 4 294 1222
Fax: +971 (0) 4 295 4444
Email: cityhot@emirates.net.ae

Accolades

★★★★☆

Airport

Dubai International Airport: 5 mins

Accommodation price guide

€

Accepted credit cards
AE DC JCB MC V

Preferred tour operator

From UK, South Africa and Australia
Arabian
Adventures Tel: +971 (0) 4 343 9966
From UK, France and Italy
ALPHA Tours Tel: +971 (0) 4 222 3229
From Germany
Travco   Tel: +971 (0) 4 343 2444

Recreational facilities

Lifestyle health club, tennis and squash courts.

Meeting/business facilities

Three conference rooms and eight meeting rooms to accommodate up to 400 delegates.

Local attractions

Deira City Centre shopping complex with a total of 280 shops; cinemas and children's indoor amusement park and entertainment centre.

Conveniently located in the heart of Dubai, the City Centre Hotel & Residence offers five-star elegance in an easy and relaxed atmosphere. Minutes away from the world-renowned Dubai Creek Golf & Yacht Club, and adjoining the largest shopping complex in town – Deira City Centre – this luxurious home from home has all the amenities and recreational facilities that you would expect from a major hotel. Excellent accommodation and friendly, efficient staff make it a must for business and leisure travellers alike.

The City Centre Hotel & Residence has something special for everyone. Relax by the pool, work out in a state-of-the-art gymnasium, or have a game of tennis or squash. Enjoy a sumptuous snack or meal poolside, sip a long cool drink in one of the fully licensed bars, or sample a mouth-watering dish or two prepared by a team of master chefs at one of the gourmet restaurants.

Year after year, visitors are drawn back to this cosmopolitan and vibrant city which complements the enigmatic beauty of Arabia. The City Centre Hotel & Residence, managed by Sofitel, has absorbed these exceptional qualities into every aspect of its operation, assuring guests a truly unique and luxurious stay.

GOLF FACILITIES
Best season for golf: October to April.

COURSES: LENGTH	PAR	FEES
Dubai Creek		
6233m	72	AED345-395
Emirates		
6221m	72	AED330-425
Dubai Golf & Racing Club		
5858m	71	AED220-295

Facilities key

327   400

HILTON BEACH CLUB DUBAI

Hotel information

Jumeirah Beach Road
PO Box 26878
Dubai
United Arab Emirates

Tel: +971 (0) 4 445333
Fax: +971 (0) 4 446222
Email: DXBHBC@emirates.net.ae
Web: www.hilton.com

Accolades

✩✩✩✩✩ De Luxe

Airport

Dubai International: 20 mins

Accommodation price guide

Accepted credit cards
AE MC V DC

Preferred tour operator

From UK
ITC   Tel: +44 (0) 1244 355400
From Germany
Airtours   Tel: +49 (0) 69 7928-0
From Switzerland
Kuoni   Tel: +41 (0) 1 277 4723

Delightfully situated on the breathtaking Jumeirah Beach, the luxurious Hilton Beach Club Dubai enjoys one of this exciting and exotic city's most prestigious locations. Besides its close proximity to internationally acclaimed golf courses, the resort is also conveniently situated within minutes of the business centres, shopping centres and night-life, making it a perfect choice for golfing business traveller and leisure visitor alike.

As privileged guests of Hilton Beach Club, the choice is open: 50 tastefully appointed suites, each with its own unique view. All the suites boast a spacious lounge, a large balcony or terrace, central music system, TV and video, air-conditioning, personal fax with PC connections and, of course, the legendary Hilton care and attention.

Besides easy access to the golf, other sports are given high priority, with one of the two pools featuring an exciting 40-metre water slide. The hotel has its own private beach and a watersports centre, and the Hilton Beach Club also offers a fully equipped health and fitness facility.

There's a classy chic cocktail bar, a sunset bar and a choice of restaurants, including Prasino's, which presents Mediterranean cuisine at its best, and the informal Sails, with its culinary tour of the world.

Recreational facilities

Seven floodlit tennis courses, three squash courses, health and fitness centre, watersports centre; two temperature-controlled outdoor swimming pools with waterslides.

Meeting/business facilities

Three rooms, for up to 120 delegates.

Local attractions

Complimentary shuttle service from the hotel to the Gold Souk and shopping malls; scuba diving, watersports; exciting desert excursions.

GOLF FACILITIES

Best season for golf: October to April.

COURSES:	LENGTH	PAR	FEES
Emirates Majlis			
	6221m	72	AED370-425
Emirates Wadi			
	6221m	72	AED330-365
Dubai Creek			
	6233m	72	AED345-395
Dubai Golf & Racing Club			
	5858mm	71	AED220-295

Three quality golf courses lie within 15-25 minutes' drive.

Facilities key

50   120

JW MARRIOTT HOTEL DUBAI

Hotel information

Abu Baker
Al Siddique Road
PO Box 16590
Dubai
UAE

Tel: +971 (0) 4 624444*
Fax: +971 (0) 4 626264*
*For both numbers please add a '2'
before the '6' effective 1/1/2000
Email: marriott@emirates.net.ae
Web: www.marriott.com

Accolades

☆☆☆☆☆ Deluxe

Airport

Dubai International: 10 mins

Accommodation price guide

Accepted credit cards
AE DC MC V

Recreational facilities

Roof-top swimming pool; gym; sauna, steam room; billiard tables; sports bar; squash courts; Hamarain shopping mall is part of the hotel complex.

Meeting/business facilities

Twelve rooms, for up to 1000 delegates; 24-hour business centre, internet access.

Local attractions

Desert safaris; shopping; night life; watersports; Wonderland and Wild Valley theme parks.

Every design detail at the JW Marriott Hotel Dubai is geared toward making any visit a success, whether it is for business, pleasure, or planning a meeting. Guests can enjoy the comfort of one of some 344 oversized guest rooms and 39 suites, equipped with remote control interactive TV, voicemail, two-line telephones, alarm clock, data ports, individual climate-control, bathrobes, in-room safe, and separate shower and bath tub.

Two ballrooms and 11 break-out rooms are there to host up to 2000 persons for corporate groups while golfing parties are especially welcome – and there are three superb courses within easy reach.

The JW Marriott has a total of ten restaurants, including the JW Steak House, Cucina (Italian Kitchen), Hofbrauhaus (German restaurant), Vienna Café, The Market Place (international), Bamboo Lagoon, Piano Lounge, Atrium Cafe, Champions, and the Awafi arabic roof-top swimming pool restaurant.

Guests can relax at the roof-top swimming pool or exercise at Griffins Health Club, with its state-of-the-art training equipment.

When in Dubai you can count on the JW Marriott Hotel Dubai to make your stay a memorable one and your trip a grand success.

GOLF FACILITIES

Best season for golf: October to May.

COURSES:	LENGTH	PAR	FEES
Dubai Creek	6233m	72	US$95
Emirates	6221m	72	US$117
Dubai Golf & Racing Club	5858m	71	US$69

Driving range, putting green, short course; tuition packages available; tournaments open to guests.

Facilities key

344 1000

NORTH AFRICA History, romance and escapism

More than most places, North Africa conjures up potent images. From the ruins of ancient Carthage in Tunisia, the Bedouin camps of the Sahara, we find societies steeped in tradition and rich in history, romance and escapism.

Morocco has a population of just under 30 million, mainly concentrated in the major cities. From the long Atlantic and Mediterranean coastline to the inland wastes of the Sahara Desert and the magnificent peaks of the mighty Atlas Mountains – snow-capped in winter – Morocco is a big land of many contrasts.

While considerably smaller, Tunisia also offers great variety, with the olive trees and orange groves of the green and fertile north giving way to the magnificent sand dunes and desert sunsets of the south. Tunis, the capital, is a lively city offering a heady mix of Southern European and North African culture.

Egypt is the great treasure house of the Middle East while its Sinai resort of Sharm El Shekh boasts not just great golf but the world's best scuba diving too.

GETTING THERE North Africa's golfing countries are now key players in the tourism business, with the infrastructure to support their continuing growth as popular destinations for both holidays and short breaks. In the more remote parts of these lands, roads are scarce and require caution with 4x4 almost mandatory.

APRÈS GOLF Though Muslim countries, Morocco and Tunisia support domestic wine industries, the latter producing some notably fine vintages to accompany the plentiful fresh fish, grilled meats and simple salads which go with the renowned *cous-cous* and ultra-hot *harissa* dip. Egypt makes good beer and fabulous buffets of the *meze* ilk. Locals enjoy a vibrant café society; visitors will find discotheques and night clubs in the major tourist resorts.

OFF THE COURSE Tunisia's beaches are among the Mediterranean's best, while the Atlantic strands of Morocco are renowned for surfing and sailboarding. Egypt's Red Sea is famed for its coral and lovely beaches.

NOT TO BE MISSED The bustle of Cairo; the Pyramids; the ruins of Tunisia's ancient Carthage and the vestiges of the French colonial heritage; camel rides and 4x4 desert safaris; bargaining in the intriguing *souks* (marketplaces).

FACTS AND FIGURES

- First-time golfers in Tunisia are often bemused by the common sight of camels being led along adjacent roads. From a distance they can appear almost as a mirage looming on the fairways!
- Morocco's royal family are long-time golfing enthusiasts and tourism is recognised as the biggest economic sector, with 53 per cent of the working population now involved in the service sector.

Lakeside putting at Golf Tabarka, Tunisia

Fast-rising star destinations in the golfing firmament, the former French colonies of Morocco and Tunisia offer not only an exotic environment but near perfect weather, with reliable year-round sunshine and low humidity. Egypt's Red Sea coast offers similar advantages and golf is taking off there too.

Morocco's golfing tradition dates back to 1917 when the British laid out some holes in Tangier. Today the country has over 25 courses, with something to suit players of every ability. Morocco's monarchs have long been obsessed by golf and almost every course seems to prefix its name with Royal. The nine-hole course at Meknes is even built in the grounds of a royal palace. While Morocco offers some of the outstanding older golf venues in North Africa, with the Red Course at Royal Dar-Es-Salam regarded as one of Robert Trent Jones' masterpieces, Tunisia has a growing reputation for uncrowded winter sunshine conditions and outstanding facilities.

The most popular months for visiting golfers are April and October when cloudless skies and mild temperatures create almost perfect conditions for a leisurely round. Booking a tee time is rarely a problem and Tunisia is often favoured by higher-handicap players seeking to improve their game.

There's more to Egypt than monuments, museums, and thousands of years of history – there's great golf too, with new courses designed by world class golf architects, including Florida's Stanford Associates, Gary Player, Karl Litten, and renowned French golf architect Yves Bureau, as well as the historic Mena House Oberoi, facing the Pyramids and built in 1917 by Englishman Roy Wilson.

NEW DEVELOPMENTS

- Both Tunisia and Morocco are ploughing money into golf – many of Morocco's existing nine-hole courses are being extended to 18 holes while Tunisia has new venues planned in the desert resort of Tozeur and on the island of Djerba.
- The influx of golfers to this exotic corner of North Africa has seen hotels respond in kind. Many offer free transfers to local courses, with preferential tee times and reduced green fees for guests.

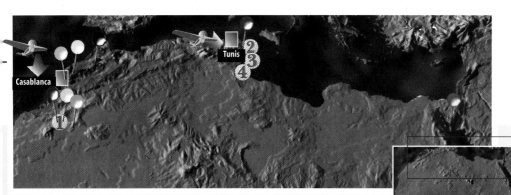

RECOMMENDED **Hertz**
CAR HIRE
UK: +44 (0) 870 848 4848
Germany: +49 (0) 180 533 3535
Website: www.hertz.com

Hotels

Favourite fairways

1 ROYAL MARRAKESH

Recently renovated and always kept in pristine condition, this is Morocco's showpiece course. Built in the 1920s, the Royal Marrakesh is situated at the bottom of the Atlas Mountains and features flat fairways, receptive greens and hanging palm trees. But although it looks beautiful, it is also a highly testing course and you need to plan carefully the best way to get round.
Par 72   Length 6200m
BP 634 Ancienne Route de Ouarzazatem, Marrakesh, Morocco
Tel: + 212 (0) 4 44 43 41   Fax: +212 (0) 4 43 00 84

2 EL KANTAOUI

El Kantaoui is one of the most popular golfing resorts in Tunisia. The Ronald Fream-designed course opened in 1979 and has recently expanded into two distinctive yet enjoyable 18-hole challenges. Holes 14 to 17 of the Sea course are played directly along the beachfront where a tough breeze is coupled with spectacular views. The Panorama course is equally testing and more strikingly beautiful.
Par 72   Length 6127m (Sea Course)
Par 72   Length 6409m (Panorama Course)
El Kantaoui Golf Course, Port El Knataoui, Sousse, Tunisia
Tel: +216 (0) 3 348 756   Fax: +216 (0) 3 348 755

3 FLAMINGO

Yet another Ronald Fream-creation, the Flamingo makes the most of its magnificent setting on a plateau shaded by olive trees and presents views across lakes and the sea. The course, to be found a few kilometres south of the city of Sousse and the international airport at Monastir, meanders over crests and hills, but includes strategically positioned water traps to surprise the unwary. There are five tee boxes for each hole which enable golfers of all abilities to enjoy the course.
Par 72   Length 6140m
Flamingo Golf Club, Route de Ouardanine, Monastir, Tunisia
Tel: +216 (0) 3 46 1095   Fax: +216 (0) 3 461 145

4 DJERBA GOLF

The beautiful island hideaway of Djerba lurks just off the coast of Tunisia, and this 27-hole resort course designed by British architect Martin Hawtree combines a championship round with a short, 'executive' nine-hole course. The Djerba Golf Club is also home to the first African David Leadbetter golf academy and therefore contains an instruction lounge and a covered practice putting green.
Par 72   Length 6500m
Djerba Golf Club, Zone Touristique, Midoun, Djerba, Tunisia
Tel: +216 (0) 5 659 055   Fax: +216 (0) 5 659 051

CONTACT

Tunisian National Tourist Office 1, Avenue Mohamed V, 1001 Tunis Tel: +216 (0) 1 341 077 Fax: +216 (0) 1 350 997
Moroccan National Tourist Office 31 Angle mRue, Oved Fes Avenue Al Abtal Agdal, Rabat, Morocco Tel: +212 (0) 7 681 531 Fax: +212 (0) 7 681 527
Egyptian National Tourist Office Misr Travel Tower, Abbassia Square, Cairo, Egypt Tel: +20 (0) 285-4509/284 1970 Fax: +20 (0) 285 4363

The most up-to-date golf travel information is always at www.golftravel4u.com

CLIMATE   Tunisia's coastal climate can be quite temperate. Inland, hot and dry desert conditions prevail. While Morocco's Atlas Mountains are often snow-capped, most of the country has a desert climate. Egypt has the world's sunniest environment, with vast tracts lying inside the Sahara.

Sample point: Tunis

Price guide €

Round of golf   Golf balls
Small beer   4/5 star hotel room

JOLIE VILLE MÖVENPICK GOLF RESORT

Hotel information

Sharm El Sheikh
Um Marikha Bay
South Sinai

Tel: +20 62 603 200
Fax: +20 62 603 225
Email: golf.sharm@moevenpick.com
Web: www.moevenpick-sharmgolf.com

Accolades

★★★★☆

Airport

Sharm El Sheikh: 10 mins

Accommodation price guide

Accepted credit cards
AE DC MC V

Recreational facilities

La Spa Jolie Ville; Water Theme Park; tennis courts; Excursion & Activity Centre; windsurfing, sailing, water skiing, parasailing, diving; billiards, darts, table tennis.

Meeting/business facilities

Six rooms, for up to 400 delegates.

Local attractions

Tours and excursions to nearby diving sites and other points of interest are easily arranged by the sightseeing and tour desk.

The spectacular Jolie Ville Mövenpick Golf Hotel & Resort is attracting visitors to Sharm El Sheikh, in the vibrant centre of South Sinai.

Drivers and snorkellers have been drawn here to the famous crystal-clear Red Sea waters, and now, this exciting resort is also attracting golfers, enthusiasts of other watersports, families and business meeting planners.

A stay at the resort offers panoramic views of the Sinai coastline, Tiran Island, lush tropical landscaping and all the luxuries, services and amenities one expects of a world-class hotel.

On the premises is Egypt's largest water theme park, which features cascading waterfalls, lakes, grottos, water slides and giant mushroom fountains.

A state-of-the-art conference facility at the Golf Clubhouse can seat 400. There are also three meeting rooms, as well as a business centre.

Le Spa Jolie Ville Health Centre offers massage, sauna, Jacuzzi, whirlpool, gym, and beauty salon.

A variety of culinary specialities is prepared daily and offered in a choice of 11 restaurants and bars.

Tours and excursions to nearby diving sites and other points of interest are easily arranged by the Jolie Ville's sightseeing and tour desks.

The 18-hole championship golf course, a par 72, features glorious sea and desert mountain views.

GOLF FACILITIES
Best season for golf: Winter.

COURSES:	LENGTH	PAR	FEES
Jolie Ville			
	6021m	72	$35-55

Driving range; golf school; pro shop; bar/restaurant; carts and caddies available.

Facilities key

245 400

LA MAMOUNIA

Hotel information

Avenue Bab Jdid
40000
Marrakesh

Tel: +212 (0) 4 44 44 09
Fax: +212 (0) 4 44 49 40
Email: marketing@mamounia.com
Web: www.mamounia.com

Accolades

☆☆☆☆☆ De Luxe
Best hotel in Africa 1998 (Gourmet magazine)

Airport

Marrakesh: 10 mins

Accommodation price guide

Accepted credit cards
AE   MC   V   DC

Recreational facilities

Pool, Jacuzzi, fitness room, tennis courts, squash courts; spa with hammam, sauna, massage; golf driving range (in-house pro); horse riding and shooting available locally; seven hectares of gardens; boutiques.

Meeting/business facilities

Four rooms, for up to 400 delegates; business centre.

Local attractions

Bahia Palace, Sa'adi tombs, souks, traditional entertainment, Berber villages and Ouarzazate oasis; arts and crafts; excursions to Atlas Mountains.

"It is the most lovely spot in the whole world." So said Winston Churchill to Franklin D. Roosevelt about Marrakesh in 1943, as they gazed at one of the beautiful sunsets for which the city is famous, tinting the distant snow-capped peaks of the Atlas Mountains into a velvet red. The hotel takes its name from the surrounding seven-hectare garden park – a wedding gift two centuries ago to Prince Moulay Mamoun from his father, the Sultan.

The 1986 renovation programme left the 1920s porch intact, opening into the '20s-style 'Salon of Honour' used for ceremonial occasions. The hotel's guest list speaks for itself: Churchill, Roosevelt, Charles de Gaulle, Charlie Chaplin, Omar Sharif, Tom Cruise, Nicole Kidman, Sylvester Stallone, Ronald and Nancy Reagan, Princess Caroline of Monaco, Prince Naruhito, Nelson Mandela and Desmond Tutu, among many others.

Themed suites include the Orient Express Suite, a replica of the train's luxury compartments, and the Au Baldaquin wedding suite, with its four-poster bed and views over the pool, gardens and olive groves to the Atlas Mountains. There are also three detached villas, connected to the hotel by underground passages. Each has its own entrance, private parking, and gardens. Restaurants feature French, Italian and traditional Moroccan cuisine.

GOLF FACILITIES
Best season for golf: All year round.

COURSES:	LENGTH	PAR	FEES
Royal	6120m	72	US$40
Amelkis	5774m	72	US$55

Tuition available; Mamounia Golf Cup, Jan 29-30, 2000.

Facilities key

230   400

LE MERIDIEN BERBERE PALACE

Recreational facilities

Outdoor swimming pool, tennis courts; health and fitness centre featuring sauna, Hammam baths, Jacuzzi and massage amenities.

Meeting/business facilities

One multipurpose room, for up to 800 delegates.

Local attractions

The beautiful kasbahs of Aït Benhaddou, just north of Ouarzazate; excursions to the Draa valley across the desolate Anti-Atlas; stunning gorges to the west.

Hotel information

Quartier Mansour Eddahbi
Ouarzazate

Tel: +212 (0) 4 88 31 05
Fax: +212 (0) 4 88 30 71

Accolades

★★★★☆

Airport

Taourirt International Ouarzazate: 10 mins

Accommodation price guide

€

Accepted credit cards
AE MC V DC

Preferred tour operator

From UK
Cadogan
Travel   Tel: +44 (0) 20 73 82 8331
From Germany
Airtours   Tel: +49 (0) 69 79 280
From France
Gallia
Voyages   Tel: +33 (0) 1 53 43 36 36
From Italy
Acentro   Tel: +39 02 6671 1811

The luxurious Méridien Berbère Palace Hotel is conveniently located right in the centre of Ouarzazate, one of Morocco's most historic old cities, and stands in its own 11 hectares of delightful gardens as a true oasis of a resort.

Constructed in the style of a traditional Berber village, it has retained traditional authenticity and combined it with every modern comfort.

The 222 guest rooms – which include duplexes, apartments and suites – are all decorated in Berber style and are air-conditioned throughout for comfort. All rooms have a large bathroom, with separate WC, as well as direct dial telephones and satellite TV.

Gourmets will appreciate the delicious international and Moroccan cuisine served in the award-winning Oasis restaurant while the less formal Teri pizzeria offers a full range of lighter meals and snacks.

A spacious outdoor swimming pool, a fitness centre offering sauna, Hammam, Jacuzzi and massage facilities and tennis courts are among the first-class leisure facilities offered by this fine hotel, while quality golf is available within easy reach.

GOLF FACILITIES
Best season for golf: All year round.

COURSES:	LENGTH	PAR	FEES
Royal Golf			
	3050m	36	US$20

Royal Golf, 15 kilometres from the hotel, offers a 45-bay driving range plus putting green.

Facilities key

222 800

LE MERIDIEN MARRAKECH

OPENING APRIL 2000

Hotel information

Avenue de France
Marrakesh

Tel: +212 (0) 4 44 87 72
Fax: +212 (0) 4 44 74 46

Accolades

☆☆☆☆☆

Airport

Menara Marrakesh: 8 mins

Accommodation price guide

Accepted credit cards
AE DC MC V

Preferred tour operator

From UK
Cadogan
Travel   Tel: +44 (0) 207 382 8331
From Germany
Airtours   Tel: +49 (0) 69 79 280
From France
Gallia
Voyages   Tel: +33 (0) 1 53 43 36 36
From Italy
Acentro   Tel: +39 02 6671 1811

Recreational facilities

Fitness centre, hammam, sauna; large swimming pool, two clay tennis courts; karting, horse riding and skiing are available locally.

Meeting/business facilities

Four rooms, for up to 150 delegates.

Local attractions

Square Jamaa Al Fna, Majorelle Gardens, Saadian tombs, Koutoubia Mosque, Menara Gardens.

Set to open in Spring 2000, this new luxury hotel is certain to make its mark quickly on the ancient city of Marrakesh, surrounded by a magnificent five-hectare parkland setting and commanding undeniably the best location in town.

Just a stone's throw away are the two finest golf courses in Marrakesh – Amelkis Golf and Golf Royal – both of which provide breathtaking views to the nearby Atlas Mountains.

The fragrance of cypress, eucalyptus, palm, olive, orange and apricot trees at the Royal Golf adds a seductive new dimension to the golfing experience, while Amelkis is a truly challenging course, with outstanding fairways and greens and obstacles to test players of all levels.

Getting to and from the courses will be a breeze, with complimentary minibus transfers from the hotel and a journey time of under ten minutes.

After an inspiring round at North Africa's finest, how better to relax and unwind than sipping a drink in a shady corner of the Andalusian gardens at Le Meridien Marrakech, the air suffused with the aroma of ripe fruits and exotic blooms?

GOLF FACILITIES

Best season for golf: All year round.

COURSES:	LENGTH	PAR	FEES
Golf Royal Marrakech			
	6120m	72	Dir350
Amelkis Golf Marrakech			
	6657m	72	Dir450
Tuition available.			

Facilities key

277   150

LE MÉRIDIEN MERINIDES

Hotel information

Borj Nord
Fez

Tel: +212 (0) 5 645226
Fax: +212 (0) 5 645225

Accolades

★★★★☆

Airport

Fes Les Saiss: 25 mins

Accommodation price guide

Accepted credit cards
AE MC V DC

Preferred tour operator

From UK
Cadogan
Travel   Tel: +44 (0) 207 382 8331
From Germany
Airtours   Tel: +49 (0) 69 79 280
From France
Gallia
Voyages   Tel: +33 (0) 1 53 43 36 36
From Italy
Acentro   Tel: +39 02 6671 1811

Recreational facilities

Swimming pool; night club at hotel; Moulay Yacoub Spa Centre; golf and tennis available locally.

Meeting/business facilities

One room, for up to 200 delegates.

Local attractions

The ravishing and mystical imperial city of Fez; Qarawiyyin Mosque (the largest mosque in North Africa and one of the world's most beautiful places of worship); richly ornamented interiors of the Mosque and Tomb of Moulay Idris II; handicraft industry.

GOLF FACILITIES
Best season for golf: All year round.

COURSES:	LENGTH	PAR	FEES
Royal Golf Fes	3168m	37	MDH280

Beautifully sited on a hill overlooking the ancient Moroccan royal city of Fes, Le Méridien Merinides is a short distance from the bustling city centre. A 15-minute drive from the hotel will bring you to Royal Golf Fes, a splendid course designed by CB Robinson in the middle of olive groves in a naturally undulating landscape.

All the 106 guest rooms feature a mini-bar, direct dial telephone, satellite TV and hair-dryer in the bathroom. A number of dining options are available. On the third floor, overlooking the Medina, the hotel's 200-seater Moroccan restaurant is the only five star hotel restaurant in Fes to offer a full programme, of entertainment including belly dancing. International food with a French touch is also served, while the atmospheric and intimate L'Italian Café has 40 covers. The Bar Eusha has 60 seats and splendid views.

The ultimate in relaxation after a great round of golf is a water treatment at the Moulay Yacoub Spa Centre, while no visit to Fes would be complete without a wander through the fascinating Medina.

Facilities key

 106 200

OCCIDENTAL HAMMAMET

Hotel information

BP 237
8050 Yasmine
Hammamet

Tel: +216 (0) 2 226 935
Fax: +216 (0) 2 226 965 / 226 315
Email: occidental.hammamet@planet.tn

Accolades

☆☆☆☆☆

Airport

Tunis-Carthage: 1 hr
Habib-Bourguiba - Monastir: 1 hr 15 mins

Accommodation price guide

Accepted credit cards
AE MC V DC

Preferred tour operator

From Germany
THR Tours   Tel: +49 (0) 211 9415 102
From Franoo
Green du
Monde   Tel: +33 (0) 494 55 97 77
From The Netherlands
Executive
Golf Travel   Tel: +31 (0) 35 543 1588

Recreational facilities

Indoor/outdoor pools; spa, solariums, terraces, gardens; beach club; tennis, sport and water activities; dinner shows; casino; beauty and hair salon.

Meeting/business facilities

Facilities for up to 360 delegates.

Local attractions

Roman and Carthaginian ruins at Dougga, El Djem (amphitheatre) and Carthage; Tarkaba Phoenician port; artists' colony village of Sidi Bou Said; troglodytic houses of Matmata.

Within just minutes of this attractive five-star hotel are the Yasmine and Citrus golf clubs, both built to meet the highest international design parameters. The courses wend their way around six lakes and 170 highly attractive hectares of olive trees and green space, with easy access to the highly popular resort of Hammamet.

The Yasmine course in particular provides wonderful views of the sea and of the lush vegetation which is so typical of the Hammamet.

Ideally placed for visiting golfers, the Occidental Hammamet is a veritable Arabian palace, set in nine hectares of citrus trees and colourful gardens. With direct access to the sea and a glorious beach, the hotel offers a spa, sports, and a children's fun club.

Each of the 262 truly magnificent guest rooms has a terrace, direct dial telephone, air-conditioning, mini-bar safe-deposit box and satellite TV. At the hotel, opportunities for leisure and relaxation abound, including a spa, sports, swimming, and the Occidental Fun Club for children.

GOLF FACILITIES
Best season for golf: October to April.

COURSES:	LENGTH	PAR	FEES
Yasmine	6115m	72	DT40
Citrus Oliviers	6178m	72	DT45
Citrus Foret	6250m	72	DT45
Flamingo	6140m	72	DT65
El Kantaoui	6127m	72	DT45

Guests may enter local tournaments subject to availability; golf practice facilities nearby; all fees include transfer.

Facilities key

262   360

LA TOUR HASSAN MÉRIDIEN

Hotel information

26 Rue Chellah
B.P. 14
Rabat

Tel: +212 (0) 7 70 42 01
Fax: +212 (0) 7 72 54 08
Email: sand@mtds.com

Accolades

★★★★☆

Airport

Rabat Salé: 15 mins

Accommodation price guide

€

Accepted credit cards
AE MC V DC

Preferred tour operator

From UK
Cadogan
Travel   Tel: +44 (0) 207 382 8331
From Germany
Airtours   Tel: +49 (0) 69 79 280
From France
Gallia
Voyages   Tel: +33 (0) 1 53 43 36 36
From Italy
Acentro   Tel: +39 02 6671 1811

Recreational facilities

Andalous garden; fitness centre, sauna, hammam baths, Jacuzzi, beauty salon for women and men; outdoor pool and solarium; clay tennis courts, surfing and waterskiing nearby.

Meeting/business facilities

Seven conference rooms, to accommodate up to 600 delegates; business centre.

Local attractions

Mausoleum of Mohammed V; Le Chellah; the Kasbah of the Oudayas; beaches at Skhirat and Bouznika.

Founded in 1914, La Tour Hassan Méridien is an integral part of the history of Rabat, the capital of Morocco. This jewel of *rbati* architecture has been totally renovated, respecting its original majesty and elegance, to enable it to offer all the modern amenities and personal attention you could wish for in a luxury hotel. Located in the city centre, just 20 minutes from the airport and the prestigious golf courses of Dar Es Salam, La Tour Hassan is your best address in Rabat. All rooms air-conditioned, and have satellite TV and direct dial telephone.

Every single aspect of the hotel is an expression of Andalusian heritage. You will find flavours of Moroccan traditional cooking at La Maison Arabe, the subtleties of the French influence at the Restaurant Impérial, and fine drinks in Le Pacha bar. With a business centre oriented to your needs, a fitness centre for your well-being, a swimming pool and Jacuzzi in the wonderful hotel garden, everything at La Tour Hassan Méridien combines to achieve your total satisfaction.

Other Méridien hotels in Morocco are: Le Mérinides in Fez, Le Berbère Palace in Ouarzazate, and Le Royal Mansour in Casablanca. Le Méridien Marrakech opens in Spring 2000.

GOLF FACILITIES

Best season for golf: All year round.

COURSES:	LENGTH	PAR	FEES
Dar Es Salam Red			
	6680m	73	US$40
Dar Es Salam Blue			
	6000m	72	US$40
Dar Es Salam Green			
	2170m	32	US$40
Mohammedia			
	5898m	72	US$40

Practice and tuition facilities available; guests may take part in local tournaments organised by the golf club; buggies for hire.

Facilities key

139   600

LE ROYAL MANSOUR MERIDIEN

Hotel information

27 Avenue de l'Armée Royale
21100 Casablanca

Tel: +212 (0) 2 31 30 11
Fax: +212 (0) 2 31 25 83
Web: www.marocnet.net.ma/mansour

Accolades

☆☆☆☆ De Luxe
Member The Leading Hotels of the World

Airport

Casablanca Mohammed V: 30 mins

Accommodation price guide

 €

Accepted credit cards
AE MC V DC

Preferred tour operator

From UK
Cadogan
Travel   Tel: +44 (0) 207 382 8331
From Germany
Airtours   Tel: +49 (0) 69 79 280
From France
Gallia
Voyages   Tel: +33 (0) 1 53 43 36 36
From Italy
Acentro   Tel: +39 02 6671 1811

 AMERICAN EXPRESS OFFER

For advance booking on American Express Card you receive **VIP treatment in room; free shining of golf shoes.**

Quote 'Great Golf Hotels offer' when you book.

Recreational facilities

Fitness club with beauty parlour, work-out room, Turkish bath, sauna; hairdresser; winter garden; evening entertainment; karting, bowling, horse riding, handicraft shopping.

Meeting/business facilities

Seven rooms, one for up to 450 delegates; business centre.

Local attractions

Hassan II Mosque; arts and crafts shopping; Casablanca souks; local beaches.

Within four superb courses within easy driving distance, the Royal Mansour Méridien, one of The Leading Hotels of the World, provides an ideal Moroccan base for the visiting golfer.

Conveniently situated in the heart of Casablanca, the country's economic capital, this highly prestigious hotel is a true luxury palace, with its own unique personality and charm – subtly offering a mixture of ultra comfort and a refinement of the colourful local splendour. Exploiting the Le Méridien group's hotel management know-how and reputation for service, the Royal Mansour Méridien is a magnificent hotel in the grand tradition.

The talents and experience of the head chefs and their devoted team ensure cuisine which is simply enchanting in its excellence and variety. Delicious Moroccan specialities are served in the sumptuous Le Douira while Le Brasserie offers the pleasures of classic European menus. Breakfast, refreshments and light meals can be savoured at the delightful Jardin d'Hiver – ensuring the Royal Mansour Meridién's role as a true haven of good food.

After a day on the local courses, return for a session in the hotel's refined health and beauty centre, take a relaxing drink at the terrace bar, enjoy fine wine and food in one of the fine restaurants and be set up perfectly for the anticipation of another great day's golf to come.

GOLF FACILITIES
Best season for golf: April to end October.

COURSES:	LENGTH	PAR	FEES
Royal Golf Mohammedia			
	5400m	72	US$20
Royal Golf Benslimone			
	6160m	72	US$20
Royal Golf Eljadida			
	6234m	72	US$30
Tuition packages at local courses.			

Facilities key

  181 **450**

SOUTH AFRICA Wild, wild, life

With its stunning scenery polyglot, culture and the great coastal cities of Cape Town and Durban, 'The Rainbow Nation' is one of the world's most appealing destinations.

You can surf the Indian Ocean, follow the famed Garden Route along the coast, tour the fabled Cape Province vineyards with their pretty Dutch colonial houses, or take a safari to Kruger National Park, Mala Mala or one of dozens of game reserves. One thing's certain, you'll need plenty of film in your camera.

GETTING THERE International services fly direct into Johannesburg and Cape Town. South Africa has no real motorways but many roads are lightly trafficked.

APRÈS GOLF South Africa's cuisine is a mix of British, French, Dutch, Portuguese and native African flavours. They do wonderful things with pumpkin and low-cholesterol ostrich is a meat to enjoy. As part of the New World craze, South Africa's wines are improving apace.

OFF THE COURSE The SA hinterland begs exploration, with its vast veldt, the mystical Karoo Desert, towering red mountains, deep gorges and whitewater rivers. There's a love of the good life in these parts – and the sports, leisure and social facilities to match.

NOT TO BE MISSED The cable car ride up Table Mountain; the enormous Kango Caves; visiting ostrich and crocodile farms.

FACTS AND FIGURES

- Out of nearly 500 courses, over 100 have excellent ratings, many being regarded as among the world's most outstanding challenges.
- Major tournaments include the Million Dollar Challenge (December) and the South African Open and Alfred Dunhill Championship, both in January.
- Three courses are situated in the bush: Sabi, Hans Merensky and Malelane, which all border the famous Kruger National Park.

CLIMATE

Cape Town has a Mediterranean-style climate, Durban is sub-tropical, while Johannesburg, set on the high Veldt, has hot and thundery Summers and Winters are dry and sunny, but cold at night.

Sample point: Cape Town

RECOMMENDED CAR HIRE

Hertz®

UK: +44 (0) 870 848 4848
Germany: +49 (0) 180 533 3535
Website: www.hertz.com

Price guide

€

| Round of golf | 🏌🏌🏌 | Golf balls | 🏌🏌 |
| Small beer | 🏌🏌 | 4/5 star hotel room | 🏌🏌🏌 |

CONTACT

South African Tourism, Private Bag X164 Pretoria 0001
Tel: +27 (0) 12 347 0600
Fax: +27 (0) 12 45 4889

Diverse courses, magnificent scenery and a mild, sunny year-round climate puts South Africa amongst the most attractive golf locations in the world.

It was over 100 years ago that the British initiated the first course, later to be known as Royal Cape Golf Club, and since then there has been no stopping the march of golf, not only across South Africa but throughout the continent.

Along with its top-class championship courses designed by the likes of Gary Player and Jack Nicklaus, South Africa has unique clubs whose fairways play host to antelope, monkeys and warthog and even hippos snorting in the pools next to the tee. It's a country where you can combine a safari, scenic or seaside holiday for the family with a golfing experience that will be hard to match.

NEW DEVELOPMENTS

- A new 'pay and play' 18-hole links course will open in April 2000 at Fancourt Hotel and Country Club at George. The club's other two courses are reserved for hotel guests.
- 2000 also sees the opening of a new 18-hole Hugh Biaocchi-designed championship course at Champagne Sports Resort in the Kwazulu Natal Drakensberg, while in the Cape Town area the Atlantic Beach course will also open during the year.

Favourite fairways

1 DURBAN COUNTRY CLUB

This course was laid out by the father of South African golf, Laurie B Waters, in 1922. The first five holes have been described as the most stunning start to any golf course in the world. Driving into the wind from the raised tee of the magnificent third hole you have the Indian Ocean as your backdrop.

Par 72   Length 6090m
Water Gilbert Road
PO Box 1504
Durban 4000
Tel: +27 (0) 31 31 31 777
Fax: + 27 (0) 31 31 31 700

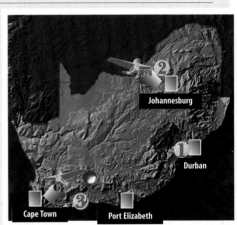

Hotels

● **Fancourt Hotel**   Page 83

2 GARY PLAYER COUNTRY CLUB

Designed by the famous South African golfer, the course was established in 1979 and is the home of the annual Million Dollar Classic championship. While comparatively flat, it is one of the longest and toughest courses in Southern Africa with water hazards and cunningly sited bunkers. The nearby desert-style Lost City course was opened in 1993.

Par 72   Length 7003m
PO Box 5
Sun City 0316
Tel: +27 (0) 14 557 1000
Fax: +27 (0) 14 557 4227

3 GEORGE

Situated on the famous Garden Route, only a few kilometres from the coast, this woodland championship course, with nine flat holes and nine in undulating country, is rated seventh in South Africa and from the clubhouse situated on a small hill you have a fine view of the first and 18th holes.

Par 72   Length 6100m
CJ Langenhoven Street
PO Box 81
George 6530
Tel: +27 (0) 44 873 6116
Fax: +27 (0) 44 874 6191

FANCOURT HOTEL & COUNTRY CLUB

Hotel information

PO Box 2266
George 6530

Tel: +27 (0) 44 804 0010
Fax: +27 (0) 44 804 0710
Email: hotel@fancourt.co.za
Web: www.fancourt.co.za

Accolades

Best Golf Resort Africa & Middle East
1999 – Hertz International Golf Travel
Awards
Best Resort Hotel & Conference Venue
1999 – Leading Venues

Airport

George: 10 mins
Cape Town: 4 hrs 30 mins (40 mins
flying time)

Accommodation price guide

Accepted credit cards
AE DC MC V

Recreational facilities

Tennis, squash, bowls, health and beauty
pavilion, gym, indoor and outdoor pools,
Jacuzzi, mini cinema, billiards, walking,
cycling, scuba diving and horse riding
available locally.

Meeting/business facilities

One large conference room and six
meeting rooms to accommodate up to
300 delegates.

Local attractions

Glorious beaches, historical sites, the
Cango Caves, ostrich farms, whale
watching, cinema, theatre, winery visits
and the Outeniqua Choo-Tjoe train.

Fancourt, South Africa's premier golfing and leisure destination, lies at the foot of the majestic Outeniqua mountain, in the heart of the world famous Garden Route. This beautifully manicured estate comprises a hotel of rare distinction, homes and leisure facilities positioned around two Gary Player-designed 18-hole championship golf courses, with a further 18-hole Links style course opening at the end of April 2000. Elegant accommodation is provided in the historic manor house or in stately garden lodges. The resort's four fine restaurants, formal and informal, cater for a variety of tastes.

A conference centre caters for up to 300 delegates and offers state-of-the-art audio-visual equipment and computerised facilities, as well as a business centre. The estate has its own luxurious health and beauty pavilion, with full resort spa facilities, gymnasium, boutique and hair salon. Squash, swimming, bowls, croquet and mini-cinema can be enjoyed at the leisure centre. Other facilities include a golf shop, warm-up area, nine hole golf school, tennis courts and a real estate office.

Fancourt is South Africa's only member of the prestigious Great Golf Resorts of the World and Preferred Hotels and Resorts Worldwide associations.

GOLF FACILITIES
Best season for golf: All year.

COURSES:	LENGTH	PAR	FEES
Outeniqua			
	5996m	72	R325
Montagu			
	5981m	72	R325
George			
	5774m	72	R150

Third on-site 18-hole Links-style course opens end April 2000; golf school and warm-up area, buggies available; twice-weekly resort competitions; four other courses within one hour's drive.

Facilities key

100   300

INDIAN OCEAN Golf in paradise

The spice island of Mauritius might be a tiny dot on the vast expanse of the Indian Ocean but it's making a major impact on the tourism list of "places to go", thanks to its natural beauty, its offshore reef protected beaches, its profusion of cultivated and wild flowers and its equally colourful multi-ethnic mix.

Equally appealing for a 'get away from it all break' are the myriad islands of the Seychelles, with Praslin as the outstanding gem in this string of pearls.

GETTING THERE As highly in-vogue tourism destinations, both Mauritius and the Seychelles are now well served with scheduled and charter services from Europe, the USA and other departure points, while light aircraft services link the smaller islands in the Seychelles.

APRÈS GOLF Cooled by the sea breeze, sipping a cocktail on the veranda as the sun sinks into the ocean – it's an everyday event hereabouts. Food reflects the ethnic mix, with fish and shellfish given star rating on the menu.

OFF THE COURSE Mauritius boasts outstanding botanical gardens, the lively capital port of Fort Louis and impressive volcanic mountain peaks. The Seychelles offer warm, shallow waters and outstanding scuba diving.

NOT TO BE MISSED Beachcomb for lustrous seashells; windsurf the lagoons in real safety; join the locals around the local bar's TV, indulging their passion for English league football.

FACTS & FIGURES

● There are six courses to be found on the two islands, with five on Mauritius – a total of just 72 holes.
● For a taste of the style and atmosphere of golf in colonial days, arrange a visit the 18-hole course at the private Gymkhana Club on Mauritius.

Both Mauritius and the Seychelles are 'paradise' destinations that have only recently started to recognise the potential of golf tourism. On both islands, government determination to control the expansion of tourism means that new developments are mostly spectacular luxury resorts, catering to the 'top end' of the market – and golf facilities are increasingly high on their agenda.

The Mauritius Open is a considerable draw – attracting players of the calibre of Scotland's Andrew Coltart – and the establishment of the Mauritius PGA means the sport's future on the island is assured.

The full golfing potential of the Seychelles has yet to be realised: serious players are restricted to the Reef Hotel's course, at Anse aux Pins south of the capital town of Victoria, though a large scale hotel and golf development is planned for Mahé following the completion of Praslin's Lémuria resort.

NEW DEVELOPMENTS

● The new Lémuria Resort on the Seychelles island of Praslin will provide the country's first 18-hole championship course, due to be ready by mid-2000.
● Guests at Mauritius' Belle Mare Plage hotel receive free green fees on the Championship Course and free play on the nine-hole course at the hotel Le St Geran.

CLIMATE Rainfall is substantial throughout the year, particularly on high ground and on the southern coasts which are most exposed to the southeast trade winds. Despite all the rain the climate is delightfully sunny.

Sample point: Port Louis

RECOMMENDED CAR HIRE *Hertz*
UK: +44 (0) 870 848 4848
Germany: +49 (0) 180 533 3535
Website: www.hertz.com

Price guide €

Round of golf	🏌🏌	Golf balls	🏌🏌🏌
Small beer	🏌🏌🏌	4/5 star hotel room	🏌🏌🏌

CONTACT

Ministry of Tourism and Leisure, Level 12, Air Mauritius Centre, John Kennedy Street, Port Louis
Tel :+230 (0) 210 1329   Fax :+230 (0) 208 6776
Seychelles Tourist Office, PO Box 92, Victoria, Mahé, Seychelles
Tel: +248 (0) 22 53 13   Fax: +248 (0) 22 40 35

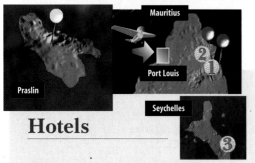

Hotels

🔵 **Belle Mare Plage**   Page 85
⚪ **Lemuria Reort of Praslin**
                        Page 86
🔵 **Le Prince Maurice** Page 87

Favourite fairways

① BELLE MARE PLAGE
Low-lying and somewhat undulating, this course, home to the Mauritius Open held every December, has been created over volcanic rock and marshy flood plain. Accuracy is crucial with cunningly placed bunkers and a punishing indigenous rough. The well-kept greens are a putter's delight; challenging, roomy and set amongst beautiful sub-tropical scenery.
Par 72   Length 6312m
Belle Mare, Mauritius
Tel: +230 (0) 415 1518
Fax: +230 (0) 415 1993

② LE SAINT GERAN
Designed by veteran Gary Player, this nine-hole gem provides a pleasant round for golfers of all abilities. Lush vegetation and the ever-present ocean views add to the charms of a course whose real challenge lies in its short and well-bunkered holes with surprisingly tricky greens.
Par 33
Poste de Flacq, Mauritius
Tel: +230 (0) 415 1825
Fax: +230 (0) 415 1983

③ REEF HOTEL GOLF CLUB
Currently the only round of golf available on the islands, this pretty nine-hole tropical course is a pleasure to play. There are few surprises and the average player will not be stretched; however, with sections built over a mangrove swamp and the occasional hazard of the crabs which have been known to steal balls, there is the guarantee of a unique golfing experience.
PO Box 388, Seychelles
Tel: +248 (0) 376 251

BELLE MARE PLAGE THE RESORT

Hotel information

Belle Mare Plage
Poste De Flacq

Tel: +230 415 1083/4
Fax: +230 415 1082
Email: chsimkt@intnet.mu
Web: www.bellemareplage.com

Accolades

☆☆☆☆

Airport

SSR International: 1 hr

Accommodation price guide

Accepted credit cards
AE MC V DC

Preferred tour operator

From UK
Sunset   Tel: +44 (0) 207 498 9922
From Germany
Airtours   Tel: +49 (0) 0070 20 250
From Sweden
Ving   Tel: +46 (0) 8555 13 302

Recreational facilities

Two swimming pools, pool bar, fitness centre, sauna; tennis on four floodlit clay courts; boat hire, excellent watersports, scuba diving, deep sea fishing; boutiques, mini club.

Meeting/business facilities

One room, for up to 100 delegates.

Local attractions

Splendid beaches; trips to coral reef; enjoying the island's unique cultural mix.

Overlooking the mountains and the sea, the 17th is the signature hole on the Belle Mare Plage's scenically located and entertaining course – designed by South Africa's talented Hugh Baiocchi and the first and only 18-hole championship course on this beautiful island.

All the guest rooms at the resort are comfortably furnished with the Prestige rooms and Deluxe suites offering even more spaciousness as well as direct access to the beach, which is protected from the ocean swell by an offshore coral reef, making it ideal for swimming and watersports.

The commendably high standards of the accommodations are complemented by superb cuisine. La Citronelle serves breakfast and dinner and is idyllically situated by the beach while Le Beach Rendez-vous and the coffee shop are open for light snacks throughout the day. The two bars are the prime meeting points in the hotel and provide lively entertainment.

Belle Mare Plage boasts a fully equipped fitness centre, featuring gymnasium, body building equipment, massage, sauna, cold swimming pool, air-conditioned squash court, hairdressing salon, beautician, aerobics, yoga and two Jacuzzis.

The hotel's on-site golf academy features the Marc Farry/Hugh Baiocchi method.

GOLF FACILITIES

Best season for golf: All year round.

COURSES:	LENGTH	PAR	FEES
Belle Mare Plage			
	6014m	72	FREE

Play at the Belle Mare course is reserved for guests; club house features the exclusive Deer Hunter restaurant; nine-hole course nearby.

Facilities key

210   100

LÉMURIA RESORT OF PRASLIN

Hotel information

Anse Kerlan
Seychelles

Tel: +248 (0) 281281
Fax: +248 (0) 281000
Email: lemuria@seychelles.net
Web: www.lemuriaresort.com

Accolades

☆☆☆☆☆ De Luxe

Airport

Praslin: 5 mins
Mahé International (air transfer to Praslin): 20 mins

Accommodation price guide

€ 🐚🐚🐚🐚

Accepted credit cards
AE DC MC V

Preferred tour operator

From UK
Elegant
Resorts   Tel: +44 (0)870 3333 380
From Germany
Trauminsel   Tel: +49 (0) 81 52 93 190
From Sweden
Select Travel   Tel: +46 (0) 86 78 15 15

Recreational facilities

Health, beauty and fitness centre; sauna, steam bath; boat house: windsurfing, pedalos, sailing, snorkelling; swimming pool; scuba diving, deep sea fishing.

Meeting/business facilities

One room, for up to 16 delegates; fully-equipped business centre.

Local attractions

Cocos de mer; turtles laying eggs in sand; huge natural garden and some of world's best beaches.

It's the ultimate dream setting: just a 15-minute drive from the enchanting Vallée de Mai which, according to local legend, was the original Garden of Eden. Here is to be found the first five-star deluxe resort to be opened in the glorious Seychelles. The attractive Lémuria Resort of Praslin comprises 88 suites, 80 of them junior, eight senior.

This is one of the best conserved sites on Praslin island, offering a breathtaking view of both Petite and Grand Anse Kerlan, two lovely beaches. Built amid luxuriant vegetation, this tropical paradise also overlooks Anse Georgette, which has been adjudged the second most beautiful beach in the world.

The Lémuria resort's three restaurants offer a variety of international and Mediterranean cuisines, blended with mouthwatering local specialities.

Opening in June 2000, the 18-hole championship Lémuria course – unique in the Seychelles – will encourage golf in the country, and complement the fully-equipped health spa and fitness centre.

Environmentally friendly watersports facilities are free to resort guests while, at extra cost, they can patronise the resort's fully-equipped dive centre and choose to go either deep sea fishing or on exciting organised excursions to the many outlying islands in this corner of heaven on earth.

GOLF FACILITIES
Best season for golf: All year round.

COURSES:	LENGTH	PAR	FEES
Lémuria			
	5751m	70	US$30

Spectacular 18-hole course designed by Rodney France, US, and Marc Farry, France.

Facilities key

88   18

LE PRINCE MAURICE

Hotel information

Choisy Road
Poste de Flacq

Tel: +230 413 9100
Fax: +230 413 9129
Email: leprince@intnet.mu
Web: www.princemaurice.com

Accolades

☆☆☆☆☆ Deluxe

Airport

SSR International: 1 hr

Accommodation price guide

Accepted credit cards
AE MC V DC

Preferred tour operator

From UK
Elegant
Resorts   Tel: +44 (0) 8703 333 380
From Germany
Airtours
Int'l   Tel: +49 (0) 69 79 28 0
From Sweden
Select Travel   Tel: +46 (0) 8678 1515

Mauritius was named after Prince Maurice Van Nassau, Stadholder of Holland and pioneer of the spice trade in the Indian Ocean. That romantic figure from the colonial past has given his name to the Le Prince Maurice, which opened its doors in mid-November 1998.

Here the smell of the warm sea mingles with the aroma of spices, their exotic perfumes imbuing the dream which the hotel enshrines of elegance from times past, of warmth, exotic fragrance and exclusive quality.

The five-star deluxe Le Prince Maurice enjoys an idyllic location on the north-east coast of one of the world's most enticing island hideaways.

Sheltered from prevailing winds and standing on 30 hectares of totally unspoilt private land which ensures privacy for guests, the resort blends naturally with the beauty and simplicity of the environment. The use of wood, stone and thatch lends a unique charm, producing an atmosphere of total tranquility and refined elegance.

The property's tropical gardens are filled with rare and luxuriant vegetation while the calm turquoise blue lagoon and secluded beaches of brilliant white sand. A natural fish reserve situated on the western part of the hotel property adds to the uniqueness and natural beauty of the site.

Recreational facilities

Boutique, mini club; watersports, scuba diving, deep sea fishing, fly fishing; fitness centre.

Meeting/business facilities

One room, for up to 16 delegates; fully equipped business centre.

Local attractions

Exploring this island gem of the Indian Ocean; visiting local beaches; shopping in Port Louis.

GOLF FACILITIES
Best season for golf: All year round.

COURSES: LENGTH	PAR	FEES
Belle Mare Plage		
6014m	72	FREE

Practice fairway; golf pro and golf tutors; weekly tournaments organised (hotel guests are welcome to play).

Facilities key

88   16

Europe

Beyond the 18th hole.

If you're looking for golf that drives you beyond the 18th hole,
look no further than Portugal, where you find, in charming surroundings, so many
courses designed by world famous architects. Hook or slice and the ball will take you
to a wonderful beach or an old manor house in the countryside.
Or if you middle the fairway and fancy your chances, have your partner buy you a
unforgettable seafood dinner, and you´ll find no finer 19th hole.
For challenging golf, all year round, it has to be Portugal.

Portugal. The choice.

Portugal

 AIR PORTUGAL

ICEP Portuguese Trade and Tourism Office • London
Tel.: (0207) 494 14 41 • http://www.portugalinsite.pt

PORTUGAL: ALGARVE   A world apart

Clean, safe, Atlantic beaches, blessed with year-round sunshine – some 3,000 hours of it – and backed with pretty, gently undulating countryside, make Portugal's Algarve an eternally popular holiday destination, especially among families and those with golf and other sporting activities in mind.

It's just 150 kilometres from the Spanish border on the banks of the Rio Guadiana to the rock-strewn Cabo São Vincente but within that relatively short distance there's lots to see and do, with tiny time-warp fishing villages interspersing bustling holiday resorts and first-rate golf courses punctuating the journey.

There are four distinct seasons, with carpets of flowers in spring and mellow autumns, but the summer heat is tempered by cooling sea breezes while winters are mild.

GETTING THERE In recent years, Faro Airport has expanded to full international capability, handling scheduled and charter flights from across Europe.

APRÈS GOLF Night birds will find plenty of lively clubs and bars but there are also plenty of places where you can take the kids. They claim a different recipe for every day of the year in the preparation of *bacualhõ* (salt cod) while the taste of fresh sardines, simply grilled, with a dash of lemon, is quite exquisite.

OFF THE COURSE Besides sunbathing and enjoying the firm, golden sands, there are all manner of sports to be savoured, including notable facilities for tennis, horse riding and a huge variety of watersports.

NOT TO BE MISSED Find your own secluded cove for a family day out; buy handicrafts and, especially, ornate Portuguese tiles and ceramics.

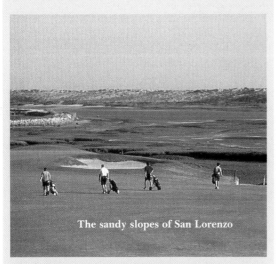
The sandy slopes of San Lorenzo

FACTS AND FIGURES

- From 54 holes in 1969, there are now 333 holes in play, with many more planned or under construction.
- As well as several Portuguese Open Championships, the Algarve has also been the venue for the World Ladies Amateur Team Championship, won by the United States, at Vilamoura in 1976.
- One Portuguese professional has won a European tour event – D. Silva in the Jersey Open.
- The new Faro airport, due for completion in 2000, will have a capacity for six million passengers, with automated direct boarding ramps.

Fun in the sun: Vale do Lobo

Tucked away below a mountain range along Portugal's southern coast, the Algarve has always seemed a world apart. Long occupied by the Moors from North Africa, countless reminders remain in the charming architecture, crafts, fruit and lifestyle of the region. The advent of charter flights and package holidays in the late 1950s brought tourism, filling the few hotels in summer and leaving them looking to provide interest and employment in the off-peak season. Golf provided the answer.

The region has a mild winter climate, with plenty of sunshine, ideal for holiday golf. Three-times British Open champion Henry Cotton designed Penina on a former ricefield, which opened in 1966. Two more courses, Vilamoura and Vale do Lobo, followed in 1969, all under British management. The formula proved a success and further courses followed.

There are now 20 courses in all along the coast, stretching from near Faro airport in the east nearly to Cape St. Vincent in the west. Daily direct flights serve numerous European cities as well as connections through Lisbon. The region can also be reached in around three hours by car from the capital.

There is golf for all, from major championship layouts by top golf architects, to smaller nine-hole gems for a more relaxed game. The spectacular coastline and ubiquitous umbrella pines add to the charm of a region that has become a golfing magnet, drawing increased numbers from the colder countries of northern Europe. A good location for families, golfing couples and small groups of both sexes.

NEW DEVELOPMENTS

- A new Championship course, Benamor, is due to open near Tavira in the eastern Algarve early in 2000.
- A new health and beauty spa, with a full range of treatments to appeal to golfers and non-golfers alike, has opened at Parque da Floresta.
- Lusotur Golfes S.A., managers of the Vilamoura courses, plan a further two golf courses to add to the 63 holes already in play along with a golf academy within the next two years.

Hotels

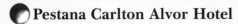
Pestana Carlton Alvor Hotel

Page 92

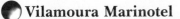
Vilamoura Marinotel

Page 93

CONTACT
Regiãode de Turismo do Algarve
Av. 5 de Outrubro 18, 8000 Faro, Algarve
Tel: +351 289 800 400   Fax: +351 289 800 489

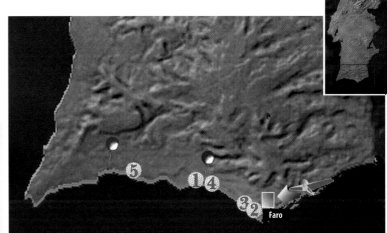

RECOMMENDED AIR CARRIER
UK Reservations: 0845 601 0932
Golf inclusive packages with
Caravela Tours: +44 (0) 020 7630 9223

AIR PORTUGAL

Favourite fairways

The most up-to-date golf travel information is always at www.golftravel4u.com

1 THE OLD COURSE, VILAMOURA
Recently revitalised in every aspect while skilfully retaining
Frank Pennink's masterful design from 1969, the Old Course
remains one of the country's finest. Laid out over rolling sandy
slopes lined with pine, this is a course of genuine class and a
permanent pleasure to play.
Par 72   Length 5988m
Vilamoura, 9125 Quarteira, Algarve
Tel: +351 289 321 652   Fax: +351 289 380 726

2 SAN LORENZO GOLF CLUB
Neatly combining big rolling slopes undulating past ranks of
umbrella pine with some spectacular holes flanking the sea, this
magnificent test by Joe Lee improves every year. Kept in fine
condition, its closing stretch bordering two large lakes calls for
nerve and no little ability.
Par 72   Length 5837m
Quinta do Lago, Vale do Lobo, 8135 Almansil
Tel: +351 289 396 522   Fax: +351 289 396 908

3 QUINTA DO LAGO
Open since 1974, this was the first 18 holes, designed by
American William Mitchell, of a luxury development now
encompassing 36 holes and much else besides. Laid out over
rolling sandy slopes encrusted with umbrella pine, this elegant
course forms part of the Ria Formosa natural park and
protected eco-system. Host to several Portuguese Opens.
Par 72   Length 5870m
Quinta do Lago, 8135 Almansil
Tel: +351 289 390 700. Fax: +351 289 394 013

4 VILA SOL
The first effort in Portugal by Donald Steel, the course makes
effective use of undulating land, with umbrella pine, fig and oak
trees, steep escarpments and various water hazards. Narrow
fairways lead to well-kept, speedy greens. A visual delight.
Par 72   Length 5880m
Alto de Semino, N.396, Km24.8, Vilamoura, 8125 Quarteira
Tel: +351 289 300 505 Fax: +351 289 300 592

5 VALE DA PINTA
American architect Ronald Fream's opening effort in Portugal
and a genuine test, worthy of a major championship. Severely
undulating land rolls past ancient olive trees, with large areas
of penal sand, mounding and numerous doglegs. Home of
Europe's fifth largest David Leadbetter golf academy.
Par 71   Length 5636m
**Pestana Golf and Resort-Carvoeiro, Apart. 11, Praia do
Carvoeiro, 8400 Lagoa**
Tel: +351 282 340 900 Fax: +351 282 342 189

CLIMATE
The combination of a southerly location and cooling sea breezes means
the Algarve's climate avoids extremes. It also provides an amazing 3000
hours of sunshine annually.

RECOMMENDED CAR HIRE
Hertz
UK: +44 (0) 870 848 4848
Germany: +49 (0) 180 533 3535
Website: www.hertz.com

Price guide
€

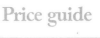

Round of golf		Golf balls	
Small beer		4/5 star hotel room	

PESTANA CARLTON ALVOR HOTEL

Recreational facilties

Outdoor swimming pool, tennis court, gardens; riding, fishing, and shooting can be arranged.

Meeting/business facilities

Six rooms, for up to 500 delegates.

Local attractions

Characteristic Portuguese fado restaurants, one of Europe's most beautiful coastlines.

The impressive five-star Pestana Carlton Alvor Hotel is renowned for its outstanding location. From the large terraced swimming pool a lift carries guests down to the secluded sandy beach of Três Irmâos, where the dramatic sandstone cliffs tower above as an added attraction.

The Carlton Alvor is the flagship of the Hotels Group Pestana, Portugal's leading hotel chain and one of the fastest growing conglomerates in the European hotel and leisure industry. The group currently owns and manages a chain of 12 hotels in Madeira and mainland Portugal – all rated four or five star – three in Mozambique and one in Brazil.

All five Pestana hotels in the Algarve benefit from the group's ownership of Carvoeiro Golf and its two courses in the Algarve, Pinta and Gramacho, both located close to the Carlton Alvor. *Golf World* and *Golf Sport* magazines voted Carvoeiro one of the top golf clubs in Europe.

Another big attraction for golfers – Pestana resorts has the only David Leadbetter Golf Academy in Portugal. The Academy enables golfers of differing ages and abilities to benefit from the expertise of one of the world's leading teachers. Tuition takes place on two purpose-built fairways, with six target greens, special chipping and bunker play areas and a large practice putting green.

GOLF FACILITIES
Best season for golf: September to April is golf high season.

COURSES:	LENGTH	PAR	FEES
Gramacha			
	5505m	72	E26
Pinta			
	5636m	71	E34
Palmares			
	5961m	71	E37

Driving ranges at all local courses, David Leadbetter Golf Academy in Pinta.

Facilities key

198   500

VILAMOURA MARINOTEL

Hotel information

8125 Vilamoura - Codex
Algarve

Tel: +351 289 389988
Fax: +351 289 389869
Email: marinotel@mail.telepac.pt
Web: www.nexus-pt.com/marinotel

Accolades

✩✩✩✩✩

Airport

Faro International: 30 mins

Accommodation price guide

Accepted credit cards
AE DC MC V

Preferred tour operator

From UK
Thomson   Tel: +44 (0) 207 387 9321
First
Choice   Tol: ı 44 (0) 1203 560777
From Germany
TUI   Tel: +49 (0) 511 5670

With its five-star features, the Vilamoura Marinotel has established itself as one of the most successful golf hotels on the entire Algarve coast. Its location between the marina and the beach in the heart of the popular resort of Vilamoura makes it an idyllic leisure hotel.

There are three hectares of attractive gardens and the hotel has its own direct access to the beach, while many activities are catered for on-site, including watersports, tennis and use of the health club, with its sauna, Jacuzzi and gym.

Special rates have been negotiated for guests wishing to play the ten superb golf courses located within a radius of ten kilometres from this welcoming modern hotel.

All 389 bedrooms feature individually regulated air-conditioning, satellite TV channels, direct dial TV, mini-bar and a terrace with lovely views over either the sea or the marina.

With its reception area open 24 hours a day, the hotel also offers such amenities as a private parking area, lavish entertainment programmes, 24-hour medical assistance, laundry service and safety boxes, and is a perfect choice for business or pleasure and especially for golf enthusiasts, who can call on the assistance of Vilamoura Marinotel's attentive golf hospitality service.

Recreational facilities

Two outdoor pools, indoor heated pool, health club, two floodlit tennis courts, shooting club, nearby riding centre, flying lessons, watersports, casino, yacht rental, four golf courses.

Meeting/business facilities

The on-site Vilamoura Congress Centre has 15 conference rooms, to accommodate 1200.

Local attractions

Casino, marina, restaurants, Roman ruins, big game fishing.

GOLF FACILITIES
Best season: October to April.

COURSES:	LENGTH	PAR	FEES
Old Course			
	6254m	73	E58
Vilasol			
	6242m	72	E58
Pinhal			
	6300m	72	E44
Valdolobo (Royal)			
	6175m	72	E78
Quinta Do Lago			
	6488m	72	E58
Salgados			
	6000m	72	E30
Laguna			
	6133m	72	E39

On-site putting green, range net; five-day golf tuition package available; guests can enter Vilamoura Marinotel Stars Week (February 5-12, 2000).

Facilities key

389   1200

PORTUGAL: LISBON COASTS Choice aplenty...

One of the world's most attractive capital cities, Lisbon, set on the estuary of the River Tagus, stands at the gateway to Portugal's playground coast.

The action centres on the elegant resort of Estoril, with its world-famous casino, smart new promenade, restaurants, bars and night spots, and the former fishing village of Cascais and encompasses the Cabo Roca – most westerly point on the European mainland – and the World Heritage hill-top town of Sintra.

GETTING THERE The coasts are a short drive from Lisbon airport, but unfortunately on the opposite side of the city and the traffic can be nightmarish.

APRÈS GOLF Enjoy simple, hearty and uncomplicated peasant fare – from salt cod and plain grilled sardines to *ameijos na cataplana*, made from clams, cockles, sausage, onions, tomatoes and potatoes all stewed together. The breads and patisserie are outstanding, so too is the coffee.

OFF THE COURSE Great surfing beaches up on the Atlantic coast towards Nazare. The walled mediaeval town of Obidos is worth a visit. Estoril is geared up for family holidays.

NOT TO BE MISSED The Portuguese national bird – the cock – adorns crockery, cotton prints and other worthy souvenirs; try *aguadente* – a potent relation of brandy – and ride Lisbon's trams and funiculars.

FACTS AND FIGURES
- Golf was first played in the Lisbon area by British telephone and railway employees. They laid out six holes near Alges in 1900, due to become the Lisbon Sports Club, founded in 1922.
- The Estoril club, long favoured by the wealthy and well-connected, was for many years the home of both the Portuguese Open and Amateur championships.

Most golfers consider the Algarve as the prime Portuguese destination for holiday golf. The attractive coasts around Lisbon, however, are catching up fast. They have nearly as many places to play (15); are easier to reach (more flights, shorter flying time); have arguably seven of the top 12 courses in Portugal; enjoy golf that is cheaper and less crowded; a climate which, although marginally higher on rainfall, has similar temperatures and, as a sophisticated urban area, greater dining choice and much more to do.

With a new motorway network, golf in this region now falls into three distinct areas. One can choose between Estoril, the longest established location, the high-class courses on the Costa Azul and two great newcomers a little north, near Obidos.

NEW DEVELOPMENTS
- A new 18-holes with sea views by Arthur Hills is under construction on the Quinta da Marinha estate.
- Aroeira will have a second 18-holes open mid-2000, designed by Donald Steel.

CLIMATE
The best time for golf is from October to April, when it is sunny and warm. Most rain falls in the period between December and February.

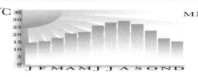

Sample point: Lisbon

RECOMMENDED CAR HIRE

UK: +44 (0) 870 848 4848
Germany: +49 (0) 180 533 3535
Website: www.hertz.com

CONTACT
Costa do Estoril Tourist Board
Arcades do Parque, 275 Estoril
Tel: +351 21 467 0793 Fax: +351 21 467 2280

Price guide

Round of golf	Golf balls
Small beer	4/5 star hotel room

RECOMMENDED AIR CARRIER
TAP Air Portugal
UK Reservations: 0845 601 0932
Golf inclusive packages
with Caravela Tours: +44 (0) 020 7630 9223

Favourite fairways

① ESTORIL PALÁCIO
Third most senior club in Portugal and longtime venue for the national Open, created on hills above the town and sea by Mackenzie Ross in 1945. A tight, strategic test with narrow holes winding past pine and eucalyptus. A genuine historic treat to savour.
Par 69   Length 5238m
Avenida da Republica, 2675 Estoril
Tel: +351 21 468 0176
Fax: +351 21 468 2796

② QUINTA DO PERU
An elegant stylish course laid out on and around an elevated, pine-encrusted ridge by American Rocky Roquemore. Large areas of strategic sand and water and superb views to distant hills and Palmela castle. The relaxed clubhouse offers a warm welcome, good menu and some fine wines.
Par 72   Length 5645m
2830 Quinta do Conde
Tel: +351 21 213 4320 Fax: +351 21 213 4321

③ PENHA LONGA
An excellent course laid out through a wooded estate below the historic palace of Sintra. Rolling slopes, good use of sand and water on more exposed holes by US designer Robert Trent Jones Jr. Venue for the Portuguese and Estoril Opens. A further nine holes are due to reopen in 2000.
Atlantico Course   Par 72   Length 5926m
Estrada da Lagoa Azul, Linho 2710 Sintra
Tel: +351 21 924 9011 Fax: +351 21 924 9024
Email: penhalongagolf@mail.telepac.pt

Hotels
● **Senhora da Guia**
Page 95

● **Hotel Quinta da Marinha**
Golf Conference Resort
Page 95

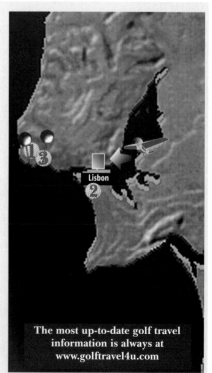

Lisbon

The most up-to-date golf travel information is always at www.golftravel4u.com

HOTEL QUINTA DA MARINHA GOLF CONFERENCE RESORT

Within easy access of Lisbon's Airport and the city, the Quinta da Marinha Conference & Golf Resort offers the widest range of facilities to meet the needs of both business and leisure visitors.

Facing its own 18-hole golf course and the Atlantic Ocean, the resort features 70 villas and a 200-room hotel. Its 100 hectares of green grounds include a golf academy, tennis courts, health centre, pools, bars, restaurants and conference facilities.

Recently renovated, the glorious golf course is set between the beautiful Sintra hills and the sea, with the fairways threading their way past pine trees and lakes. The 13th hole is one of the famed golf *ex-libris* of this popular golfing region. Special conditions to other golf courses, sports and tours are available.

Hotel information

Guia Quinta da Marinha
Casa 36
2750 Cascais, Lisbon

Tel: +351 21 486 9881
Fax: +351 21 486 9032
Email: marinhagolf@mail.telepac.pt
Web: www.quinta-da-marinha.com

Accolades

★★★☆

Airport

Lisbon International: 30 mins

Accommodation price guide

Accepted credit cards
AE DC MC V

Local attractions

Cascais; casino in Estoril; beaches, walks, historic palaces at Sintra, Lisbon.

Meeting/business facilities

Six rooms, for up to 500 delegates.

Recreational facilities

Six tennis courts, tennis academy, cycling; health centre with indoor pool; kids club; watersports & riding locally.

GOLF FACILITIES

Best season: All year round.

COURSES:	LENGTH	PAR	FEES
Q. da Marinha	6014m	71	E30
Int'l Golf Academy	1805m	62	E15

Driving range, putting green; individual and group tuition.

Facilities key

270 500

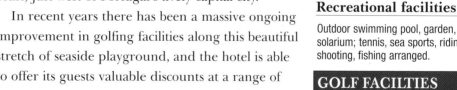

SENHORA DA GUIA

The welcoming Estalagem Senhora da Guia has established for itself a solid reputation as one of the leading golfing hotels on the beautiful Estoril coast, just west of Portugal's lively capital city.

In recent years there has been a massive ongoing improvement in golfing facilities along this beautiful stretch of seaside playground, and the hotel is able to offer its guests valuable discounts at a range of highly entertaining and sporting courses which provide play for golfers of all abilities, all within a short and pleasant drive.

The hotel provides a cosy and warmly welcoming environment, with comfortable rooms and attentive service. The Senhora da Guia restaurant features first-class Portuguese and international cuisine.

Hotel information

Estrada do Guincho
2750 Cascais

Tel: +351 21 486 9239
Fax: +351 21 486 9227
Email: senhoradaguia@mail.telepac.pt

Accolades

★★★★☆

Airport

Lisbon: 40 mins

Accommodation price guide

Accepted credit cards
AE DC MC V

Local attractions

Extensive sports: golf, tennis, watersports, riding; glamorous Estoril plus city attractions of Lisbon.

Meeting/business facilities

Two rooms, for up to 60 delegates.

Recreational facilities

Outdoor swimming pool, garden, solarium; tennis, sea sports, riding, shooting, fishing arranged.

GOLF FACILTIES

Best season: November to March.

COURSES:	LENGTH	PAR	FEES
Quinta da Marinha	6014m	72	E51
Estoril Palacio	5997m	72	E42
Quinta da Beloura	817m	73	E32
Penha Longa	6228m	72	E32
Praia D'el Rey	6467m	72	E69

Practice facilities at Quinta da Marinha, tuition at Quinta da Beloura; good golf discounts available to guests.

Facilities key

42 60

PORTUGAL: MADEIRA The garden of golf

Portuguese, yes, most definitely – and proudly so – but, set far out in the Atlantic Ocean, the spectacular island of Madeira has an ambience which is very much its own and, while long a popular tourist destination, it has managed to preserve a strong sense of tradition, from the white and red national costume to the ancient trade in the fortified wines which bear the island's name.

Funchal, home to half the island's 260,000 population, is the prime visitor magnet, with its pretty streets, little squares and historic buildings, but there's lots more besides to this truly mountainous outpost of one of Europe's smallest but proudest nations.

Breathtaking ravines, towering sea cliffs and a profusion of flowers – with two-thirds of Madeira a conservation area – make it a magical place for rambling, made easier by the paths which run alongside the distinctive 'levada' irrigation ditches winding around the hillsides.

GETTING THERE Daily direct flights to Funchal (one of the world's more dramatic landing strips) from most major European airports.

APRÈS GOLF With its year-round mild climate, Madeira tends to attract the older visitor, leading to a relaxed atmosphere where taking afternoon tea is of more import than hitting the discos. Food is Portuguese, with an emphasis on the freshest of locally caught fish and seafood.

OFF THE COURSE Madeira has very few beaches but offers dramatic cliff walks instead. It's also a haven for flora and fauna and garden-lovers will adore it.

NOT TO BE MISSED Watch the comings and goings of the cruise ships in Funchal's busy harbour; take a thrilling sledge ride over steep cobbled streets leading down from the heights into town; enjoy a wine tasting and learn to tell your Malmsey from your Sercial and Verdelho.

FACTS AND FIGURES

● **Santo da Serra was inaugurated in 1937 by a group of British wine producers. They invited five star golf professionals of the time, JH Taylor, Alf Padgham, Abe Mitchell, Bill Cox and Allan Dailey, who sailed on the Arundel Castle, to play an exhibition.**
● **The PGA European Tour has held the Madeira Open on the successor course since 1993.**
● **Superb botanical gardens, with a wealth of specimen trees from around the world, form a legacy surrounding the Palheiro golf course.**

A giant volcanic outcrop jutting out from the Atlantic, level with the western rim of Africa, Madeira has been described as a 'floating tropical garden'. Since its discovery by the Portuguese in 1420, its mild, sub-tropical climate has encouraged visitors for the spectacular views, wealth of flowers and crops such as bananas, sugar and wine. The latter trade, founded by British expatriates, led to the creation of nine holes of golf in 1936 on an elevated mountain plateau at Santo da Serra, one of the few semi-level spots on the island.

Recent expansion of the golf has boosted tourism. Santo da Serra, revamped in 1991, now has 27 holes, followed by Palheiro in 1994. Spectacular mountain golf with sensational views; a golf buggy is essential. Best for mature golfing couples.

A well kept secret, Porto Santo

NEW DEVELOPMENTS

● **Santo da Serra recently opened the third nine holes – Serras 2930 metres par 36 – to create 27 in total. Palheiro Golf launched the Estalagem Casa Velha, the former hunting lodge of the Count de Carvalhal, an exquisite 25-room country house hotel in the heart of the golf course with a dining room already drawing high praise.**

CLIMATE Madeira's position, so far out in the Atlantic, gives the island a moderate climate, despite being so far south. Winters are mild, and summers are seldom too hot.

Sample point: Funchal

RECOMMENDED CAR HIRE *Hertz*
UK: +44 (0) 870 848 4848
Germany: +49 (0) 180 533 3535
Website: www.hertz.com

Price guide €

Round of golf   Golf balls
Small beer   4/5 star hotel room

CONTACT
Madeira Tourist Office
Posto Do Funchal, Av. Arriaga 18, 8000 Funchal
Tel: +351 291 225658 Fax: +351 291 232151

RECOMMENDED AIR CARRIER
TAP Air Portugal
UK Reservations: 0845 601 0932
Golf inclusive packages
with Caravela Tours: +44 (0) 20 7630 9223

Favourite fairways

1 CLUBE DE GOLFE SANTO DA SERRA

Described as 'golf in heaven', the course was re-designed as 18 holes by Robert Trent Jones in 1991. Flowing over a high plateau which skirts severe chasms and steep mountain slopes, this is a wonderful test of golf and concentration, with mature trees and spectacular views down to remote coastal villages and the Atlantic Ocean.
Par 72   Length 5496m
Santo Antonio da Serra, 9200 Machico
Tel: +351 291 552 345
Fax: +351 291 552 367

2 PALHEIRO

A creditable effort by architect Cabell Robinson over what is in places a very steeply sloping site above Funchal. Plenty of fine specimen trees (it edges on to the exotic gardens of Quinta da Palheiro) and superb views, especially down over the town from the fourth green. Make sure to take a golf buggy and, after your golf, drink in one of the great clubhouse views from the verandah.
Par 71   Length 5847m
Sitio do Balançal, São Gonçalo, 9050
Funchal   Tel: +351 291 792 116
Fax: +351 291 792 456

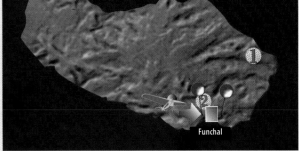
Funchal

Hotels
● **The Cliff Bay Resort Hotel** Page 97
● **Hotel Madeira Palácio** Page 98

The most up-to-date golf travel information is always at www.golftravel4u.com

THE CLIFF BAY RESORT HOTEL

Hotel information

Estrada Monumental 147
9004 - 532 Funchal
Madeira

Tel: +351 291 707700
Fax: +351 291 762524
Email: info@cliffbay.com
Web: www.cliffbay.com

Accolades

☆☆☆☆☆
Gold Awards '96, '97, '98 – Thomson
Gold Medal of Tourism Merit 1997
Member of Porto Bay Hotels & Resorts Group

Airport

Funchal Sta. Catarina: 20 mins

Accommodation price guide

Accepted credit cards
AE DC MC V

Recreational facilities

The Spa at Cliff Bay, featuring sauna, steam room, Jacuzzi, aerobics studio, gymnasium, hairdresser, manicure, pedicure, reflexology, beauty and health treatments; two swimming pools, tennis, table tennis; watersports and horse riding available nearby.

Meeting/business facilities

Two function rooms, to accommodate up to 80 delegates.

Local attractions

Madeira wine cellars; Cabo Girão – the second highest sea cliff in the world; the levadas (agricultural canals); all the cultural and natural attractions of this sub-tropical island.

Set in sub-tropical cliff-top gardens, The Cliff Bay Resort Hotel perches above the Bay of Funchal. It combines hotel, a health club and a sports resort. Most rooms enjoy Atlantic views, with private balconies, marbled bathrooms, twin or king-sized beds and cable TV, and are air-conditioned.

Madeira is excellent for golf, possessing two picturesquely sited 18-hole courses. The hotel is a founder member of the Palheiro Golf Course, where guests have guaranteed starting times. Reduced green fees are available at both the Palheiro and Santo da Sera courses.

Guests can choose between a cliff-edge heated freshwater pool or the salt-water, sea-level Blue Lagoon Pool. Tennis, aerobics classes and a gymnasium are there for the active. A private jetty gives direct access for watersports, including scuba diving, sailing, windsurfing and parasailing. Boat trips and deep-sea fishing are arranged in waters which have some of the world's best big game fishing. In the interior of the island, activities include jeep safaris "levada" walking, riding and canoeing. For relaxation, you can linger in the sauna and steam room while, for more personal attention, massage, physiotherapy and reflexology are also available.

GOLF FACILITIES
Best season for golf: All year round.

COURSES:	LENGTH	PAR	FEES
Palheiro	6015m	72	E55
Santo da Sera	3062m	71	E40

The Palheiro and Santo da Sera courses both offer a 30 per cent green fee discount to Cliff Bay guests, as well as providing club rental, caddies, electric buggy hire, driving net, putting green and group and individual lessons from PGA and APGP pros.

Facilities key

201   80

MADEIRA PALACIO
— *Resort Hotel* —

Hotel information

Estrada Monumental 265
9001-853 Funchal
Madeira

Tel: + 351 291 702 702
Fax: + 351 291 702 703
Email: mpalacio@mail.telepac.pt
Web: www.madinfo.pt/hotel/mpalacio

Accolades

★★★★☆

Airport

Funchal: 25 mins

Accommodation price guide

Accepted credit cards
AE MC V DC

Recreational facilities

Tennis, table tennis, billiards, massage, sauna; surrounded by tropical gardens, ideally situated in a quiet setting with spectacular views overlooking the sea; three souvenirs shops; rent a car.

Meeting/business facilities

Six rooms, for up to 250 people.

Local attractions

Walks along the 'levadas', toboggan run down into Funchal, Madeira wine visits, floral displays.

Totally renovated, the Madeira Palácio Resort Hotel is surrounded by colourful tropical gardens, quietly situated overlooking the sea.

Santo de Serra was the first golf course to be built on Madeira, constructed by a prominent Madeiran businessman and a frustrated retired English golfer. The present clubhouse gives views over the Atlantic Ocean. The course is a short drive from Funchal and less than 15 minutes from Santa Cruz airport. It is surrounded by mountains to the north and has views over the Atlantic to the south.

Nearby Palheiro was designed by Cabell Robinson. He has exploited the hills, ridges and deep valleys of the area to challenge golfers of a wide range of abilities.

Madeira has been part of Portugal since the 15th century. About 640 kilometres off the African coast west of Casablanca and 800 kilometres south west of Lisbon, it has a sub-tropical climate and a year-round warm sea. Summer heat is tempered by Atlantic breezes, while winter sunshine allows good conditions for golf all year round.

GOLF FACILITIES
Best season for golf: All year round.

COURSES: LENGTH		PAR	FEES
Palheiro			
	various	71	E 58
Santo da Serra			
	6015m	72	E 47

Guests are entitled to special 30 per cent green fee discounts at the island's two 18-hole courses and can also book guaranteed tee-off times.

A special 7-night golf package is offered between 5 January - 20 December 2000, priced at E784 per person (based on two people sharing a double room). The package includes American buffet breakfast, flowers and fruit basket, two dinners in the main restaurant 'Cristovão Columbo', seven days car rental (per couple) and five green fees at either course.

Facilities key

253 250

SPAIN: CANARIES Golf's islands of charm

Contrasts: that's the key word where the Canary Islands are concerned. Not only is each of these holiday paradise islands dramatically different from its neighbours – low, windswept Lanzarote, for instance, contrasting dramatically with Tenerife, which is dominated by huge Mount Teide – but they each pack enormous variety.

GETTING THERE Each of the main islands has direct flight connections – scheduled and chartered – with a range of European departure points.

APRÈS GOLF Dine late – then go out partying! Specialities include tropical fruits, spit-roast pork, succulent tomatoes and potatoes coated in salt then cooked in a sealed pot without water – delicious!

OFF THE COURSE Most beaches feature unusual jet black sand. The waters are warm and generally safe for bathing and watersports. Thanks to its Atlantic winds, Lanzarote is renowned for windsurfing. Tenerife is a big island which will take a week to explore. Gran Canaria features a spectacular volcanic crater.

NOT TO BE MISSED The moon-like landscape on the slopes of Mount Teide and in Lanzarote's 'Valley of Fire' where locals impress by digging holes down to the molten lava inches below the surface.

FACTS & FIGURES

- The Canaries have been the traditional winter retreat for the British middle classes since the 19th Century. They built the first course on Gran Canaria in 1891.
- The islands have been extensively developed for mass tourism in the past thirty years.

RECOMMENDED CAR HIRE

UK: +44 (0) 870 848 4848
Germany: +49 (0) 180 533 3535
Website: www.hertz.com

CONTACT

Gran Canaria Regional Tourist Authority, Plaza de los Derechos Humanos, Las Palmas Tel: +34 928 361 156
Tenerife Regional Tourist Authority, Edificio Usos Multiples 2 C/Jose Manuel Guimera 8, Santa Cruz de Tenerife, Tenerife Tel: +34 922 476500

The main attraction of the Canary Islands is the weather. Far down in the Atlantic off the Moroccan coast near to the Tropic of Cancer, the five main islands of Lanzarotte, Fuerteventura, Gran Canaria, Tenerife and La Palma are protected from the heat by cool sea breezes, and from the rain of Europe by their latitude.

Tenerife has six courses, Gran Canaria has two, and Lanzarote has just one, at Teguise. Seven new courses are under construction, with more planned. While the Canaries is not perhaps a destination for the serious golfer seeking a challenge, it is ideal for people mixing a resort holiday with a few rounds of golf. Both the Golf del Sur and the Amarilla courses on Tenerife have hosted European PGA events, and MacKenzie Ross designed the Real Club on Gran Canaria in 1956, so there is some class here as well.

For beginners the nine hole, par three course at Los Palos is well run, and the Golf Las Americas, a John Jacobs development, is a taxi ride from Tenerife's main resort Playa de las Americas.

NEW DEVELOPMENTS

- The Canaries are expanding at an extraordinary rate. There are new developments on all the islands: new hotels, new roads, and new shops, indeed an on-going radical upgrading of the entire region's tourism infrastructure.
- Santo da Serra recently opened a third nine holes to create 27 in total.
- For golfers who want to combine a two centre Spanish holiday with a cruise, there is a new regular service between Majorca and Gran Canaria.

CLIMATE

Geographical variety, latitude, and the effect of the trade winds all influence the varied climates of the Canary Islands. The north of Tenerife is wet and lush, the south almost desert-like, with only three or four days of rain a year.

Sample point: Canaries

Price guide €

Round of golf		Golf balls	
Small beer		4/5 star hotel room	

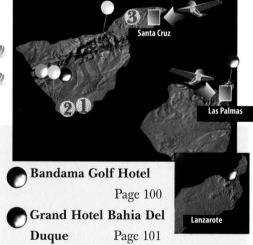

Santa Cruz

Las Palmas

Lanzarote

Favourite fairways

① GOLF DEL SUR

By imaginative use of the barren land and the black volcanic ash, which are such a feature of Tenerife, Spanish designer Pepe Gancedo has done wonders to create this interesting and pleasant 27-hole course by the sea. It's even good enough to attract the PGA from time to time. The likes of Ernie Els, Phil Mickelson and Jose Maria Olazabal have all played here.
Par 70/72 Length: Course A, 2957m; Course B, 2469m; Course C, 2913m.
Urb. Golf del Sur, San Miguel de Abona, Tenerife
Tel: +34 922 738170   Fax: +34 922 738272

② AMARILLA

The greens on this Atlantic Ocean course right at the southern tip of Tenerife are just wonderful. The course was designed by Donald Steel and opened in 1989. The course is tight in places, bordered by volcanic rock and unforgiving scrub. The ocean plays a big part in this course, coming into play on the fifth and 12th, and the amenities are good.
Par 72   Length 6077m
38639 San Miguel de Abona, Tenerife.
Tel: +34 922 730319   Fax: +34 922 785557

③ EL PEÑÓN

El Peñón, which opened in 1932, is the home of the Royal Golf Club of Tenerife. Situated in the northern, wetter, part of the island, it is much more lush than the island's other courses. It is 600 metres above sea level, and many of the holes are lined with mature pines, bay and eucalyptus trees.
Par 72   Length 5694m
Real Club de Golf, Tacoronte, Tenerife
Tel: +34 922 636607   Fax: + 34 922 636480

Bandama Golf Hotel   Page 100

Grand Hotel Bahia Del Duque   Page 101

Melia Salinas   Page 102

Hotel Botanico   Page 103

Hotel Jardin Tropical   Page 104

Hotel Jardines de Nivaria   Page 105

BANDAMA
GOLF & COUNTRY HOTEL

Hotel information

Caldera de Bandama El Lugar 14
Tafira Alta
Gran Canaria

Tel: +34 928 35 33 54
Fax: +34 928 35 12 90
Email: hsport@step.es
Web: www.step.es/canarias-golf

Accolades

✩✩✩Small Hotels With Charm
Hotels With Golf, Recommended by 'Guia
Mundial Assistance' Hotels and
Restaurants in Spain 1999

Airport

Las Palmas de Gran Canaria: 20 mins

Accommodation price guide

Accepted credit cards
AE MC V DC

Preferred tour operator

From UK
Lotus
Supertravel Tel: +44 (0) 20 7962 9494
Longshot   Tel: +44 (0) 1730 268 621
From Germany
Sportcheck   Toll free: +0180 500 1197
From Sweden
SLG   Tel: +46 (0) 87 89 89 80

Situated in an area of outstanding natural beauty, 400 metres above sea level, the Bandama Golf & Country Hotel is just 15 metres from the first tee of the Royal Las Palmas Golf Club. The hotel is dramatically perched on the edge of the incredible 300-metre deep, sheer-walled, crater of the extinct Bandana volcano.

Founded by the British in 1891, the Royal Las Palmas is the oldest golf club in Spain. The beautiful new course, designed by the famed Mackenzie Ross, is unique in that you almost never have the ball on a flat lie. The holes are diverse as well as technical and entertaining, forcing players to use their heads and all their golf clubs. The rough is full of Canarian flora, mimosa, palm trees and pine trees, with greens well protected by bunkers.

The cozy Bandama Golf & Country Hotel is able to offer service which is perfect yet truly personal, combining Spanish friendliness with modern efficiency. Golf is included in the room rates, with pre-booked tee times.

The hotel's famous wine bodega specialises in Riojas and other Spanish districts, as well as local wines, which guests are invited to sample with cheese. The 19th hole is a popular meeting place and stays open until the last guest has gone to bed.

Recreational facilities

Massage, swimming pool, sauna, solarium, tennis courts, horse riding, gardens, wine cellar, video library.

Meeting/business facilities

Two rooms, for up to 30 delegates.

Local attractions

Hotel is in a protected area; panoramic view over ocean and mountains; local wineries; Las Palmas beach and shopping area.

GOLF FACILITIES
Best season for golf: All year round.

COURSES: LENGTH PAR FEES
Royal Club
          5915m   71   free*

Two putting greens, driving range; tuition by seven golf pros; pro shop; tournament open to guests three times a week.

*GREEN FEES INCLUSIVE FOR HOTEL GUESTS

Facilities key

27   30

GRAN HOTEL BAHIA DEL DUQUE

Hotel information

C/. Alcalde Walter Paetzman s/n
38660 Costa Adeje
Tenerife

Tel: +34 922 74 69 00
Fax: +34 922 71 26 16
Email: comercial@bahia-duque.com
Web: www.bahia-duque.com

Accolades

☆☆☆☆☆ Luxe
GEBTA National Hotel of the Year 1998

Airport

Reina Sofia (Tenerife South): 15 mins
Los Rodeos (Tenerife North): 1 hr 15 mins

Accommodation price guide

€

Accepted credit cards
AE DC MC V

Preferred tour operator

From UK
Elegant
Resorts   Tel: +44 (0) 1244 897011
From Germany
TUI   Tel: +49 (0) 511 5670

Recreational facilities

Five swimming pools, fitness centre, beauty centre with massage and sauna; three tennis courts, two squash courts, putting green, jogging circuit, mountain bikes; observatory, internet café.

Meeting/business facilities

19 rooms, for up to 1000 delegates, internet facilities.

Local attractions

Excursions to Mount Teide, Spain's highest mountain, with its lunar landscapes; the resort of Playa Las Americas, excursions to other islands, boat charters, riding, deep-sea sport fishing, sailing, diving.

The stunning Gran Hotel Bahia Del Duque, styled after a classic Spanish village, stands in Adeje, one of the most beautiful areas of southern Tenerife, where it rises above a breathtaking estate bordering the sea.

Set like a jewel in the Atlantic, the westerly island of Tenerife enjoys the advantages of a gentle climate, making golf a highly enjoyable pastime throughout the year.

The Gran Hotel Bahia Del Duque has been designed for those experienced travellers who appreciate the notable difference of an establishment whose foundations are based on the charm and values of your own individuality.

This veritable oasis has 362 rooms, 38 of which are sumptuous suites, distributed through 19 inter-connected houses which reflect early 20th Century Canarian architecture, providing a true synthesis of the Victorian and Venetian influences of that more leisured age. In recognition of the excellence of the hotel's cuisine, the chef of the Restaurant El Duque has been awarded first prize in the National Gastronomical Competition.

This hotel constitutes, without doubt, the perfect holiday resort for those who seek paradise, a haven of nature surrounded by a myriad of colours set in spacious gardens covering some five hectares.

GOLF FACILITIES
Best season for golf: All year round.

COURSES:	LENGTH	PAR	FEES
Costa Adeje	6330m	72	E52
Las Americas	6039m	72	E48
Golf del Sur	5870m	72	E48
Amarilla Golf	6077m	72	E41
Golf Los Palos	913m	3	E21

Bahia del Duque works closely with all Tenerife's golf courses, which provide equipment hire for those without clubs; tee time reservations, transfers to courses and tuition can be arranged by the hotel, which has its own putting green and is just five minutes from two major courses.

Facilities key

362   1000

GRAN MELIÁ SALINAS THE GARDEN VILLAS

Hotel information

Urbanizacion Costa Teguise
35509 Lanzarote (Las Palmas)
Islas Canarias

Tel: +34 928 59 00 40
Fax: +34 928 59 11 10
Email: gran.melia.salinas@solmelia.es
Web: www.solmelia.es

Accolades

☆☆☆☆☆ Grand Luxe

Airport

Arrecife: 10 mins

Accommodation price guide

€

Accepted credit cards
AE DC MC V

Preferred tour operator

From UK
Thomson Tel: +44 (0) 207 387 9321
First
Choice Tel: +44 (0) 1293 560777
From Germany
TUI Tel: +49 (0) 511 5670

Within easy reach of the airport, the five-star Gran Meliá Salinas is surrounded by the deep blue Atlantic and spectacular volcanic landscape on the fascinating island of Lanzarote.

The hotel is just five minutes from the Golf Club Costa Teguise, an 18-hole facility designed by seasoned golfing architect John Harris and reminiscent of earlier courses where comfort and plenty of elbow room went hand in hand with good testing play.

An unusual feature is the black volcanic sand in the bunkers – something which makes it much easier to spot the ball.

Panoramic views across the island and the ocean are pleasant additions to the course's general charms and challenges, making it a perfect venue for high and low handicap golfers alike.

With its unrivalled front-line location on Las Cucharas Beach, Gran Meliá Salinas, which was totally renovated and refurbished last year, boasts the most comprehensive sports facilities to be found on the island.

The hotel has recently been officially recognised as being an important part of the cultural heritage of Lanzarote for its various masterpieces of architectural detail from Cesar Manrique.

A major part of the attraction is highly personalised service of a standard which always puts the needs of guests first. There are five restaurants on site, offering a wide range of cuisine.

Recreational facilties

Gymnasium, tennis, basketball, volleyball, health and beauty centre with sauna and massage, fully equipped entertainment area, surfing, diving, sailing available locally.

Meeting/business facilities

Five rooms, for up to 375 delegates; brand new state-of-the-art business centre with all facilities.

Local attractions

Close to local market and shopping centre; good beaches; sand dune camel rides.

GOLF FACILITIES

Best season for golf: All year round.

COURSES:	LENGTH	PAR	FEES
Costa Teguise			
	6000m	72	E41

Guest tournaments organised by entertainment team; practice facilities including pitch and putt, mini golf.

Facilities key

320 375

HOTEL BOTANICO

Hotel information

Avda Richard Yeoward 1
38400 Puerto de la Cruz

Tel: +34 922 430100
Fax: +34 922 383993
Email: hotelbotanico@hotelbotanico.com
Web: www.hotelbotanico.com

Accolades

☆☆☆☆☆ De Luxe
'Best A La Carte Accommodation', Gold
Award 1997 & 1998 – Thomson, 'Holly'
award 1998/99 – TUI, Best Hotel Resort
In Spain 1998 – Magic Travel Group.

Airport

Tenerife Los Rodeos: 20 mins
Tenerife Reina Sofia: 1 hr

Accommodation price guide

€ ◖◖◖

Accepted credit cards
AE MC V DC

Preferred tour operator

From UK
Elegant
Resorts   Tel: +44 (0) 1244 897777
From Germany
TUI   Tel: +49 (0) 51 15 67 43 65
From Sweden
Fritidsresor Tel: +46 (0) 8 720 7200

On the lush north coast of delightful Tenerife, the resort town of Puerto de la Cruz is the traditional choice location for tourism in the Canary Islands, offering what many count as the best climate in the world. Locals and visitors alike benefit from clear seas and non-polluted air for the healthy option. Another advantage is the flora and fauna to be seen all year round. The temperature during winter and summer rarely moves far from 20°C.

Long hours of sunshine contrast with the drama of the often snow-covered Mount Teide, Spain's highest peak, which can be admired from the hotel.

The Hotel Botánico is the only member of The Leading Hotels of the World in the Canary Islands. Among its excellent facilities is a modern health centre providing advanced procedures for such special treatments as stress cures, face packs and non-surgical face, bust and body liftings.

Local culture is to be found in the hotel's panoramic Bar Hall, with its permanent exhibition of 19th and 20th Century Canarian art. A choice of restaurants offers traditional Spanish, Italian and Asian cuisine, or just a light lunch by the pool.

An 18-hole putting green, bunker and driving range adjoins the Hotel Botanico, while the par 71 Royal Golf Club El Peñon, founded in 1932, is located just 15 minutes away.

Recreational facilities

Two swimming pools – one fresh water, one sea water; whirlpool bath, fitness room, sauna; Vital centre with beauty and relax treatments, massage; two floodlit tennis courts, billiards, library, private yacht; 18 hole putting green with bunker and driving range; live music every night; two-and-a-half hectares of botanical gardens with lake.

Meeting/business facilities

Nine rooms, for up to 500 delegates.

Local attractions

Wide choice of restaurants in old Canarian-style houses with local and international cuisine; golf, scuba diving, yachting, riding, squash, paddle, fishing, whale watching, mountain biking; Loro Parque zoological parrot park, National volcanic park, ethnological park.

GOLF FACILITIES
Best season for golf: May to October.

COURSES:	LENGTH	PAR	FEES
Real Club de Golf			
	5800m	70	E 35
Golf del Sur			
	5870m	72	E 51
Golf Las Americas			
	6039m	72	E 51

On-site 18-hole putting green (5000m²) with driving range and bunker.

Facilities key

252   500

HOTEL JARDIN TROPICAL

Hotel information

Calle Gran Bretaña s/n
E-38660 Adeje
Tenerife

Tel: +34 922 746 000
Fax: +34 922 746 060
Email: golf@jardin-tropical.com

Accolades

☆☆☆☆
The 100 Best Hotels of the World, 1995
and 1996 – Tui-Holly
Relais du Golf

Airport

Reina Sofia: 15 mins

Accommodation price guide

€ ◖◖◖◖

Accepted credit cards
AE MC V DC

Preferred tour operator

From Germany
Airtours Int'l   Tel: +49 (0) 69 79 28 262
From Holland/Belgium
Pin High Golf   Tel: +31 (0) 23 561 53 05
From Switzerland
Columbus
Tours   Tel: +41 (0) 56 460 73 79

Situated on the Costa Adeje, in the south of Tenerife, the Hotel Jardin Tropical's seafront position, exclusive atmosphere and tropical surroundings combine to make it a dream come true. Exotic Moorish architecture, lush vegetation, sub-tropical gardens, bougainvilleas and palm trees provide the natural backdrop for relaxation.

Decorated in soft, warm colours, all guest rooms benefit from private bathrooms, air-conditioning, direct dial telephone, minibar, satellite TV, private safe, 24-hour room service, and a striking view from the terrace. The suites are like luxury villas – comfortable and well appointed.

Not even the most demanding guest will be able to resist the exquisite gastronomy of the hotel's five restaurants. Breakfast at the buffet restaurant Las Mimosas is an endless parade of colours and flavours, while lunch can be enjoyed by the pool, in the snack bar or in the Restaurant Las Rocas. Dinner may be taken in Las Mimosas, in the *à la carte* Las Cuevas or in the Las Rocas Beach Club. Finally, the exceptional El Patio has been awarded 'Best Restaurant of Tenerife' on several occasions. To complete a perfect evening, guests can enjoy live music in the Lobby Bar or Champagne Bar, or take in one of the nightly shows in the Café de Paris.

Recreational facilities

Sauna, Turkish baths, gym, massage, health and beauty treatments on offer in the Bio Centre; fresh water and sea water swimming pools; watersports available locally.

Meeting/business facilities

Two rooms, which can accommodate up to 60 delegates each.

Local attractions

All kinds of excursions including Mount Teide, Loro Parque, Eagles Park, Piramides de Guimar.

GOLF FACILITIES

Best season for golf: All year round.

COURSES:	LENGTH	PAR	FEES
Del Sur			
	5543m	72	E46-51
Las Americas			
	5860m	72	E48-60
Costa Adeje			
	6190m	72	E42-51

Practice facilities at all courses; tuition at Golf Costa Adeje; buggies available; tournaments open to guests.

Facilities key

434 **120**

SPAIN: CANARIES: TENERIFE

JARDINES DE NIVARIA

Hotel information

C/París S/N
Playa Fañabé
Costa Adeje - 38660

Tel: +34 922 713333
Fax: +34 922 713340
Email: nivaria@nexo.es

Airport

Tenerife Reina Sofia: 20 mins

Accommodation price guide

Accepted credit cards
AE MC V DC

Preferred tour operator

From UK
Simply Golf   Tel: +44 (0) 161 926927
From Germany
Airtours
International Tel: +49 (0) 697 928 287
From Sweden
Ving   Tel: +46 (0) 209 959 955

This delightful hotel is situated in the quiet area of Costa Adeje, with direct access to the sandy beach of Fañabé. Elegantly constructed in the traditional style of the island, it is surrounded by spacious green areas complete with waterfalls, fountains and an open-air stage for shows.

Crowning the principal building is a remarkable dome representing in colourful leaded glass the constellations at the Spring equinox. The hotel's luxurious accommodations are situated in the other buildings, offering a variety of rooms including single use, connecting rooms, non-smoker, rooms for disabled people, junior suites and suites.

Mouth-watering international cuisine is offered, with snack-bar restaurant 'La Cascada' at the pool, International Buffet 'Solandra' with show-cooking, *à la carte* restaurant 'La Cúpula' and Specialities Restaurant. Orchestral music and international shows are presented in the ballroom 'Armstrong', with live music in the piano bar 'Tiffany'.

There is a putting green on site, and the hotel can organise bookings at special rates for all the island's golf courses, and also arranges free entrance to the Casino. The hotel has a fitness centre, a health and beauty centre with facial and body treatments, a hairdresser, a floodlit tennis court with artificial grass, squash, table tennis, bowls and a playground. There are two adult sea water swimming pools, one heated all year, as well as another for children, also heated, complete with its own Jacuzzi.

Recreational facilities

Floodlit tennis court with artificial grass, squash, table tennis, french boules, giant garden chess; Jacuzzi at pool, massage, turkish bath; free bicycle loan; free putting green on site for golfers with handicap; direct beach access.

Meeting/business facilities

Five rooms, for up to 350 delegates.

Local attractions

Aquatic sports at Playa Fañabé, with direct access: riding, sailing, diving, sea trips, trekking, hangliding.

GOLF FACILITIES
Best season for golf: All year round.

COURSES:	LENGTH	PAR	FEES
Costa Adeje			
	6201m	72	E18
Las Américas			
	6002m	72	E18
Amarilla Golf			
	6077m	72	E18

Garages for car parking; putting-green with free club loan for golfers with handicap; storage room for golf clubs; free club loan.

Facilities key

271   350

SPAIN: BALEARICS Sun, sand, sea and superb golf

If variety is truly the spice of life then Spain's Mediterranean island of Mallorca has to be one of the world's hottest destinations. Contrast the nightlife of El Arenal and Magaluf with the peace of the Formentor peninsula; the mountains around Deia and Soler in the north with the gently rolling interior; fashionable Palma with villages where life has seemingly stood still for years. They've even got two native languages – Spanish and Catalan – with English also very widely spoken.

GETTING THERE Palma's airport has recently been extended to cope with the huge numbers coming into what is the Mediterranean's most popular holiday island.

APRÈS GOLF Mallorca's big tourist resorts are geared to the mass holiday market. If you don't want to disco the night away, head instead to a country *bodega* to sample the local wines, or to one of several truly gourmet restaurants sited in converted manor houses.

OFF THE COURSE Country walks, mountain biking and all manner of watersports are all on the agenda. Many, though will be drawn by the opportunity simply to relax in the sun here in the favoured retreat of the likes of George Sands and Frederic Chopin.

NOT TO BE MISSED The mystic caves of Drac; the train ride from Palma through the mountains to Soler with its picturesque harbour; local ceramics and handcrafts.

Facts & figures

- There are 17 courses to be found on the islands, with 14 on Mallorca – a total of 235 holes.
- Designed by FW Hawtree and opened in 1961, Golf Son Vida outside Palma is the islands' oldest course.
- The six artificial lakes at Capdepera mark it out as one of the few courses in Europe designed by American Dan Maples, best known for his work in North Carolina and Florida.

Since Prince Rainier of Monaco inaugurated golf on Mallorca in 1961 by hitting the first shot at Golf Son Vida (finishing up in the bushes, incidentally), enthusiasts have flocked to the Balearics for year-round sun and for the variety of the courses that continue to flourish. Away from Mallorca there are only three opportunities to play, and despite the exclusive, 'away from it all' atmosphere on Menorca or Ibiza the serious golfer will stay on the main island.

Prices remain reasonable after the excesses of ten years ago, and Mallorca has much to attract the family. Using a little ingenuity it is possible to plan outings to clubs like Poniente, a mere stone's throw from the Portals Vells beach, with its white sand, yachts and restaurant/bar, or to Capdepera, close to the dunes of Cala Mesquida, the former smugglers' haunt, set against the backdrop of undulating mountains. If one can avoid worst excesses of the midday sun and the problems of crowded tees, an early morning or evening round at Santa Ponsa or Canyamel is an experience not to be missed.

NEW DEVELOPMENTS

- **Santa Ponsa III, a nine-hole course designed by Francisco Lopez Segales, opened in February 1999. This large residential development plans two further courses.**
- **Recently reconstructed, Menorca's idyllic Golf Son Parc now has a full 18 holes.**

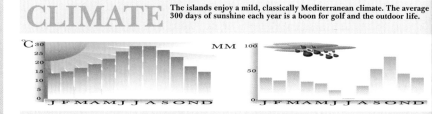

CLIMATE The islands enjoy a mild, classically Mediterranean climate. The average 300 days of sunshine each year is a boon for golf and the outdoor life.

Sample point: Mallorca

RECOMMENDED CAR HIRE *Hertz*
UK: +44 (0) 870 848 4848
Germany: +49 (0) 180 533 3535
Website: www.hertz.com

Price guide €
Round of golf / Golf balls
Small beer / 4/5 star hotel room

CONTACT
Balearic Tourist Board, Calle Montenegro, 5, 07012 Palma Mallorca
Tel: +34 971 176191 Fax: +34 971 176185

Favourite fairways

① REAL CLUB DE BENDINAT
Though extended in 1995, this is not a large course, but you will need a buggy if you plan to join the King of Spain (a regular player) for a tricky, hilly round. Designer Martin Hawtree has excelled himself on the elevated and difficult-to-hit greens. Care is needed on the tight fairways where balls can be easily lost amidst the olive and pine trees. Sea breezes provide welcome relief from the heat, but can cause a few surprises.
Par 70   Length 5596m
Urbanization Bendinat, E-07015 Bendinat, Mallorca
Tel: +34 971 40 52 00 Fax: +34 971 70 07 86

② PONIENTE
This John Harris designed course is quite flat and is as easy on the eye as it is on the feet – there are spectacular views of the mountains, and skilful use has been made of the natural features of the landscape in laying out the holes. The 396-metre par 4 tenth, with a lake to the right and two huge bunkers down the left hand side, is one of the finest holes on the island, while the long downhill par five 18th is guaranteed to leave you with a big smile on your face.
Par 72   Length 6082m
Poniente Ctra. Cala Figuera, Calvia
Tel: +34 971 690211 Fax: +34 971 693364

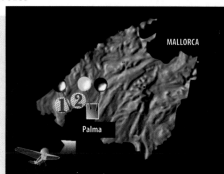

MALLORCA

Palma

Hotels

- **Arabella Sheraton Golf Hotel** — Page 107
- **Hotel Son Vida** — Page 108
- **Meliá de Mar** — Page 109

ARABELLASHERATON GOLF HOTEL

Recreational facilities

Indoor and outdoor pools; Jacuzzi, steam bath, sauna, beauty farm, fitness house; five tennis courts; watersports and sailing locally.

Meeting/business facilities

Three rooms, for up to 90 delegates.

Local attractions

Palma Cathedral; opera, theatre and concerts in Palma; Drach's Caves, Valdemossa, Formentor for climbers and walkers – the rugged Sierra de Tramontana has nine peaks over 1000m.

Hotel information

Carrer de la Vinagrella s/n
07013 Palma de Mallorca

Tel: +34 971 799 999
Fax: +34 971 799 997
Email: arabella@arabella.es

Accolades

☆☆☆☆☆
Sheraton Luxury Collection

Airport

Son San Juan: 15-20 mins

Accommodation price guide

Accepted credit cards
AE MC V DC

Close to Palma, set amongst Mediterranean-style gardens and adjacent to the prestigious Son Vida golf course, stands the magnificent five-star ArabellaSheraton Golf Hotel and the new Son Muntaner course. Designed in the style of a Spanish mansion, the hotel's 93 guest rooms offer the highest standards of quality, comfort and facilities.

The hotel is fortunate in enjoying not only a mild Mediterranean climate but also an ideal location in a verdant landscape of exceptional tranquility. As a consequence, guests are able to benefit from the optimum conditions in which to play golf, and can also get the best out of all the other types of sport and alternative forms of relaxation on offer.

The ArabellaSheraton features a beauty and holistic centre which specialises in gentle, natural beauty treatments and, for those who wish to explore, areas of natural beauty, cultural attractions and all kinds of entertainment are close by.

A mouthwatering choice is available at the hotel's restaurants. The Plat d'Or serves a well-balanced interpretation of Mediterranean specialities, while the Foravila offers a more rustic style: local *tapas*, fresh salads, abundant seafood and Iberian meats.

GOLF FACILITIES

Best season for golf: September to June.

COURSES:	LENGTH	PAR	FEES
Son Muntaner	6347m	72	on request
Golf Son Vida	5740m	72	E39
Bendinat Real	5600m	72	E41
Bendinat Real	5600m	72	E41
Poniente	6400m	72	E41
Santa Ponça	6543m	72	E41

New Son Muntaner course opens Spring 2000; special green fee deals for guests; driving range, pitch and putt, tuition packages; tournaments open to guests; golf carts for hire; host to PGA Open; 13 golf courses within one hour.

Facilities key

93 90

HOTEL SON VIDA

Hotel information

C/Raixa 2
07013 Palma de Mallorca

Tel: +34 971 790 000
Fax: +34 971 790 017
Email: hsonvida@balears.net
Web: www.hsonvida.balears.net

Accolades

☆☆☆☆☆

Airport

Son San Juan (Palma): 20 mins

Accommodation price guide

Accepted credit cards
AE DC MC V

Preferred tour operator

From UK
Thomson Tel: +44 (0) 207 387 9321

From Germany
TUI   Tel: +49 (0) 511 5670

From Switzerland
Kuoni   Tel: +41 (0) 1 277 4444

Recreational facilities

Swimming club in spacious gardens, tennis courts, health club, jewellery shop, boutiques, hairdresser, beauty farm offering massage and acupuncture.

Local attractions

Cathedral, theatre and concerts at Palma, Drach's caves, Valldemosa, Formentor; for climbers and walkers, the rugged Sierra de Tramontana has nine peaks over 1000 metres; five kilometres from Puerto Portals, the world's most famous yachting harbour.

A 13th century castle, the Hotel Son Vida underwent a thorough conversion into a hotel in 1961, combining old architecture with modern facilities. Surrounded by 500 hectares of sub-tropical parkland, its 18-hole golf course commands magnificent views over the bay of Palma.

It has had an illustrious guest list, including the Prince and Princess of Monaco, Emperor Haile Selassie the Lion of Judah, King Saud Ibn Abdul Aziz of Arabia, King Feisal, Prince Juan Carlos de Borbon and Princess Sofia (today King and Queen of Spain), Queen Sirikit of Thailand, President of China Jiang Zemin, Truman Capote, Yehudi Menuhin, John Lennon, Brigitte Bardot and Marlene Dietrich.

The hotel is located five kilometres from Palma city centre and 15km from the airport. All rooms offer direct-dial telephone, 16 channels of satellite TV, a safe deposit box, mini-bar, air-conditioning and central heating, bathrobe and hair dryer, and electricity at 220V.

The health club provides an indoor heated swimming pool, Jacuzzi, fitness room, sauna, Turkish bath and massage. Four tennis courts are available, while the beauty farm offers facial and body treatments, massage and acupuncture.

GOLF FACILITIES
Best season for golf: All year round.

COURSES:	LENGTH	PAR	FEES
Son Vida			
	5740m	71	E40
Stanta Ponça			
	6543m	72	E44
Bendinat			
	5650m	70	E49
Son Muntaner (opens March 2000) (exclusive for hotel guests)			
	6347m	72	E57

Guests benefit from reductions of 10-20 per cent on green fee rates for all golf courses on Mallorca; there are tournaments open to guests at Easter and Christmas; the given green fee rates are special rates for hotel guests.

Facilities key

170   200

MELIÁ DE MAR

Hotel information

Paseo de Illetas 7
Illetas
07015 Mallorca

Tel: +34 971 40 25 11
Fax: +34 971 40 58 52
Email: melia.de.mar@solmelia.es
Web: www.solmelia.es

Accolades

★★★★☆

Airport

Palma de Mallorca: 25 mins

Accommodation price guide

Accepted credit cards
AE DC MC V

Preferred tour operator

From UK
Thompson Tel: +44 (0) 171 387 9321
From Germany
TUI   Tel: +49 (0) 11 6546 516711
From Spain
Mundicolor Tel: +34 91 456 8600

Recreational facilities

Beach, tennis, heated indoor swimming pool; 18 000m² of gardens; children's playground, entertainment programme in summer; watersports nearby.

Meeting/business facilities

Five rooms, for up to 250 delegates.

Local attractions

Palma cathedral, international standard shopping, island tours, arts and crafts, Caves of Drac.

GOLF FACILITIES
Best season for golf: October to end of March.

COURSES:	LENGTH	PAR	FEES
Royal Golf Bendinat			
	5650m	70	E45
Son Vida			
	5740m	72	E48
Santa Ponça			
	6543m	72	E48

Within easy reach of the local golf courses, the Meliá de Mar is ideally situated in the residential area of Illetas, just ten minutes from the centre of Palma and right on the sea front. The Royal Bendinat Golf Course is just 500 metres away while the Poniente and Santa Ponça golf courses are also easily reached. The hotel has 133 double rooms, four junior suites and seven grand suites, all with private terrace and breathtaking views.

The Amaranto restaurant and Del Jardin *à la carte* restaurant both have views over the sea and the gardens. The Di Mare Italian restaurant overlooks coast and swimming pool, while the Ultramar Beach Club combines cafeteria service with an excellent grill. The Marfil Bar has music every night, and on summer nights there is dancing on the terrace.

Tennis courts and a heated indoor swimming pool are available, together with five meeting rooms and banqueting rooms to accommodate up to 250 persons. The hotel also offers 24-hour room service, its own private parking area, and a fast and efficient laundry and ironing service.

Key persons in politics, the arts and business, have already sampled the exquisite quality of the hotel's cuisine, and the success of their meetings and incentives have been guaranteed by the touch of class and the personalised service offered.

Guests may rest assured that the Meliá de Mar will provide the ideal setting for the enjoyment of great golf in relaxing and peaceful surroundings.

Facilities key

    144 250

SPAIN: ANDALUCIA & MURCIA The Golf Coast

Spain's Costa del Sol is blessed by year-round sunshine, beautiful countryside punctuated by the famed 'white villages', bustling cities which wear their Moorish heritage with pride, and a lively cosmopolitan community which matches Spanish locals with resident expats – usually of the well-heeled variety – and incoming tourists and holidaymakers.

For many, this is real Spain – and if you take a day trip down the coast to Gibraltar or a short ferry trip across the Straits to Tangier you can leaven those traditions with the history of Britain's great naval outpost and the exotic charms of Morocco.

This is the land of expansive golden sands, of swaying palms, mountains which stretch down to the coast, ancient forts and castles, marinas chock-a-block with expensive yachts, and night life which stretches way into the small hours.

GETTING THERE Málaga and Gibraltar airports both have busy scheduled and charter services from a wealth of UK and Continental departure points and, along with the key resorts, are linked by a brand new motorway which hugs the coast and also puts Madrid within reach. Car hire is easy to arrange and taxis are not expensive.

APRÈS GOLF Marbella and Puerto Banus are two of the world's most fashionable resorts, where the game is to see and be seen. Designer clothes, expensive cars and stylish eating out are almost de rigeur. Local Spanish cuisine heavies on fresh fish and seafood but an international clientele ensures you'll find everything from pizzas to sushi, from bratwürst to balti – and there'll be a cocktail to match every occasion.

OFF THE COURSE Watersports of each and every kind – from sailboarding to water skiing, swimming to snorkelling, are key activities, along with sightseeing to great cities like Granada and Seville. There are plenty of discos, nightclubs and cultural festivals to be savoured.

FACTS AND FIGURES

- The oldest course in Andalucia is Real Club de Campo de Malaga, designed in 1925 by legendary Englishman Tom Simpson.
- Rated No.1 in Europe by *Golf World*, Valderrama started life in 1975 as the New Sotogrande course. As Las Aves, it staged the Ladies' Spanish Open in 1982 and, fully renovated in 1985 as Valderrama, was the annual venue for the Volvo Masters and, in 1997, the Ryder Cup.
- The world's most valuable private museum devoted to historic golfing artefacts is exhibited in the Valderrama clubhouse.
- Golf La Dama de Noche is a 2928-metre nine-hole golf course near Marbella and the only course fully floodlit for night-time play.

Set among oaks and olives – the joyful Valderrama

Mention holiday golf to a European and his or her first thoughts are of the Costa del Sol – that stretch of the southern Andalucian coast known, with good reason, as the 'Costa del Golf'. This is where the modern concept of holiday golf – hotel, adjacent golf course, resort facilities, integrated real estate – was born. Guadalmina opened its doors, with 18 holes by Javier Arana nudging the seashore, in 1959. By 1968, five courses were available along the coast. Now Andalucia has 58 golf clubs, with no less than 36 of them sited among the colourful developments of the Costa del Sol.

This matches England's south-east as the greatest concentration of golf in Europe, exceeded only by such US destinations as Myrtle Beach and Palm Springs. It pays to be selective where you play. Green fees vary considerably, generally in relation to the quality of the course, and now most clubs require production of a handicap certificate. There are many teaching academies plus a number of par three courses for beginners, overcoming some of the past problems of slow play and poor course etiquette. For families, golfers of all abilities and hedonists.

Despite the first 36 holes at La Manga opening in 1971, golf in Murcia still has room for expansion. The La Manga resort, however, is easily the most complete sports holiday complex in Europe. It has three golf courses plus an executive layout, a sizeable tennis centre, squash, bowling, facilities for football, volleyball and basketball; also a private beach club. Recommended for committed holiday sports persons.

NEW DEVELOPMENTS

- The Almenara course at Sotogrande opened a four-star hotel in September 1999 and plans a further nine holes in 2000, a golf academy and three practice holes. It is part of a US$45 million development which will also see two further 18-hole courses and an additional nine holes on the La Canada course.
- The five-star Hotel Principe Felipe at La Manga now has a casino next door.
- Golfers wishing to play Valderrama, venue of the 1997 Ryder Cup, must reserve tee-off times in advance, which are available at 15-minute intervals between 12pm and 2pm.

Hotels

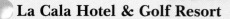

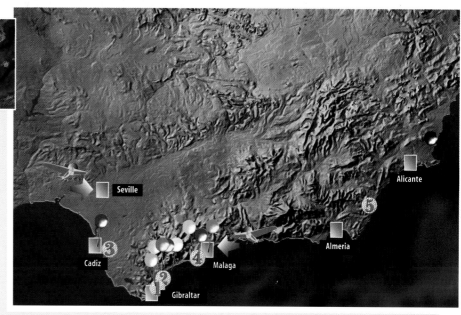

RECOMMENDED CAR HIRE

Hertz

UK: +44 (0) 870 848 4848
Germany: +49 (0) 180 533 3535
Website: www.hertz.com

Favourite fairways

① VALDERRAMA

Originally laid out by American master Robert Trent Jones in 1975, this course has been considerably improved, making it a superb setting for the 1977 Ryder Cup. The ultimate private club, kept in immaculate condition, it represents a course all good golfers should play once despite the high green fee. Venue for the World Golf Championship in November 1999.
Par 72   Length 5983m
Apartado 1, 11310 Sotogrande (Cadiz)
Tel: +34 956 795 775   Fax: +34 956 796 028

② SOTOGRANDE

The first creation of Robert Trent Jones in Spain and one of the earliest Costa del Sol courses (1962). A pure test of golf running out over level holes with palm-fringed water and up into cork-oak embroidered hillside. An exclusive private club that has hosted many top tournaments, both amateur and professional. It accepts visitors and has always appealed to better players.
Par 72   Length 5853m
Paseo del Parque, s/n, Sotogrande (Cadiz)
Tel: +34 956 795 050   Fax: +34 956 795 029

③ MONTECASTILLO HOTEL & GOLF RESORT

A majestic test of golf by Jack Nicklaus, his first in southern Spain. It is the current host to the end-of-term Volvo Masters. Laid out over undulating ground, with some elevated tees and greens, it always offers a view of the problem however demanding. Plenty of sand and water, in true American style.

Castellated clubhouse and hotel on site.
Par 72   Length 6043m
Ctra. de Arcos, Km.9.5, 11406 Jerez de la Frontera (Cadiz)
Tel: +34 956 151 200   Fax: +34 956 151 209

④ TORREQUEBRADA

Former Spanish amateur champion Pepe Gancedo set this challenging course over plunging hills and chasms in 1972. Fairer than it seems, the course has hosted the Spanish Open and needs to be played with caution and finesse. Plenty of sloping lies and great Mediterranean views from the clubhouse.
Par 72   Length 5513m
Apartado de Correos 120, C.N. 340 Km.220, 29630
Benalmadena-Costa (Malaga)
Tel: +34 952 442 742   Fax: +34 952 561 129

⑤ LA MANGA CLUB

Very much an 'island' resort, aiming to provide every facility the sporting family could possibly want, all on one site. An attractive setting, embraced by low hills behind and views of the Mar Menor and the sea. With all the palms, sand and strategic water, you could well be Stateside. The golf courses can cover all abilities; the South Course is the toughest.
South Course Par 70, Length 5475m, North Course Par 72, Length 5951m, West Course Par 73 Length 5680m
Los Belones, Cartagena, 30385 Murcia
Tel: +34 968 175 000   Fax: +34 968 137 272

The most up-to-date golf travel information is always at www.golftravel4u.com

CLIMATE

Golf is enjoyed year-round in Southern Spain. With summer temperatures rising to 30°C, some may be more comfortable playing later in the year when 18°-20°C is the norm. But no-one need worry about rain!

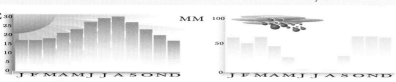

Sample point: Málaga

CONTACT

Turisimo Andaluz, Ctra. Nac. 340 km, 189.6, 29600, Marbella
Tel: +34 95 28 38 785   Fax: +34 95 283 63 69

Price guide   €

| Round of golf | 🐚🐚🐚 | Golf balls | 🐚🐚🐚🐚🐚 |
| Small beer | 🐚🐚 | 4/5 star hotel room | 🐚🐚🐚 |

LA CALA RESORT

Hotel information

La Cala de Mijas
29647 Mijas-Costa
Málaga

Tel: +34 95 266 9000
Fax: +34 95 266 9039
Email: lacala@lacala.com
Web: www.lacala.com

Accolades

★★★★☆

Airport

Málaga: 40 mins

Accommodation price guide

Accepted credit cards
AE MC V

Recreational facilities

Sauna, whirlpool, tennis, gym, football pitch, squash, shops; mountain biking, hiking and horse riding.

Meeting/business facilities

Three rooms, for up to 70 delegates.

Local attractions

Marbella – jet-set seaside resort and Puerto Banus; Mijas – old whitewashed village; Ronda; Sierra de la Nieves National Park; Málaga.

One of the most successful of the recently constructed major golf resorts in Europe, La Cala Resort, with its five-star hotel and two magnificent 18-hole courses is set a convenient 35 kilometres from Málaga Airport in the spectacular hinterland of Mijas Costa and dazzling Marbella.

The attractive hotel commands a central position in the heart of the fabulous La Cala golf courses and comprises 100 deluxe double/twin rooms.

All rooms offer superb views of the La Cala South Course and are luxuriously furnished in a traditional style, blending with the hotel's classical Andalusian architecture. They all are equipped with satellite TV, electronic safe, hairdryers, direct dial telephone plus message service, central heating, air-conditioning and luxuriously appointed bathroom with bathrobes and heated floor.

Recreational possibilities include tennis courts, football pitch, indoor swimming pool, saunas, games rooms, outside pool and Jacuzzi, hill walking, mountain biking and horse riding. The Resort's two restaurants, La Terraza (at the hotel) and Los Olivos (at the clubhouse), offer a selection of national and international cuisines, and each features a splendid terrace overlooking the golf courses.

GOLF FACILITIES

Best season for golf: January to December.

COURSES: LENGTH	PAR	FEES
La Cala North		
6187m	73	E51
La Cala South		
5966m	72	E51

The two fine 18-hole courses both designed by the American Architect Cabell B Robinson are complemented superbly by an elegant and comfortably-appointed colonial-style clubhouse and the David Leadbetter Golf Academy that includes a six-hole par-three 'executive' course.

Facilities key

106   70

GRAN MELIÁ DON PEPE

Hotel information

José Meliá s/n
29600 Marbella
Málaga

Tel: +34 95 277 03 00
Fax: +34 95 277 99 50/54
Email: gran.melia.don.pepe@solmelia.es
Web: www.solmelia.es

Accolades

☆☆☆☆☆ Grand Luxe

Airport

Málaga: 45 mins

Accommodation price guide

Accepted credit cards
AE MC V DC

Recreational facilities

Two outdoor pools, heated indoor pool; fully equipped sporting club: sauna, Turkish baths, massage; two tennis courts; golf; free entry to Marbella Casino.

Meeting/business facilities

Five rooms, for up to 350 delegates.

Local attractions

Marbella nightlife, the yacht harbour of Puerto Banus.

Surrounded by beautiful tropical gardens and looking directly over the beach, Gran Meliá Don Pepe is just five minutes from the centre of Marbella, one of the most prestigious tourism destinations in the world.

Visitors will find guest rooms with all the comfort and elegance that distinguish the Gran Meliá chain of superior hotels. The 202 rooms and suites are furnished with the most modern facilities and amenities, almost all of them enjoying splendid views of the blue Mediterranean.

Every small detail is take care of, both in quality of service and presentation, to make the hotel's high quality cuisine truly memorable.

Nor are leisure moments overlooked. Surrounded by the most magnificent of facilities, guests may choose to swim in the pools or simply soak up the sun and enjoy the pleasant sea breezes, attended at all times by courteous terrace service.

Magnificent golf is also at hand, along with tennis, keep-fit and an extensive programme of activities organised by the expert team of professionals from the hotel's own sports club.

GOLF FACILITIES
Best season for golf: Spring, Autumn, Winter.

COURSES:	LENGTH	PAR	FEES
La Quinta			
	3006m	36	E35
Los Naranjos			
	6457m	72	E39
Guadalmina South			
	6012m	72	E41
Guadalmina North			
	5825m	71	E41
Practice facilities at La Quinta.			

Facilities key

202   350

HOTEL BYBLOS ANDALUZ

Recreational facilities

Louison Bobet Thalassotherapy/Spa centre; La Prairie beauty centre; two fresh-water and one indoor heated sea-water pool, five tennis courts, mountain bikes, gymnasium, horse riding.

Meeting/business facilities

Eight rooms, for up to 300 delegates.

Local attractions

Mijas (12 km) – a typical white Andalusian village; Málaga (30 km); the spectacularly sited mountain town of Ronda (85 km); further afield, Gibraltar and North Africa both beckon.

Hotel information

Mijas Golf
Apt. 138
Fuengirola

Tel: +34 95 246 02 50
Fax: +34 95 247 67 83
Email: byblos@spa.es
Web: www.hotel-byblos.com

Accolades

Member The Leading Hotels of the World

Airport

Málaga: 20 mins

Accommodation price guide

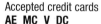

Accepted credit cards
AE MC V DC

Located in the glorious south of Spain, between Málaga and Marbella in the heart of Andalucia, overlooking two 18-hole golf courses, stands the Hotel Byblos Andaluz.

The hotel is built in the Moorish Andalusian tradition, characterised by ceramic fountains, patios and gardens. It offers 144 bedrooms and suites, three restaurants, two bars – the Saint-Tropez and, at the poolside, The Minaret – and eight conference and banqueting rooms with capacity ranging from ten to 300 people. There is a 60-seat projection room and a banqueting terrace for up to 400.

Sporting and relaxation facilities include two 18-hole golf courses, three pools, five tennis courts, the acclaimed Louison Bobet Thalassotherapy/Spa Centre – with its treatments based on seawater at body temperature, ideal for revitalising the body – and the La Prairie Beauty Centre. In the unlikely event of guests needing a change from golf and the ambience of the Byblos, the typical Andalusian 'white village' of Mijas is only 12 km away. Málaga is just 30 km, as is the international jet-set resort of Marbella/Puerto Banus.

Further afield, at 85 km, but well worth a visit, is Ronda, a small mountain town overlooking the Tajo and home to the oldest bullring in Spain. There are also two aqua-parks a few kilometres from the hotel.

GOLF FACILITIES
Best season for golf: All year round.

COURSES: LENGTH	PAR	FEES
Los Olivos		
5545m	72	E42
Los Lagos		
5975m	71	E42

Start times can be booked either with hotel reservation or after arrival; golf carts and cars available; practice area 100m from hotel; golf dressing room service in hotel; equipment and shoe cleaning; bar service on course; classes and clinics; tournaments arranged.

Facilities key

144   300

HOTEL EL PARAÍSO

Hotel information

Ctra. Cádiz, Km 167
29680 Estopona (Málaga)

Tel: +34 95 288 30 00
Fax: +34 95 288 20 19
E-mail: hparaiso@jet.es
Web: www.costadelsol.spa.es/hotel/paraiso

Accolades

★★★☆

Airport

Malaga: 45 - 60 mins

Accommodation price guide

Accepted credit cards
AE MC V DC

The Hotel El Paraíso has a stunning hilltop location in the privileged district of El Paraíso, commanding wonderful views of the Mediterranean Sea. Just next door is the Gary Player-designed El Paraíso golf course, a mecca for golfers of all ages and abilities, with lush fairways flanked by palm trees and an abundance of exotic flora. Guests benefit from reduced green fees rates there and at 17 other fine courses within easy reach.

Facilities at the hotel include indoor and outdoor swimming pools, a naturist solarium, extensive gardens, children's playground, tennis courts, hairdresser, beauty parlour and shop, and free transport to the beach and golf course. Next door is a centre offering traditional Chinese medicine (acupuncture, acupressure, etc), natural medicine (anti-stress, anti-tobacco etc) and homeopathy, plus saunas, Turkish steam bath and gym.

All rooms are en-suite, with air-conditioning, minibar, satellite TV, pay video, safe and a terrace with views out to the sea or golf course. Three restaurants give guests a great choice of dining: La Pergola offers a large breakfast buffet, including home-made bread and pastries, La Piramide is the hotel's *à la carte* restaurant, while the Restaurant Diet provides delicious and healthy choices.

Recreational facilities

Live music every night; Beach Club Costalita, beach restaurant with hammocks and parasols for rent; heated indoor swimming pool and Jacuzzi; naturist solarium; hairdresser, beauty parlour and shop; outdoor swimming pool, tennis, watersports, riding and country walks.

Meeting/business facilities

Three rooms, with capacity up to 120 persons.

Local attractions

Puerto Banus – one of the world's most famous yachting harbours; Marbella old town and beach; the towns of San Pedro de Alcántara and Estepona; Andalusian countryside; traditional Chinese medicine centre situated next to the hotel.

GOLF FACILITIES

Best season for golf: October to March.

COURSES:	LENGTH	PAR	FEES
El Paraíso	6131m	71	E36
Atalaya Old	5856m	72	E42
Guadalmina South	6012m	72	E46
Los Arqueros	5874m	72	E42
Monte Mayor	5593m	70	E40
La Quinta	3006m	36	E46

The El Paraíso golf school, staffed by fully qualified professionals; buggies for hire; tournaments open to guests; wide choice of local courses; special reduced rates for guests.

Facilities key

188   120

HOTEL MELIÁ SANCTI PETRI

Hotel information

Urbanizacion Novo Sancti Petri
11.130 Chiclana
Cádiz

Tel: +34 956 491200
Fax: +34 956 497053
Email: meliasptri@bitmailer.com
Web: www.solmelia.es

Accolades

☆☆☆☆☆ Grand Luxe

Airport

Jerez: 40 mins
Gibraltar: 1 hr
Seville: 1 hr 30 mins

Accommodation price guide

€

Accepted credit cards
AE MC V DC

Preferred tour operator

From Germany
Airtours   Tel: +49 (0) 69 7928 631
TUI   Tel: +49 (0) 56 4959 01

With the famed Valderrama course just one-and-a-half hours' drive away and five other courses all within one hour, the outstanding five-star Hotel Meliá Sancti Petri has the much-acclaimed Severiano Ballesteros designed 27-hole Novo Sancti Petri course right on its doorstep.

This pretty modern hotel, taking its cues from traditional Andalusian architecture, styled around the shady cloisters surrounding its tranquil inner courtyard, overlooks the fabulous La Barrosa beach. Designed by the architect Alvaro Sans, the entire hotel imbues an ambience of peace and tranquility.

226 spacious, beautifully decorated and air-conditioned bedrooms overlook the sea and the hotel's vast and truly magnificent pool, while starting with the magnificent breakfast buffet, and continuing through the day, the Meliá Sancti Petri is a gourmet's pleasure house. Guests can enjoy international specialities in the exquisite Alhambra *à la carte* restaurant, the exclusive El Patio restaurant and the finest Italian dishes in San Marco.

Natural beauty is the very essence of Andalucia and the Hotel Meliá Sancti Petri makes the very most of this truly magical setting to provide a truly unforgettable experience.

Recreational facilities

Swimming pool, Jacuzzi, sauna, billiards; golf, tennis, horse riding, cycling available locally.

Meeting/business facilities

Five rooms, for up to 350 delegates.

Local attractions

Sierra de Grazelema mountains, Cádiz, Conil, Veier.

GOLF FACILITIES
Best season for golf: All year round.

COURSES: LENGTH	PAR	FEES
Novo Sancti Petri		
6484m	72	E33
Campano		
3072m	72	E36
Montenmedio		
5990m	72	E61
Costa Ballena		
6220m	72	E24
Valderrama		
6234m	72	E135

Guest of the hotel get discounted green fees at Novo Sancti Petri.

Facilities key

226   350

HYATT REGENCY LA MANGA

Hotel information

Los Belones
30385 Cartagena
Murcia

Tel: +34 968 33 1234
Fax: +34 968 33 1235
Email: enquiries@cesser.com
Web: www.lamanga.hyatt.com

Accolades

☆☆☆☆☆
European Golf Resort of the Year 1999
Hertz International Golf Travel Awards

Airport

Murcia (San Javier): 20 mins
Alicante: 1 hr 15 mins

Accommodation price guide

Accepted credit cards
AE DC MC V

N estling amid the rolling hills which separate the crystalline Mediterranean from the warm waters of the Mar Menor lagoon, La Manga Club is blessed with a year-round Mediterranean climate. Lush green golf courses meander around palm trees and pine woodland, bordered by lemon groves, scented jasmines and colourful bougainvillaeas.

At the very heart of the resort, surrounded by two of the three championship golf courses – hosts to numerous major international tournaments since the resort opened in 1972 – are the 192 superbly appointed rooms and suites of the luxury five-star Hyatt Regency La Manga. In addition, there are 60 fully-equipped apartments, ranging from studios to three-bedroom units. Across the resort is a tantalising selection of restaurants and bars, as well as a casino.

Golf at La Manga is unparalleled. With a choice of three great courses, diverse in style and terrain, there's something to challenge golfers of all ages and abilities. The long championship South Course, designed by Robert D. Putman, was recently remodelled by Arnold Palmer. The North Course is slightly shorter, but no less exciting. Completing the total golf experience is the Dave Thomas-designed West Course, with its pine-fringed, undulating fairways. Complementing the courses are a renowned golf academy, comprehensive practice facilities, a well-equipped clubhouse and pro shop.

Recreational facilities

Three 18-hole championship golf courses on-site, 18-court tennis centre, bowls, climbing wall, diving school (seasonal), fitness centre and spa, international standard soccer pitches, mini-golf, children's club, paddle tennis, squash, heated and unheated swimming pools, beach. Go-karting, hill walking, climbing, horse riding, watersports, mountain biking – available nearby.

Meeting/business facilities

400m² ballroom accommodating up to 400 theatre style, divisible into four distinct sections, plus four separate meeting rooms for up to 16.

Local attractions

Cartagena Roman ruins and archaeological museum, Murcia's Baroque cathedral and museums, boat excursions and watersports on Mar Menor – Europe's largest saltwater lagoon.

GOLF FACILITIES

Best season for golf: All year round.

COURSES:	LENGTH	PAR	FEES
La Manga South	6065m	72	US$55
La Manga North	5518m	71	US$55
La Manga West	5689m	73	US$55

Floodlit driving range with more than 80 bays; practice bunker, putting and chipping greens; 18-hole par 47 pitch and putt course; mini golf; five-day academy courses plus private coaching; three guest tournaments weekly.

Facilities key

192 **400**

LE MÉRIDIEN LOS MONTEROS

Hotel information

Carretera de Cádiz, km 187
29600 Marbella

Tel: +34 95 277 1700
Fax: +34 95 282 58 46
Email: hotel@monteros.com
Web: www.monteros.com

Accolades

☆☆☆☆☆ De Luxe

Airport

Málaga AGP: 30 - 40 mins
Gibraltar: 45 mins - 1 hr

Accommodation price guide

€

Accepted credit cards
AE MC V DC

Preferred tour operator

From UK
British Airways
Holidays   Tel: +44 (0) 87024 24 249
From Germany
Airtours Int   Tel: +49 (0) 69 792 8444
From Sweden
Golf Tours   Tel: +46 (0) 831 03 97

Recreational facilities

18-hole golf course; swimming pool, tennis; sub-tropical gardens; beach club; boutiques.

Meeting/business facilities

Three rooms, for up to 300 delegates; audio-visual equipment available.

Local attractions

The Rock of Gibraltar, Marbella night-life, hill town of Ronda.

Often acclaimed as one of Europe's premier resort hotels and luxuriously refurbished during 1999, the renowned Hotel Le Méridien Los Monteros stands amid its own beautiful sub-tropical gardens, just five kilometres from Marbella's town centre. There are several swimming pools, as well as bars, restaurants, lounges and shops decorated in an attractive contemporary style.

This prestige five-star grand luxe establishment has 168 beautifully appointed air-conditioned rooms, with terrace, mini-bar, satellite TV and other amenities. Host to many famous personalities and members of royalty over the years, Los Monteros offers true sophistication. Attractions include regular evening dances and the elegant El Corzo Grill, which offers dining *à la grande carte*, as well as the famous La Cabane Beach Club with its swimming pool. The hotel also has its own tennis courts.

The hotel offers its guest reduced green fees at a selection of golf gourses in the area, including Río Real, the 18-hole golf course associated with the hotel, and can prebook tee-off times.

GOLF FACILITIES

Best season for golf: September to May.

COURSES:	LENGTH	PAR	FEES
Río Real			
	6057m	72	E37
La Quinta			
	5500m	72	E33
Alhaurín			
	5857m	72	E33
Los Arqueros			
	5900m	72	E33
Atalaya			
	5856m	72	E33
Estepona Golf			
	6001m	72	E33

Driving range at Río Real; private tuition; pre-booked tee-off times and reduced green fee of E33 per person for 18 holes on seven local courses available to hotel guests.

Facilities key

168   300

GOLF HOTEL GUADALMINA

Hotel information

Guadalmina Baja
29678
Marbella

Tel: +34 95 2882211
Fax: +34 95 2882291
Email: hotel_guadalmina@spa.es
Web: www.spa.es/hotel_guadalmina

Accolades

✩✩✩✩

Airport

Malaga: 1 hr
Gibraltar: 1 hr

Accommodation price guides

Accepted credit cards
AE DC MC V

Local attractions

Excursions to Ronda, Granada, Seville, Gibraltar and Tangier (Morocco).

Ideally located in the 'paradise of golf', just 60 km from Málaga International Airport, Golf Hotel Guadalmina is the exclusive hotel for seekers of a combination of golf, leisure and business.

Enjoying fabulous views across to Gibraltar and North Africa, guests can make the most of the setting right on the beachfront and adjacent to the tenth hole of the Guadalmina South golf course.

Built in 1959 and the setting for the movie 'A Touch Of Class', starring Oscar winner Glenda Jackson, the Golf Hotel Guadalmina has recently been extended and extensively re-decorated and now offers 177 rooms and updated facilities.

The hotel has a renowned restaurant, whose terrace overlooks the golf course and the sea.

Meeting/business facilities

Three rooms, for up to 390 delegates.

Recreational facilities

Two seawater swimming pools; watersports 800 metres away, gym and tennis nearby; 30 golf courses locally.

GOLF FACILITIES

Best season: November to May.

COURSES:	LENGTH	PAR	FEES
Guadalmina Nth	5874m	71	US$55
Guadalmina Sth	5674m	72	US$55

Practice facilities; tuition available; discounted fees at local courses.

Facilities key

177 **390**

LAS DUNAS BEACH HOTEL & SPA

Hotel information

La Boladilla Baja
Crta. Cádiz, Km 163,500
29689 Estepona, Málaga

Tel: +34 95 279 43 45
Fax: +34 95 279 48 25
Email: reservas@las-dunas.com
Web: www.las-dunas.com

Accolades

✩✩✩✩✩ Grand Luxe
Member of the Leading Hotels of the World
Five Star Diamond Award

Airport

Gibraltar: 40 mins
Málaga: 50 mins

Accommodation price guide

Accepted credit cards
AE DC MC V

Local attractions

Everything you could want for relaxation and fun is in the Marbella-Estepona area.

Located between Marbella and Estepona, a short distance from some of the best golf courses on the coast, the deluxe La Dunas Beach Hotel and Spa offers many top quality facilities, including the most luxurious accommodation, excellent service, and the best of the culinary art, as well as a first-class health clinic and spa.

Reduced green fees have been negotiated for hotel guests at many of the courses along the coast, and tee times can be arranged at any course. Special conditions are offered at the affiliated La Quinta Golf & Country Club and its golf academy, and the in-house golf pro will look after all your golfing requirements. Enjoy the ultimate combination of excellent golf and personal well-being!

Meeting/business facilities

One conference and meeting room, to accommodate 80 theatre-style.

Recreational facilities

Swimming pool, watersports, health and beauty treatments at the spa, fitness.

GOLF FACILITIES

Best season: All year round.

COURSES:	LENGTH	PAR	FEES
La Quinta	5792m	72	tbc
Los Arqueros	6028m	72	tbc
Monte Mayer	5589m	71	tbc

Practice facilities; tuition packages; reduced green fees at most courses.

Facilities key

106 **80**

MARBELLA CLUB HOTEL

Located on the southern coast of Spain, at the heart of the well-known 'Golden Mile', between fashionable Marbella and the exclusive harbour of Puerto Banus, stands the luxurious Marbella Club Hotel surrounded by subtropical gardens.

This Andalusian-styled, year-round beach resort, counts with 136 guest rooms, including nine bungalows on a broad selection of suites.

Guests enjoy preferred conditions at the nearby Dave Thomas designed 18-hole golf course – owned by the Marbella Club and the Puente Romano.

The Marbella Club Hotel features its own Beach Club, and guests are able to make full use the superb leisure facilities available at its adjacent sister resort, the Hotel Puento Romano.

GOLF FACILITIES
Best season for golf: All year round.

COURSES:	LENGTH	PAR	FEES
Marbella Club Golf Resort	6050m	71	E36

The Marbella Club course, designed by the world renowned player and designer Dave Thomas, offers 18 holes and comprises water features and demanding bunkers – encouraging players to find the most advantageous approach to the greens.

Meeting/business facilities

Two rooms, for up to 200 delegates.

For recreational facilities, see Puente Romano below.

Facilities key

136   **200**

HOTEL PUENTO ROMANO

Marbella is a golfer's heaven, as well as probably the most elegant and exclusive resort on the Costa del Sol. The Hotel Puente Romano nestles beside the Mediterranean coast, at the foot of the stunningly beautiful Sierra Blanca mountains.

The hotel comprises a series of low-rise horizontal buildings constructed in traditional Andalusian style and offering secluded and spacious demi-suite rooms with terraces or balconies overlooking waterfalls, fountains and lush subtropical gardens.

Its excellent restaurants offer a wealth of gastronomic delights, including spectacular buffets and a range of traditional dishes.

The hotel's wide range of leisure facilities includes tennis, swimming pool and fitness club.

Local attractions

Aquarium at Puerto Banus; all kinds of sports available in Marbella; superb local restaurants: La Meridiana and Los Corrales, serving international cuisine.

Meeting/business facilities

Four meeting rooms, for up to 160 delegates.

Recreational facilities

Tennis, sauna, gymnasium, Turkish baths and massage; tennis and fitness club; watersports on season; three swimming pools; shopping arcade; beach club.

GOLF FACILITIES
See Marbella Club (above).

Facilities key

226   **160**

SPAIN: CATALONIA & VALENCIA The hidden gem

Europe's premier holiday playground, the northern section of Spain's Mediterranean coast has much more to offer than just the renowned sun, sand, sea and sex so beloved of the package holiday hordes.

First off, from Port Bou, close by the French border, past the Costa Brava resorts of Tosa and Lloret and the cosmopolitan city of Barcelona and on south to Valencia, the Costa Blanca resort of Benidorm and historic Alicante, there's one of the world's finest and most varied coastlines.

There are sophisticated resorts too, and mediaeval hill towns scarcely touched by time. From the foothills of the Pyrénées down the spine of the coastal massif it's mountainous country, with jagged peaks interspersed by steep valleys full of woodlands and fruit groves.

This is Catalonia, a country within a country; part of Spain, yet with its own language, culture, pace of life and a great deal of autonomy. The cities are lively and fascinating – a kaleidoscope of heritage and modernity.

GETTING THERE From north to south of the region, Gerona, Barcelona, Valencia and Alicante all have modern international airports. The modern coastal motorway helps minimise transfer times. Inland, roads can be narrow, twisting and slow but present endlessly delightful vistas.

APRÈS GOLF People here rise late, don't go out to dinner until 10pm or so and then stay up partying all night – especially in Lloret, Benidorm and the other beach resorts. There's a wealth of things to do, from visiting ancient castles and monasteries to every kind of sporting activity to taking the de rigeur evening stroll strutting your stuff along the Ramblas. Food and drink are serious topics here, with tapas to fend off the hunger pangs and delicious Catalan stews for when things get serious.

OFF THE COURSE Every kind of watersport, from diving to windsurfing is well catered for. Mountain rambles and horse rides and the abundant flora and fauna vie for attention with such attractions as the Salvador Dalí museum at Figueras and his former home in nearby Cadaques. There are endless colourful fiestas to enjoy too, including the famed and riotous 'Moors v Christians' celebrations – and nobody enjoys a good firework display more than the Spanish.

NOT TO BE MISSED The ancient monastery at Montserrat; a day-trip to the tiny country of Andorra, which is ruled jointly by the Bishop of Urguel and the President of France.

FACTS AND FIGURES

- More than 50 courses are available for play in the two regions, with several of genuine class.
- Apart from the new test of Golf de Catalunya, major events have been held at Real Club de Golf El Prat, Club de Golf Escorpion and Campo de Golf El Saler, the latter possibly the best public golf course in Continental Europe.
- The head professional at Club de Campo Mediterraneo near Castellon – a very fine golf course which presents an excellent but fair challenge – has another claim to fame: Victor Garcia is the father of new European golfing sensation, Sergio.

Golf is a fairly recent phenomenon around the coasts of Spain, its history closely linked to a rising demand from holiday players. In the late 1950s, the market for overseas holidays altered radically with the introduction of charter flights and cheap package holidays. Suddenly the opportunity to go abroad to the sun became a real possibility for many.

People came in the summer and the first resort golf courses followed, closely linked to the building and sale of second or retirement homes within the golf development. It is interesting to note that, in those early days, the Costa Brava in Catalonia was just as important a destination for golf as the Costa del Sol, having three courses in play to the latter's four.

There have been many changes over the intervening years, not least the emphasis on golf in the southern part of the country. The regions of Catalonia and Valencia, where the first course (El Saler) opened in 1968, deserve to be better known. Although the overall coastline is identical in length to that stretching from Alicante round to the border with Portugal, with more than fifty courses to entice the visitor, hardly any of the major golf tour operators feature them.

With a gentle climate, mild in winter and not too hot in summer, there is a feast of golf to enjoy. Still comparatively undiscovered, with many of the courses planned for local members and thus less busy midweek with lower green fees. A region with appeal for families and golfers of all abilities.

NEW DEVELOPMENTS

- The newest course in Spain, the PGA Golf de Catalunya, is sited close to Barcelona and was the venue for the Sarazen World Open in October 1999. At 6584 metres on a demanding site, it has been designed to test the best professional players in a major tournament and is predicted to be rated amongst the best in the country.
- Due to open in June 2000, Golf Serres de Pals will add a further course to the Pals coastal region. Next to ricefields and marshes, with their extensive variety of wildlife, this slightly elevated 6308-metre course by designer Ramon Espinosa enjoys magnificent views over the surrounding countryside.

Hotels

RECOMMENDED CAR HIRE

Hertz
UK: +44 (0) 870 848 4848
Germany: +49 (0) 180 533 3535
Website: www.hertz.com

Favourite fairways

The most up-to-date golf travel information is always at www.golftravel4u.com

1 PALS

Not far from the seashore, this excellent course, designed by Englishman Fred Hawtree and opened in 1966, has proved a genuine examination for golfers of all levels. The narrow fairways, lined with impenetrable umbrella pine, are laid out on sandy soil and lead to small greens, normally in excellent condition. A European PGA Qualifying School is held here.
Par 73   Length 5940m
Carretera de Pals, E-17256 Pals (Girona)
Tel: +34 972 636 006   Fax: +34 972 637 009

2 PGA GOLF DE CATALUNYA

This is the newly opened dream of the European PGA, set near Barcelona. Designed by Neil Coles and Angel Gallardo, the course combines wooded areas of cork oak and pine, heath and parkland over undulating terrain to provide an excellent test with views of the Pyrénées for good measure. A further 18 holes and a hotel are due to follow.
Par 72   Length 6226m
Caldes de Malavella, Nacional N2, km. 701, 17455 Girona
Tel: +34 972 472 577   Fax: +34 972 470 493

3 EMPORDÁ

In what will eventually be 36 holes of golf, designer Robert von Hagge, creator of Seignosse in France, has crafted much variety between sandy links, lakes and tree-bordered parkland over three nine-hole loops. Typical grassy mounds and deep, excellent greens. Already considered one of the top ten courses in Spain.
Par 71   Length 5855m (East Course)
Ctra de Palafrugell a Torroella, 1725 Gualta (Girona)
Tel: +34 972 760 450   Fax: +34 972 757 100

4 EL SALER

A triumph for master architect Javier Arana and rated in a global top 50 by *Golf World*. Combining pine-lined holes with sandhills and truc linksland by the sea, open to any offshore breeze. Tough off the back tees, a genuine test of all aspects of the game. Very natural, which is its strength, if it also means a touch less manicuring than some. Not to be missed.
Par 72   Length 6042m
Parador Nacional 'Luis Vives', E-46012 El Saler (Valencia)
Tel: +34 96 161 1186   Fax: +34 96 162 7016

5 EL BOSQUE

West of Valencia on land elevated above acres of olive groves, Robert Trent Jones has created an American-style layout of great charm. The land is hilly, with ravines, rocks and some steep slopes. There are also some blind elevated greens on a demanding but attractive, sculptured, usually extremely well-kept course.
Par 72   Length 5915m
Carretera Godelleta km. 4.1, 46370 Chiva (Valencia)
Tel: +34 96 180 4142   Fax: +34 96 180 4009

CLIMATE

The northern Costas offer the Mediterranean's most exotic climate, with the mix of high mountains and sea sometimes leading to spectacular weather changes.

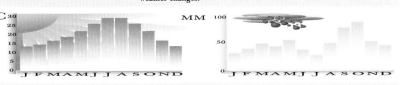

Sample point: Barcelona

Price guide

€

Round of golf	€€€		Golf balls	€€€€€	
Small beer	€€		4/5 star hotel room	€€€	

CONTACT

Turismo Catalonia, Passeig de Gracias 105, 08008 Barcelona
Tel: +34 93 237 9045 Fax: +34 93 415 6442
Turismo Valencia, Paz 48-46003, Valencia

HOTEL LA COSTA

Hotel information

Av. Arenales De Mar 3
17256 Pals
Costa Brava

Tel: +34 972 66 7740
Fax: +34 972 66 7736
E-mail: info@lacostahotel.com
Web: www.lacostahotel.com

Accolades

☆☆☆☆

Airport

Girona: 45 mins
Barcelona: 1 hr 30 mins

Accommodation price guide

Accepted credit cards
AE DC MC V

Preferred tour operator

From UK
Thomson   Tel: +44 (0) 207 387 9321
From Germany
Birdie Golf &
Reisen   Tel: +49 (0) 41 949 9990

Recreational facilties

Tennis, paddle courts, gym, saunas, Jacuzzi, games, multi-dimensional swimming pool, bicycles; sailing, riding, flying, cruises, scuba diving, microlite and ballooning locally.

Meeting/business facilities

Five rooms, for up to 250 delegates.

Local attractions

Many sites of historical interest, from Greek and Roman ruins at Empúries to mediaeval quarters in Pals and Peratallada; the Islas Medes nature reserve; the Peralada Casino; the Dalí Museum in Figueres.

Pals is a beautifully restored mediaeval walled village at the heart of the Costa Brava, at the northern end of Spain's Mediterranean coast. The comfortable Hotel La Costa adjoins the 18-hole Golf de Pals course and is 100 metres from the beach.

Opportunities for golf abound in these parts, with seven 18-hole courses within 45 minutes of the hotel, all with special green fees for residents. Tee-time bookings, payment of fees and information about lessons and courses can all be dealt with at the hotel reception. All the courses offer a full range of facilities both on and off the fairway.

The area is rich in cultural diversions, with many other mediaeval villages nearby, including Peratallada, Palau-sator, Vulpellac, Sant Martí d'Empúries, Bellcaire d'Empordà and Cruïlles. Empúries is especially notable for its ruins of ancient Greek and Roman colonies. Girona, the provincial capital, is remarkable for its historical treasures, particularly the best-preserved Jewish quarter in Europe, while its impressive cathedral has the widest Gothic nave ever built.

In contrast, Figueres is the home of the famous Dalí Museum. Many of Salvador Dalí's greatest works are here, in the building which also houses his tomb. Look closely and you will see the many golf balls he hid in his paintings!

GOLF FACILITIES

Best season for golf: Spring and Autumn.

COURSES:	LENGTH	PAR	FEES
Pais			
	6238m	73	E26-40
Emporda			
	6160m	71	E25-39
Girona			
	6100m	72	E26-36
Serres de Pals			
	6308m	72	E30-39

Tuition available, buggies for hire, guests may play in two tournaments: Trofeo La Costa and Parera-Vilar.

Facilities key

120   250

HOTEL TERMES MONTBRIÓ

Hotel information

c/Nou 38
43340 Montbrió Del Camp
Tarragona

Tel: +34 977 81 4000
Fax: +34 977 82 6251
Email: termes@ctv.es
Web: www.ctv.es/termes

Accolades

★★★☆

Airport

Reus: 20 mins
Barcelona: 1 hr

Accommodation price guide

Accepted credit cards
AE DC MC V

Recreational facilities

Thermal spa centre; outdoor swimming pool; bicycle hire; extensive garden (four hectares) and botanical gardens; equestrian school near the resort; mountain sports; diving centre at Cambrils fishing village.

Meeting/business facilities

19 rooms, for up to 900 delegates; dedicated conference centre offering variety of set-ups and newly extended state-of-the-art facilities.

Local attractions

City of Tarragona; Cistercian monasteries; Escornalbou castle; Delta del Ebro national park; mediaeval city Vila Ducal of Montblanc; many organised excursions, including Joan Miro tour; boat trips on the Ebro estuary; Universal's Port Aventura fun park.

Set in Montbrió del Camp, in the region of Costa Daurada, the resort complex of Hotel Termes Montbrió enjoys an exclusive and peaceful setting. The climate is pleasant all year round and the region offers visitors a whole variety of landscape, from beach to mountains, including the natural riches of the Delta del Ebro national park and three excellent 18-hole golf courses.

A harmonious combination of turn-of-the-century and ultra-contemporary architecture, the Hotel Termes Montbrió has 200 elegant and regally decorated rooms, featuring all the comforts of a state-of-the-art hotel, plus suites which give an unbeatable combination of space and services. Guests can stroll and relax in the expansive four-hectare gardens, which are alive with fountains and fascinating botanical species – the perfect complements for an enchanting spectacle of light and colour.

The best anti-stress therapy of all is to be found in the 41°C thermal waters of Montbrió, which emerge into the spa, where the most advanced treatments are on offer to promote health and beauty. Also unmissable is the meticulously prepared gastronomy of the Hotel Termes Montbrió, with its wide variety of quality international *à la carte* French and Mediterranean cuisine.

GOLF FACILITIES

Best season for golf: Spring, summer and autumn.

COURSES: LENGTH	PAR	FEES
Bonmont Terres Noves		
6202m	72	E29
Reus Aiguesverds		
6293m	72	E36
Costa Dorada		
6223m	73	E30

Facilities key

200 900

MAS DE TORRENT

Hotel information

Afores de Torrent
S/n- 17123
Torrent
Girona

Tel: +34 972 30 32 92
Fax: +34 972 30 32 93
Email: mtorrent@intercom.es
Web: www.mastorrent.com

Accolades

Best Hotel In Spain - Gourmetour Guide
1998 – Welcome Trophy Relais et
Chateaux

Airport

Barcelona: 2 hrs
Perpignan: 1 hr

Accommodation price guide

Accepted credit cards
AE DC MC V

Created from an 18th century farmhouse, this luxury hotel retains the structure and rural atmosphere of its origins. There are 20 guest rooms, including ten which are located in the farmhouse and are furnished with antiques of the region, while the bathrooms are absolutely modern.

The other 20 rooms have been built in an area adjacent to the swimming pool, with sensitivity to the traditional architecture and landscape of the Costa Brava. In evenings and afternoons when the weather is pleasant, the hotel restaurant spills out onto the terrace of the farmhouse, which is covered in beautifully kept plants. Breakfasts are also served on the terrace during the warmer months, as well as in the gardens of the bungalows.

A wide choice of sporting possibilities is available, including tennis, racquet and paddleball, as well as mountain bikes on which to enjoy the hotel's own bike trails. The beaches nearby offer a variety of exciting watersports.

The hotel lies at the heart of the Costa Brava, within easy reach of Barcelona, the French border and the sea. Nearby are the old town of Girona, the Dalí Museum at Figueras and fascinating ancient Greek and Roman ruins.

Recreational facilities

Golf, swimming pool, tennis, mountain biking on the hotel's bike trails.

Meeting/business facilities

Two rooms, for up to 80 delegates.

Local attractions

Lively Barcelona; historic Girona with its beautiful old quarters; the Costa Brava coast; the Dalí Museum and a fascinating toy museum at Figueras; Greco-Roman ruins at Ampurias; quaint mediaeval towns of Pals, Peratallada and Torroella de Montgrí.

GOLF FACILITIES

Best season for golf: All year round.

COURSES:	LENGTH	PAR	FEES
Empordà			
	6160m	71	E25-39
Pals			
	6222m	73	E36-60
D'Aro Mas Nou			
	6218m	72	E30-39
Costa Brava			
	5573m	70	E33-45

Driving range and putting green; range of fine courses within half hour drive.

Facilities key

30   80

HOTEL GOLF COSTA BRAVA

Urb. Golf Costa Brava
17246 Santa Cristina d'Aro
Girona

Tel: +34 972 83 51 51
Fax: +34 972 83 75 88
Email: hgolf@santacristina.net
Web: www.santacristina.net/hotelgolf.htm

Accolades

☆☆☆☆

Airport

Girona: 20 mins, Barcelona: 1 hr

Accommodation price guide

€

Accepted credit cards
AE DC MC V

Local attractions

Greek, Roman and prehistoric monuments; mediaeval and modernist architecture; monasteries, castles, beautiful countryside.

Perfectly located in Santa Cristina de Aro, between the first tee and the 18th green of the Golf Costa Brava course, Hotel Golf Costa Brava is a wonderful place to relax and enjoy both the golf and the myriad attractions of this fascinating region.

Guests appreciate the cultivated atmosphere of this delightful hotel managed so lovingly by the Sureda family. All 99 rooms are all air-conditioned, with direct-dial telephones, fridge and TV. Many also feature a terrace or balcony overlooking the swimming pool and golf course. During the winter, a 12-suites residence is available for exclusive hire.

Seven local courses offer specially reduced fees for guests of Hotel Golf Costa Brava, and the new PTA Catalunya course is just 20 minutes away.

Meeting/business facilities

One conference room and two meeting rooms, for up to 130 delegates.

Recreational facilities

Semi-Olympic pool, games room, walking and cycling tours; large garden; horse club, tennis and gym nearby.

GOLF FACILITIES
Best season: March to October.

COURSES:	LENGTH	PAR	FEES
Costa Brava	5573m	72	US$28-40
D'Aro	6210m	72	US$28-40
Girona	6100m	72	US$28-40

On-site practice range and pitch and putt; tuition available; buggies for hire.

Facilities key

99   130

MELIÁ ALTEA HILLS RESORT

Urbanizacion Altea Hills
332 Carretera Nacional KM 163,5
03590 Altea

Tel: +34 96 6881006
Fax: +34 96 6881024
Email: melia.altea.hills@solmelia.es
Web: www.solmelia.es

Accolades

☆☆☆☆☆

Airport

Alicante: 40 mins
Valencia: 1 hr 15 mins

Accommodation price guide

€

Accepted credit cards
AE DC MC V

Local attractions

Beaches, countryside, Benidorm resort.

Picturesquely situated on a rocky hillside overlooking the sea, just three kilometres from the charming town of Altea, the five-star Meliá Altea Hills features elegant and welcoming décor in charming surroundings. The 50 spacious suites offer every modern amenity plus spectacular Mediterranean views from their large balconies.

Sport, fitness and health facilities – including indoor and outdoor pools and a fully equipped leisure centre – keep guests in perfect shape and the Don Cayo golf course is just five minutes away. For 'aprés golf' winding down, guests may choose from the comfortable lobby bar, the tropical-style Palapa, the Les Penyes cafeteria or the sophisticated Altaya restaurant, with its delicious *à la carte* specialities.

Meeting/business facilities

Four rooms, for up to 800 delegates.

Recreational facilities

Indoor and outdoor pools, Jacuzzi, sauna, spa; beauty centre; gymnasium; squash.

GOLF FACILITIES
Best season for golf: All year round.

COURSES:	LENGTH	PAR	FEES
Don Cayo	6156m	36	E6
La Sella	6028m	36	E12
Javea	6070m	36	E9

Driving range, putting green, approach zone; buggies on request.

Facilities key

51   800

HOTEL SIDI SALER

Though located within minutes of Valencia's busy downtown, the five-star Hotel Sidi Saler is an oasis of calm and peace, set directly on the beach and bounded by the pine woods, rice paddies, lakes and canals of the beautiful Albufera nature reserve.

Four-season-long sunshine and close proximity to some of Spain's premier golf courses add to the appeal. There's a putting green and range right on site and the renowned El Saler course – ranked in the world's top 50 – is four kilometres away. Two other championship courses, El Bosque and Escorpion, are within 20 minutes' drive.

All rooms and suites meet the most exacting standards in comfort, and the hotel is a convincing place to do business without sacrificing leisure.

Hotel information

Playa Del Saler
E - 46012
Valencia

Tel: +34 96 161 04 11
Fax: +34 96 161 08 38
Email: sidisaler@ctv.es
Web: www.hotelessidi.es

Accolades

★★★★★

Airport

Valencia: 20 mins

Accommodation price guide

Accepted credit cards
AE DC MC V

Local attractions

Golf courses, horse riding, gardens, beach, beauty farm.

 AMERICAN EXPRESS OFFER
For advance booking on American Express Card you receive a **golf gift on arrival.**

Meeting/business facilities

Seven rooms, for up to 300 delegates.

Recreational facilities

Gardens, beach, beauty centre; tennis, squash, swimming pools, bicycle hire.

GOLF FACILITIES

Best season for golf: All year round.

COURSES:	LENGTH	PAR	FEES
El Saler	6355m	72	E60
El Bosque	6276m	72	E60
El Escorpion	6319m	72	E60
Putting green, driving/approach ranges.			

Facilities key

276   300

HOTEL SIDI SAN JUAN

Six kilometres from the old city of Alicante and directly on San Juan Beach, this friendly hotel's elongated architecture ensures the building fits in with its natural surroundings and has all rooms facing the sea. The only five-star establishment in the locality, Hotel Sidi San Juan is an oasis of tranquility, set amid more than 200 palm trees.

The hotel's inventive cuisine is prepared by a master chef who is a master of intriguing surprises, as well as creating healthy low-calorie menus.

Health is also firmly on the agenda at the hotel's on-site full-facility beauty farm and relaxation centre. There are also six tennis courts and a tennis school. Golfers will find a number of first-rate courses within very easy reach.

Hotel information

Playa De San Juan
E - 03540
Alicante

Tel: +34 96 516 13 00
Fax: +34 96 516 33 46
Email: sidisanjuan@ctv.es
Web: www.hotelessidi.es

Accolades

★★★★★

Airport

Alicante: 20 mins, Valencia: 1 hr

Accommodation price guide

Accepted credit cards
AE DC MC V

Local attractions

Re-enactment fiestas; Roman ruins; Benidorm.

 AMERICAN EXPRESS OFFER
For advance booking on American Express Card you receive a **golf gift on arrival.**

Meeting/business facilities

Seven rooms for up to 350 delegates.

Recreational facilities

Swimming pools, bicycle hire; tennis; beauty centre.

GOLF FACILITIES

Best season for golf: All year round.

COURSES:	LENGTH	PAR	FEES
Alicante Golf	6270m	72	E45
Bonalba	6367m	72	E45
Alenda	5901m	71	E45

New Ballesteros-designed Alicante course five minutes away; ten prestige courses within easy reach, all set in prime locations, offering superb play.

Facilities key

176   350

Your mark of excellence

The Great Golf Hotels Organisation, Big Publishing Ltd, 22 Stephenson Way, London NW1 2HD, United Kingdom
Tel: +44 (0) 20 7383 2335   e-mail: ggh@bigpublishing.com

FRANCE: SOUTH The golf gourmet's paradise

You only need enter a local restaurant to define south rather than north when you're in France. Above the Massif Central, it's a dairyland, the cuisine based on a rich combination of cream, butter and eggs. Follow the sun south and you'll find that if they aren't cooking with duck or goose fat then olive oil has surely taken over.

The people are different too, more Latin in temperament, more relaxed and unhurried in their approach to life – creating a great ambience for a pleasant golfing break.

France has taken to the sport enthusiastically in recent times and you will find a concentration of good courses on the South West Atlantic Coast around Biarritz, strung along the Riviera and in the glorious setting of the Alps. Those three regions help define the diversity which is the core of the French experience.

Windswept dunes – including lofty Mont Pilat, the highest sand dune north of the Sahara – and vast flat pine forests mark out the Landes; sophisticated resorts dapple the Côte d'Azur, and the French Alps are Western Europe's highest mountains.

GETTING THERE There are direct flights from many major European mainland and UK airports into such regional centres as Biarritz, Toulouse, Perpignan, Marseilles and Nice while many more destinations can be accessed by flights via Paris. TGV high speed train services put the south within four or five hours' relaxed journey time of the capital, whisking along at 300 km/h. While there is now an extensive autoroute (motorway) system throughout the south, don't miss the pleasures of France's web of quiet and picturesque D-roads.

APRÈS GOLF France's seaside resorts are as lively as any in Europe, with abundant discos, night clubs and late night bars and restaurants. Head a few kilometres inland, however, and there's a dramatic change. Here people rise early and retire again soon after dark. French food has strong regional diversity: in the south it is the cooking of Provence, redolent with olive oil, peppers, herbs and the sunny flavours of the Mediterranean, which is the undoubted culinary star though South West specialities are also brilliant and you might well be as tempted to drink a rosé as a red or white. This is the land of cheap local wines – but don't forget the majestic glories of Bordeaux.

OFF THE COURSE Sunworshippers: you've arrived! If you can tempt them away from the beach – by the sea or at the lake – take the family for a country ramble or to visit ancient castles and churches or to enjoy one of the famed *son et lumière* historic presentations.

NOT TO BE MISSED Visit the great wine châteaux of Bordeaux: many give guided tours and tastings; Dordogne with its Franco/English history; bustling Marseilles, with its North African connections; explore the majestic Alps; get lost in the narrow alleyways of old Nice; play the casinos in Biarritz, Cannes or Monte Carlo.

FACTS AND FIGURES

● **Golfing tourists spend an annual 800 million francs during their stay.**
● **The region has two of the three oldest golf clubs in Continental Europe – Pau (1856) and Biarritz (1888).**
● **A Basque, Arnaud Massey, from Biarritz, remains the only Frenchman to win the British Open (at Hoylake in 1907).**
● **At Golf du Médoc, near Bordeaux, each of the 36 holes is dedicated to a fine wine château, which is replicated on the clubhouse restaurant wine list.**

The Alpine splendour of Golf de Chamonix

Golf in the southern half of France has much in its favour, not least the good weather, especially along the Mediterranean. Most of the courses here are comparatively new, designed for holiday visitors, often in spectacularly beautiful locations.

Highlighting the new, one should not ignore the old. For here, in the south-western corner of the country, is where it all began. Expatriate Englishmen at Pau, nearly 150 years ago, introduced the game and, with the popularity of Biarritz as a winter retreat in the earlier part of this century for those with the means, it flourished.

Recent course developments mean that Aquitaine, in a green coastal strip from the winefields of Bordeaux south almost to the border with Spain, offers more great tests of golf than any other region of France. Courses like Médoc, Pessac, Gujan, Moliets, Hossegor, Seignosse, Chiberta, Makila, Arcangues and Nivelle provide a golfing feast for real players. As an alternative to the long drive south, a car ferry to Santander or Bilbao in northern Spain is a short drive away around the corner.

Golf de Frégate, at Bandol

The southern half of France can offer a fine variety of locations to suit all tastes and interests. As an alternative to the vineyards and seaside resorts of Aquitaine, one can sample the craggy, colourful, historic charms of Provence or go for snow-capped mountain vistas and relaxed golf in the French Alps.

Sun-lovers will doubtless head for the Mediterranean-hugging curve of the Cote d'Azur and its fashionable delights. Recommended for better golfers, nature lovers and gourmets.

NEW DEVELOPMENTS

● **It is now reckoned that one million of the annual foreign visits to France are linked to golf. The British form the largest group coming to play the game, followed by German, Dutch, Belgian, Italian and Swiss golfers. This group together accounts for 85% of French golf holidays.**
● **As one might expect, the British and Swiss prefer courses on the coast or in the countryside while the Dutch choose courses in the mountains. The most popular tourist areas are, in the main, also those most popular for golf.**

Hotels

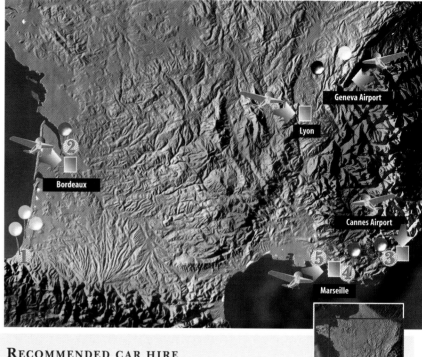

RECOMMENDED CAR HIRE

Hertz
UK: +44 (0) 870 848 4848
Germany: +49 (0) 180 533 3535
Website: www.hertz.com

Favourite fairways

The most up-to-date golf travel information is always at www.golftravel4u.com

① GOLF DE SEIGNOSSE

Possibly the toughest test of the game in France, it is Jose Maria Olazabal's preferred practice location. The course flows narrowly over steep hills and through a wooded valley with a number of water hazards, pine and cork oaks with grass as well as sand bunkers. Superbly demanding.
Par 72   Length 5774m
Avenue du Belvedere, 40510 Seignosse
Tel: +33 (0) 5 5841 6830 Fax: +33 (0) 5 5841 6831

② GOLF DU MÉDOC

A 36-hole complex. One course, Les Châteaux, offers a fine examination over an undulating, virtually treeless setting; the other, Les Vignes, is partly carved through a pinewood. Les Châteaux, the tougher test, has many links characteristics with huge, well-designed greens.
Les Châteaux: Par 71, Length 5765m
Les Vignes: Par 71, Length 5694m
Chemin de Courmateau, 33290 Le Pian Médoc Louens
Tel: +33 (0) 5 5670 1190 Fax: +33 (0) 5 5670 1199

③ ROYAL MOUGINS

Visually tight, with sloping terrain demanding careful strategy and precision play. This relatively new but lavishly-built course by Robert von Hagge has generous use of water which comes into play on 12 holes, not least at the par three second, played down a tumbling waterfall.
Par 71   Length 5697m
424, Avenue du Roi, 06250 Mougins
Tel: +33 (0) 4 9292 4969 Fax: +33 (0) 4 9292 4970

④ GOLF DE FRÉGATE

Challenging golf in a truly spectacular setting overlooking the sea just south of Marseille. American Ronald Fream has made good use of demanding slopes, olive trees and occasional rocky outcrops. Beautifully landscaped but tough to score. A course where you can play across the corner of a vineyard and then enjoy the vintage in the 19th. Also an executive nine holes.
Par 72   Length 5847m
Route de Bandol, 83270 Saint-Cyr sur Mer
Tel: +33 (0) 4 9432 5050 Fax: +33 (0) 4 9429 9694

⑤ GOLF DE MONTPELLIER MASSANE

This is a course for good players and high-handicap masochists. On a relatively level site, American Ronald Fream has used all his design skills to create a superb test from the back tees. Mounded sloping greens, strategic bunkers, plenty of water hazards – all demand that you know your game and play within it. Winter home of the European PGA Tour.
Par 72   Length 6044m
Mas de Massane, 34670 Baillargues
Tel: +33 (0) 4 6787 8787 Fax: +33 (0) 4 6788 8790

CLIMATE

Inland, south-west France can get very cold in winter, but golf is playable all year round, while the season in the Rhône-Alpes runs from April through to October. On the Med, the weather is idyllic for most of the year.

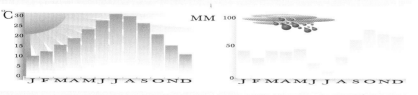

Sample point: Marseilles

CONTACT

French Tourist Board
Maison de la France, 8 Avenue de L'Opéra, 75001 Paris
Tel: +33 (0) 1 42 66 26 28 Fax: +33 (0) 1 49 24 96 56

Price guide   €

		Golf balls	
Round of golf			
Small beer		4/5 star hotel room	

CHÂTEAU DE LA BÉGUDE

Hotel information

Route De Roquefort-Les-Pins
06650 Opio

Tel: +33 (0) 4 93 12 37 00
Fax: +33 (0) 4 93 12 37 13
Email: begude@worldnet.fr

Accolades

☆☆☆
Châteaux & Hotels de France
Recommended by Guide Michelin

Airport

Nice: 20 mins

Accommodation price guide

Accepted credit cards
AE MC V

Preferred tour operator

From Denmark
Tee-off
Travel   Tel: +45 (0) 45 767699
From The Netherlands
Dutch Golf   Tel: +31 (0) 38 444 1888

Recreational facilities

18-hole golf, putting green, driving range; outdoor swimming pool; Restaurant La Begude with terrace overlooking the golf course.

Meeting/business facilities

Two conference rooms, for up to 60 delegates.

Local attractions

Skiing in Alps, musical events, and all the delights of the Riviera.

Located in the heart of the French Riviera, between sea and mountains, the Opio-Valbonne Golf Course, which was designed 30 years ago by Donald Harradine, provides a year-round welcome.

Imagine an 18-hole course in the middle of a hilly 220-hectare park, shaded by hundred-year-old trees: on one side, the beautiful Mediterranean coast, on the other, the snow-capped Alps.

A *savoir-faire* in approaches and your irons are required on the way in, while a long and regular handling of your woods is necessary on the way back. Practice facilities and a pro shop are provided.

Exceptionally situated on the oldest French Riviera golf course, the hotel of Le Château de la Bégude is a member of the famous chain of Châteaux et Hotels de France. It welcomes guests from January to December in its 17th century country manor and invites you to discover one of its 35 delightful rooms, all newly renovated in Provençal style.

Enjoy the renowned restaurant, offering classic French cuisine, and its beautifully situated terrace overlooking the arrival of the ninth hole and the beginning of the tenth. Do not hesitate to inquire about the tempting golf packages which are on offer.

GOLF FACILITIES
Best season for golf: March to June and September to October.

COURSES:	LENGTH	PAR	FEES
Opio Valbonne			
	5586m	72	E44
Cannes-Mougins			
	5904m	72	E59
Saint-Donat			
	5572m	71	E45

Practice facilities; three pros available for tuition; pro shop; tournaments are arranged for guests.

Facilities key

35   60

DOMAINE DE CHÂTEAUNEUF

Hotel information

RN60
8380 Nans les Pins

Tel: +33 (0) 494 789006
Fax: +33 (0) 494 786330
Email:
chateauneufhotel@opengolfclub.com
Web: www.opengolfclub.com/ch9/

Accolades

☆☆☆☆

Airport

Marseilles: 45mins
Toulon: 1hr
Nice: 1hr 30 mins

Accommodation price guide

Accepted credit cards
AE MC DC V

Preferred tour operator

From UK
French Golf
Holidays   Tel: +44 (0) 1277 374374
From The Netherlands
Pin High Golf
Travel   Tel: +31 (0) 23561 5305

Recreational facilities

Outdoor swimming pool, golf, two tennis courts, table tennis, petanque, jogging, walking; horse riding and hunting (in season) available locally waymarked walking trails.

Meeting/business facilities

Two rooms, for up to 70 delegates.

Local attractions

Basilica of St. Maximin, the Ste Baume mountain, Aix en Provence, Marseille, Canyon of Verdon, the Calanques cliffs.

On the site of a restful stopover for Holy Land-bound pilgrims, Domaine de Châteauneuf is a picturesque 18th Century mansion, framed with greenery and standing in the foothills of La Sainte Baume at the very heart of glorious Provence.

With its finely decorated interiors, gourmet restaurant and shaded terraces, this luxurious old house induces guests to relax and to enjoy the unforgettable charms of the unhurried Provençal lifestyle. Its 30 air-conditioned rooms, including four suites, have been fully restored during 1999.

The local sightseeing round is just tremendous: the ancient city of Aix en Provence, the bustle of Marseille and its Old Port, the Notre Dame de la Garde church, the castle of If, secluded rocky coves, the La Sainte Baume Mountain, St. Maximin and its basilica are all waiting to be explored, while neighbouring producers offer enticing wine tastings.

Nearby, traditional Provençal cuisine can be savoured at Château de Nans while famed French chef Alain Ducasse has opened a new restaurant at Abbaye de la Celle to much acclaim. Visiting golfers will not wish to stray too far though, for Golf de la Sainte Baume is recognised as one of Europe's finest courses, nestling at the foot of the spectacular mountain of La Sainte Baume. What's more, a further ten courses lie within an hour's easy drive.

GOLF FACILITIES
Best season for golf: Spring and Autumn.

COURSES:	LENGTH	PAR	FEES
La Sainte Baume			
	6172m	72	E32-42
Barbaroux			
	6367m	72	E35-45
Saint Endréol			
	6219m	72	E42-51

Driving range (10 covered, 20 uncovered); tuition packages available, tournaments open to guests.

Facilities key

30   70

DOMAINE DE DIVONNE

Hotel information

Avenue des Thermes
F - 01220 Divonne-les-Bains

Tel: +33 (0) 4 50 40 34 34
Fax: +33 (0) 4 50 40 34 24
Email: info@domaine-de-divonne.com
Web: www.domaine-de-divonne.com

Accolades

☆☆☆☆ De Luxe
Member of Leading Hotels of the World

Airport

Geneva International Airport: 15 mins

Accommodation price guide

Accepted credit cards
AE DC MC V

Recreational facilities

Three tennis courts, outdoor heated swimming pool in summer, fitness club (sauna, Jacuzzi, gym); archery, mountain bikes, riding, hiking, excursions; casino and night club with 355 slot machines and traditional games; watersports on Lakes Geneva and Divonne; downhill and cross country ski; all winter sports.

Meeting/business facilities

17 meeting rooms, for up to 250 people and free access to a business centre.

Local attractions

Lake Geneva and Lake Léman cruises; Geneva - old town and United Nations; cheesemaking in Gruyères; classical music festival in June; wineries in France and Switzerland; Château de Coppet; Chamonix and the Aiguille du Midi; helicopter flights around Mont Blanc; Lausanne, Montreux.

Situated in France on the Swiss border, facing the dramatic Mont Blanc panorama and just 15 kilometres north of Geneva, the Domaine de Divonne enjoys an outstanding locating and agreeable climate, in which the invigorating air of the French Jura is softened by nearby Lake Geneva.

The Domaine's grounds cover five hectares in the centre of the charming village of Divonne-les-Bains, with its famous Sunday food and flea market.

The Grand Hôtel is made up of two buildings, the main one dating from 1931. A recent renovation has carefully respected the original art déco style, and the Domaine de Divonne now comprises the golf course, the Grand Hôtel, with 135 deluxe rooms and suites (all providing air-conditioning plus internet access), a choice of five restaurants and a casino, allowing it to fulfil its vocation as a tourist complex for an international clientele.

The 18-hole golf course was one of the first ever created in France, back in 1932. Set in undulating grounds and featuring many outstanding trees, this highly characteristic championship course is one of France's most attractive, commanding views across the French Alps and Mont Blanc.

Guests have free access to the casino, with its 355 slot machines, blackjack and roulette, and can dance until late at the nightclub. The Domaine's extremely easy access makes it an ideal weekend destination.

GOLF FACILITIES

Best season for golf: March to October.

COURSES:	LENGTH	PAR	FEES
Domaine de Divonne			
	6030m	72	E23-46
Bonmont			
	5855m	71	E57
Domaine Imperial			
	6297m	72	E57

Two pros; equipment rental available; several golf courses in France and Switzerland in the area between Geneva and Lausanne, with which golf tours can be organised.

Facilities key

135   250

GOLF-HÔTEL DE SEIGNOSSE

Hotel information

Avenue du Belvedere
40510 Seignosse

Tel: +33 (0) 5 58 41 68 30
Fax: +33 (0) 5 58 41 58 31
Email: golfseignosse@wanadoo.fr
Web: www.golfseignosse.com

Accolades

☆☆☆ hotel, ☆☆☆☆ golf,
Member of Best Western, Best Golf
Course in France 1996 – ABTOF.

Airport

Biarritz Parme: 30 mins

Accommodation price guide

Accepted credit cards
AE DC MC V

Preferred tour operator

From UK
French Golf
Holidays   Tel: +44 (0) 1277 374 374
From Netherlands
Pin High
Golf Travel Tel: +31 (0) 2356 15305
From Sweden
Birdie Golf
Tour   Tel: +46 (0) 831 01 99

Recreational facilities

18-hole golf course, outdoor swimming
pool, riding, tennis, aqua park, beach
and surfing locally.

Meeting/business facilities

One room, for up to 30 delegates.

Local attractions

The beautiful Basque country, Landes
forests, the Pyrenees mountains, miles of
spectacular surfing beaches.

Unquestionably one of Europe's finest golf
resorts, the peerless reputation of the Golf-
Hôtel Seignosse comes from both its setting, in the
beautiful Landes, just north of Biarritz, and its
superb championship golf course, designed by the
eminent American architect Robert Van Hagge.

Rated the best course in France by British golf
tour operators and 15th best in Europe by *Golf
World* magazine, Seignosse is a famous modern
masterpiece. Threading its way through pine trees
and cork-oaks, over steeply undulating terrain and
past daunting water hazards, the layout takes
players through magnificent virgin woodland.

This is France's best golfing region, and keen
golfers will purchase the 'Golf Pass Biarritz', giving
access to four other top courses in the area: Moliets,
Biarritz le Phare, Arcangues and Bassussarry.

Built to a striking design in traditional Louisiana
style, the adjoining hotel furnishes fine views over
the golf course and glimpses of the Atlantic Ocean
in the distance. The 45 comfortable rooms offer
every modern convenience, and the popular
restaurant specialises in the distinctive local cuisine
of the Basque country.

If you are looking for a complete change, try this
unspoilt corner on the hospitable coastline of South
West France – it's hard to beat.

GOLF FACILITIES

Best season for golf: April to
November.

COURSE	LENGTH	PAR	FEES
Seignosse			
	6124m	72	E26-49
Moliets			
	6172m	73	E34-50
Biarritz Le Phare			
	5379m	69	E34-52

Covered driving range and putting
green on-site, 20 per cent discount
at local courses; international
amateur tournament.

Facilities key

45   30

HÔTEL DU GOLF DE CHANTACO

Hotel information

Route d'Ascain
64500 St. Jean de Luz

Tel: +33 (0) 5 5926 1476
Fax: +33 (0) 5 5926 3597
Email: resa@hotel-chantaco.com
Web: www.hotel-chantaco.com

Accolades

☆☆☆☆

Airport

Biarritz: 10 mins
Pau: 1 hr
Bordeaux: 2 hrs

Accommodation price guide

€

Accepted credit cards
AE MC V DC

Recreational facilities

Golf, swimming pool, tennis.

Meeting/business facilities

Three rooms, for up to 80 delegates.

Local attractions

Atlantic beaches, the Pyrénées, casino.

Standing amid the open green spaces of the glorious Basque countryside next to an oftimes lauded championship golf course, the charming Hôtel de Chantaco has been welcoming honoured guests since 1930 with its magical setting and delightful atmosphere. Beautifully decorated rooms and suites provide gracious accommodations, while the finest modern French cuisine can be savoured, whether by the splendid open fireplace or on the shady patio looking out on flower-filled gardens.

The Golf de Chantaco's world-renowned master pro, Jean Garaïalde, is on hand to offer tuition to guests at preferential rates while the 18-hole course, laid out in 1928 by Harry Colt, takes every advantage of the magnificent Pyrénéean backdrop.

This golf course, pride of the Pays Basque comprises two sections: nine holes set in a forest-fringed valley, and a further nine featuring outstanding water obstacles. The course is remarkable for the sheer variety of trees with which it is lined – including maritime, Parasol and Nordmann pines, Douglas firs and a number of rare species, providing an ambience of serenity away from the cares of the outside world.

It is this wonderful setting and the superb play of the course which explains why it is so often chosen to host major international tournaments including, most notably, the French Open.

GOLF FACILITIES
Best season for golf: Spring and Autumn.

COURSES:	LENGTH	PAR	FEES
Golf de Chantaco			
	5722m	70	E32-41
Golf de la Nivelle			
	5590m	70	E27-40
Golf d'Arcangues			
	6142m	72	E35-46
Golf de Bassussary			
	6176m	72	E32-44

Professional golf tuition available; guests can play in some tournaments.

Facilities key

23   80

HÔTEL DU GOUVERNEUR

Hotel information

Chateau Du Breuil
F - 01390 Monthieux

Tel: +33 (0) 4 72 26 42 00
Fax: +33 (0) 4 72 26 42 20
Email: info@golfgouverneur.fr
Web: www.golfgouverneur.fr

Accolades

☆☆☆☆
Golf and hotel recommended by Relais
du Golf (PGA Europe)

Airport

Lyon Satolas: 30 mins

Accommodation price guide

Accepted credit cards
AE MC V DC

Recreational facilities

Golf, swimming pool, tennis, billiards,
table tennis; fly-fishing centre with black
bass; riding, shooting and fishing
arranged locally.

Meeting/business facilities

Six rooms, for up to 200 delegates.

Local attractions

Medieval city of Perouges; the Beaujolais
wine district; Lyon 30 minutes away;
Dombes circuit and Natural Birds
Regional Park.

The motto of the Hotel & Golf du Gouverneur is "Let pleasure govern". Amidst the protected environment of the Dombes, Le Gouverneur's 235 hectares are home to the largest golf resort in the Rhone-Alpes region.

Beginners and experienced players alike will enjoy the 18-hole courses spreading amongst the lakes, trees and hills. In addition, the site avails of a driving range on water, another on grass, two putting greens, one chipping green, a nine-hole beginner's course and the training centre run by Corinne Soules, four-times national champion and once world team vice-champion.

Le Gouverneur has the distinction of being a Relais du Golf (Officially Recommended Hotel and Resort of the PGA of Europe). Everyone here can fulfill their expectations, whatever they may be: the junior club for children, the clubhouse in a 14th Century castle, the fly-fishing centre, the tennis court, the swimming pool and the shady summer terrace, a well-stocked pro shop, public rooms finely panelled in burr-poplar, with billiards, chessboards and bridge tables. The traditional restaurant, La Table d'Antigny, adds the final note to make Le Gouverneur a paradise for all.

GOLF FACILITIES

Best season for golf: Mid-March to
Mid-November.

COURSES:	LENGTH	PAR	FEES
Le Breuil			
	6578m	72	E50
Montaplan			
	5880m	71	E50
Bresse			
	6177m	72	E45

Six of Germany's most beautiful courses
within 20 kilometres.

Facilities key

53 200

HÔTEL DU PALAIS

Hotel information

1 Avenue de l'Impératrice
F - 64200 Biarritz

Tel: +33 (0) 5 59 41 64 00
Fax: +33 (0) 5 59 41 67 99
Email: manager@hotel-du-palais.com
Web: www.hotel-du-palais.com

Accolades

★★★★☆

Airport

Biarritz: 15 mins
Funtarrabia (Spain): 45 mins

Accommodation price guide

Accepted credit cards
AE MC V DC

Preferred tour operator

From UK
The Leading Hotels
of the World   Freefone 0800 181 123
Concorde
Hotels   Freefone 0800 181 591
From USA & Canada
The Leading Hotels
of the World   Toll free 1-800 223 6800

 AMERICAN EXPRESS OFFER

For advance booking on American
Express Card you receive a **15%
discount on rack rate**.

Quote 'Great Golf Hotels offer' when you book.

Empress Eugénie, wife of Napoleon III, persuaded her husband to build a palace in Biarritz, the scene of her childhood holidays. Season after season, Villa Eugénie entertained most of Europe's royalty and nobility. Its illustrious clientele were not put off by the deposition of Napoleon III and the transformation of the palace into the Hotel du Palais. Guests subsequently included Queen Victoria and Edward VII. Suffice to say that the hotel's standards have not fallen since then.

With ten 18-hole golf courses in the area, Biarritz is famous as the beachhead of golf in the south-west, its Atlantic breezes providing a good climate for greens. The century-old Phare course is situated in the heart of the town. Amateurs will find all they need in the Ilbarritz International Golf Centre.

Biarritz's reputation, of course, goes before it. Since the 1920s, writers, painters and film-goers have turned the town into a fashionable place to go. Spring comes early in the year, but summer is cooled off by the sea breeze, autumn warmed by the south winds and winter tempered by the Gulf Stream. The more energetic will be attracted by Biarritz's reputation for surfing. It is also a centre for traditional Basque sports.

Recreational facilities

Private heated seawater swimming pool with direct access to beach; sauna, fitness club; hairdresser, boutique; gardens.

Meeting/business facilities

Seven meeting rooms, for 15-250 delegates.

Local attractions

Walks to the Rocher de la Vierge –'The White Madonna' – and the unusual Musée de la Mer; the picturesque village of Saint-Jean-de-Luz is 20 km away and San Sebastian is 40 km, just over the Spanish border.

GOLF FACILITIES
Best season for golf: All year round.

COURSES:	LENGTH	PAR	FEES
Biarritz Le Phare			
	5379m	69	E44-66
Anglet Chiberta			
	5901m	70	E48-66
Golf de Arcangues			
	6092m	72	E44-60
Golf De Bassussarry			
	6176m	72	E46-60
Golf De Chantaco			
	5722m	70	E52-68
Golf De La Nivelle			
	5587m	70	E46-54

All courses have shop, equipment hire, practice facilities, putting green, restaurant and club cars; the international golf training centre of Ilbarritz looks out over the sea.

Facilities key

156   250

RELAIS DE MARGAUX HOTEL

Hotel information

Chemin de L'Ile Vincent
33460
Margaux
France

Tel: +33 (0) 557 88 38 30
Fax: +33 (0) 557 88 31 73
Email: relais-margaux@relais-margaux.fr
Web: www.relais-margaux.fr

Accolades

☆☆☆☆ Luxe

Airport

Bordeaux: 35 mins

Accommodation price guide

Accepted credit cards
AE DC MC V

Preferred tour operator

From UK
Golf Par
Excellence   Tel: +44 (0) 1737 721 1818
From Germany
Classic Golf
Tours   Tel: +49 (0) 6109 30 99 60
From Switzerland
Fert   Tel: +41 (0) 22 7304 751
From Holland
Label
Travel   Tel: +31 (0) 20 646 3656

Recreational facilities

Swimming pool, tennis court, driving range, putting green/approach, billiards; large riverside park, sun terrace; two 18 hole courses locally; beach 45 minutes.

Meeting/business facilities

Seven rooms for up to 350 delegates

Local attractions

Touring world-renowned wine châteaux; Bordeaux's 18th Century architecture.

The four-star de luxe Relais de Margaux is situated in the heart of the famous Médoc vineyards, alongside the River Gironde, just 30 minutes from historic Bordeaux and only 15 minutes from the Golf du Médoc with its two fine 18 hole courses, the Les Châteaux and Les Vignes.

The hotel has 59 comfortable rooms and five suites, all with a cosy Bordeaux-style décor. The gastronomic restaurant and the hotel bar, with its mellow stone walls, are situated in one of the ancient wine cellars of the world-renowned Château Margaux. The pleasant terraces allow guests to savour the peace and quiet of the 55-hectare park while there are swimming pool, driving range, putting green and approach and tennis court facilities on site.

Many world-famous wine châteaux are just minutes away – Château Mouton Rothschild, for instance, is an easy 15 minutes drive. Reservations can be made for châteaux visits and wine tastings.

With its lofty philosophy of "the art of living", the Relais de Margaux provides an accomplished blend of a prestigious past and all the modern facilities of a top-class hotel.

GOLF FACILITIES
Best season for golf: All year round.

COURSES:	LENGTH	PAR	FEES
Golf de Médoc Châteaux			
	6316m	71	E42
Golf de Lacanau			
	5932m	72	E37
Golf de Médoc Vignes			
	6220m	71	E42

Two courses in Médoc wine country, 15 minutes' drive; 18 and nine hole courses close to ocean – 45 minutes away.

Facilities key

64   350

FRANCE: NORTH *Vive la golf revolution!*

Get an Eiffel of this!

For many years the game was only to be found in those seaside spas favoured by the well-off and well-connected. But recently, golf in France has undergone a revolution. Spurred on by domestic interest and the lure of tourist income, courses sprouted throughout the country, with those in the northern regions prospering through their ease of access from Britain and the low countries.

There are now more than 500 courses in France, many in resort areas, designed for holiday visitors. Whether seaside or parkland with château, being mostly new the courses are of good quality and normally not overcrowded, especially midweek. Green fees are reasonable and, as one would expect in France, clubhouse dining can be of a very high standard. Good for small groups and families.

NEW DEVELOPMENTS

● Golf in France now boasts probably the best organsiation to aid the visiting player. 'France Golf International' – an initiative of the French Tourist Office and the French Golf Federation – ensures adequate quality of courses, facilities and multi-lingual reception.
● The 125 approved clubs are promoted internationally and an annual guide book and map of all participating courses are available free from the Maison de la France.

CLIMATE

Northern France has a variable climate, especially near the Channel. Head south for the Loire Valley or Burgundy and things get progressively warmer.

Sample point: Paris

RECOMMENDED CAR HIRE — Hertz

UK: +44 (0) 870 848 4848
Germany: +49 (0) 180 533 3535
Website: www.hertz.com

Price guide €

| Round of golf | | Golf balls | |
| Small beer | | 4/5 star hotel room | |

CONTACT

French Tourist Board, Maison de la France, 8 Avenue de L'Opéra, 75001 Paris
Tel: +33 (0) 1 42 66 26 28 Fax: +33 (0) 1 49 24 96 56

The most up-to-date golf travel information is always at www.golftravel4u.com

The rich variety of its landscape, its fascinatingly complex history, its art, its cultural and its gastronomic tradition have all helped make France by far and away the world's leading tourism destination.

With less than 55 million inhabitants in a country more than twice the size of the UK there's room to breath here and the whole country is geared to sports, leisure and the good things in life.

GETTING THERE France's world-leading network of TGV high speed trains, efficient regional airports, autoroutes and main roads all help make it the most accessible of countries. Paris Roissy Charles De Gaulle is one of the great international airports, supplemented by Orly and Le Bourget, while the local airports at Lille, Le Touquet and Beauvais are useful to visiting golfers.

APRÈS GOLF They say the English eat to live but the French live to eat – and it's true, but restaurants close early. For value stick to the fixed price set menus. By the Channel go for the wonderful fish dishes, accompanied by the good local beers. And in Burgundy the world's greatest white wines and some of the best reds are happily married to classic French cuisine at its finest.

OFF THE COURSE In north and central France you will find peaceful countryside, a relaxed and unhurried way of life and a rich culture and sense of history. There are family diversions too, such as Disney World Europe and the Asterix theme park, while the shores of the Opal Coast offer miles of wide, firm sandy beaches.

NOT TO BE MISSED The great cathedrals at Rheims, Beauvais, Amiens, Blois; the Normandy Invasion D-Day beaches; battle sites and museums; beautiful Loire châteaux; vineyard visits (Loire, Champagne, Burgundy); the great cities: Lille, Nancy, Metz, Lyons, St. Etienne, Clermont Ferrand; the Franco/Germanic cultural mix of Alsace.

FACTS AND FIGURES

● **The northern coast of France is the world's oldest holiday golf destination. The British have been visiting to play golf for more than 100 years, firstly at Dinard (1887), then Le Touquet (1904) and Wimereux (1907).**
● **'18 Holes & 18 Chefs' is an annual competition at Golf de St. Jean-de-Monts, where local culinary experts prepare specialities for competitors beside each green.**

Favourite fairways

1 CHAMP DE BATAILLE

Relatively unknown but a positive delight. From the majestic chateau/clubhouse, the course wanders through a centuries-old protected forest where tall pines give way to vivid banks of rhododendrons and other flowering shrubs. Strategic lakes along a wooded valley add interest.
Par 72   Length 5600m
27110 Le Neubourg
Tel: +33 (0) 2 3235 0372
Fax: +33 (0) 2 3235 8310

2 LES GOLFS D'HARDELOT

Two courses, Pines (1931) and Dunes (1990), contrast two different eras of golf architecture. The Pines course is a classic by Tom Simpson, with well-placed hazards and subtle greens. The Dunes is hilly, with a number of doglegs and blind shots.
Les Pins: Par 72, Length 5871m
Les Dunes: Par 73, Length 6031m
3 Avenue du Golf, 62152 Hardelot
Tel: +33 (0) 3 2183 7310
Fax: +33 (0) 3 2183 2483

3 LA BRETESCHE

Designed by a British architect, Bill Baker, and much favoured by British holiday players. This parkland course winds through a forested estate, finishing by the trademark fairytale château seemingly moored on the edge of a picturesque lake.
Par 72   Length 5809m
Domaine de la Bretesche, 44780 Missilac
Tel: +33 (0) 2 5176 8686 Fax: +33 (0) 2 4088 3628

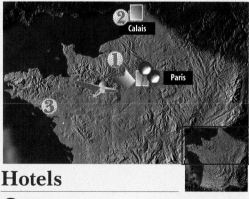
Calais
Paris

Hotels

◐ **Domaine de Roncemay**
Page 142

◐ **Domaine & Golf de Vaugouard**
Page 143

DOMAINE DU RONCEMAY

Hotel information

Château du Roncemay
F-89110
Aillant sur Tholon

Tel: +33 (0) 386 73 50 50
Fax: +33 (0) 386 73 69 46
Email: roncemay@aol.com

Accolades

☆☆☆☆

Airport

Paris Orly: 1 hr 15mins
Paris Charles de Gaulle: 1 hr 45 mins

Accommodation price guide

Accepted credit cards
AE DC MC V JCB

Recreational facilities

On-site golf course, swimming pool, tennis, fitness centre, bike rental; hammam baths opening February 2000.

Meeting/business facilities

One room, for up to 30 delegates.

Local attractions

Historic towns of Auxerre, Joigny and Sens; river cruises; visits to Chablis wineries; church and hill of Vezelay, Cistercian abbey of Fontenay (both World Heritage Sites).

Discover the calm and beauty of the Domaine du Roncemay, a large Burgundian estate amid glorious countryside close to Auxerre.

This charming hotel recreates the atmosphere of a fine 19th Century manor house, with each of its rooms decorated in its own unique style, including antique furniture and original engravings.

The Domaine du Roncemay golf course, skillfully landscaped by Jean Garaïade and Jérémy Pern, stretches out over more than 80 hectares. The plateau, often likened to Scottish links, the valley with its three lakes, and the forest fairways bordered with century-old oaks, all make Roncemay one of the top golf courses in France. Opposite the golf course, in the splendid dining rooms, with their panoramic views, or out on the terrace, guests can appreciate the original cuisine of a bold young chef while sipping a classic Burgundy wine.

The hotel's Moroccan hammam baths will open in Spring 2000. Together with the swimming pool, gym, badminton and tennis courts, they will offer guests the ideal location to tone up or just unwind.

Burgundy's immensely rich cultural, natural and gastronomic heritage holds plenty in store for the more inquisitive guest, and the area surrounding the Domaine du Roncemay entices with its interesting and diverse attractions.

GOLF FACILITIES

Best season for golf: April to October.

COURSES:	LENGTH	PAR	FEES
Domaine du Roncemay			
	6270m	72	E23-32
Domaine de Vaugouard			
	5914m	72	E26-43

Tuition packages available; practice facilities; tournaments open to guests.

Facilities key

16   30

DOMAINE & GOLF DE VAUGOUARD

Recreational facilities

Covered and floodlit tennis, swimming pool, riding school, trekking in the forest, fitness centre with sauna, golf course.

Meeting/business facilities

Seven rooms, for up to 120 delegates.

Local attractions

Châteaux of the Loire, Faiencerie de Gien; historic Auxerre and Voigny; royal towns of Orleans and Fontainebleau; Chablis vineyards; Sologne Lake and Forest natural parks.

Hotel information

Chemin des Bois
45210 Fontenay-sur-Loire

Tel: +33 (0) 2 38 89 79 00
Fax: +33 (0) 2 38 89 79 01
Email: domaine.golf.vaugouard@wanadoo.fr
Web: www.vaugouard.com

Accolades

★★★☆

Airport

Paris Orly: 45 mins
Paris Roissy-Charles de Gaulle: 1 hr 15 mins

Accommodation price guide

Accepted credit cards
AE MC V DC JCB

An hour's drive from Paris, near the glorious châteaux de la Loire, between the vineyards of Burgundy and those of the Loire, nestles Le Domaine et Golf de Vaugouard, a haven of peace and comfort. The hotel is a synthesis of the charm and character of a stylishly renovated farmhouse with all the comfort and facilities of a modern hotel. Moreover, it has its own wooded golf course, complete with well-set obstacles and a river at the beginning and at the end.

The hotel's recreational facilities extend far beyond golf: there are five tennis courts, a covered course for the hotel's own riding school and a health club with sauna facilities. The swimming pool, with its poolside grill, allows guests to combine physical exercise or relaxation with the culinary delights of traditional French cuisine. For a fuller exploration of the latter, meals are served inside the château and on the terrace, with its view of the golf course, during summer months.

The simple pleasures of exploration can be found by trekking in the forest around the hotel, or, further afield, visiting the famously beautiful châteaux of the Loire and the Faiencerie de Gien.

Charles Baudelaire could have been thinking of Vaugouard when he wrote: "There, all that is orderly, beautiful, luxurious, calm and pleasurable."

GOLF FACILITIES

Best season for golf: March to November.

COURSES:	LENGTH	PAR	FEES
Vaugouard			
	5545m	72	E29-53

Covered driving range; two putting greens; tuition available; buggy, trolley and clubhire; pro shop, many other golf courses within easy reach; practice facilities and tuition packages.

Facilities key

44   120

SCOTLAND The historic home of golf

Tartan, bagpipes, pictures of stags at bay: that's the old and hackneyed image of Scotland. Truth is that 'The Land Of The Brave' is today one of Europe's most vibrant regions, offering sophisticated shopping, a vast wealth of entertainments (you'll need to book very early if you want to attend the world-famous Edinburgh Festival, which takes place each August).

As capital of the nation, Edinburgh is jam-packed with history, from the castle perched on its rock to the Queen's Scottish residence of Holyrood House. It also has a wealth of superb restaurants and lively pubs and the famed shopping along Prince's Street.

'Second City of the Empire' during the Victorian era, Glasgow has bounced back from the doldrums to reclaim its rightful place as a truly international destination, its own proud and distinctive culture counterpointed with a truly cosmopolitan flavour.

Golfers will be most drawn though to the Borders and to the great links courses of the east and west coasts – and especially to St. Andrew's, the hallowed birthplace of the game.

GETTING THERE Edinburgh International airport is strongly networked into the rest of the UK and Europe beyond while Glasgow International offers all that plus transatlantic flights. North American visitors can also reach Scotland through Prestwick, a short drive from Glasgow.

APRÈS GOLF Though their hearty soups and stews, pies, dumplings and, wait for it, deep-fried Mars bars, make many Scots notoriously unhealthy eaters you will not have to look far for food of truly gourmet provenance. What helps, of course, is one of the world's most richly endowed larders, stocked full with game, succulent beef, fine salmon and the most exquisite raspberries in the world. Sample the vast array (more than 200) of malt whiskies.

OFF THE COURSE There are castles and stately homes to visit plus truly spectacular mountain and coastal scenery.

NOT TO BE MISSED Follow the whisky trail round the great distilleries. Walk to the top of a 'Munroe' (a peak over 600 metres). Admire Glasgow's Charles Rennie Mackintosh architectural heritage.

FACTS & FIGURES

- Golfing holidays are a growing sector for Scottish tourism, with visitors spending more than £100m each year.
- The world's largest Rolex has clocked in at Carnoustie's Golf Course Hotel and Resort. The 2.8 metre timekeeper was mounted on the front on the new £8.5m luxury hotel in April 1999.
- The quantity and quality of golf is amazing, with nearly 500 courses (around 8,500 holes), boasting the oldest golfing societies and clubs in the world as well as newer developments that maintain the peerless standards of the past.

The Links at Nairn

Scotland is the home of golf. It gave the game to the world, but a golfing holiday in 'The Land of the Brave' is as much about enjoying the country and its people as birdies and bogies. It is also about value for money, and although the game is no longer as inexpensive as it was, it will still make a far smaller dent in your pocket here than almost any other country. Golf lovers who are happy to avoid the big name courses can have a week's golf for the price of a couple of rounds in more fashionable areas.

The contrasts are also spectacular. Where else in the world could you play the most famous of venue, the Old Course at St Andrews, where just about every great player in the game has walked over the ancient Swilcan Bridge, and the following day retreat to the Highlands where the sheep trim the fairways and an honesty box is left out to collect the modest green fees?

With diversity like this in an area where there are nearly 500 courses, the real problem is being spoiled for choice. But this is the ultimate destination for those who want to devise their own itinerary and combine the great championship links with humbler nine-hole layouts in a wide diversity of enjoyable settings.

Those who watched the 1999 Open at Carnoustie know the ferocious challenge that Scottish golf can offer, but as Ryder Cup assistant captain Sam Torrance explained: "For me, Scotland is still, and always will be, the greatest place in the world to play golf. Apart from the fact that it is recognised as the historical home of the game, I can think of no other country where you can find so many coursees of such high quality, variety and accessibility, all within such a comparatively small area."

Battling the elements is an integral part of golf in these parts, though surprisingly it doesn't rain in Scotland nearly as much people suppose, with the north and east comparing well with the driest parts of England. The high latitude means summer evenings stretching to after midnight in the north, with visibility generally good in Scotland compared with more industrialised nations.

NEW DEVELOPMENTS

- Golf continues to be a vital part of Scotland's tourist industry, with more famous courses per square kilometre than any other part of the world.
- Golf Pass Scotland offers three- to five-day golf in some of the most scenic parts of Scotland from only £7.50 per round. There are various discounts in all areas. For information on Golf Pass Scotland call +44 (0) 990 133 206.
- Since April 1999 Gleneagles' golf courses have been open to visiting players, companies and private individuals alike.
- 'Welcome golfer' – an intitative from the Scottish Tourist Board – is aimed at increasing golf club access to vistors and offering extra facilities such as drying areas and storage for clubs.

Hotels

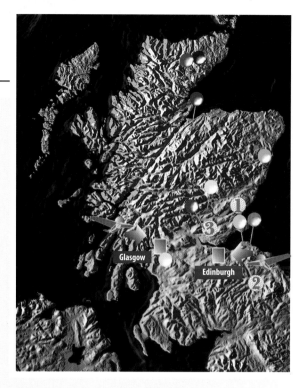

RECOMMENDED CAR HIRE

UK: +44 (0) 870 848 4848
Germany: +49 (0) 180 533 3535
Website: www.hertz.com

Favourite fairways

① CARNOUSTIE

Who would dare challenge Carnoustie's Championship Course after watching the demise of Jean van de Velde in the 1999 Open? When the wind is blowing, anyone who stands on the 15th tee needing four pars to win the championship fully deserves the trophy. There are three 18-hole courses, the Championship Course, Burnside Course and Buddon Links.
Par 75   Length 6347m (Championship Course)
Carnoustie Golf Links, Links Parade, Carnoustie DD7 7JE
Tel: +44 (0) 1241 853789   Fax: +44 (0) 1241 852720

② ROXBURGHE

A top class golf course created in the grounds of Sunlaws House Hotel by The Duke of Roxburghe and designed by Dave Thomas to attract the low handicapper seeking a challenge and the less talented who wants to enjoy a round in the beautiful Borders countryside.
Par 73   Length 6283m
Sunlaws House Hotel, Heiton, Kelso, TD5 8JZ
Tel: +44 (0) 1573 450331   Fax: +44 (0) 1573 450611

③ GLENEAGLES HOTEL GOLF COURSES

Gleneagles offers two moorland 18 hole courses, and a third parkland course – a golfing haven that prompted Lee Trevino to say: "If Heaven's like this, I sure hope they have a tee time left." Now non hotel residents can play the course, and rounds vary from £55 to £100.
Monarchs course designed by Jack Nicklaus: Par 74, Length 6474m
Gleneagles Hotel Golf Courses, Auchterarder PH3 1NF,
Tel: +44 (0) 1764 662231   Fax: +44 (0) 1764 662134

④ CARNEGIE GOLF LINKS

In 1992 this became the first links to be built in Britain for over half a century. It blends perfectly with a majestic Highland setting, magnified by the clear, northern light. Membership confers use of the incomparable Skibo Castle.
Designed by Donald Steel, Par 72, Length 6100m
Skibo Castle, Dornoch, Sutherland IV25 3RQ
Tel: +44 (0) 1542 832236   Fax: +44 (0) 1542 894601

⑤ CRUDEN BAY

The embodiment of the seaside links, on this stretch of the Aberdeenshire coastline the dunes contain a turbulent air and all the holes are a test of adaptability and ingenuity.
Designed by Tom Morris and Archie Simpson: Par 72, Length 5848m
Aulton Road, Cruden Bay, Peterhead, Aberdeenshire, AB2 7NN
Tel: +44 (0) 1799 812285   Fax: +44 (0) 1799 812945

The most up-to-date golf travel information is always at www.golftravel4u.com

CLIMATE

Very long summer evenings make a midnight round feasible on northern courses. Even in deepest winter, Scotland often enjoys surprisingly mild weather, though it's often dull and damp and gets dark early.

MM 100

J F M A M J J A S O N D

J F M A M J J A S O N D

Sample point: Edinburgh

Price guide €

Round of golf	💶💶💶	Golf balls	💶💶💶💶	
Small beer	💶💶	4/5 star hotel room	💶💶💶	

CONTACT

Scottish Tourist Board, Thistle House, Beechwood Park North, Inverness, IV2 3ED
Tel: +44 (0) 1463 716 996 Fax: +44 (0) 1463 717 266

BALBIRNIE HOUSE

Hotel information

Balbirnie Park
Markinch Village
By Glenrothes
Fife
KY7 6NE

Tel: +44 (0) 1592 610066
Fax: +44 (0) 1592 610529
Email: balbirnie@btinternet.com
Web: www.balbirnie.co.uk

Accolades

☆☆☆☆ AA
1998 Golf International Hotel of the Year
Macallan Taste of Scotland Hotel of the Year
RAC Blue Ribbon

Airport

Fife: 5 mins
Edinburgh: 30 mins
Glasgow: 1 hr

Accommodation price guide

Accepted credit cards
AE DC MC V

The three keys to a great golfing break? Location! Location! Location! – and Balbirnie scores on all three counts, being set in the very heartland of golf past and present. Voted 'Golf International Hotel of the Year', Balbirnie is a unique destination, with a superb parkland course right on its doorstep.

With more than 100 courses located within an hour, including, just a half hour away, St. Andrews – "the home of golf" – Balbirnie can spoil its guests with a choice factor which also applies to the other amenities provided by this delightful Grade A listed and privately owned and managed 30-bedroom house, set in its own 160-hectare country estate.

Views from the house extend over natural hillocks and flowing vistas to Balbirnie Park Golf Course, an undulating and scenic par 71 challenge which was recently awarded nine out of ten by the prestigious *Golf Monthly* magazine.

The many fine courses of Fife are easily accessible, including Leven Links, Lundin Links, Elie, Crail and Ladybank. Those looking for the ultimate need only drive for 45 minutes, crossing the River Tay to find the wonderful Carnoustie, possibly the hardest golfing test of them all. Back at the hotel, delicious cuisine, fine wines and comfortable lounges and bedrooms await returning players to complete the perfect day.

Recreational facilities

Gardens, craft centre, croquet, woodland walks, snooker; luxury guided tours and falconry demonstrations arranged.

Meeting/business facilities

Eight rooms, for up to 250 delegates.

Local attractions

Falkland Palace, Scone Palace, Glamis Castle, Stirling Castle, Edinburgh Castle, the Royal Yacht Britannia, Bannockburn battle site.

GOLF FACILITIES
Best season for golf: All year round, perfect from March to November.

COURSES:	LENGTH	PAR	FEES
Balbirnie Park	5589m	71	£23
St. Andrews Old	6300m	72	£72
Carnoustie	6350m	72	£57

Buggies available; practice facilities locally; host of Scottish Tartan Tour.

Facilities key

30   250

CULLODEN HOUSE HOTEL

Hotel information

Culloden
Inverness
IV2 7BZ

Tel: +44 (0) 1463 790461
Fax: +44 (0) 1463 792181
Email: info@cullodenhouse.co.uk
Web: www.cullodenhouse.co.uk

Accolades

✩✩✩✩ AA & STB
Two rosettes for food
Taste of Scotland

Airport

Inverness Dalcross: 10 mins
Glasgow: 3 hrs
Edinburgh: 2 hrs 50 mins

Accommodation price guide

Accepted credit cards
AE DC MC V JCB Delta Switch

Preferred tour operator

From UK
Golf
International Tel: +44 (0) 1292 313388
Golf
Scotland   Tel: +44 (0) 1292 478772
From Germany
Airtours   Tel: +49 (0) 69 79280
From USA
Grasshopper Tel: +1 630 858 1660

Recreational facilities

Tennis, badminton, boules, croquet on site; horse riding, fishing, shooting available locally.

Meeting/business facilities

Three rooms, for up to 60 delegates; teleconferencing, fax and internet.

Local attractions

Bonnie Prince Charlie's 1746 Culloden Battlefield (ended the '45 Rebellion), Fort George, Caledonian Canal, Loch Ness, whisky distillery tours.

Lauded in *The Scottish Highlands Hidden Gems Golf Experience*, delightful Culloden House is a gracious Palladian mansion where princes past and present have enjoyed an ambience which is in a class of its own. Here, traditional Scottish Highland hospitality has been elevated to an art form without having become too formal, stuffy or reserved.

With a number of world-renowned championship courses close by – 35 within a 45-minute drive – golfers are made especially welcome. The respected *Gourmet* magazine put it well: "It isn't like a hotel at all, but more like being a guest in someone's home."

Arriving here you could be forgiven for thinking you had strayed into a majestic private house. Culloden House was designed and built by the near-genius architect John Adam, incorporating the original fortified residence used by Bonnie Prince Charlie on the eve of his fateful battle on Culloden Moor. The bedrooms are all individually furnished, many featuring four-poster beds.

Eating here is a real event and highlights the very finest of fresh and smoked Scottish produce, exquisitely prepared and presented by an award-winning chef to provide the essence of local cuisine with an inspired Continental touch. A cellar stocked with more than 120 wines, plus more than 30 local malt whiskies, complements the cuisine.

GOLF FACILITIES

Best season for golf: February to December.

COURSES:	LENGTH	PAR	FEES
Royal Durnoch			
	6106m	72	£60
Nairn Championship			
	6135m	72	£60
Fort Rose			
	5858m	71	£24

Two net driving tees, pitching area; tuition available (minimum two people); 35 golf courses within a 45-minute drive.

Facilities key

28   60

KINLOCH HOUSE HOTEL

Hotel information

By Blairgowrie
Perthshire
PH10 6SG

Tel: +44 (0) 1250 884 237
Fax: +44 (0) 1250 884 333
Email: reservations@kinlochhouse.com
Web: www.kinlochhouse.com

Accolades

☆☆☆ (Red) AA ☆☆☆☆☆ STB
Three AA rosettes

Airport

Edinburgh: 1 hr 30 mins
Glasgow: 1 hr 30 mins

Accommodation price guide

Accepted credit cards
AE MC V DC

AMERICAN EXPRESS OFFER

For nearly 20 years, Kinloch House Hotel has been taking care of its discerning guests golfing requirements. Nestled in beautiful grounds, situated in the heart of sporting Perthshire and only 90 minutes from Edinburgh, Glasgow and Aberdeen, Kinloch House is uniquely placed to provide a complete yet varied golfing experience, having 30 golf courses within an hour's drive.

This magnetic appeal is coupled with a critically acclaimed three-rosette dining room, with daily changing menu. Beautifully appointed rooms, a health and fitness centre and other amenities also ensure this is a perfect venue for a golfing break.

A sportman's room, complete with full drying and storage facilities, plus attentive personal service makes this red star hotel an essential port of call for golfing visitors to Scotland.

Full golfing intineries can be arranged, including transportation, the booking of tee-off times, tuition and club hire. The fact that 85 per cent of guests return time and again underlines that this is an experience not to be missed.

Recreational facilities

Fully maintained Victorian walled garden; mountain bikes, sail boat, coarse fishing, croquet, walks; health and fitness facilities including spa bath, swimming pool, sauna, steam room, multi-gym and masseuse (by arrangement).

Meeting/business facilities

One room, for up to 16 delegates; secretarial services, overhead projector, flipchart.

Local attractions

Scotland's great East Coast courses all within easy reach; Balmoral and Royal Deeside; St. Andrews, Dundee and Aberdeen.

GOLF FACILITIES

Best season for golf: Spring, Summer and Autumn.

COURSES:	LENGTH	PAR	FEES
Rosemount/Blairgowrie			
	6588m	72	£50
Landsdown/Blairgowrie			
	6802m	72	£40
Alyth			
	6205m	71	£25

30 golf courses within one hour's drive; tuition; club hire.

Facilities key

20 16

LETHAM GRANGE RESORT

Hotel information

Letham Grange Resort
"Carnoustie Country"
Colliston
By Arbroath
Angus
DD11 4RL

Tel: +44 (0) 1241 890373
Fax: +44 (0) 1241 890725
Email: lethamgrange@sol.co.uk
Web: www.lethamgrange.co.uk

Accolades

✩✩✩✩ AA, RAC, STB
Taste of Scotland
One of Scotland's Hotels of Distinction

Airport

Dundee: 30 mins
Aberdeen: 1 hr
Edinburgh: 1 hr 30 mins
Glasgow: 2 hrs

Accommodation price guide

Accepted credit cards
AE MC V DC

AMERICAN EXPRESS OFFER

For advance booking on American Express Card you receive **ten per cent off rack rate plus room upgrade when available, or ten per cent off Eagle Golf packages.**

Quote 'Great Golf Hotels offer' when you book.

At the very heart of Carnoustie country, Letham Grange is a charming superbly restored Victorian castle-like mansion, which offers golfing guests the very best of Scottish history and tradition.

Elegant sculpted ceilings, rich oak panelled lounges and dining rooms are supported by the most modern of facilities and skilled professional management to enhance the joy of country style living on a sporting estate which boasts two magnificent golf courses, earning it the well deserved appellation "The Augusta of Scotland".

The mansion's elegant bedrooms have been individually designed to reflect the charm of traditional country living, but there are also modern bedrooms on the estate – perfect for golfing parties seeking comfort, privacy and a quiet retreat. Some of the bedrooms have direct views of and access to the fairways.

The hotel's award-winning chef specialises in preparing Scotland's richly endowed national larder – salmon, venison, Angus beef, fresh local lobsters and seafood included – to create traditional and international dishes which are served in the luxurious Rosehaugh restaurant, while lighter meals can be enjoyed in the Conservatory.

In winter Letham Grange is Scotland's favourite ice curling centre and features the world's most chandilered indoor rink for the sport.

Letham Grange's appeal is strong at all four seasons and golfers can play year round.

Recreational facilities

Two 18-hole championship golf courses on-site, golf academy; croquet lawn, indoor curling rink; country estate with wildlife, lake and streams; swimming pool, tennis, fishing, sailing and Carnoustie golf course nearby.

Meeting/business facilities

Six rooms, for up to 300 delegates (summer), 40 (winter).

Local attractions

Beautiful rugged coastline; easy access to Highlands; shopping in Dundee; salmon fishing; castles; distillery visits.

GOLF FACILITIES

Best season for golf: May to mid-October

COURSES	LENGTH	PAR	FEES
Letham Grange Old			
	6240m	73	£35
Letham Grange Glens			
	5324m	68	£20
Carnoustie			
	6426m	71	£62

Practice driving range, bunkers, putting greens, tuition packages; hotel course was site for Peter Allis BBC TV golf tuition series; host course for Scottish Amateur Championships 2000. Some 60 courses within 60 minutes. Hotel residents receive 30 per cent discount on hotel-owned courses.

Facilities key

44 400

THE LINKS

Hotel information

Mid Links
Montrose
Angus
DD10 8RL

Tel: +44 (0) 1674 671 000
Fax: +44 (0) 1674 672 698
Email:
reception@merproleisure.demon.co.uk

Accolades

⭐⭐⭐ AA, member of Best Western

Airport

Aberdeen: 45 mins
Edinburgh International: 2 hrs
Glasgow International: 2 hrs

Accommodation price guide

Accepted credit cards
AE   DC   MC   V

Preferred tour operator

From UK
Alliance   Tel: +44 (0) 1674 671 000

Recreational facilities

Jazz club, night club in hotel; cycling, walking; stalking, shooting and salmon fishing can be arranged locally.

Meeting/business facilities

Two rooms, for up to 120 delegates.

Local attractions

House of Dun, Montrose Museum, Basin Wildlife Centre, Carnoustie, Fettercairn, Glamis Castle, whisky distillery trail.

Gloriously situated in the heart of Scotland's near-legendary golfing country, the Links Hotel is a fine Edwardian townhouse, with all 25 of its guest rooms decorated and appointed to the very highest standards.

Dining, both informal and formal, is superb, with the restaurant offering a highly inventive *à la carte* menu and a fixed price set dinner option, created using only the very finest of Scotland's bounteous fresh produce.

With a setting just minutes away from the excellent and suitably challenging Montrose Medal Course – the ninth oldest golfing venue in the world – the location of the Links Hotel allows its guests to thoroughly enjoy the splendour of more than 50 golf courses within a 45-minute drive, all of them matching spectacular views to their individual playing characteristics.

Arguably the king of them all is Carnoustie, venue of the 1999 Open Golf Championships, with its superlative links challenge.

GOLF FACILITIES

Best season for golf: April to October.

COURSES:	LENGTH	PAR	FEES
Montrose Medal			
	6000m	72	£30
Edzell			
	5900m	71	£26
Carnoustie			
	6326m	75	£70
Letham Grange			
	6200m	73	£32
Arbroath			
	5600m	70	£20
Forfar			
	5700m	70	£22

Tuition and golf packages available; reception staff will assist guests with golf bookings and tee-off times; buggies for hire.

Facilities key

25   120

THE LINKS & ROYAL MARINE HOTELS

Hotel information

Golf Road
Brora
Sutherland KW9 6QS

Tel: +44 (0) 1408 621252
Fax: +44 (0) 1408 621181
Email: highlandescape@btinternet.com
Web: www.highlandescape.com

Accolades

☆☆☆☆ Scottish Tourist Board
Taste of Scotland member
One AA rosette

Airport

Inverness: 1 hr 15 mins

Accommodation price guide

Accepted credit cards
AE DC MC V

Local attractions

Salmon and trout fishing; beaches, hill walking; seal colonies, dolphin watching; Dunrobin Castle, Clynelish and Glenmorangie Whisky Distilleries.

A mid stunningly wild and spectacular Highland scenery, a warm welcome awaits in the village of Brora at The Links and Royal Marine hotels.

The Links Hotel overlooks James Braid's famous 18-hole links course, whilst the Royal Marine sits at the mouth of the River Brora close by.

The Royal Marine is a family-run hotel offering traditional Highland hospitality, a fully-equipped leisure centre and an AA-rosette awarded restaurant. The Links Hotel additionally offers luxury Links View Apartments in its grounds, and its Seaforth restaurant uses the very best of local produce and seafood to create memorable dishes.

With the challenging Brora course just steps away, and Royal Dornoch, Golspie and Tain courses easily reached, golfing guests are spoilt for choice.

Meeting/business facilities

Four rooms, for up to 100 delegates.

Recreational facilities

Indoor pool, Jacuzzi, solarium, gym, sauna, steam room; snooker; four-lane curling rink (October to March).

GOLF FACILITIES

Best season: Spring, Summer, Autumn.

COURSES:	LENGTH	PAR	FEES
Brora	5587m	69	£20
Royal Dornoch	6018m	70	£57
Golspie	5336m	68	£20

James Braid's 18-hole Brora links course; many other classic links courses.

Facilities key

44   100

PRESTWICK OLD COURSE HOTEL

Hotel information

13 Links Road
Prestwick
Ayrshire
KA9 1QG

Tel: +44 (0) 1292 477446
Fax: +44 (0) 1292 478316
Email: paul@prestwickochotel.co.uk
Web: www.prestwickochotel.co.uk

Accolades

☆☆☆

Airport

Prestwick: 2 mins
Glasgow International: 30 mins

Accommodation price guide

Accepted credit cards
AE MC V

Local attractions

Isle of Arran, Burns country, Culzean Castle, Scottish Borders; visits to local whisky distilleries.

O verlooking the 14th and 18th greens of Prestwick Golf Club, the original Open Championship course, and with 20 courses within 20 minutes' drive, this family-run hotel is the ideal base for your golfing breaks in the west of Scotland.

Just two minutes from Prestwick airport and railway station, it offers en-suite accommodation, excellent service in comfortable surroundings, and time to relax from your busy schedule.

The lounge bar and restaurant facilities are adorned with golfing memorabilia and photographs and offer an extensive menu of traditional and local produce. The hotel staff would be delighted to tailor-make golfing itineraries for you, including tee-times and transport.

Meeting/business facilities

Three rooms, for up to 70 delegates.

Recreational facilities

Garden/lawn area

GOLF FACILITIES

Best season: April to October

COURSES:	LENGTH	PAR	FEES
Prestwick Old	5964m	71	£75
Prestwick	5377m	70	£40
St. Nicholas			
Royal Troon	6454m	73	£125

Local driving range, caddied; tuition packages available; various tournaments open to guests.

Facilities key

7   70

RUSACKS HOTEL

Opened in 1887, Rusacks Hotel preserves a genuine warmth and intimacy of style which makes it a St. Andrews tradition. With just 48 rooms and suites, the hotel has a peaceful, club-like mood and quality of service which foster a sense of well-being, with magnificent windows looking out on green panoramas, shining seas and limitless skies.

Here St. Andrews celebrated Old Course is no more than a firm putt from your door. An easy chip brings you to the beckoning shops and history of St. Andrews, and a full three-wood is all you need to reach one of Scotland's finest miles of sand.

Blend your golfing pleasures with the comforts of the bar and the acclaimed restaurant, overlooking the first tee and 18th green of the Old Course.

Hotel information

Pilmour Links
St. Andrews
Fife KY16 9JQ

Tel: +44 (0) 1334 474 321
Fax: +44 (0) 1334 477 896
Email: HeritageHotels_StAndrews.Rusacks
@forte-hotels.com
Web: www.heritage-hotels.com

Accolades

☆☆☆☆ AA / RAC   AA rosette

Airport

Edinburgh International: 1hr

Accommodation price guide

Accepted credit cards
AE DC MC V

Local attractions

The 'Home of Golf', with 99 holes outside the door of the hotel; British Golf Museum, historic St. Andrews Abbey, the Fife coast.

Meeting/business facilities

Three rooms, for up to 100 delegates.

Recreational facilities

Riding, shooting and fishing arranged.

GOLF FACILITIES

Best season for golf: Spring, Summer and Winter.

COURSES:	LENGTH	PAR	FEES
St. Andrews Old	6339m	72	£75
St. Andrews New	6038m	71	£35
The Eden	5588m	70	£23

Tuition; driving range on the Links; club facilities open to guests; pro shop; pre-booking for 30-plus courses arranged.

Facilities key

48   100

THE MARINE HOTEL

The Marine Hotel, a gloriously embellished example of Victoriana, is picturesquely located at the heart of East Lothian's popular golfing coast.

The Marine actually overlooks the 16th hole of North Berwick's championship West Links course, which threads its way along the edge of the Firth of Forth and includes one of golf's most copied holes – the infamous par three 15th 'Radan'. Real golfing aficionados should take one of the 40 sea view rooms and suites at the rear where they can watch fellow players tackling the West Links course.

There are no fewer than 18 golf courses within an easy drive, including Muirfield (British Open venue 2002), and the hotel makes an ideal base for touring the Borders and Fife.

Hotel information

Cromwell Road
North Berwick
East Lothian EH39 4LZ

Tel: +44 (0) 1620 892 406
Fax: +44 (0) 1620 894 480
Email: heritagehotels_berwick.marine
@forte-hotels.com
Web: www.heritage-hotels.com

Accolades

☆☆☆ AA RAC

Airport

Edinburgh International: 40mins

Accommodation price guide

Accepted credit cards   **AE DC MC V**

Local attractions

Outstanding coastline; Edinburgh, Dirleton Castle.

AMERICAN EXPRESS OFFER
For advance booking on American Express Card you receive a **free room upgrade (subject to availability).**

Meeting/business facilities

Five rooms, for up to 350 delegates.

Recreational facilities

Sauna, solarium, multi-gym, two tennis courts, outdoor pool, landscaped garden, 18 hole putting green.

GOLF FACILITIES

Best season for golf: Spring, Summer and Autumn.

COURSES:	LENGTH	PAR	FEES
N. Berwick West	5792m	72	£45
Gullane 1 & 2	5912m	71	£45
N. Berwick Glen	5568m	69	£31

Facilities key

83   350

IRELAND: EAST & NORTH   The Emerald's jewel

There's an Irish folk tale that you can play a ball from course to course clear across the Emerald Isle. That's an exaggeration, of course, but it's true that there are now more than 400 listed courses in Ireland and, conveniently, many of them are to be found clustered in a crescent around the lively capital of Dublin.

That's doubly fortunate since the city offers a vast amount of things to do – from visiting the Guinness brewery and taking the writers' trail round the pubs in the footsteps of Swift, Wilde, Joyce, Behan and the rest, to marvelling at the splendour of Dublin Castle and visiting the many museums and galleries.

Just to the south of Dublin are the magical Wicklow mountains while inland you will enter horse country, with its many studs and world-renowned race courses.

In the north, Belfast and its environs offer many attractions. Wonderful shopping, attractive Victorian buildings – including the mighty City Hall – and award-winning restaurants will draw you to the city while further afield there's the beautiful Antrim Coast Road, the Devil's Causeway and vast Lough Neagh.

Bustling Dublin

GETTING THERE Now a major international business centre, Dublin has air links with Europe and North America. Belfast International and Belfast City are important regional airports while Derry also has good air links. Car ferries run from Wales, England and Scotland, connecting Rosslare, Dun Laoghaire, Dublin and Belfast.

Irish roads are generally fairly quiet. There's a motorway ring round around Dublin and Northern Ireland is well served with motorways.

APRÈS GOLF One of Ireland's prime attractions is the 'craic', that magical mix of story telling, laughter, impromptu singing and general bonhomie which makes this "The land of one hundred thousand welcomes". Food has improved beyond belief and to those traditional hearty breakfasts and mixed grills can now be added the hautest of cuisine.

OFF THE COURSE Country lifestyle is one of Ireland's great drawing cards – so too is an enormous range of sporting activity, of both the participant and spectator kind. Try to catch a game of hurling or of Gaelic football, spend a day at the races or sample the best river, lake and sea angling in Europe.

NOT TO BE MISSED See the *Book of Kells* in Dublin's Trinity College; visit the Abbey Theatre; visit Bray, Wicklow or any of the delightful little harbour towns along the coast. In the north, see where the Mountains of Mourne really do "sweep down to the sea".

FACTS & FIGURES

- There are 374 golf clubs affiliated to the Golfing Union of Ireland, which was established in 1881. Ninty-three of them are in the six counties of Northern Ireland.
- Ireland has 30 per cent of all the links courses in the world.
- The Ryder Cup will be played in Ireland for the first time in 2005.
- Access to this region is good. There are major airports at Belfast and Dublin and regional airports at Derry. Ferry services run from the UK mainland to Dun Laoghaire (Dublin) and Larne and Bangor (for Belfast).

One of Ireland's famed 'thousand shades of green' – Druid's Glen

Two of the best golf courses in the world, Royal Portrush and Royal County Down, are in Northern Ireland. They are so good that many of the world's greatest golfers regularly use them to hone their links skills in the days leading up to the Open.

In many ways these two great courses set the scene on golf in the north-east region of this island, which stretches from the wild coast of Sligo, round to the northern tip in Derry and down past Belfast to the capital of Eire, Dublin.

Although there are 52 courses in the Dublin area alone and 18 around Belfast, it is the sheer majesty of these two great courses, which set the standard for all the rest. They are rugged, windswept and tough, but above all natural links.

Overall the standard of courses in this region is high. There are more than enough courses to suit every level of player and they are all easily accessible along well signposted, if twisty, roads. Many are very old. County Down, for example, was opened in 1889.

There are also a number of newer parkland courses like the 'K' Club, designed by Arnold Palmer and venue for the 2005 Ryder Cup, and Druid's Glen. Both are fine golf courses, but traditionalists would question the wisdom of travelling all the way to Ireland to play what are essentially 'American' courses. That said, they do add to the range of experiences in an area which is a feast of golf.

The climate is, it has to be said, a problem. It rains a lot, but it is seldom cold between April and November and there are plenty of interesting things to do away from the golf course in what is a charming and beautiful part of the world.

NEW DEVELOPMENTS

- Golf in Ireland is growing at a phenomenal rate. Five years ago approximately 175,000 people travelled to Ireland to play the game. By 1997 the traffic had grown to 245,000. Half a million are expected in 2000.
- All the major car hire companies (Hertz, Europcar, Avis etc) have multiple outlets.
- Roads are good, and traffic is light except around Dublin and Belfast.
- There is a wide choice of accommodation, ranging from good bed and breakfast priced from about £25 per person per night up to five star hotels charging international rates. Hiring a cottage for a week starts from about £200.
- The vast majority of hotels take all major credit cards; many offer special deals with local courses.
- The Irish Tourist Board publishes an official guide to golf and accommodation in the region.

Favourite fairways

① ROYAL PORTRUSH

One of the best golf courses in the world. It was designed chiefly by God. It's very difficult and a caddy is a good investment if you have any sort of bet on. A good score on this course is a trophy.
Par 72   Length 6072m
Portrush, Co Antrim. BT56 8JQ
Tel: +44 (0) 1265 822311 Fax: +44 (0) 1265 823139

② ROYAL COUNTY DOWN

This beautiful course is pitched just at the point where the mountains of Mourne sweep down to the sea. The ninth hole is wondrously beautiful. Although it's a great test, it's also fair and a joy to play.
Par 71   Length 6435m
Royal County Down, Newcastle BT33 OAN
Tel: +44 (0) 13967 23314 Fax: +44 (0) 13967 26281

③ MOUNT JULIET

This Jack Nicklaus course opened in 1991 and is regularly used on the professional circuit. Like many courses the great man has designed, Mount Juliet can be a brute for mere mortals with handicaps, but it's still a very charming course.
Par 72   Length 6073m
Mount Juliet, Thomastown, Co Kilkenny
Tel: +353 (0) 56 73000 Fax: +353 (0) 56 73019

④ DRUID'S GLEN

A 30-kilometre drive from Dublin, Druid's Glen abounds with streams and lakes which have been manicured into a picture postcard course looking over the sea towards the Welsh mountains. The Irish Open is regularly held here.
Par 72   Length 5987m
Druid's Glen Golf Club, Kilcoole, Co Wicklow
Tel: +353 (0) 1 287 3600 Fax: +353 (0) 1 287 3699

⑤ THE 'K' CLUB

Purists cringe at the thought that anyone would travel all the way to Ireland to play an inland 'American' course designed by Arnold Palmer that is the pride of a golf-mad millionaire, and costs IR£130 a round to play. However, it has to be said that this is a very fine course, good enough indeed to be the venue for the 2005 Ryder Cup.
Par 72   Length 6163m
The 'K' Club, Straffan, Dublin
Tel: +353 (0) 1 601 7300 Fax: +353 (0) 1 601 7399

CONTACT

Northern Ireland Tourist Board, St.Anne's Court, 59 North St. Belfast BT1 1NB
Tel: +44 (0) 1232 246609 Fax: +44 (0) 1232 312 424
Bord Failte (Irish Tourist Board), Baggot Street Bridge, Dublin
Tel: +353 (0) 1 602 4000 Fax: +353 (0) 1 602 4100

Hotels

The most up-to-date golf travel information is always at www.golftravel4u.com

CLIMATE

The Gulf Stream effect provides Ireland with a temperate climate where the rain is euphemistically described as 'soft mist'. The locals claim: "The sun always shines on Ireland, even if it is sometimes from behind a cloud."

Sample point: Dublin

RECOMMENDED CAR HIRE *Hertz*

UK: +44 (0) 870 848 4848
Germany: +49 (0) 180 533 3535
Website: www.hertz.com

Price guide   €

| Round of golf | | Golf balls | |
| Small beer | | 4/5 star hotel room | |

MOUNT JULIET

Hotel information

Thomastown
County Kilkenny

Tel: +353 (0) 56 73000
Fax: +353 (0) 56 73019
Email: info@mountjuliet.ie
Web: www.mountjuliet.ie

Accolades

★★★★ AA Hotel of the Year 1999
RAC Gold Ribbon Award

Airport

Dublin: 2hrs

Accommodation price guide

Accepted credit cards
AE MC V DC

Recreational facilities

Tennis, equestrian centre with horse riding, archery, clay pigeon shooting, fishing; leisure centre with spa.

Meeting/business facilities

Six rooms, for up to 200 delegates.

Local attractions

Kilkenny Castle, Waterford Crystal.

Often referred to as "The Augusta of Ireland", Mount Juliet's outstanding Jack Nicklaus signature course has hosted the Irish Open on three occasions, winning unanimous praise from the European Tour players.

Also unique in Europe is the 18-hole putting course, which combines bunkers, water hazards and dog legs in a par 53. Expert tuition is available all year round from the resident professional and players of all abilities are welcome.

Easy to reach from Europe's major cities and just an hour and a half's drive from Dublin International Airport, Mount Juliet is set within a 600-hectare walled estate of woodland, pasture and formal gardens. Mount Juliet House itself retains an aura of 18th Century grandeur, offering 32 en-suite bedrooms of individual character and ambience. Just a two-minute walk away is Hunter's Yard – centre of Mount Juliet's many sporting activities.

The en-suite courtyard bedrooms provide a rustic contrast to the grandeur of the house, while the Rose Garden Lodges, each with two en-suite bedrooms, lounge room and kitchen, are popular for longer stays.

GOLF FACILITIES

Best season for golf: May to September.

COURSES:	LENGTH	PAR	FEES
Mount Juliet			
	7142m	72	E63-76*

Driving range, pitching green, 18-hole putting course, three-hole golf academy; tuition packages available.
*Fees for hotel residents.

Facilities key

59 200

PORTMARNOCK HOTEL & GOLF LINKS

Recreational facilities

Clay pigeon shooting, sailing and horse riding can be arranged; fitness centre nearby; two restaurants on site: The Osborne, for formal dining, and The Links, less formal, for lunch, dinner and snacks.

Meeting/business facilities

Three meeting rooms, the largest seating 350 theatre-style; business centre; fax and modem points in most rooms.

Local attractions

Sightseeing, shopping and dining in Dublin City, which is just 18 km away.

Hotel information

Portmarnock
County Dublin

Tel: +353 (0) 1 846 0611
Fax: +353 (0) 1 846 2442

Accolades

☆☆☆☆

Airport

Dublin: 15 mins

Accommodation price guide

€

Accepted credit cards
AE MC V DC

Portmarnock Hotel & Golf Links is the venue for a truly outstanding Irish golfing break. You will enjoy the formidable challenge of a Bernhard Langer designed championship links course and a deluxe hotel offering great comfort and the best of traditional Irish hospitality.

Course and hotel lie side by side against the dunes of Ireland's east coast, not far from the city of Dublin and just minutes from Dublin Airport.

Laid out on classic dunesland of hillocks, wild grasses and gorse, the gently undulating fairways of the Portmarnock Links are negotiated past 98 strategically placed bunkers to large, fast greens. Inspirational use of natural features, elevated tees and greens, and acute dog-legs, coupled with ever-present sea breezes, conspire to keep the brain working through every round.

Originally the home of the Jameson whiskey family, the grand 19th Century house has been enlarged to offer a choice of accommodation ranging from de luxe bedrooms and executive suites to a number of 'Jameson Suites', complete with period features and four-poster beds.

A choice of two restaurants and three bars includes the award-winning Osborne for fine dining, and the Jameson Bar, with its oak panelling and homely open fire.

GOLF FACILITIES

Best season for golf: March to November.

COURSES:	LENGTH	PAR	FEES
Portmarnock Links			
	5904m	71	IR£38-60
Portmarnock (Old)			
	6270m	72	IR£70-90
The Island			
	5962m	72	IR£50-60

Portmarnock Links offers putting green, practice ground, chipping area, fully-equipped clubhouse with showers, lockers, bag storage, pro shop, bar and restaurant; two-night packages including golf start from IR£127 per person - call for details.

Facilities key

103   350

RATHSALLAGH HOUSE GOLF & COUNTRY CLUB

Hotel information

Dunlavin
Co. Wicklow

Tel: +353 (0) 45 403112
Fax: +353 (0) 45 403343
Email: info@rathsallagh.com
Web: www.rathsallagh.com

Accolades

'One of Top 50 Hotels In Ireland' -
Food & Wine
Member Blue Book
Three times National Breakfast Awards winner
Bridgestone 100 Best Places to Stay in Ireland
Gilbey's Gold Medal for Excellence in Catering

Airport

Dublin: 1 hr

Accommodation price guide

Accepted credit cards
AE MC V

Preferred tour operator

From UK
Wilkinson Golf
& Leisure   Tel: +44 (0) 1383 861000
From Germany
Golfen
In Ireland   Tel: +49 (0) 6198 50 21 96
From Sweden
ECstay AB   Tel: +46 (0) 822 8070

Converted from elegant Queen Anne stables in 1798, Rathsallagh is a spacious four-star Grade 'A' country house, idyllically situated in 215 hectares of peaceful parkland, with a walled garden and its own 18-hole par 72 championship golf course, designed by the redoubtable Christy O'Connor Jnr.

Rathsallagh is a family-run establishment and has a happy and relaxed atmosphere, with log and turf fires in the bar and drawing rooms. The food is country cooking at its very best, using ingredients organically produced by local growers and in Rathsallagh's gardens. Game in season and the freshest of fish are specialities, while breakfast is an experience in itself and has won the National Breakfast Awards three times.

As well as having access to the golf course at a special rate, guests at Rathsallagh may also avail themselves of its indoor heated pool and sauna, billiard room and tennis court. Clay pigeon shooting, fishing, archery and horse riding are available by prior arrangement.

Rathsallagh is well within an hour's drive of four more of the nation's premier golf courses: Portmarnock, Druids Glen, Mount Juliet and the 'K' Club – home of the 2005 Ryder Cup.

Recreational facilities

Indoor pool, sauna; billiard room; tennis court; 215 hectares of parkland; walled garden; fishing, shooting; horse racing and bloodstock sales nearby.

Meeting/business facilities

One conference room and three meeting rooms, for up to 40 delegates; helipad.

Local attractions

The glorious Wicklow Mountains; the Irish National Stud and Japanese gardens; The Curragh – home of the Irish classics; Nass and Punchestown racecourses and Goffs Bloodstock Sales; Dublin one hour away.

GOLF FACILITIES

Best season for golf: Spring, Summer and Autumn.

COURSES:	LENGTH	PAR	FEES
Rathsallagh	6303m	72	E32-45
	(special fee for guests only)		
The 'K' Club	6542m	72	E178
Druids Glen	6403m	72	E108
Mount Juliet	6482m	72	E95-108

Tuition packages are available; buggies for hire in the Summer season.

Facilities key

17   40

SILVERWOOD GOLF HOTEL

Hotel information

40 Kiln Road
Lurgan
Craigavon
County Armagh
BT66 6NF

Tel: +44 (0) 2838 327722
Fax: +44 (0) 2838 325290

Accolades

☆☆☆

Airport

Belfast City: 20 mins
Belfast International: 20 mins

Accommodation price guide

Accepted credit cards
AE DC MC V Switch Delta

Recreational facilities

Golf, ski centre and gardens at the hotel; watersports, sailing, angling and birdwatching available locally.

Meeting/business facilities

One conference room and two meeting rooms, accommodating up to 300 delegates.

Local attractions

Lough Neagh and its Discovery Centre; parks and gardens; National Trust properties.

The moment you enter the Silverwood Golf Hotel, you are welcomed by friendly staff who enjoy extending real Irish hospitality to a cosmopolitan clientele.

Although the setting is pleasant and rural, Belfast's air and sea ports are just 20 minutes away. Rooms are bright, spacious and newly refurbished to the highest standards, and the hotel is decorated throughout with very fine paintings and prints of famous golf courses.

The hotel overlooks the Silverwood, an entertaining 18-hole parkland course with well-irrigated sand-based greens, incorporating lakes in the third and tenth holes. There is also a nine-hole par three course, pitch and putt, putting greens and floodlit driving range.

After a great day's golf, you can select from a varied *à la carte* menu and extensive wine list at the hotel's restaurant. The lounge bar serves food all day long, and entertainment is provided both there and in the Topaz Suite, a most exciting night-spot.

The hotel has established a reputation for golf packages, and can also book other courses in the area. Other hotel-related activities include skiing, watersports, sailing angling and birdwatching.

GOLF FACILITIES

Best season for golf: March to October.

COURSES:	LENGTH	PAR	FEES
Silverwood	5640m	72	£15
Lurgan	5816m	70	£20*
Portadown	5848m	70	£18*
Banbridge	4560m	67	£20*

Practice and tuition facilities, tournaments, booking for other courses; packages including room, breakfast dinner and golf; one day £40, two days £75, three days £110 (per person sharing).

*rate for weekend

Facilities key

29   300

SLIEVE DONARD HOTEL

Hotel information

Downs Road
Newcastle
County Down BT33 OAH

Tel: +44 (0) 28 4372 3681
Fax: +44 (0) 28 4372 4830
Email: res@sdh.hastingshotels.com
Web: www.hastingshotels.com

Accolades

✩✩✩✩ AA, RAC, NITB

Airport

Belfast City: 1 hr
Belfast International, Aldergrove: 1hr, 20 mins

Accommodation price guide

Accepted credit cards
AE MC V DC

Nestled in the heart of County Down, just where the Mountains of Mourne truly do "sweep down to the sea", the architecturally acclaimed Slieve Donard Hotel stands in two-and-a-half hectares of private grounds which lead to both an extensive golden beach and the renowned Royal County Down golf course, ranked sixth in the world. With no less than eight golf courses within a 30km radius, the Slieve Donard is the ideal location for all golf enthusiasts.

Recently refurbished to celebrate its centenary, the Slieve Donard is a hotel of luxury and prestige. Each guest room is exquisitely decorated and furnished to provide an environment which draws guests back time and again. In the Oak Restaurant, the ultimate culinary experience is complemented by the charm of its huge central fireplace and magnificent wood panelling.

Named after the famed comic actor, who visited the hotel in 1921, Chaplin's Bar provides the perfect ambience for a quiet drink and a little 'craic' while, located in the hotel's grounds, the Percy French Inn is a cosy and informal bar and restaurant providing quality entertainment and sumptuous food and is regarded as the perfect 19th hole.

For 'après golf' relaxation, the Elysium Health Club and Beauty Salon provides a sanctuary of sheer indulgence for body and mind, with state of the art facilities providing everything from a pulse-raising work-out to a relaxing massage.

Recreational facilities

Elysium health club and beauty salon, fully equipped gym, steam room, Jacuzzi, swimming pool; table tennis, lifesize chess set.

Meeting/business facilities

16 conference/meeting rooms with secretarial access; computer access and full support services.

Local attractions

Newcastle's seaside attractions, the Mountains of Mourne, Silent Valley, Tullymore Forest, Tropicana Fun Aqua Park, Coco's Adventure Playground.

GOLF FACILITIES

Best season for golf: Temperate climate facilitates year-round play.

COURSES:	LENGTH	PAR	FEES
Royal County Down			
	7037m	71	£65-75
Kilkeel			
	6615m	72	£16-20
Warrenpoint			
	6000m	71	£20-27

Host to 1999 British Amateur Open, staged at Royal County Down and Kilkeel, as will be the 2000 British Senior Open.

Facilities key

  126 **825**

ROSAPENNA HOTEL & GOLF LINKS

Hotel information

Rosapenna
Downings
Letterkenny
Co. Donegal

Tel: +353 (0) 74 55301
Fax: +353 (0) 74 55128
Email: rosapenna@eircom.net
Web: www.rosapenna.ie

Accolades

☆☆☆☆

Airport

City of Derry: 1 hr 15 mins
Belfast International: 2 hrs 30 mins

Accommodation price guide

€

Accepted credit cards
AE DC MC V

Local attractions

Adjacent fishing village of Downings,
Glebe Gallery, Glenveagh National Park.

Lovely Rosapenna Hotel is proudly set on its own private 18-hole links course, designed in 1893 by 'Old Tom' Morris. This glorious course runs alongside the beautiful Tramore Beach and then loops around Coastguard Hill and back to the hotel. Designed by Pat Ruddy, a second 18-hole links layout is scheduled to open for play by 2001.

Built on the Muslack headland between two magnificent beaches on one of Ireland's most outstanding stretches of coastline, the family-run Rosapenna Hotel is on the outskirts of the village of Downings, some 38 kilometres from Letterkenny.

Accommodations include new spa suites and deluxe rooms overlooking Sheephaven Bay, while the dining room is renowned for its seafood.

Meeting/business facilities

Two rooms, for up to 75 delegates.

Recreational facilities

Leisure centre; snooker, table tennis; hotel is located on a beach.

GOLF FACILITIES

Best season for golf: March to October.

COURSES:	LENGTH	PAR	FEES
Rosapenna	5734m	71	free
Portsalon	5376m	69	E13-16

Practice facilities; tuition packages available.

Facilities key

53   75

FAITHLEGG HOUSE HOTEL

Hotel information

Faithlegg
Co. Waterford

Tel: +353 (0) 51 382000
Fax: +353 (0) 51 382010
Email: faithleg@iol.ie
Web: www.towerhotelgroup.ie

Airport

Waterford: 10 mins
Dublin: 2 hrs

Accommodation price guide

€

Accepted credit cards
AE DC MC V

Local attractions

Historic Waterford city, with its Viking heritage; Dunmore East, picturesque local fishing village.

Overlooking the picturesque estuary of the River Suir, Faithlegg House Hotel is located on the renowned Faithlegg championship golf course. This enticing parkland challenge was designed by Patrick Merrigan, who believes that: "The design solution is in the landscape." It features strategically placed water hazards and some challenging slopes and burrows on the immaculate greens and undulating fairways.

The pretty 18th Century manor house has been tastefully extended to incorporate 82 bedrooms and a unique fitness, health and beauty club. A very special feature of the house is the elegant Billiards Room, with its original oak-beamed ceiling and dramatic views across the 18th green.

First class facilities and a superb location make this is an ideal venue, for pleasure and business.

Meeting/business facilities

Four rooms, for up to 180 delegates.

Recreational facilities

Golf on site; gym, steam room, sauna, Jacuzzi, beauty therapy; riding, water activities, angling, surfing, walking.

GOLF FACILITIES

Best season: Spring, Summer, Autumn.

COURSES:	LENGTH	PAR	FEES
Faithlegg	6079m	72	E12-15
Tramore	6055m	72	E15
Waterford	5722m	71	E15

Practice facilities, tuition; competitions; special green fees/tee times for guests.

Facilities key

82   180

Helen Alfredsson
Seve Ballesteros
Nick Faldo
Tommy Horton
David Leadbetter
Nick Price

the greatest names in golf write exclusively for Golf International

For subscription details,
ring **+44 (0)1795 414854** or fax **+44 (0)1795 414555** or e-mail **golfint@galleon.co.uk**

Essential reading from the best in the game
golf
INTERNATIONAL
the best instruction on the planet

Golf International, 10 Buckingham Place, London SW1E 6HX

IRELAND: SOUTH & WEST Concentrated golf goodness

There's an air of romance and mystery about Ireland's south and west. This is the land from which the people left in such numbers all those years ago – and it's the place to which their descendants, and many others too are now flocking back.

However, Ireland's resident population today is still not much more than half what it was back in 1840, at the start of the Great Famine, which means there's an air of space and solitude which is part of the appeal.

Add to that lofty mountains, windswept moors, rushing rivers teeming with trout and salmon just waiting to be hooked, mystical lakes and unspoilt villages and you're beginning to get the picture – though you'll also need to paint in the multi-hued attractions of the lively cities of Waterford, Cork, Limerick and Galway, the clean, Atlantic storm-lashed beaches of the West, the towering Cliffs of Moher, the flower-bedecked limestone plateau of The Burren and lots more besides.

GETTING THERE Shannon International Airport – where the 'duty free' concept was invented, incidentally – started life as a transatlantic refuelling post. Despite its remote location it is still a major airport serving many US cities as well as Europe.

There is a train service from Dublin to both Cork and Killarney while roads, though mainly single carriageway, are relatively lightly trafficked.

APRÈS GOLF Find a snug bar in a country pub and a group of locals is sure to find you, leading to a memorable night of yarn telling and conversation over a few pints of 'the black stuff'. Try some Irish whiskey, champ – the most delicious mashed potato ever, thanks to the addition of spring onions – and local fish and seafood. Once a gastronomic desert, Ireland now offers a wealth of fine restaurants – many of the best adjacent to fine golf courses.

OFF THE COURSE Cruise from course to course by taking a holiday afloat on the mighty River Shannon; go horse riding or mountain walking, savour an Irish country market day. With its light traffic, Ireland is a paradise for cycling.

NOT TO BE MISSED Explore wild Donegal and Connemara and visit the spot near Clifden where Alcock and Brown landed after their epic pioneer flight across the Atlantic. Sample Galway Bay oysters; buy some tweeds.

FACTS & FIGURES

● Access to the region is good. There are international airports at Dublin in the east and Shannon in the west. There are also local airports at Cork, Killarney and Waterford.
● Car ferries go into Dublin, Rosslare and Cork. All the major car rental companies have fleets at Dublin and Shannon.
● The roads are mostly single lane and twisty, but there is not much traffic. Leave plenty of time to get to the course.
● Accommodation is plentiful and varied. Most golfers travelling round the south move from one B&B place to another. Hiring a cottage, usually for four, is also popular.
● Booking in advance is wise in July and August.

The mighty cliffs of Moher

In the swing at Old Head of Kinsale

Ireland has 374 golf courses. Many of the best ones are in the south and west. There are few other places in Europe where there are so many good courses in a relatively small area.

Golf in the region is dominated by the westerly weather that flows in from the Atlantic. On a calm dry day great links courses like Ballybunion, Waterville and Lahinch are magnificent challenges. When it blows and rains however, they are a nightmare and best avoided. Even the more sheltered courses like Killarney and Limerick County become a slog in the rain. Conditions can be very different just a few miles away, so it is always advisable to have a flexible itinerary and to check the weather forecast before deciding exactly where to go.

The best time to visit the area is from May to September. Golf has been played in this part of Ireland for over 200 years. In addition to the championship links which everyone wants to play and which are therefore sometimes booked up on peak days, the region abounds with good courses. It is especially welcoming for non-playing spouses and families. There are many things to see and do.

A car is essential because many of the courses are in out of the way places. The exception is Cork where there are 11 within a short taxi ride.

NEW DEVELOPMENTS

● Golf is big business in this part of Ireland. It's on the European professional tour and golfers from all over the world are welcomed. Many of the clubhouses have displays of photographs of famous golfers who have played there recently, including Tiger Woods and Mark O'Meara.

Favourite fairways

1 DINGLE (CEANN SIBEAL)
The most westerly course in Europe, Dingle is a scenic delight. A traditional links, the main feature of this championship course is a stream that comes into play on 14 holes.
Par 72   Length 6123m
Ceann Sibeal, Ballyferriter, County Kerry
Tel: +353 (0) 66 915 6255   Fax:+353 (0) 66 915 6409

2 WATERVILLE
This is where Tiger Woods and Mark O'Meara practiced before O'Meara won the Open at Royal Birkdale in 1998. He described the Waterville links as 'the dream of a lifetime'.
Par 72   Length 6569m
Waterville House and Golf Links, Ring of Kerry, Co. Kerry
Tel:+353 (0) 66 74102   Fax:+353 (0) 66 74482.

3 LAHINCH (OLD COURSE)
Frequently referred to as 'the St Andrews of Ireland', Lahinch was the brainchild of Old Tom Morris, four times Open winner. Master designer Dr. Alistair MacKenzie, who also worked on Augusta, Pebble Beach and Cypress Point, later improved it.
Par 72   Length 6175m
Lahinch, Lahinch, County Clare
Tel:+353 (0) 65 81003   Fax:+353 (0) 65 81592

4 BALLYBUNION
This famous links features in most 'world top ten' lists. With the Atlantic waves crashing in on the huge wild sand dunes, this is one of the gems of the world of golf. It's an adventure as well as a joy to play.
Par 71   Length 6038m
Ballybunion, County Kerry
Tel:+353 (0) 68 27146   Fax:+353 (0) 68 23787

5 TRALEE
Designer Arnold Palmer said he had never before come across a piece of land so ideally suited for a golf course as the links of Tralee. The fact that so many people come back to the course year after year is a measure of the special place it holds in Irish golf.
Par 71   Length 6288m
Tralee, West Barrow, Co Kerry
Tel:+353 (0) 66 36379   Fax:+353 (0) 66 36008

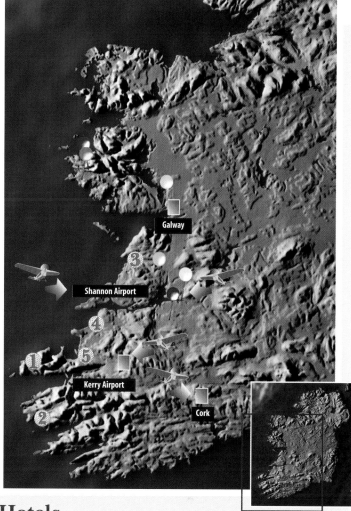

Hotels

Adare Manor & Adare Golf Club
Page 164

Ballynahinch Castle Hotel
Page 165

Castletroy Park Hotel
Page 166

Dromoland Castle
Page 167

Glenlo Abbey Hotel
Page 168

CLIMATE

Most courses in Ireland remain open year round but the best playing conditions are from April to October. It's generally mild and temperate, as a result of the warming effects of the Gulf Stream – but can be very windy.

Sample point: Limerick

Price guide

Round of golf		Golf balls	
Small beer		4/5 star hotel room	

CONTACT
Bord Failte (Irish Tourist Board), Baggot Street Bridge, Dublin 2
Tel: +353 (0) 1 6024000 Fax: +353 (0) 1 6024100

ADARE MANOR & ADARE GOLF CLUB

Hotel information

Adare
County Limerick

Tel: +353 (0) 61 396 566
Fax: +353 (0) 61 396 124
Email: reservations@adaremanor.com
Web: www.adaremanor.com

Accolades

Airport

Shannon: 40 mins

Accommodation price guide

€ ⊙⊙⊙⊙

Accepted credit cards
AE MC V DC

Recreational facilities

Championship golf course; indoor pool, gym, massage therapy and sauna; fishing, horse riding, clay pigeon shooting.

Meeting/business facilities

Meeting rooms for up to 250 delegates.

Local attractions

Adare Village Heritage Centre, pubs and antique shops; the Ring of Kerry; the Cliffs of Moher.

Home to the Dunraven family for the past two centuries, Adare Manor has entered a new era. Tucked into the natural seclusion of its 340-hectare estate beside the picture-postcard village of Adare, this showpiece of Irish architecture combines delicate local craftsmanship with the finest design influences from Europe. The aristocratic heart of Adare remained the home of the Quin family and the Earls of Dunraven until the 1980s, when Thomas Kane and family restored the Manor, lovingly transforming it into a luxury resort.

The Manor house has 63 bedrooms, and its candlelit restaurant overlooks the peacefully flowing River Maigue. The newly opened Golf Village, close to the Manor House, includes a clubhouse with 11 bedroom suites, extensive conference facilities, 25 Garden Townhomes, an indoor swimming pool, fitness centre, sauna and equestrian facilities.

The Manor's championship golf course lies within the estate's rolling countryside. The front nine is dominated by two man-made lakes, while the River Maigue forms the backbone of one of the best finishing nines in Ireland. The course, carving through 200-year-old trees, ranks among the best ever designed by Robert Trent Jones Senior.

GOLF FACILITIES

Best season for golf: Spring, Summer and Autumn.

COURSES:	LENGTH	PAR	FEES
Adare			
	6505m	72	E 70-76

Designed by Robert Trent Jones Snr, lined by 200-year-old trees, with two artificial lakes and River Maigue within hotel grounds; driving range, golf tuition; Ballybunion: 1 hr drive from hotel; Lahinch: 1 hr 30 mins from hotel.

Facilities key

  63 250

BALLYNAHINCH CASTLE

Hotel information

Ballynahinch
Connemara
County Galway

Tel: +353 (0) 95 31006
Fax: +353 (0) 95 31085
Email: bhinch@iol.ie
Web: www.commerce.ie/ballynahinch

Accolades

☆☆☆☆ ITB, AA, Two Rosettes

Airport

Galway: 1 hr
Shannon: 2 hrs 30 mins
Dublin: 4 hrs

Accommodation price guide

Accepted credit cards
AE MC V DC

Recreational facilities

Wild salmon and trout fishing; tennis, cycling; 140 hectares of grounds for walks; clay shoot; sea angling and horse riding available locally.

Meeting/business facilities

Boardroom, for up to 12 delegates.

Local attractions

Connemara National Park and Joyce's Country; day trips to Aran Islands; sea fishing; Letterfrack; climbing on the Twelve Bens.

Ballynahinch Castle is set in the heart of Connemara and stands proud and majestic overlooking the famous Ballynahinch River. The Castle has been intertwined in the history of Connemara and its people for many centuries.

The Connemara Golf Club, 27 kilometres from Ballynahinch Castle, offers a fitting challenge to any golfer. The par 72 is rarely achieved on this most challenging Atlantic links, described by James W Finegan as "a perfect reflection of the austere beauty that is the world of Connemara."

The hotel has a charm which can best be described as 'Casual Country Elegance'. Open log fires glow in the reception rooms and all your needs will be attended to by the friendly professional staff. Soft and restful colour schemes harmonise with the natural charm of the surroundings in the tastefully decorated bedrooms. Local fresh produce is used to create culinary delights for the dining room, with its panoramic view of Ballynahinch River.

Ballynahinch Castle is surrounded by 140 hectares of woodlands, rivers and lakes which offer miles of scenic walks. Tennis, pony trekking and hill climbing are all close at hand, and Ballynahinch Fishery is world-renowned as one of the finest salmon and sea trout rivers in Ireland. Fishing is reserved for guests of the hotel. Also here are 5250 hectares of prime woodcock shooting.

GOLF FACILITIES

Best season for golf: April to October.

COURSES:	LENGTH	PAR	FEES
Connemara			
	6611m	72	E46

The championship Connemara course is just a half hour from Ballynahinch; practice facilities and carts/buggy hire.

Facilities key

40   12

CASTLETROY PARK
HOTEL & CONFERENCE CENTRE

Hotel information

Dublin Road
Limerick

Tel: +353 (0) 61 335566
Fax: +353 (0) 61 331117
Email: sales@castletroy-park.ie
Web: www.castletroy-park.ie

Accolades

☆☆☆☆
1995 Business Hotel of the Year - Egon
Ronay Jameson Guide

Airport

Shannon International: 30 mins

Accommodation price guide

Accepted credit cards
AE MC V C

Recreational facilities

Castletroy Club; fully equipped gym; 20-
metre deck level pool, sauna, steam room,
Jacuzzi; half-mile outdoor jogging track.

Meeting/business facilities

15 rooms, for up to 400 delegates.

Local attractions

King John's Castle, the Hunt Museum,
and the Cliffs of Moher.

The Castletroy Park Hotel lies at the heart of the
south-west of Ireland. Standing in six hectares
of beautifully landscaped gardens, it overlooks the
Clare Hills, just a short stroll from the meandering
River Shannon, at the entrance to the 200 hectares
of Plassey Park.

The hotel is comprised of 107 individually
appointed bedrooms, including two presidential
suites, to meet the needs of the discerning traveller.
Traditionally styled, the Castletroy Park offers
varied dining, from McLaughlin's Gourmet
Restaurant, with a reputation for its contemporary
interpretations of international and local cuisine, to
the Merry Pedlar Pub, a well-known meeting place
for a carvery lunch or bistro-style dinner.

Guests are ideally located for some of the 23
courses in the region, from Castletroy Golf Club,
one kilometre away, to the renowned Bullybunion
Golf Links in County Kerry. Guests enjoy preferred
green fees and tee-times at many courses.
Arrangements can be made to co-ordinate the
complete golfing need for groups of any size.

Relax and unwind in the early evening at the
Castletroy Club, with state-of-the-art gym
equipment, deck level pool, Jacuzzi, steam room
and sauna. Attractions in the surrounding area
include the spectacular Cliffs of Moher.

GOLF FACILITIES
Best season for golf: April to
October.

COURSES:	LENGTH	PAR	FEES
Castletroy			
	5807m	71	E19
Ballybunion			
	6050m	71	E70
Lahinch			
	5703m	71	E57

Preferred green fees and tee times at
many courses; complete golfing needs
can be arranged for groups of any size.

Facilities key

107 **400**

DROMOLAND CASTLE

Hotel information

Newmarket on Fergus
Ennis
Country Clare

Tel: +353 (0) 61 368 144
Fax: +353 (0) 61 363 355
Email: sales@dromoland.ie
Web: www.dromoland.ie

Accolades

✩✩✩✩✩

Airport

Shannon International: 20 mins

Accommodation price guide

Accepted credit cards
AE MC V

Recreational facilities

Indoor swimming pool, golf, fishing, health and fitness centre, beauty spa, clay pigeon shooting, mountain biking; horse riding available locally.

Meeting/business facilities

Five rooms, for up to 450 delegates.

Local attractions

Bunratty Folk Park and castle, The Burren National Park, Hunt Museum, Cliffs of Moher, King John's Castle.

Dromoland Castle is one of Ireland's most famous baronial castles and dates back to the 16th Century. Today, the castle is among Europe's leading resort hotels. Its rooms and suites blend period pieces with the best of modern comfort and it boasts one of the largest collections of portraits, most notably one of Lucius O'Brien, the 17th Baron Inchiquin, painted by Michael Dahl.

The 150-hectare wooded estate offers scenic walks, jogging trails and a serene 17th Century rose garden. Large trout have been caught in the lake and the River Rine, which flows through the estate. More energetic activities available include tennis, riding and mountain biking.

The dining room gives panoramic views of the lake and the golf course. The internationally renowned David McCann, head chef, presents house specialities such as lamb with foie gras and steamed fillets of turbot with fennel. Casual dining can be experienced in the golf club's Fig Tree restaurant. There is an extensive list of wines from the cellar, which guests are welcome to visit.

The 18-hole par 71 Dromoland Golf Course, established since 1961, is set against the backdrop of the castle, encompassing rolling hills, water hazards and century-old trees.

GOLF FACILITIES
Best season for golf: April to October.

COURSES:	LENGTH	PAR	FEES
Dromoland			
	5719m	71	E31
Shannon			
	6874m	72	E28
Lahinch			
	6123m	72	E43

Practice fairways, bunkers, putting greens; tuition available with club pro; buggy hire, pro shop.

Facilities key

100   450

GLENLO ABBEY HOTEL

Hotel information

Bushypark
Galway

Tel: +353 (0) 91 526666
Fax: +353 (0) 91 527800
Email: glenlo@iol.ie
Web: www.glenlo.com

Accolades

☆☆☆☆☆ Irish Tourist Board
RAC Blue Ribbon, AA Red Star
Member of Small Luxury Hotels of the
World

Airport

Galway: 20 mins
Shannon: 1 hr 20 mins
Dublin 2 hr 30 mins

Accommodation price guide

Accepted credit cards
AE MC V DC

Recreational facilities

Fishing, boating on lake, clay pigeon
shooting.

Meeting/business facilities

12 rooms, for up to 250 delegates;
business service bureau, ISDN lines.

Local attractions

Connemara, Galway City, Aran Islands,
The Burren.

A member of the prestigious Small Luxury Hotels of the World consortium for the past five years, Glenlo Abbey – the only five-star hotel in beautiful County Galway – is situated just four kilometres from Galway City. Sitting on a 55-hectare lakeside golf estate, Glenlo Abbey is the perfect retreat for a weekend break or a corporate and incentive event.

Glenlo Abbey's unique nine-hole Double Green Golf Course is favourite amongst locals and repeat guests. With the Murphy Sweeney Golf School operating out of the on-site state-of-the-art driving range, all hooks and slices can be cured before teeing off at the first.

There are 46 luxury bedrooms, many of which have fabulous views of Loch Corrib, the second-largest lake in Ireland. The award-winning River Room restaurant is perfect for an intimate dinner while the unique Pullman Restaurant is housed aboard two vintage Orient Express carriages, one of which dates back to 1927 and served on the Paris-Istanbul-St. Petersburg route hosting such personages as Sir Winston Churchill and Sir Laurence Olivier, besides featuring in the classic movie 'Murder On The Orient Express'.

There is also an on-site log barn, which can host a wide range of themed nights for groups – including country & western, Arabian nights, French Revolution and Caribbean samba events.

GOLF FACILITIES
Best season for golf: All year round.

COURSES:	LENGTH	PAR	FEES
Glenlo Abbey			
	6500m	71	E15
Galway			
	5698m	70	E25
Galway Bay			
	6500m	72	E25
Barna			
	6900m	72	E25
Connemara			
	6611m	72	E25

Unique nine-hole double green, driving range with tuition. Guests can play in selected tournaments.

Facilities key

46   250

Hotels

RECOMMENDED CAR HIRE *Hertz*®

UK: +44 (0) 870 848 4848
Germany: +49 (0) 180 533 3535
Website: www.hertz.com

The most up-to-date golf travel information is always at
www.golftravel4u.com

Favourite fairways

① ROYAL BIRKDALE

Recognised by the professionals as one of the fairest courses, the fairways are devoid of the knobs of land so often found on links courses that can divert a good drive into the rough. The dunes surrounding each green add to the drama of a course, designed by Hawtree and Taylor, that remains one of the favourites of the great Seve Ballesteros.
Par 72   Length 6097m
Waterloo Road, Birkdale, Southport, Merseyside, PR8 2LX
Tel/fax: +44 (0) 1704 567920

② ROYAL LIVERPOOL (HOYLAKE) 1

Host to ten Open Championships, a course designed by Robert Chambers and George Morris, Hoylake is steeped in history and highly vulnerable to the elements. You can play the first nine holes with barely a breeze and finish in a gale. The ninth, 10th, 11th and 12th run along the River Dee and are a particularly stiff test.
Par 76   Length 6496m
Meols Drive, Hoylake, Wirral, Merseyside, L47 4AL
Tel: +44 (0) 151 623 3101   Fax: +44 (0) 151 632 6737

③ GANTON

Lying in the lovely Vale of Pickering some 11 miles south-west of Scarborough, this unique course was created by the joint efforts of architects Dunn, Vardon, Braid and Colt and hosted the 1949 Ryder Cup. The design calls for accurate play. Best visited in late summer when the gorse is in full bloom.
Par 74   Length 6137m
Ganton, Scarborough, North Yorks, YO12 4PA
Tel: +44 (0) 1944 710329   Fax: +44 (0) 1944 710922

④ KESWICK GOLF CLUB

Dominated by the Saddleback mountain, this course is part parkland, part moorland with tree-lined fairways and streams. Right in the heart of the Lake District, the beautiful Derwentwater is never far away. The course was designed by Eric Brown, and green fees can be as little as £17.
Par 72   Length 6038m
Threlkeld Hall, Threlkeld, Keswick
Tel/fax: +44 (0) 17687 79013

⑤ CASTLETOWN GOLF LINKS

With more coastal frontage than perhaps any other course in the world, its other natural hazards are gorse, bracken and rocks. If the weather is good and the greens holding, fine. But when the wind whips in and the rain lashes, it's a different story. The first few holes are relatively straightforward, but once you hit the long dog-leg fifth, it's a fight to the finish.
Par 72   Length 6116m
Fort Island, Derbyhaven, Castletown, Isle of Man, IM9 IUA
Tel: +44 (0) 1624 822201   Fax: +44 (0) 1624 824633

CLIMATE

Wind is an almost universal factor on golf courses on both the east and west coasts. In winter, it gets dark around 4pm, so early rounds are the order of the day, while, in contrast, the summer can provide long, balmy evenings.

°C 30 25 20 15 10 5 0
J F M A M J J A S O N D

MM 100 50 0
J F M A M J J A S O N D

Sample point: Birmingham

Price guide €

Round of golf	💶💶	Golf balls	💶💶💶💶
Small beer	💶💶	4/5 star hotel room	💶💶💶💶

CONTACT

English Tourist Board
Thames Tower, Blacks Road, Hammersmith, London W6 9EL
Tel: +44 (0) 20 8846 9000   Fax: +44 (0) 20 8846 0302

ENGLAND: NORTH & MIDLANDS Where quantity meets quality

Nowhere has the nature of golf changed more than in England. Once an elitist affair, the domain of bank managers and company directors, the sport now has a following which transcends age and social background.

At the very heart of the nation, the Midlands are the land of Shakespeare. You can visit his home of Stratford and the battlefield at Bosworth where Richard III intoned: "A horse, a horse, my kingdom for a horse!"

There are Civil War sites to visit too, and historic towns like Lincoln, Nottingham, Worcester and Hereford, with their notable cathedrals. Lively Birmingham was the capital of the Industrial Revolution and is today Britain's second city.

Further north you come to the youth-oriented cities of Liverpool and Manchester and the picturesque walled cities of Chester and York. This is the land of vast upland moors, the brooding Pennines, the picture postcard Lake District and the lush Yorkshire Dales.

GETTING THERE Manchester is now a major international airport, with regular long-haul flights, while Birmingham International is one of Europe's busiest regional airports and Leeds/Bradford, Teesside, and Newcastle also have Continental links. Fast inter-city trains and a network of modern motorways help cut journey times, though rural roads are often winding and narrow, city roads horrendously crowded.

APRÈS GOLF Northerners swear their beer – darkish, bitter and served at room temperature – is far superior to the southern variety and all those imported lagers. Food tends towards the basic, but you can find oases of haute cuisine even way out in the countryside. There's a host of historic houses to visit, while kids will just love the top-class theme parks and the glitter of Blackpool, Britain's most lively seaside resort.

OFF THE COURSE Gateshead and Sheffield boast two of Europe's largest shopping malls, while Manchester too is a great retail experience. Industrial heritage is one of the great tourism themes in these parts, as are fascinating themed trails like the Bronte Country Experience, Captain Cook Country and Herriott Country.

NOT TO BE MISSED The Roman Hadrian's Wall, striding across country between Carlisle and Newcastle; the Granada Studios TV Tour in Manchester; narrow boat canals; and trips through the Pennines.

FACTS AND FIGURES

- Yorkshire, England's biggest county, has 175. Lancashire, the Isle of Man and Cumbria boast 167 courses.
- Ian Woosnam's county golf as an amateur was played for Shropshire in company with Sandy Lyle, who was raised at Hawkstone Park.
- Seve Ballesteros played his first stroke in open competition at Royal Birkdale.
- The composer Edward Elgar was a great golf lover who sought musical inspiration from the Worcestershire Golf Club at Malvern Wells.

Here is an area rich in quantity and quality of courses, that is easily accessible by rail, road and air links. It graduates from the relatively benign geography and climate of the southern Midlands, to the rugged beauty of the Lakes and the bracing challenge of the Lancashire links courses.

Heading north from south a suggested first stop is Northampton, with two new courses close to the city. Collingtree boasts an American-style design, while the relocation of Northampton Golf Club on Lord Spencer's Estate at Althorp blends a challenging course in a lovely natural landscape. The Belfry, host to the Ryder Cup and close to Birmingham, is naturally worth a visit.

South of the Mersey, Royal Liverpool and Hoylake, with its championship links, is the second oldest seaside course in England and has hardly changed in character since its foundation in 1869.

In the North West the real neglected gems of English golf can be found in the Lake District, England's 'Little Switzerland'. Ulverston Golf Club in South Lakeland is a parkland course kept in immaculate condition, with spectacular mountain views. Windermere is known as 'the Gleneagles of the Lakes', a marvellous creation considering the country that the architect, George Lowe, had to work with. Steve Rooke, the professional there for more than 20 years, calls it "a wonderful place to play golf, especially when the sun is going down and casting its amazing light on the Langdale Pikes."

Northumberland offers a heady combination of seascape, woodland, farmland and lonely moor. A classic course is Berwick-upon-Tweed at Goswick, with some enchanting holes between the dunes that open up views of the ancient ground of Holy Island.

NEW DEVELOPMENTS

- Hawkstone Park, a hotel complex north of Shrewsbury with popular golfing facilities, has recently added a much upgraded second course.
- The Tytherington, near Macclesfield, is a modern parkland course built 12 years ago and now home to the women's European Tour.
- Durham is celebrating the opening of The Ramside, a 27-hole course attached to the popular Ramside Hall Hotel.
- The Ryder Cup returns to The Belfry in 2001, following a £2.4 million renovation to the Brabazon course by the original architect Dave Thomas.
- The Lea Marston Hotel In Warwickshire stages a two-day golf school for beginners on Sundays and Mondays for £155 per person, including all meals and accommodation. Tel: +44 (0) 1675 470468.

THE BELFRY

Hotel information

Wishaw
North Warwickshire
B76 9PR

Tel: +44 (0) 1675 470033
Fax: +44 (0) 1675 470256
Email: enquiries@thebelfry.com
Web: www.thebelfry.com

Accolades

☆☆☆☆
Two AA rosettes for French Restaurant

Airport

Birmingham International: 10 mins

Accommodation price guide

Accepted credit cards
AE MC V DC

Recreational facilities

Full leisure club – The De Vere Club at The Belfry; Aqua Spa; The Shop; three golf courses, putting green, driving range; jogging trail, tennis courts, squash; Bel Air Nightclub.

Meeting/business facilities

21 rooms, for up to 400 delegates.

Local attractions

Warwick Castle, Drayton Manor theme park and zoo, Stratford-upon-Avon, Cadbury World.

The Belfry is unique as the only venue to have staged the Ryder Cup Matches – the biggest golf event in the world – three times, with a fourth visit set for 2001. While set in 200 hectares in the middle of beautiful English countryside, the venue is just ten minutes' drive from Birmingham International airport and railway station and close to the M42 motorway.

The Brabazon at The Belfry is widely regarded as a truly great championship course, with some of the most demanding holes in golf – simply breathtaking and unforgettable. Alternatively, guests can pit their golfing skills against a new legend in the making – the superb PGA National Course, which has won plaudits from near and far.

For those who prefer their golf a little easier or wish to get back into the swing gently, The Derby course is ideal. There is also a putting green on site, plus a floodlit driving range. The Belfry caters for golfers at every level of ability and development, running courses for beginners and residential golf schools for more experienced players.

But The Belfry is more than simply a great golf venue. It also boasts a capacious 324-bedroom four-star hotel, 21 conference and meeting rooms, five restaurants and eight bars. There is a well-equipped leisure club, Aqua Spa, and the Bel Air Nightclub is in the hotel grounds.

GOLF FACILITIES

Best season for golf: Spring, Summer, Autumn.

COURSES: LENGTH	PAR	FEES
The Brabazon		
6487m	72	closed/£90
The PGA National		
6140m	72	£45/£60
The Derby		
5476m	69	£20/£30

N.B. Rates given are for low/high season and are valid until 31.10.2000.

Europe's largest on-course golf leisure and lifestyle shop; Ryder Cup venue 1985, 1989, 1993 and 2001; practice facilities; tuition by arrangement.

Facilities key

324   400

HAWKSTONE PARK HOTEL

Hotel information

Weston-under-Redcastle
Shrewsbury
Shropshire
SY4 SUY

Tel: +44 (0) 1939 200611
Fax: +44 (0) 1939 200311
Email: info@hawkstone.co.uk
Web: www.hawkstone.co.uk

Accolades

☆☆☆ Silver ETC

Airport

Birmingham: 1 hr
Manchester: 1 hr

Accommodation price guide

Accepted credit cards
AE MC V DC

Set in 160 hectares of Shropshire parkland designated by English Heritage as Grade One landscape, Hawkstone Park boasts two 18-hole courses, each offering contrasting and challenging games. The Hawkstone course opened for play in 1920 and is built around the 12th Century Red Castle. The Windmill course has many American-style features, such as round and oval tees, fairways lined with uniform mounds and large, gently undulating greens.

To support these championship courses there is a six-hole par Academy Course, a driving range and practice areas, plus a purpose-built golf centre. This complex incorporates a reception/registration area, deluxe changing facilities, PGA Professional Services, a golf shop with an extensive range of equipment and leisurewear, a Corporate Day sales office, and the Terrace Bar and Restaurant. The hotel also has a range of meeting rooms, perfect for conferences, banquets and dinner-dances.

This unique location is complemented by the 18th Century Park and Follies – a woodland fantasy of caves, cliffs and grottoes which has been described as a lost world in the heart of Shropshire. Hawkstone Park is, without question, one of Britain's greatest historic parklands.

Recreational facilities

Historic park and follies. English Heritage designated Grade One landscape with caves, cliffs and grotto.

Meeting/business facilities

Three conference rooms and three meeting rooms, to accomodate up to 200 people.

Local attractions

Iron Bridge Gorge museums.

GOLF FACILITIES

Best season for golf: May to October.

COURSES:	LENGTH	PAR	FEES
Windmill			
	5902m	72	£30-38
Hawkstone			
	5916m	72	£30-38
Academy (six holes)			
	664m	3	£5-6

Facilities key

66   200

RUDDING PARK HOUSE & HOTEL

Hotel information

Rudding Park
Follifoot
Harrogate
North Yorkshire
HG3 1JH

Tel: +44 (0) 1423 871 350
Fax: +44 (0) 1423 872 286
Email: reservations@rudding-park.co.uk
Web: www.rudding-park.co.uk

Accolades

☆☆☆☆
Yorkshire Tourist Board Hotel of Year

Airport

Leeds/Bradford: 15 mins

Accommodation price guide

Accepted credit cards
AE MC V DC

Recreational facilities

18-hole golf course; nearby (5 km) Academy Health Club and Spa with gym, pool, sauna, solarium, tennis, spa and beauty treatments.

Meeting/business facilities

14 rooms, for up to 230 delegates; on-site field available for activities – team building, falconry, go-karts, archery, team games.

Local attractions

Spa town of Harrogate, York (Railway Museum), Leeds (Royal Armories), Harwood House, Ripley Castle, Castle Howard.

Voted "Hotel of the Year 1998" by the Yorkshire Tourist Board, Rudding Park is the ideal place from which to explore the county's many sights. After 27 years of careful restoration by the Mackaness family, this 800-hectare estate located just south of Harrogate now includes a superb four-star hotel and an 18-hole, parkland golf course.

Rudding Park Hotel, the estate's latest addition, complements the original architecture of the Regency House, whilst its interior design is more contemporary, with bold colours in the public areas blending with the cherrywood and paler colours of the bedrooms. Rudding Park's Clocktower Bar & Restaurant, with its imaginative cooking style, has already become a local favourite.

The relaxing atmosphere of Rudding Park lends itself to guests seeking a tranquil, weekend break, whilst keen golfers find Rudding Park's mature parkland course a delight. The 18-hole, par 72, golf course was designed by Martin Hawtree and has won several awards for its environmental awareness.

All guests staying at Rudding Park have complimentary use of the nearby Academy Health Spa, with its gym, swimming pool, sauna and steam room. For an extra charge guests may partake in a myriad of health and beauty treatments, and also use the indoor and outdoor tennis courts.

GOLF FACILITIES

Best season for golf: May to October.

COURSES:	LENGTH	PAR	FEES
Rudding Park			
	6871m	72	E 29-34

18-bay covered floodlit driving range; tuition packages available; tournaments open to guests.

Facilities key

50   230

STAKIS PUCKRUP HALL

Recreational facilities

Heated pool, sauna, spa bath, steam room, beauty salon, state-of-the-art gym.

Meeting/business facilities

13 rooms, for up to 250 delegates.

Local attractions

Gloucester docks, Royal Worcester factory, Cheltenham racecourse.

Hotel information

Puckrup
Tewkesbury
Gloucestershire GL20 6EL

Tel: +44 (0) 1684 296200
Fax: +44 (0) 1684 850788

Accolades

★☆☆☆

Airport

Birmingham International: 40 mins

Accommodation price guide

€

Accepted credit cards
AE MC V DC

Formerly a regency manor house, now sympathetically extended into a luxury country house hotel, Puckrup Hall is a welcome retreat on the edge of the Cotswolds. The hotel is conveniently situated for the M5 motorway, midway between historic Worcester, with its famous cathedral and cricket ground, and the well-known racecourse and beautiful shops of Cheltenham.

The 16 bedrooms in the old hall retain individuality and charm, ranging from cozy double rooms 'under the eaves' to four-posters in large high-ceilinged rooms. Each has its own en-suite bathroom, as do the rooms in the new part of the hotel, some of which offer particularly fine views over the golf course. Some junior and grand suites with balconies are also available at a supplement.

The 18-hole par 70 course, set in 60 hectares of parkland around the hotel, with its natural water hazards, mature trees and wonderful views of the Malvern Hills, is a challenging game of golf for the novice and experienced golfer alike. Host to the PGA West Region Tournament for three years from 1994, the course is acknowledged as being one of the finest in the area.

GOLF FACILITIES

Best season for golf: May to October.

COURSES:	LENGTH	PAR	FEES
Puckrup Hall			
	5641m	70	£46

Practice ground on site, tuition available, buggy hire; PGA West Region Tournament held here 1994 to 1996.

Facilities key

84   250

STAPLEFORD PARK

Hotel information

Nr. Melton Mowbray
Leicestershire
LE14 2EF

Tel: +44 (0) 1572 787522
Fax: +44 (0) 1572 787651
Email: reservations@stapleford.co.uk
Web: www.stapleford.co.uk

Accolades

✪✪✪✪ (red) AA, RAC

Airport

East Midlands: 40 mins
Birmingham International: 1 hr
London Heathrow: 2 hrs

Accommodation price guide

Accepted credit cards
AE DC MC V

Recreational facilities

Health and leisure centre with indoor pool; five hectares of formal gardens, 200 hectares of parkland; clay target shooting, archery, school of falconry, croquet, lake fishing, riding stables.

Meeting/business facilities

10 rooms, for up to 200 delegates; ISDN2 data line.

Local attractions

Lincoln Cathedral, Belvoir Castle, Burghley House, historic old town of Stamford; country walks, antique shops.

Set in 220 hectares of glorious Capability Brown landscaped parkland in the heart of the Shires, luxurious Stapleford Park is the complete destination for a weekend away and provides standards of hospitality and elegance found in only a few hotels and resorts worldwide.

The Donald Steel designed golf course draws its inspiration from the Scottish links courses. Using the natural features of the land, drawing on the beautiful views over classic English countryside, and at just over 6300 metres, this is a rewarding course in all respects, for novice and expert alike.

In an atmosphere of informal luxury, Stapleford Park's house guests experience the unique ambience of rich warmth and friendliness in which the finest things in life can be properly enjoyed. The menu changes daily and complements the cellar of fine wines. The Grinling Gibbons dining room, with its ornately carved woodwork, must be one of the most elegant in England.

The 50 wonderful individually designed and furnished bedrooms, sumptuous reception rooms, Carnegie Clarins health spa and swimming pool, equestrian centre and golf academy are all complemented by a great team of friendly staff.

Privately situated in the classically beautiful English countryside of rural Leicestershire, Stapleford Park's accessibility from London brings a new meaning to the pleasures and enjoyment of being a house guest at a splendid country house.

GOLF FACILITIES
Best season for golf: April to October.

COURSES:	LENGTH	PAR	FEES
Stapleford Park			
	6309m	73	£50
Belton Woods Lakes Course			
	6180m	72	£22-25
Greetham Valley Course			
	5099m	68	£24-28

Driving range and putting green; range of fine courses within half hour drive.

Facilities key

51   200

WELCOMBE HOTEL & GOLF COURSE

Hotel information

Warwick Road
Stratford upon Avon
Warwickshire
CV37 0NR

Tel: +44 (0) 1789 295 252
Fax: +44 (0) 1789 414 666
Email: sales@welcombe.co.uk
Web: www.welcombe.co.uk

Accolades

☆☆☆☆☆ de luxe AA, ☆☆☆☆☆
Highly recommended Heart of England
Tourist Board, two AA rosettes for
cuisine.

Airport

Birmingham International: 25 mins
London Heathrow: 1hr 30 mins

Accommodation price guide

Accepted credit cards
AE DC MC V

Preferred tour operator

From UK
British Airways Holidays
Tel: +44 (0) 870 2424 249
Crystal Holidays
Tel: +44 (0) 208 240 3336
Superbreak
Tel: +44 (0) 1904 628 992

The Welcombe Hotel is a spectacular listed 19th Century Jacobean-style mansion set within 60 hectares of parkland once owned by William Shakespeare, featuring formal gardens, mature trees, lakes and a waterfall.

It enjoys a reputation for exceptional comfort, fine cuisine and traditional English country house ambience. Each room is decorated with fine antique furniture and an individual elegance. The Trevelyan Bar is perfect for pre- or after-dinner drinks.

The hotel's latest development is a health and beauty salon. Set in the peaceful garden wing, its facilities include a hair salon, treatment rooms, solarium and fitness room.

The 18-hole Welcombe Golf Course has recently benefitted from an intensive period of lavish attention. An extensive fairway watering system now ensures lush fairways, and greens that run fast and true. The last three holes are especially noteworthy. The 16th is a superb par 5 slight dog-leg right, while the 17th requires a full carry over a picturesque lake. The 18th provides a reasonably gentle par five finish for the weary golfer.

Recreational facilities

18-hole golf course, health and beauty salon, two outdoor tennis courts, mini fitness room, solarium, team building for groups – by arrangement; swimming, horse riding, fishing, river boating all available locally.

Meeting/business facilities

Seven meeting rooms, for up to 110 delegates, secretarial services.

Local attractions

Formal Italian gardens, walks in the Welcombe Hills, Shakespeare Theatre and the historic riverside town of Stratford upon Avon.

GOLF FACILITIES
Best season for golf: Excellent conditions throughout the year.

COURSES:	LENGTH	PAR	FEES
Welcombe			
	5750m	70	£50

On-site 18-hole course, practice range, putting green; tuition available; stunning views across River Avon.

Facilities key

65   110

HILL VALLEY GOLF HOTEL & COUNTRY CLUB

Hill Valley's magnificent 5944-metre par 73 Emerald course, originally designed by Peter Aliss and David Thomas, features undulating fairways and American-style greens protected by strategically placed bunkers and an abundance of water to present a true test for all golfers. The 4390m Sapphire course is a stern test of the short game, with water featured on no less than 14 of its holes.

Splendidly located within the Clubhouse area are 28 spacious and well-appointed bedrooms all with private bathrooms, TV, radio, tea and coffee making facilities and telephones. Other first-class facilities provided at the Clubhouse include restaurants, bars, a carvery, a substantial function suite and a fully equipped leisure centre.

Hotel information

Terrick Road
Whitchurch
Shropshire
SY13 4JZ

Tel: +44 (0) 1948 663584/667788
Fax: +44 (0) 1948 665927
Email: info@hill-valley.co.uk
Web: www.hill-valley.co.uk

Airport

Manchester: 1 hr
Liverpool: 1 hr
Birmingham: 1 hr 30 mins

Accommodation price guide

Accepted credit cards
AE DC MC V

Local attractions

Historic city of Chester; Horseshoe Pass; mountains of Snowdonia.

Meeting/business facilities

Fully equipped Eagle Suite accommodates up to 250 for dances, dinners, wedding receptions and party nights; specialists in catering for group and society packages.

Recreational facilities

Leisure centre, snooker, pool.

GOLF FACILITIES

Best season for golf: All year round.

COURSES:	LENGTH	PAR	FEES
Emerald	5943m	73	£15-27.50
Sapphire	4390m	66	£7-12.50

Brand new fully stocked pro shop; over 40 buggies available all year round; driving range; tuition by PGA pro.

Facilities key

28   250

KENWICK PARK HOTEL

The Kenwick Park Hotel stands in the grounds of the Kenwick Park Estate, itself set amid a designated Area of Outstanding Natural Beauty.

Approached through a magnificent avenue of majestic broadleaf trees, the hotel has been created by carefully converting the imposing Georgian-style Kenwick Hall. It stands within a few yards of the ninth and 18th greens of the superb Kenwick Park Golf Course, where play is exclusive to members and to overnight guests of the hotel.

Special holiday packages are available for visiting golfers, and there is lots in the immediate area for accompanying families to enjoy. Kenwick Park Hotel provides an oasis of rural pursuits, both on the estate and in the surrounding Lincolnshire Wolds.

Hotel information

Kenwick Park
Louth
Lincolnshire LN11 8NR

Tel: +44 (0) 1507 608806
Fax: +44 (0) 1507 608027
Email: enquiries@kenwick-park.co.uk
Web: www.kenwick-park.co.uk

Accolades

☆☆☆ Two AA rosettes

Airport

Humberside: 30 mins
East Midlands: 1 hr 30 mins

Accommodation price guide

Accepted credit cards
AE DC MC V

Local attractions

Thriving market town of Louth; coastal resorts of Cleethorpes, Mablethorpe and Skegness; historic city of Lincoln; Lincolnshire Wolds.

Meeting/business facilities

Four rooms, for up to 100 delegates

Recreational facilities

Adjacent golf course; gardens; health and leisure facilities, including pool, sauna, Jacuzzi, steam room, aerobics, gym, sunbed, creche; tennis, squash.

GOLF FACILITIES

Best season: April to October.

COURSES:	LENGTH	PAR	FEES
Kenwick Park	6398m	72	£30

Parkland course with undulating terrain, nine water features and mature woodland; indoor and outdoor driving range.

Facilities key

24   100

ENGLAND SOUTH & WALES   Planning for the perfect tour

White cliffs, imposing castles, thatched cottages, country churches and pubs, golden fields of wheat and cities filled with dreaming spires and so much history – the South of England could have been created with the travel writer's book of clichés specifically in mind.

Canterbury, Salisbury, Exeter, Oxford, Cambridge, Bath – these and others are cities of rare charm, and these days offer gourmet quality food, even at pub level, street entertainment and an air of lively vitality to all the time-honoured heritage and culture. Nor should we forget London, a particular magnet in this first year of the new century, thanks to the vast Millennium Dome, the towering London Eye Ferris wheel and year-long celebrations.

Wales too has a truly picture postcard quality. Deep, thickly wooded valleys, where you will truly find Tom Jones's vaunted 'Green, Green Grass Of Home', contrasted with vast stretches of open moorland, the smooth, rounded Brecon Beacons and the more dramatic mountains of Snowdonia.

GETTING THERE Four international airports – Heathrow, Gatwick, Stansted and Luton – surround London, the world's most exciting city of the moment. To this can be added a network of regional airports. The South also has an extensive motorway network.

APRÈS GOLF Take time out in London and you are hitting one of the world's great entertainment capitals – but make sure to book show tickets well in advance. Good theatre can also be found in smaller towns and cities while music of all kinds is heard in abundance.

OFF THE COURSE Sightseeing is a major pre-occupation in a land full of natural beauty as well as abundant remembrances of Celtic, Roman, Saxon, Danish, Norman and subsequent civilisations. Southern England and Wales can boast a myriad things to do and have ample opportunities for every kind of leisure opportunity, from cruising the River Thames or the mighty Severn, hang-gliding off the Downs and watching world-class sport to bird-watching, studying archaeology and horse riding.

Royal St David's in Wales

NOT TO BE MISSED There's a surfeit of cathedrals, castles, stately homes and royal palaces. Outstanding gems include Canterbury, Winchester, Exeter and Salisbury cathedrals; the castles at Dover, Leeds (Kent), Windsor, Norwich, Caernarfon and Conway; admire Buckingham Palace and Hampton Court. Visit the Cotswolds, the Norfolk Broads, Suffolk, Snowdonia.

FACTS AND FIGURES

- The South of Britain has the highest concentration of golf courses in the world.
- Bring a valid handicap certificate (and a letter of introduction for the top courses).
- Access is easy, with international airports at London, Bristol and Cardiff and many regional airports.
- There are train and ferry links with mainland Europe and the region abounds with car hire outlets.
- Beware – the roads are congested.
- Accommodation is plentiful, but advance booking is recommended between June and September.

The first documented evidence of golf in England and Wales dates from the middle of the 15th Century and the sport has been growing ever since. We all know about the great courses like Wentworth, Sunningdale and Royal St George's, and there are quite literally hundreds of other courses here, old and new.

As you'd expect, the biggest concentration of venues is around London, but there is nowhere in the region that doesn't abound with courses. The key to arranging a successful golfing holiday here is planning ahead. Although Southern England and Wales looks a relatively small area on the map, it is wise not to select courses located too far apart. The whole area has frequently congested roads, so it is wise to plan your play within a maximum 80-kilometre radius.

Adding the wonderful wild courses like Princes and Royal Cinque Ports along the Kent coast to a London-based itinerary might sound attractive, but you'd probably spend more time in the car than on the greens. In the West Country and Wales things are easier, but even here the roads get clogged up at peak holiday time. So if you decide to take on Jack Nicklaus's monster at St. Mellion at Saltash, then choose nearby courses like St. Enodoc at Wadebridge or Trevose.

It is also wise to book ahead and to plan according to your pocket. Great courses around London like Wentworth and Woburn are expensive and often difficult to get on. In the countryside, though, rates as low as £20 can still mean good golf. The Cambridge Meridian course, for example, is a wonderful test of lakes and woodland, yet only charges £18 at weekends. In the West Country the historic links at Royal North Devon, the oldest in England, charges just £24.

In Wales there are even more bargains. The fine Cardigan Golf Course on the Teifi estuary is £15 mid week and £20 at weekends, while right at the top of the Welsh league, St Pierre at Chepstow is £40 mid week and £50 at weekends. Great value indeed.

NEW DEVELOPMENTS

- In the past decade more than 180 new courses have been built in the region.

Hotels

● Stoke Park	Page 180
○ Vale of Glamorgan Hotel	Page 181
◐ Woodbury Park Hotel	Page 182

Favourite fairways

① THE OLD COURSE SUNNINGDALE

Founded in 1900 the Old Course was designed by Willie Park. Every hole is joy on what is considered by many to be the most attractive inland course in Britain. Visitors cannot play on Friday, Saturday or Sunday, and both a handicap certificate and a letter of introduction are necessary. The green fee, at £105 per day, is money well spent.
Par 70   Length 5779m
Sunningdale, Ridgemount Rd., Sunningdale Ascot SL5 9RR
Tel:+44 (0) 1344 621681   Fax:+44 (0) 1344 624154

② ROYAL ST GEORGE'S

Opened in 1887, St George's is the famous Kent links course where Sandy Lyle won the 1985 Open by one shot from Payne Stewart. Offshore breezes quickly turn into gales outside the summer months and make the course, with its deep bunkers and huge sand hills, virtually unplayable. If it's blowing don't go there – it's just too difficult.
Par 70   Length 5983m
Royal St George's Sandwich, Kent, CT13 9PB
Tel: +44 (0) 1304 613090   Fax: +44 (0) 1304 611245

③ WOODHALL SPA

Classified as the "finest inland course in the British Isles" by the English Golf Union, which recently bought it to use as its headquarters, Woodhall is a delightful heathland course in the flatlands southeast of Lincoln. It is noted for its friendly atmosphere, but it has become so popular that its wise to ring before you go.
Par 73   Length 6308m
Woodhall Spa, Lincolnshire, LN10 6PU
Tel: +44 (0) 1526 352778   Fax: +44 (0) 1526 352511

④ ST PIERRE (OLD COURSE)

Set in 160 hectares of glorious deer park, this relatively new course demands good shot-making if you're not to be snookered by the huge mature oak and ash trees. The feature lake, a wildlife sanctuary, gives this premier Welsh course a fresh feel. There are fine views down to the Severn Bridge, which links Wales and England across the Bristol Channel.
Par 71   Length 5224m
St Pierre, St Pierre Park, Chepstow, Monmouthshire, NP6 6YA
Tel: +44 (0) 1291 625261   Fax: +44 (0) 1291 629975

⑤ YELVERTON

This excellent little course in the wilds of Devon is a fine example of the hidden gems of the English countryside. It's pretty, friendly, has wonderfully fast greens and is just a pleasure to play. No pushover either, this is typical of so many good private courses which visitors miss out on to their cost when they just concentrate on the big names. At £30 a round it's a bargain.
Par 71   Length 5799m
Yelverton, Golf Links Rd, Yelverton, Devon. PL20 6BN
Tel: +44 (0) 1822 852824   Fax: +44 (0) 1822 854824

CLIMATE

Though it's said you can experience all four seasons in a single day, England and Wales have temperate climates. Rainfall is unpredictable, though. Whatever the season, prepare for anything and you can't go too far wrong!

Sample point: London

Price guide €

Round of golf	🪙🪙🪙	Golf balls	🪙🪙🪙🪙
Small beer	🪙🪙	4/5 star hotel room	🪙🪙🪙🪙🪙

CONTACT

English Tourism Council
Thames Tower, Blacks Road, Hammersmith, London W6 9EL
Tel: +44 (0) 20 8563 3000   Fax: +44 (0) 20 8563 0302

STOKE PARK CLUB

Hotel information

Park Road
Stoke Poges
Buckinghamshire
SL2 4PG

Tel: +44 (0) 1753 717171
Fax: +44 (0) 1753 717181
Email: info@stokeparkclub.com
Web: www.stokeparkclub.com

Accolades

★★★★☆
Member The Leading Hotels of the World
Gold Accolade from Tourist Board

Airport

London Heathrow: 15 mins
London Gatwick: 45 mins

Accommodation price guide

Accepted credit cards
AE MC V DC

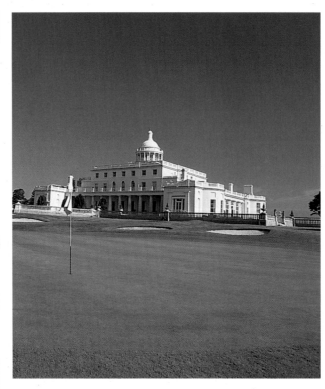

Recreational facilities

Historic gardens, fountains, lakes; 27-hole championship golf; four all-weather and five grass tennis courts; snooker, croquet, fishing; swimming available locally.

Meeting/business facilities

Seven rooms, for up to 110 delegates.

Local attractions

Windsor Castle, Royal Ascot race course, Legoland, Thorpe Park theme park, Eton College, boating on the Thames.

A magnificent 18th Century mansion built in 1791, Stoke Park Club sits at the pinnacle of a quintessentially English country estate. Historic gardens, landscaped by the renowned Capability Brown, and the 27-hole championship golf course, created in 1908 by Harry Colt and described by many as one of the finest parkland courses in the world, surround the house, affording the most spectacular views from every room.

Stoke Park Club's interior is truly palatial, with tall ceilings, fine works of art, antiques and original etchings. The guest bedrooms, too, are exquisite, featuring the finest interior design and elegant period furniture. The marble bathrooms are luxurious and boast every possible extra.

Within the mansion there is an abundance of spacious drawing rooms, and guests can enjoy the traditional Presidents Bar, filled with pictures illustrating years of historic golf.

Stoke Park Club is a beautiful estate with enticing golf. However, guests can also simply sit on the terrace or in the gardens and relax.

GOLF FACILITIES

Best season for golf: Spring, Summer, Autumn.

COURSES:	LENGTH	PAR	FEES
Stoke Poges Lane Jackson			
	2766m	36	£110-180*
Stoke Poges Alison			
	2916m	35	£110-180*
Stoke Poges Colt			
	2934m	36	£110-180*
			*per 18 holes

Facilities key

20   110

VALE OF GLAMORGAN HOTEL
GOLF & COUNTRY CLUB

Hotel information

Hensol Park
Hensol
Vale of Glamorgan
South Wales

Tel: +44 (0) 1443 667800
Fax: +44 (0) 1443 667801

Accolades

★★★☆

Airport

Cardiff International: 20 mins
London Heathrow: 1hr 30 mins

Accommodation price guide

Accepted credit cards
AE MC V DC

Recreational facilities

18-hole championship course, nine-hole course; Jacuzzi, indoor heated pool, gym, squash, tennis, sauna, steam room, extensive spa facilities and treatments; horse riding, falconry and off-road driving locally.

Meeting/business facilities

Nine rooms, for up to 250 delegates; executive club.

Local attractions

Cardiff – capital city of Wales, Llanerch Vineyard, Castle Coch.

In the heart of South Wales' most beautiful countryside, the Vale of Glamorgan Hotel, Golf & Country Club enjoys an enviable location, just 15 minutes from the centre of bustling Cardiff and 20 minutes from Cardiff International Airport.

Surrounded by 100 hectares of glorious parkland, the hotel's design is based on the elegant Georgian manors of the 18th Century. Traditionally furnished, the hotel combines elegance with comfort and the most breathtaking views from most rooms. Peace and tranquility can be found in abundance here. In addition to the two excellent golf courses, there are extensive sports facilities, including tennis and squash courts, swimming pool, gymnasium, saunas and Jacuzzi. Heron's Spa offers an extensive range of health and beauty treatments.

The Lake course is a par 72 championship layout, taking full advantage of the setting, with its towering trees and strategically placed bunkers and lakes. The signature 12th hole is particularly challenging, the green being surrounded by water and only accessible via a narrow stone bridge. Comparisons with the famous 13th at Augusta are inevitable.

The nine-hole Hensol course is perfect for clients seeking a challenge but with little time to play. This lay-out offers cleverly landscaped holes, providing many interesting and difficult shots and appealing to players of all levels.

GOLF FACILITIES

Best season for golf: March to September.

COURSES:	LENGTH	PAR	FEE
The Lake			
	5852m	72	£25
The Hensol			
	2845m	36	£12.50

20-bay driving range, sand bunker, chipping area, 18-hole putting green, video analysis.

Facilities key

143   250

WOODBURY PARK HOTEL, GOLF & COUNTRY CLUB

Hotel information

Woodbury Castle
Woodbury
Exeter
Devon
EX5 1JJ

Tel: +44 (0) 1395 233382
Fax: +44 (0) 1395 234701
Email: woodbury-park@eclipse.co.uk
Web: www.woodburypark.co.uk

Airport

Exeter: 15 mins

Accommodation price guide

Accepted credit cards
MC V

Recreational facilities

Swimming pool, Jacuzzi, sauna, gym, dance studio, squash tennis, football; beauty treatments; Nigel Mansell World of Racing.

Meeting/business facilities

Four rooms, for up to 150 delegates, with video conferencing and PowerPoint presentation facilities.

Local attractions

Bicton Gardens, Crealy Adventure Park; 15 mins from the coast.

Former Formula One world motor racing champion Nigel Mansell has poured a huge investment into this little piece of glorious Devon, creating a superb golf and country club hotel for the ultimate in leisure experiences.

Based on a grand country mansion, Woodbury Park invites all its guests to relax in style amid elegant surroundings – and there's a very special welcome for golfers with an exceptional mature course which was designed by J. Hamilton Stutt, the doyen of British golf architecture. It carries all the master's hallmarks: wide fairways, expansive bunkers and huge, rippling greens while still being a challenge to play, with its many bending fairways.

The 18-hole Oaks course covers 6218 metres, with a par of 72, while Acorns is a splendid 2743-metre nine-hole with a par of 33. The hotel has a well-stocked golf shop – a superb retail outlet offering the very latest equipment at competitive prices, plus top fashion accessories, which include the exclusive Nigel Mansell range. The popular leisure club incorporates a sparkling 20-metre swimming pool, spa pool, sauna, fully equipped gymnasium and squash courts while the food offer is also outstanding, thanks to a team of prestige chefs.

GOLF FACILITIES

Best season for golf: April to October.

COURSES:	LENGTH	PAR	FEES
Burnham and Berrow			
	5843m	71	£30
Saunton			
	6150m	73	£30
Royal North Devon			
	6080m	72	£30
Bowood			
	6688m	74	£30
St. Mellion			
	6079m	72	£30
Lanhydrock			
	5653m	70	£25

18-bay covered driving range, pitching area, putting greens; tuition on request; guests can play at various competitons during the year.

Facilities key

56   150

SWEDEN & DENMARK A breath of fresh air

For those who want a holiday that's simply more refreshing, the pure air of Sweden and Denmark will help to clarify one of golf's best kept secrets.

Many of Southern Sweden's courses are designed by the world's leading golf architects, but this high standard is not restricted to the south. At Björklidens, on the country's northernmost point, golfers can enjoy the stimulating experience of playing under the midnight sun.

The best golf, however, is found in the south-west, nicknamed the 'Costa del Golf' by locals. This area boasts 40 courses all within an hour's drive – perfect for the golfing fanatic or for those who feel like a lot of practice. Over in Denmark, an abundance of undulating countryside and sparkling lakes are used to good effect in its more than 100 courses.

NEW DEVELOPMENTS

● **Many courses have 27 or 36 holes, but several of the former are being extended to 2x18 holes. A further 200 courses are planned within the next five years.**

Copenhagen's little maiden

Though slightly larger than California, Sweden is home to just 8.9 million people, with the greatest concentration in the southern cities of Gothenburg, Malmö and Stockholm, one of Europe's grandest and most historic capitals. That means there's lots of open space, much of it forested, with a profusion of lakes and mountains.

Denmark, with a population of 5.4 million in a far smaller area, maintains strong ties with its neighbour – underlined by the new road and rail links between the countries, making life easier for touring golfers.

GETTING THERE Stockholm and Copenhagen are major international airports, while Gothenburg is one of Europe's busiest regional destinations.

APRÈS GOLF Scandinavians like to drink socially, despite the steep prices. Fish, venison, and the vast buffets known as smorgåsbord are a great attraction, as are Denmark's lavish open sandwiches and patisserie.

OFF THE COURSE With all that water, fishing – sea, river and lake – is extremely popular, as are hiking, mountain biking and, in the colder months, cross-country skiing. Quality handicrafts and highly collectable antiques can be found in tiny village boutiques.

NOT TO BE MISSED Spare five or six days of your holiday for a fabulous trip down the Gota Canal on a 100 year old ship; visit Denmark's original Legoland at Billund and the famed Tivoli Gardens in Copenhagen.

CLIMATE

Thanks to the Gulf Stream effect, the west coast of Sweden has a temperate climate, as does the Danish peninsula of Jutland. Further north, there's the added advantage of long, clear Summer nights.

Sample point: Copenhagen

RECOMMENDED CAR HIRE *Hertz*
UK: +44 (0) 870 848 4848
Germany: +49 (0) 180 533 3535
Website: www.hertz.com

Price guide €

	Round of golf	Golf balls
Small beer		4/5 star hotel room

CONTACT
Swedish Travel & Tourism Council
Kungsgated 36, Box 3030, 10361 Stockholm, Sweden
Tel: +46 (0) 8 725 55 00   Fax: +46 (0) 8 725 55 31
Danish Tourist Bureau Bernstorffsgade 1, DK - 1577, Copenhagen V, Denmark Tel: +45 (0) 33 11 13 25 Fax: +45 (0) 93 49 69

FACTS AND FIGURES

● **With more than 430,000 golfers among its 8.3 million inhabitants, Sweden has one of the highest ratios of golfers per head of population in the world. There are 381 golf clubs, the first of which opened in 1904.**
● **Denmark has more than 100 golf courses.**

Favourite fairways

1 ESBJERG

At 78 years, this Jutland club is one of Denmark's oldest. It has two courses: the 18-hole Marbaek and the nine-hole Myrtue, which can be played twice. Set in hilly terrain amid coniferous forests and heather on the west coast, the Marbaek was designed by leading Danish course architect Frederic Dreyer.
Par 71   Length 5728m (Marbaek)
Par 71   Length 4977m (Myrtue)
Sonderhedevej 11, 6710 Esbjerg, Denmark
Tel: +45 (0) 75 26 92 19 Fax: +45 (0) 75 26 94 19

2 BÅSTAD

Designed by Hawtree, Taylor and Nordstrom, these delightful courses opened in 1930. Both offer an enjoyable challenge with tight fairways, water hazards and mature trees. For those of an all-round sporting nature Båstad is also the home of Swedish tennis.
Par 71   Length 5521m (Course 1)
Par 72   Length 5654m (Course 2)
Box 1037, 26921 Bastad, Sweden
Tel: +46 (0) 431 731 36 Fax: +46 (0) 431 733 31

3 BARSEBÄCK

With two outstanding courses designed by Steel and Bruce in 1969, this PGA European Tour course is one of Europe's best venues. Barseback, which will play host to the 2004 Solheim Cup match, is situated in a pine forest close to the sea and is strangely reminiscent of Scottish links.
Par 72   Length 6255m (Old Course)
Par 72   Length 6290m (New Course)
24655 Loddekopinge, Sweden
Tel: +46 (0) 46 776 230 Fax: +46 (0) 46 772 630

Hotels

● Hotel Store Kro	Page 184
● Skjoldenaesholm	Page 184

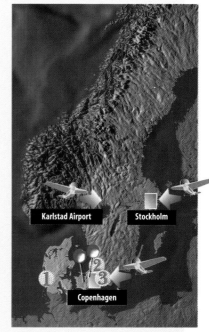
Karlstad Airport — Stockholm — Copenhagen

HOTEL STORE KRO

Hotel Store Kro was built by King Frederik IV in 1723 for guests who visited him at Fredensborg Castle, and ever since it has been the setting for countless special occasions. Naturally, much has changed over the years, but the style, ambience and quiet elegance still pervade the historic buildings and their classical architecture.

No fewer than ten golf courses are to be found in easy reach of the hotel, and you are close to many other attractions: the beautiful Fredensborg Castle, Kronborg Castle and the famous Frederiksborg Castle and museum, Louisiana and the Karen Blixen Museum, beautiful beaches and much more. In short, North Zealand's myriad of attractions are all conveniently located within a short drive.

Hotel information

Slotsgade 6
DK-3480 Fredensborg

Tel: +45 (0) 4840 0111
Fax: +45 (0) 4848 4561
Email: reservations@storekro.dk
Web: www.fredensborg.storekro.dk

Airport

Kastrup: 45 mins

Accommodation price guide

Accepted credit cards
AE DC MC V

Local attractions

Fredensborg Castle (only 100 metres away) open in July; Castle Park; Frederiksborg Museum; Louisiana Art Museum; beaches just ten kilometres away.

Meeting/business facilities

Five rooms for up to 100 delegates.

Recreational facilities

Large private garden, living rooms.

GOLF FACILITIES

Best season: March to November

COURSES:	LENGTH	PAR	FEES
Fredensborg	5829m	72	DKr270
Gilleleje	5900m	72	DKr375
Simons	6268m	72	DKr300

Facilities key

49 100

SKJOLDENÆSHOLM HOTEL & CONFERENCE CENTRE

At Skjoldenæsholm it is not hard to imagine what life must have been like in bygone days.

A stroll through the halls and salons of this gracious former manor house reveals elaborately decorated panelling and a wealth of antiques – a perfect historical gem which has been carefully converted to satisfy the expectations of even the most demanding of guests.

Close to this estate is Skjoldenæsholm's superb 18-hole golf course. Challenging and varied, it features small lakes, creeks and wooded areas, and affords players the added pleasure of enjoying rich and diverse wildlife. For the lure of culture, the fascinating city of Copenhagen is within easy reach.

Hotel information

Skjoldenaesvej 106
DK-4174 Jystrup

Tel: +45 (0) 57 528104
Fax: +45 (0) 57 528855
Email: hotel@skj.dk
Web: www.skj.dk

Airport

Copenhagen Kastrup: 45 mins

Accommodation price guide

Accepted credit cards
AE DC MC V

Local attractions

Country walks, local inns and restaurants.

Meeting/business facilities

Three rooms, for up to 50 delegates.

Recreational facilities

Tram museum on site; waymarked walking paths, large garden and park, lake fishing; tennis courts locally.

GOLF FACILITIES

Best season: April to October.

COURSES:	LENGTH	PAR	FEES
Skjoldenæsholm	5922m	71	US$48
Soro	5693m	71	US$35
Korser	5773m	71	US$35

Driving range; par 3 nine-hole course; tuition packages; guest tournaments.

Facilities key

38 50

GERMANY

Spectacular diversity at Europe's heart

Europe's most populous country – home to around 90 million people – Germany encompasses a vast range of scenery, from the Baltic sand dunes and low country to the rolling uplands of the delightful Black Forest and the high Alpine mountains on the Austrian border.

Most of the serious golfing interest focuses towards the south, where Bavaria and its neighbouring states offer courses set amid delightful hill and mountain country where green is not just a political statement but a reality. Here are to be found some truly historic cities – like Nuremberg where, at one time, more than 80 per cent of all the world's books were printed, and be-spired Munich, with its picturesque 16th and 17th Century heart.

Ulm boasts the world's tallest cathedral spires, Augsburg offers classic German half-timbered architecture, and the region is dotted with vineyards, pine forests, great rivers and other delights, including the magnificent Lake Constance.

GETTING THERE Germany pioneered the motorway concept and today has a comprehensive network of high-speed autobahns which bring its golf courses closer together. Frankfurt and Munich are major international airports while Stuttgart and other regional centres are also well served.

APRÈS GOLF The popular image of foaming steins of beer, meaty sausages and raucous beer cellars isn't far from the truth, but the delights of the German table can be subtle as well as hearty, with lots of usage of cooked fruits to accompany game and other meats. The south offers outstanding white wines and some memorable reds too, many of which never make it beyond the country's borders. Schnapps and other liqueurs dazzle with their quality and variety.

OFF THE COURSE While centuries-old houses abound, Germany is a thoroughly modern country, with all the sophisticated entertainment and leisure facilities that implies. Shopping is a joy, and the land that produced the genius of Goethe, Beethoven, Bach and Schiller is not short on culture either.

NOT TO BE MISSED — Street stall bratwürst sausages and some of the world's best beers year round but especially at the Munich Beer Festival in October; Christmas markets; Rhine and Elbe river cruises.

Watch the action from the clubhouse at Feldafing Golf Club

From its origins as a sport for the social elite, golf in Germany has expanded into one of the country's most popular pastimes. There are almost 350 18-hole golf courses in Germany, most of them located around major cities or in popular tourist regions, and offering an extremely high standard and range of facilities.

Among the most attractive golfing areas in Germany are Murnau in Bavaria and the wine valleys of the Rhine, although the cities of Berlin, Frankfurt and Munich also offer an entertaining variety of courses to complement their spectacular architecture, outstanding restaurants and a multiplicity of entertainments.

Many people hold a preconceived view that life in Germany is strictly regimented but, in truth, it is an astonishingly diverse country featuring dense forests, rolling hills, mountains, rivers and some of the most exciting and historical cities in Europe. Whether you wish to travel to the Black Forest, home to those fairytale castles which spring romantically from a cluster of trees on some Wagnerian mountainside, or visit the reunified Berlin with its pulsating nightlife and complex culture, Germany offers a stay to remember.

An excellent railway and air system, coupled with first-class, smooth-flowing autobahns, adds to the ease of the vacation while those in need of further relaxation can visit one of the many beer festivals which take place throughout much of the year.

In addition to outstanding golf courses, Germany also offers an abundance of health spas and other outdoor sporting activities.

FACTS AND FIGURES

● **For a more adventurous holiday, try visiting East Germany as reunification has led to the development of several new resorts such as Motzener-See or Semlin-am-See near Berlin.**

NEW DEVELOPMENTS

● **Golf, increasingly, is becoming one of Germany's most popular sports with a growing variety of courses to choose from. Most of them are located near to the major cities or popular tourist areas although the main drawback of that policy is that they can be fairly busy at weekends.**

Hotels

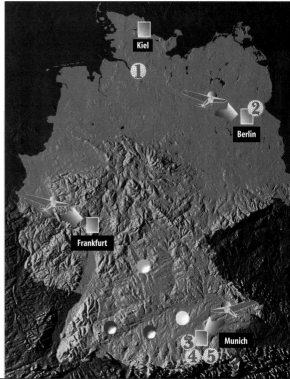

RECOMMENDED CAR HIRE

UK: +44 (0) 870 848 4848
Germany: +49 (0) 180 533 3535
Website: www.hertz.com

Hertz

Favourite fairways

The most up-to-date golf travel information is always at
www.golftravel4u.com

❶ GUT KADEN

This course on the outskirts of Hamburg has staged the Deutsche Bank-SAP Open TPC of Europe four times during the mid-1990s. Opened in 1984, it has often been blitzed by low scores from the top players. Despite being fairly straightforward as a test of golf, Gut Kaden has a picturesque setting and is an ideal venue for golfers in search of a layout to massage their egos.

Par 72   Length 6076m

Kadenerstrasse 9, 25486 Alveslohe, Germany
Tel: +49 (0) 41 939 9290   Fax: +49 (0) 41 939 92919

❷ BERLIN WANNSEE

Worth visiting just to check out the oldest course in Berlin. This was designed by FA Harris in 1895 and then extensively re-modelled in 1920s. Wannssee is not a demanding course, but it provides a pleasant way to waste an afternoon. All that is required is to hit straight to the fairways and miss the trees.

Par 72   Length 6088m

Golfweg 22, 14109 Berlin, Germany
Tel: +49 (0) 30 806 7060   Fax: +49 (0) 30 806 70610

❸ BEUERBERG

Combining spectacular views over the Bavarian Alps with a masterpiece of a course, Beuerberg in Gut Sterz is designed by Donald Harradine to include worrying water hazards and tricky bunker greens.

Par 74   Length 6036m

Gut Sterz, 82547 Beuerberg, Germany
Tel: +49 (0) 8179 617/728   Fax: +49 (0) 8179 5234

❹ GOLF CLUB FELDAFING

A traditional Bavarian resort and a fine parkland course, dating from 1926, skirting the shores of the Starnberger See. Majestic trees, which form a strategic feature here, are in fact, older than the course itself. They were part of the royal park of King Maximillian II, who created the fairy castle of Neuschwanstein nearby. Enjoyable holiday golf in a beautiful setting.

Par 71   Length 5708m

Tutzingerstrasse 15, D-8133 Faldafing/Obby, Bavaria
Tel: +49 (0) 8157 7005

❺ TEGERNSEER GOLF CLUB

Perched up on high ground overlooking the placid waters of the Tegersee, this friendly members' club welcomes visitors. Redesigned by Donald Harradine in 1982, it combines open rolling slopes with some narrow fairways carved out of the steep hillside above the charming rustic farm building that serves as clubhouse. A club with character, which has an annual 99-hole competition played on the longest day.

Par 70   Length 5483m

Robognerhof, Postfach 506, 8182 Bad Wiesee, Bavaria.
Tel: +49 (0) 8022 8769

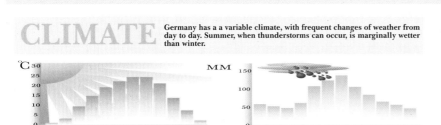

CLIMATE

Germany has a a variable climate, with frequent changes of weather from day to day. Summer, when thunderstorms can occur, is marginally wetter than winter.

Sample point: Munich

Price guide   €

| Round of golf | 🏌🏌🏌🏌 | Golf balls | 🏌🏌🏌🏌 |
| Small beer | 🏌🏌🏌 | 4/5 star hotel room | 🏌🏌🏌🏌 |

CONTACT

Deutsche Zentrale für Tourismuse.V(DZT),Beethovenstrasse 69, D-60325, Frankfurt am Main
Tel: +49 (0) 69 212 38800   Fax: +49 (0) 69 212 37880

GOLF HOTEL BODENSEE

Hotel information

Lampertsweiler 51
88138 Weissenberg

Tel: +49 (0) 8389 89100
Fax: +49 (0) 8389 89142
Email: info@golfhotel-bodensee.de
Web: www.golfhotel-bodensee.de

Accolades

☆☆☆☆

Airport

Friedrichshafen: 20 mins
Zürich: 90 mins
Munich: 2 hrs

Accommodation price guide

Accepted credit cards
MC V DC

Preferred tour operator

From UK
Abba   Tel: +44 (0) 1993 823923
From Germany
Frank   Tel: +49 (0) 69 95 88 34 38
From Germany
Frank   Tel: +49 (0) 69 95 88 34 38

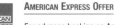

The four-star Golf Hotel Bodensee is situated directly on the Bodensee golf course, which was designed by Robert Trent Jones Senior. This charming establishment, built in country house style, offers all the facilities a discerning guest would expect of an excellent golfing hotel. The Golf Hotel Bodensee is located close to the historic island of Lindau in Lake Constance, five kilometres away. You will appreciate the privacy and intimacy of the hotel, and the hospitality and friendliness of its staff.

The kitchens of the Golf Hotel Bodensee use the freshest of produce, garnered from the lake and the surrounding region, to produce outstanding interpretations of regional and international dishes. On warm summer days you can sip a drink and follow the play on the first and 18th holes without having to move from the terrace.

After a challenging day on the fairways, you can relax and enjoy the excellent facilities of the wellness centre, with its sauna, steambath, whirlpool, solarium and massage. Alternative activities include watersports on Lake Constance, tennis, mountain excursions and sightseeing flights. As evening comes around, nothing is more pleasant than to meet up in the Rossi Bar bar to try a few cocktails – a speciality of the house.

Recreational facilities

Wellness centre with sauna, steambath, whirlpool, solarium and massage; watersports on Lake Constance; tennis and circular flights available very close by; mountains 30 mins.

Meeting/business facilities

Three conference rooms and two meeting rooms to accommodate up to 80 delegates.

Local attractions

Lake Constance, Island of Lindau, flower island of Mainau, Castle Neuschwanstein, St. Gallen Bibliothek, Zeppelin Museum at Friedrichshafen; open-air festival of Bregenz.

GOLF FACILITIES

Best season for golf: March to October.

COURSES:	LENGTH	PAR	FEES
Bodensee			
	6112m	72	E 28-38
Bad Schachen			
	5263m	72	E 31-41

The golf course at Bad Waldsee is just 40 minutes away; tuition is available at the golf academy; driving range, putting green; several tournaments are open to hotel guests.

Facilities key

26   80

HOTEL ALPENHOF

Hotel information

Ramsachstrasse 8
D-82418
Murnau

Tel: +49 (0) 8841 4910
Fax: +49 (0) 8841 5438
Email: info@alpenhof-murnau.com
Web: www.alpenhof-murnau.com

Accolades

☆☆☆☆ One star Michelin restaurant

Airport

Munich Franz-Joseph-Strauss:
1 hr 30 mins

Accommodation price guide

Accepted credit cards
AE MC V

Preferred tour operator

From UK
Abercrombie
& Kent   Tel: +44 (0) 1993 823923
From Germany
DER Tour
Frankfurt   Tel: +49 (0) 69 95 88 34 38

Recreational facilities

Outdoor and indoor swimming pools, health and beauty centre with resident doctor, sauna, tepidarium, solarium, fitness room, sun terrace, garden, tennis, watersports, walking, hiking available locally.

Meeting/business facilities

Six rooms, with latest facilities, for up to 200 delegates.

Local attractions

Murnauer Moos nature reserve, castle museum, Gabriel Münter House, castles of King Ludwig II, the Zugspitze – highest mountain in Germany.

GOLF FACILITIES

Best season for golf: Spring, Ssummer and Autumn.

COURSES:	LENGTH	PAR	FEES
Iffeldorf			
	5904m	72	E46-56
St. Eurach			
	6270m	71	E51
Werdenfels			
	5962m	72	E25-36

Six of Germany's most beautiful courses within 20 kilometres.

Right on the doorstep of Munich, the most magnificent city of South Germany, this wonderful holiday paradise – of a kind you will not find anywhere else in Germany – opens itself up to be enjoyed by the discerning visitor.

Artists of the renowned 'Blue Rider' school valued Murnau for the subtle colours of its moors, the incandescent violet of the mountains and the quality of the light reflected from its lake.

Besides super golf, leisure activities in the region are abundant and boundless. In this little piece of heaven, situated right on the border of the glorious Murnauer Moos nature reserve, you will find the Alpenhof Murnau, which has been a member of Relais et Chateaux since 1972 and is more a stylish country house than a hotel.

The Alpenhof has 77 rooms and suites, decorated in the traditional and elegant alpine style.

The Michelin one-star Reiterzimmer gourmet restaurant and the Moosberg Castell conservatory are known far beyond the region for their excellent cuisine. These comfortable and welcoming venues offer an ideal setting for private or business arrangements, and are the perfect starting points for projects of any kind.

Facilities key

77   200

KUR UND SPORTHOTEL TANNECK

Hotel information

Hartenthaler Strasse 29
86825 Bad Wörishofen

Tel: +49 (0) 82 47 30 70
Fax: +49 (0) 82 47 30 72 80
Email: tanneck@t-online.de
Web: www.tanneck.com

Accolades

★★★★

Airport

Munich: 1 hr 30 mins
Stuttgart: 2 hrs

Accommodation price guide

Accepted credit cards
AE MC V

Recreational facilties

Clay tennis courts, horse riding, swimming, country walks, large garden and park area; jetstream, whirlpool, sauna, gym, solarium, beauty salon; comprehensive health and fitness centre, including Kneipp therapies, massage, hydrotherapy, reflexology, lymph drainage, Qi-Gong, in-house medical team.

Local attractions

Elegant town of Bad Wörishofen, with excellent clothes shopping; beautiful landscapes; historic cities and architecture; less than one hour to the Alps by car.

Individuality, excellence and the finest hospitality in a dream location – that is the promise of the Kur und Sporthotel Tanneck. This luxurious hotel and spa complex is located on the southern fringes of Bad Wörishofen, an elegant town some 60 kilometres south-west of Munich, made famous by Sebastian Kneipp, founder of the renowned Kneipp therapy still practised there today.

The Tanneck is dedicated to your complete relaxation and invigoration, with a comprehensive range of facilities to entice you into healthy, active living. A golf practice area set in the hotel's extensive parkland enables guests to prepare themselves for the wide choice of 18-hole courses in the surrounding area, while tennis, riding, swimming and country walks also beckon. Perhaps the greatest pleasures await you in the spa – pamper yourself with a sauna or a dip in the whirlpool, or try massage, hydrotherapy, Qi-Dong, reflexology, or any of the many other therapies on offer, including, of course, the classic Kneipp therapy.

Modern elegance is the keynote of the hotel's rooms and apartments, while the final ingredient in this great escape from stress is the Tanneck's first-class cuisine – sumptuous food which is also designed to look after your well being.

GOLF FACILITIES

Best season for golf: April to November.

COURSES:	LENGTH	PAR	FEES
Bad Wörishofen			
	5952m	71	E46
Gut Ludwigsberg			
	6159m	72	E41
Memmingen			
	6178m	72	E51
Allgäuer			
	6215m	72	E41
Feldafing			
	5721m	71	E61

Facilities key

137

WALD & SCHLOSSHOTEL FRIEDRICHSRUHE

Hotel information

74639 Friedrichsruhe

Tel: +49 (0) 7941 60870
Fax: +49 (0) 7941 61468
Email: schlosshotel_friedrichsruhe@t-online.de
Web:
www.integra.fr/relaischateaux/waldschloss

Accolades

☆☆☆☆☆
One Michelin star

Airport

Stuttgart: 1 hr
Frankfurt: 1 hr 30 mins

Accommodation price guide

Accepted credit cards
AE MC V DC

Preferred tour operator

From Germany
Relais et
Châteaux   Tel: +49 (0) 180 533 3431
From USA
Relais et
Châteaux   Tel: +1 212 856 0115
From Japan
Relais et
Châteaux   Tel: +81 3 3444 3551

Recreational facilities

Beauty farm, indoor and outdoor pool, sauna; French gourmet restaurant on site plus local cuisine.

Meeting/business facilities

Three rooms, for up to 60-80 delegates.

Local attractions

Many medieval towns and castles.

The Magnificent Wald & Schlosshotel Friedrichsruhe, an imposing large white-walled and red-roofed mansion, is pleasingly located in the hilly and thickly wooded Hohenlohe country. It was built in 1712 by the Fursten of that ilk and is owned today by the Furst Kraft zu Hohenlohe Oehringen. This wonderful old edifice has been converted into a very superior hotel (a Relais & Chateaux member), was partly renovated last year, and is today run in lordly style by manager/chef Lothar Eirmann, who provides some of the most ambitious cooking to be found anywhere in Germany – or, for that matter, Europe.

Guest rooms are to be found in the old mansion or located along with the restaurant in a stylish modern extension which is fully in keeping with the welcoming ambience of this much favoured hotel.

Indoor and outdoor swimming pools, tennis and a health and fitness centre are among the hotel's many amenities while golfers will find a superb 18-hole course within a few steps. Beginners are catered for, expert tuition is available, and there are tournaments which guests may compete in.

GOLF FACILITIES

Best season for golf: April to November.

COURSES: LENGTH	PAR	FEES
Heilbronn Hohenlohe		
6039m	72	E46
Hofgasse		
6270m	71	E51

The 18-hole Golf Club Heilbronn Hohenlohe is only 200 metres from the hotel and can be booked for exclusive group use; trial golf courses for beginners; guests can play in most of the tournaments.

Facilities key

29 80

Golf- & Landhotel Semlin

Key Facts

Golf and Country Hotel Semlin
Ferchesarer Straße
D-14715 Semlin
Phone: +49 (0)3385 / 554-0
Fax: +49 (0)3385 / 554-400

Rooms
72 double rooms and 3 suites,
also available as singles

Prices
Single room: DM 140.00 – 175.00
Double room: DM 190.00 – 250.00
Suites: DM 250.00 – 350.00
All rates include breakfast

Credit Cards
Amex, Diners, Eurocard, Visa

Nearest Airport / City
Berlin-Tegel 75 km,
Rathenow 5 km

Fitness / Wellness
18-hole championship golf
course, state-of-the-art video
teaching equipment, individual
lessons, 2 tennis courts, fitness
facilities with solarium, steam
and dry sauna, riding, sailing,
surfing, bathing beach at nearby
Lake Hohenauer, beauty salon,
hairdresser, crèche

Golf- und Landclub Semlin am See

Golf Course
Gentlemen: 6.082 metres / 6.374 metres
Ladies: 5.423 metres / 5.640 meters
Par: 72, SSS: 72/73
50 practice tees (5 of which are covered)

Green Fee
Day Pass
Weekdays: DM 80.00
Saturday / Sunday / Bank Holidays: DM 120.00
Green Fee for the 18-hole course
Weekdays: DM 60.00
Saturday / Sunday / Bank Holidays: DM 90.00
Juniors / Students / Hotel Guests: concessions

Non-members
Non-members are welcome.
A club membership card is required.
On Saturday / Sunday / Bank Holidays guests
must be accompanied by a handicap player.

Golf & Landhotel Ahaus

Key Facts

Golf & Country Hotel Ahaus
Schmäinghook 36
D-48683 Ahaus-Alstätte
Phone: +49(0)2567 / 38-0
Fax: +49 (0)2567 / 38-200

Rooms
49, 33 double rooms,
12 apartments,
4 suites

Prices
Single room: DM 185.00
Double room: DM 220.00
Duplex: 280.00
Apartment as double room:
DM 320.00
Each additional person: DM 60.00

Credit Cards
Amex, Diners, Eurocard, Visa,
EC-Cash

Nearest Airport / City
Düsseldorf approx. 110 km
Münster approx. 60 km
Enschede (Netherlands)
approx. 15 km
Hotel transfer on request

Fitness / Wellness
3 x 9-hole golf course = 27 holes,
walking, cycling, sauna, steam
bath, Turkish bath, fitness studio,
Beauty Relax Centre, solarium,
beauty treatments

Golf- und Landclub Ahaus e.V.

Golf Course
Gentlemen: 5.810 metres / 6.109 metres
Ladies: 5.099 metres / 5.405 metres
Par: 72/1, SSS: 72/71

Green Fee
Weekdays: DM 60.00
Saturday / Sunday / Bank Holidays: DM 80.00
Driving range: DM 10.00

Non-members
Non-members are welcome.
A club membership card with handicap
certificate (36) is required.

Fairway Hotel am Golfplatz

Key Facts

Fairway Hotel am Golfplatz
Fremersbergstraße 125
D-76530 Baden-Baden
Phone: +49 (0)7221 – 3015-0
Fax: +49 (0)7221 – 3015-500

Rooms
103, 27 single rooms,
65 double rooms,
11 suites/maisonettes

Prices
Single room: DM 150.00 – 190.00
Double room: DM 180.00 – 250.00
Suites/Maisonettes: DM 290.00

Credit Cards
Amex, Visa, Eurocard, Diners,
EC-Cash

Nearest Airport / City
Stuttgart airport 100 km
Baden airpark 15 km
Karlsruhe 25 km

Fitness / Wellness
Tennis, golf, sauna, steam bath,
fitness room, beauty salon,
massage

Golf Club Baden Baden e.V.

Golf Course
Gentlemen: 4.413 metres
Ladies: 3.956 metres
Par: 64, SSS: 64
50 practice tees (5 of which are covered)r

Green Fee
Weekdays: DM 65.00
Saturday / Sunday / Bank Holidays: DM 90.00
Juniors / Students under 21: concessions
Guests on Saturday / Sunday: DM 140.00

Non-members
Non-members are welcome.
A club membership card with handicap certificate
(36) is required.
VcG members are only permitted to play from
Mondays to Fridays

Hotel Öschberghof

Key Facts

Hotel Öschberghof
Golfplatz 1
D-78166 Donaueschingen
Phone: +49 (0)771 / 84-0
Fax: +49 (0)771 / 84-600
Internet: http://oeschberghof.com
E-mail: info@oeschberghof.com

Rooms
53 , 17 single rooms,
36 double rooms

Prices
Single room: DM 212.00
Double room: DM 313.00

Credit Cards
Amex, Eurocard, Visa, Diners,
EC-Cash

Nearest Airport / City
Stuttgart 100 km, Zurich 80km

Fitness / Wellness
9-hole golf course, 18-hole golf
course, golfing tuition, swimming
pool, whirlpool, sauna, steam
bath, Thermarium, massage,
oxygen treatment, beauty oasis,
bicycle rental

Land- und Golf-Club Öschberghof

Golf Course
Gentlemen: 6.448 metres / 5.970 metres / 4.120 metres
Ladies: 5.656 metres / 5.223 meters / 3.570 meters
Par: 74, SSS: 72/62
40 practice tees (10 of which are covered)

Green Fee
Weekdays: DM 90.00
Saturday / Sunday / Bank Holidays: DM 120.00
Hotel guests: DM 50.00
Juniors / Students: 50 % of the above rates

Non-members
Non-members are welcome.
A club membership card with handicap certificate
(36) is required.

Hotel-Restaurant Gut Höhne

Gut Höhne
Düsseldorfer Straße 253
D-40822 Mettmann
Phone: +49 (0)2104 7780
Fax: +49 (0)2104 778778

Rooms
136, 35 single rooms,
96 double rooms,
4 apartments, 1 suite

Prices
Single: DM 170.00 - 330.00
Double: DM 270.00 - 440.00
Apartments: DM 330.00 - 530.00

Credit cards
Eurocard, American Express, Visa,
Diners Club

Nearest airport/city
Düsseldorf airport 20 km, Düsseldorf 10 km, Cologne 45 km, Wup-
pertal 15 km, Duisburg 15 km

Fitness/wellness
36-hole golf course, 18-hole golf
course, 3 sand tennis courts,
football pitch, badminton court,
volleyball lawn, table-tennis hall,
skittle alley, fitness studio with
coach, 'Space Curle', pool, carom
billiards, Neanderthal spa with
various adventure pools, open-air
pool with lawn and resting area,
Finnish sauna, steam sauna, solarium, sport massages, shiatsu,
beauty farm with 3 different
treatment rooms, water
gymnastics, aqua aerobics

Kosaido Int. Golfclub Düsseldorf e. V.
Golf Course
Gents: 5.193 m/5.549 m
Ladies: 4.728 m/5.042 m
Par: 71, SSS: 71
10 range tee-offs (covered)
Green Fee
Weekdays: DM 80.00, from 4 p.m. DM 45.00,
Weekends/bank holidays: DM 110.00 on appointment,
from 5 p.m. DM 65.00, Young people up to 18 years of
age: 50% reduction, Driving range: DM 20.00
Non-members
Club card with Hdc entered (36/54) is required.

Golf Club Hubbelrath e. V.
Golf Course
Gents: 6.040 m (east course), 4.325 m, (west course)
Ladies: 5.322 m (east course), 3.800 m (west course)
Par: 72, SSS: 72, 20 range tee-offs (10 covered)
Green Fee
Weekdays: DM 100.00 (east course), DM 80.00 (west course)
Weekends/bank holidays DM 120.00 (east course),
DM 100.00 (west course), Young people obtain 50% reduc-
tion, Driving range: DM 20.00 (weekdays), DM 30 (weekends)
Non-members
Club card with Hdc entered (28/36) is required.

Hotel-Restaurant im Golf Park Gut Düneburg

**Hotel-Restaurant im Golfpark
Gut Düneburg**
Düneburg 1
D-49733 Haren
Phone. +49 (0)5932 72740
Fax: +49 (0)5932 6686

Rooms
11 double and 60 holiday homes

Prices
Single: DM 90.00
Double: DM 130.00
All rates include breakfast

Credit cards
Eurocard, Visa, EC-Cash

Nearest airport/city
Münster/Bremen
airport approx. 1 hour

Fitness/wellness
Golf: tournament course and
public course, riding, cycling,
hiking; in the direct vicinity:
swimming pool, sauna, solarium,
massages, cosmetics

Golfclub Gut Düneburg e. V.

Golf Course
Gents: 5.618 m
Ladies: 4.918 m
Par: 72, SSS: 70
9 all-weather range tee-offs
Target-practice, chipping and putting greens

Green Fee
Weekdays: DM 45.00
Weekends/bank holidays: DM 55.00
Young people obtain 50% reduction
Driving range: free
Public course: DM 25.00
Club, trolley and Electro-cart hire

Non-members
Guests are always welcome.
Club card with course permission entered (PE)
25% reduction on green fees for hotel residents 50%
reduction on green fees for holiday home residents.

Golf- & Landhotel Balmer See

**Golf & Country Hotel
Balmer See**
Drewinscher Weg 1
D-17429 Neppermin-Balm
Phone: +49 (0)38379 / 28-0
Fax: +49 (0)38379 / 28-222

Rooms
88, 66 double rooms,
18 junior suites

Prices
Double room: DM 85.00 – 140.00
Junior suite: DM 115.00 – 155.00
Suite: DM 130.00 – 170.00

Credit Cards
Amex, Eurocard, Visa, Diners

Nearest Airport / City
Berlin-Tegel 250 km,
Heringsdorf 30 km

Fitness / Wellness
Golf, sports centre, activity area,
indoor swimming pool, whirlpool,
aroma grotto, Finnish sauna,
steam sauna, Thalasso therapy

Golfclub Balmer See – Insel Usedom e.V.

Golf Course
Gentlemen: 5.053 metres / 6.035 metres
Ladies: 5.328 metres / 5.328 metres
Par: 73, SSS: 72
30 practice tees (4 of which are covered)

Green Fee
Weekdays: DM 50.00
Saturday / Sunday / Bank Holidays: DM 70.00
Golfing lessons: 30 minutes / DM 35.00
Driving range: DM 10.00
Hotel guests:
day ticket DM 25.00
3 days DM 60.00
7 days DM 120.00

Non-members
Non-members are welcome.
A club membership card is required.

Kur- und Sporthotel Königshof

**Kur– und Sporthotel
Königshof mit
Privatsanatorium**
Mühlenstraße 16
D-87534 Oberstaufen im
Allgäu
Phone: +49 (0)8386 4930
Fax: +49 (0)8386 493125
http://www.koenigshof.de
E-Mail: info@koenigshof.de

Rooms
61, 31 single rooms,
30 double rooms

Prices
Single: DM 135.00 to 175.00
double: DM 120.00 to 170.00
All rates include breakfast

Credit cards
EC-Cash, Eurocard, Visa, Amex

Nearest airport/city
Munich, Stuttgart, Zürich 150
to 180 km

Fitness/wellness
Golf, gymnastics, tennis, hiking,
cycling, cross-country skiing,
Alpine skiing, bobsled runs
(also in summer), rafting,
Canada rafting, mountain-
biking, canyoning, cave tour,
bungee jumping, paragliding,
swimming pool, sauna, solarium, massages, cosmetics, hair
stylist, doctor's surgery

Golfclub Oberstaufen-Steibis e. V.
Golf Course
Gents: 4.812 m/5.448 m
Ladies: 4.491 m/5.088 m
Par: 70, SSS: 7026 range tee-offs (3 covered)
Green Fee
Weekdays: DM 70.00 (hotel residents: DM 49.00)
Weekends/bank holidays DM 85.00(hotel residents: DM 64.00)
Driving range: DM 15.00 Golf-cars
Non-members
Guests are always welcome, Club card with Hdc (36) entered is
required.

Golfclub Riefensberg-Sulzberg
Golf Course
Gents: 5.444 m/5.702 m
Ladies: 4.794 m/5.033 m
Par: 71, SSS: 71
20 range tee-offs (6 covered)
Green Fee
Weekdays: 460 Sch. (hotel residents: DM 55.00)
Weekends/bank holidays 590 Sch. (hotel residents: DM 55.00)
Driving range: 70 Sch., 9-hole course: DM 45.00, Golf-cars
Non-members
Club card is required.

Sunderland Hotel

GolfSport Sorpesee

Golf Course
9-hole course (from July 1999)
Gentlemen: 1.762 metres
Ladies: 1.445 metres
Par: 31, SSS: 31
45 practice tees
Floodlit driving range (from March 1999)
Par 3 6-hole course (from May 1999)

Green Fee
Full week: DM 40.00
Juniors: DM 20.00
Driving range: free of charge

Non-members
Non-members are welcome.

Hotel Walkershof

Golfclub St. Leon-Rot e.V.

Golf Course
Gents: 6.047 m/6.587 m
Ladies: 5.329 m/5.752 m
Par: 72, SSS: 72/74
Range tee-offs: 12 covered
9-hole course par 62

Green Fee
Weekdays: DM 120.00
Weekends/bank holidays DM 150.00
Young people up to 18 years of age obtain
50% reduction
Driving range: DM 20.00
9-hole: DM 30.00 - 40.00

Non-members
Guests are always welcome. Club card with Hdc (36)
entered is required.
Appointments necessary at weekends/on bank
holidays. Soft spikes required.

Landhotel Dreiklang

Gut Kaden Golf and Country Club
Golf Course
Gentlemen: 6.076 m/6.234 m
Ladies: 5.192 m/5.392 m
Par: 72, SSS: 71/73
9-hole, 100 practice tees (of which 13 are covered)
Green Fee
Weekdays: DM 70.00, Saturday/Sunday/Bank Holidays:
DM 90.00, Daily green fee for 9-hole course: DM 40.00,
Saturday/Sunday/Bank Holidays: DM 50.00
Non-members
Non-members are welcome.

Golf Club Gut Waldhof e. V.
Golf Course
Gentlemen: 6.044 m
Ladies: 5.318 m
Par: 72, SSS: 72
40 practice tees (of which 7 are covered)
Green Fee
Weekdays: DM 50.00, Saturday/Sunday/Bank Holidays:
DM 70.00, Winter fees: DM 40.00/50.00, VcG members
weekdays: DM 75.00, Saturday/Sunday/Bank Holidays:
DM 105.00, Driving range: DM 10.00
Non-members
Non-members are welcome.

AUSTRIA Welcome to Klammer country!

Within its compact area of less than 84,000 square kilometres, Austria provides a staggering variety of panoramas, from towering Alpine passes to rolling pasturelands, and a legacy of architecture, art and music which stretches back many centuries.

Austria's nine constituent provinces form a single political entity but are widely different in their scenic and cultural attractions.

Vienna's stately elegance dates back to the golden age of the Dual Monarchy; Burgenland, in the extreme east, is a region of fertile plains flanking Lake Neusiedl; Lower Austria is hills, woods and vineyards; with its mountains and vast forests; Styria is the country's green heartland; sun-blessed Carinthia offers bathing lakes and Austria's loftiest peak (Grossglockner, 3797m); Salzburg was Mozart's birthplace; the Tyrol strings delightful towns pearl-like along its deep valleys.

GETTING THERE A thoroughly modern country with a high standard of living, Austria has a major motorway system (toll sticker required) and reliable trains, including high-speed inter-city services. The world's major airlines fly into Vienna while several busy regional airports have pan-European services.

APRÈS GOLF Austrian food is hearty and filling – just the bill to follow a strenuous round of golf. The *Viener schnitzel* is a world-renowned way of preparing a pork or veal, apple strudels are out of this world and the dumplings are to die for. Don't believe the French: the *croissant* was invented by Viennese pastrycooks to celebrate the raising of the Turkish siege. Austrian wines, especially the whites, have recovered their reputation after the adulteration scandals of some years back. Shopping is a must, especially in stylish Vienna, where everyone still wears hats.

OFF THE COURSE Hiking, mountaineering, yachting, windsurfing, canoeing, cycling, mountain biking, hang-gliding and summer skiing are just some of the many things you can do in Austria - and tour operators offer a wide range of specialist holidays and short breaks to which golf can be added. Music lovers will find much of interest in this land of Mozart, Beethoven, Schubert and Strauss.

NOT TO BE MISSED Vienna is truly one of the most beautiful, and lively, cities in the world, combining majestic palaces, churches and mansions with all modern amenities; Innsbruck is a famed winter sports centre which is also attractive in summer; Salzburg is the spiritual heart of the modern classical music world, offering a year round concert programme.

FACTS AND FIGURES

- There are no large golf complexes in Austria; they are virtually all just 18 holes. In the mountains, where space is a problem, many are just nine holes.
- At the high plateaux courses above 1500 metres the air is thin and the ball travels about a club further than at sea level.
- Many of the regional tourist offices sell special passes giving discount green fees on local courses.
- Some of the larger hotels will arrange for visitors to take part in local tournaments at no extra cost.

The picturesque Golf am Fuschlsee

About ten years ago, so the story goes, a passionate crowd of over a hundred non-golfers ringed the first tee at a small remote Carinthian club to watch a five-handicapper tee off in an insignificant local amateur tournament.

How much that single event has contributed to the explosion of golf in Austria is open to debate, but there is no doubt that because the man was Franz Klammer, a sports icon of extraordinary influence in his home country, thousands of Austrians swapped their skis for golf clubs. It's not just that the most famous man in Austria plays golf – it's the uninhibited, joyous way he smashes a ball around even the most daunting course that has shown the youth of Austria what a fun game golf can be. Klammer takes all the aggression, verve and sheer exuberance that won him a record number of downhill world championships onto the golf course, and it has rubbed off on millions of his adoring fans.

There is no doubt that golf in Austria has also benefited hugely from the excellent tourism infrastructure that has been built up by the skiing industry. There are thousands of good hotels crying out for business in the off-season summer months, and plenty of well trained staff looking for work during the golf months. Another key factor is the lower value of the Austrian schilling which has fallen from its stay-away exchange rate of 8.3 to the US dollar of six years ago, to a much more attractive 12.9 as we go to press.

The quality of golf courses and the amenities that go with them is high, as you'd expect in a country with such a high standard of living. Many courses are concentrated around the relatively flat region near the northeast Czech and Slovak borders, but there are also plenty to be found to the west of Salzburg and in the high mountain plateaux areas.

NEW DEVELOPMENTS

- More than half of the 124 golf courses listed in the official Austrian Tourist Board's golf guide have opened in the past six years.
- By the end of 2000 there will be nearly 20 more golf venues – this in a mountainous country half the size of Florida, which has a population of just 7.5 million and is covered in snow half the year.
- Being located on natural pasture, many of Austria's new courses have a much more mature feel about them than their age would suggest.

Hotels

Golf Hotel Rasmushof	Page 196
Grand Hotel Sauerhof	Page 197
Hotel Klosterbräu	Page 198
Hotel Schloss Pichlarn	Page 199
Hotel Geisler	Page 200
Hotel St. Peter De Luxe	Page 200

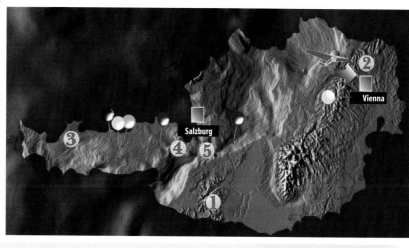

Favourite fairways

1 BAD KLEINKIRCHHEIM

There are 27 holes at this Carinthian resort in the southern part of Austria. Situated in a wooded upland area, there are some stunning holes cut out from undulating pastureland. The practice area is particularly good and there are even eight heated tee areas for the cooler spring and autumn mornings. Visitors staying in Bad Kleinkirchheim hotels which are members of the 'Golf in Austria' scheme get a reduction on the 550-600 schilling green fee.

Par 72   Length 6047 m

Bad Kleinkirchheim, Post Box 9, A-9546 Bad Kleinkirchheim
Tel: +43 (0) 4275 594   Fax: +43 (0) 4275 504

2 WALDVIERTEL GOLF CLUB

The European Tour PGA Austrian Open has been played three times at this venue. It has been voted 'Golf Course of the Year' by visitors three times in the past decade. Set in hilly moorland reminiscent of some lowland Scottish courses, this is a real test of golf in outstandingly beautiful countryside.

Par 72   Length 6059 m

Waldviertel Haugschlag, A-3874 Haugschlag 160
Tel: +43 (0) 2865 8441   Fax: +43 (0) 2865 8441-22

3 SEEFELD-WILDMOOS

English designer Donald Harradine has created a lovely course here, set in high mountain meadows 1300 metres above sea level. Many of Austria's top amateur events are held at this resort, which is in the middle of a mountain conservation area. Guest tournaments take place every Wednesday, and visitors are welcome to join weekend events as well. A handicap certificate and letter of introduction are needed.

Par 72   Length 5967 m

Golfclub Seefeld-Wildmoos A-6100 Seefeld, Tirol
Tel: +43 (0) 5212 3003   Fax: +43 (0) 5212 372222

4 ZELL AM SEE-KAPRUN

This development is at the centre of the Europa Sportregion in a valley surrounded by the high Salzburg mountains. The two fine 18-hole championship courses run a wide programme of tournaments for visitors, and there is a reduction of 30 per cent on the 750 schilling green fees for people staying at local hotels. Norman, Langer, Ballesteros and Laura Davis have all been tournament winners here.

Par 72   Length 6218 m

Zell Am See Golfclub, Golfstrasse 25, A-5700 Salzburg
Tel: +43 (0) 6542 56161   Fax: +43 (0) 6542 56161-16

5 SCHLADMING-HAUS GOLF AND COUNTRY CLUB

Bernard Langer set out to bring a flavour of Florida to this pristine golf course, which sits in a natural suntrap between the wooded Dachstein hills. The course is manicured very much along US lines, and the American feel extends to the modern clubhouse, huge pro shop, difficult water hazards, and high-class restaurant. It's even got white golf carts.

Par 71   Length 5860 m

A-8967 Schladming-Haus Oberhaus 59
Tel: +43 (0) 3686 2630   Fax: +43 (0) 3686 2630-15

CLIMATE

A country which is not only landlocked but is surrounded by high mountains, Austria usually experiences glorious summers and very cold, snowy winters, during which interest focuses on skiing rather than golf.

Price guide

Round of golf	€€€	Golf balls	€€€€
Small beer	€€€	4/5 star hotel room	€€€

CONTACT

Austrian National Tourist Office
Osterreich Werberg, Margaretenstrasse N1, 1040 Vienna
Tel: +43 (0) 1 587 2000 Fax: +43 (0) 1 588 6648

GOLF-HOTEL RASMUSHOF

Recreational facilities

Indoor swimming pool, steam bath, sauna, tennis; big garden with mountain view, music nights; great hiking and mountain biking locally.

Meeting/business facilities

Three rooms, for up to 100 delegates.

Local attractions

The old town of Kitzbühel; ATP tennis tournament at end of July; mountain walks, beautiful Alpine scenery; the Rasmushof and its golf course are situated right at the finish line of the Hahnenkamm downhill skiing race.

Hotel information

Ried Ecking 15
A - 6370 Kitzbühel

Tel: +43 (0) 5356 65252
Fax: +43 (0) 5356 6525249
Email: rasmushof@netway.at
Web: www.tiscover.com/rasmushof

Accolades

☆☆☆☆

Airport

Salzburg: 1 hr
Innsbruck: 1 hr
Munich: 1 hr 30 mins

Accommodation price guide

€ ◉◉◉◉

Accepted credit cards
AE MC V DC

The great champions of the skiing world race down the famous Hahnenkamm slope right in front of the Rasmushof's door to celebrate their victories in the grandest of style. There you will also find a challenging and conveniently located three-par golf course surrounding this cosy and welcoming hotel. It's an ideal place to train your golfing skills, providing the latest in tuition, regardless of whether you are a beginner or an experienced golfer with a handicap card to prove it.

There are 12 fine 18-hole courses at distances of from three to 60 kilometres from the hotel, all waiting to be enjoyed. Guests can also play tennis on the hotel's own well-groomed courts or relax by the enticing pool and in the fitness centre.

Within the hotel are several attractive 'Stüberl' dining rooms, furnished in century-old panelling from traditional Tyrolean farmhouses to lend an atmosphere of homespun Austrian *Gemütlichkeit*, matched by the traditional Austrian cooking which complements the hotel's modern cuisine.

Kitzbühel has been known for a century as a fabulous wintersports resort. Now it starts the new millennium determined to build itself another sparkling reputation as 'the premier golf centre of the Alps'. Why not discover it for yourself? The welcome-mat is always out.

GOLF FACILITIES
Best season for golf: Spring, Summer, Autumn.

COURSES:	LENGTH	PAR	FEES
Kaps			
	6044m	72	Sch622
Schwarzsee			
	6156m	72	Sch803
Kaiserwinkel			
	5927m	73	Sch739

Par three nine-hole golf course at hotel; driving range, putting and chipping practice greens; pro shop.

Facilities key

30   100

GRAND HOTEL SAUERHOF

Hotel information

Weilburgstrasse 11-13
A - 2500 Baden bei Wien

Tel: +43 (0) 2252 41251
Fax: +43 (0) 2252 48047
Email: sauerhof@rtk.at
Web: www.sauerfhof.at

Accolades

★★★★☆
Two 'tocques' for restaurant – Gault-Millau

Airport

Vienna Schwechat: 40 mins

Accommodation price guide

€

Accepted credit cards
AE MC V DC

Preferred tour operator

From Austria
East Europe
Travel   Tel: +43 (0) 1 597 4918
Mondial
Reiseburo   Tel: +43 (0) 1 58804
From Switzerland
Kuoni Travel Tel: +41 (0) 1 325 2111
From Germany
DER Tour
Frankfurt   Tel: +49 (0) 69 95 88 34 38

Recreational facilities

Marbert Beauty Farm; wine cellar dating
from 1419; wedding and christening
chapel; indoor swimming pool, tennis,
bicycle hire.

Meeting/business facilities

Six meeting rooms, for up to 220 people.

Local attractions

Casino Baden – the largest casino in
Europe; stadttheater (theatre and
operetta festival); cycle tours through
vineyards; trotting races; Baden, city of
spas and Beethoven.

Beethoven was among the Sauerhof's many illustrious guests at the pinnacle of Baden's popularity in the 19th century. Much has changed since the days of the great composer, but the Grand Hotel Sauerhof still provides traditional service of the very best kind, recognising that remarkable guests require a remarkable setting.

This Biedermeier-style palace is lavishly decorated, with spacious suites and rooms redolent of an age of opulence, yet its service and technology meet the highest modern standards.

A lush and elegant green-belt surrounds the hotel, with six 18-hole golf courses nearby, pride of which is the superb 18-hole Golf & Sports Club Fontana. Beautifully sited, this course is a member of both The Leading Golf Clubs of the World and Leading Golf Courses of Austria.

The restorative power of the Sauerhof's hot sulphur springs provides the basis for a wide range of health and beauty facilities, including traditional spa treatments, a fitness centre, and the Marbert Beauty Farm. The hotel's main restaurant, winner of the prestigious Two Chef's Hats ('tocques') award from Gault-Millau, combines the best of the traditional culinary arts with a modern taste for fresh, light, natural flavours.

GOLF FACILITIES
Best season for golf: Spring,
Summer and Autumn.

COURSES:	LENGTH	PAR	FEES
Fontana	6360m	72	Sch1200
Ebreichsdorf	6246m	72	Sch700
Enzesfeld	6048m	72	Sch750

Golf Arena Baden has six courses, maximum
35 mins away; practice and tuition facilities;
buggies for hire at all courses.

Facilities key

88   220

HOTEL KLOSTERBRÄU

Hotel information

Sonnenplatzl 1
A - 6100 Seefeld

Tel: +43 (0) 5212 2621
Fax: +43 (0) 5212 3885
Email: info@klosterbraeu.com
Web: www.klosterbraeu.com

Accolades

 De Luxe

Airport

Innsbruck: 25 mins

Accommodation price guide

Accepted credit cards
AE MC V DC

For six generations, the Seyerling family, owners of the five-star Klosterbräu, have been placing their entire focus on the comfort of their guests. Some 150 employees help provide round-the-clock service to fulfill the highest concepts of hospitality, holiday pleasure and splendid gastronomy.

The hotel is right in the middle of Seefeld village but vehicular access is permitted and underground parking is available. With its incomparable ambience, this gracious monastery castle hotel honours each of its guests in truly royal fashion.

The nearest 18-hole championship golf course is set some four kilometres to the west of Seefeld on the Wildmoos Plateau, with its spectacular views. This fantastic mountain panorama, with its peaceful birch and larch-studded meadows, provides one of the most beautiful golf courses in all Europe.

Just 300 metres away is the Golfacademy Seefeld, which teaches the most up-to-date techniques in Europe. Based upon scientifically founded sports knowledge and kinetics, the 'neutral technique' (also known as the basic swing model) helps the golfer to optimise his or her own personal golf swing.

Awarded 15 points by Gault Millau, the hotel's Ritter Oswald Stube, together with its Klosterhof, offers guests an outstanding dining experience.

GOLF FACILITIES
Best season for golf: May to October.

COURSES:	LENGTH	PAR	FEES
Seefeld-Wildmoos			
	5353m	72	US$42
Innsbruck-Rinn			
	4680m	70	US$42
Innsbruck-Lans			
	4260m	70	US$42
Garmish-Partenkirchen			
	5830m	72	US$42
Iffeldorf			
	6220m	72	US$42
Hohenpähl			
	4880m	71	US$42

Putting green; golf academy; tuition packages; guest tournaments; special discount rates; the Tirol Golf Card, allowing play on a different course in Seefeld and surroundings each day for five days, is available for Sch2500.

Facilities key

103   180

HOTEL SCHLOSS PICHLARN

Hotel information

A – 8952 Irdning
Steiermark

Tel: +43 (0) 36 82 22841-0
Fax: +43 (0) 36 82 22841-6
E-mail: schloss.pichlarn@vip.at
Web: www.pichlarn.at

Accolades

★★★★☆

Airport

Salzburg: 1 hr 30 mins
Graz: 1 hr 30 mins
Vienna: 2 hr 30 mins

Accommodation price guide

Accepted credit cards
AE DC MC V

Schloss Pichlarn, an impressive mediaeval castle, is located in one of the most beautiful mountain and farming regions in all of Europe, between Schladming and Admont monastery, just one hour from the world-renowned musical city of Salzburg.

This legendary Austrian edifice, historic home of royalty, celebrities and Pope Pius II, now offers the highest standard of luxury hotel accommodation.

Surrounded by an 18-hole golf course, with on-site golf academy, Hotel Schloss Pichlarn is romantically situated in peaceful woodlands and has been a favoured resort for generations.

Guests will find the hotel decorated with antiques, chandeliers, marble floors, paintings, fruit baskets and vases of fresh flowers. There is a variety of lounges with fireplaces, along with welcoming restaurants and bars, as well as conference facilities.

The hotel's four restaurants combine Styrian and international specialities in a masterful bill of fare. The castle cellar contains wines from the best European regions, and the cellar-master cultivates the great Austrian wines with particular care.

The 110 furnished rooms include 60 suites and junior suites. The hotel also offers a range of treatments in its health and beauty club, including thalassotherapy, phytobiothermic and Thalacap cosmetic treatments, massages and AyurVeda. Guests can also avail themselves of outdoor and indoor swimming pools, tennis and horse riding.

Recreational facilities

Riding, tennis, fishing, croquet, massage treatments, indoor and outdoor swimming pool, sauna, steam bath, solarium, biking facilities, meditation park in the Schloss area, cross-country skiing.

Meeting/business facilities

Six rooms for up to 300 delegates, full organisation of incentive programmes and conferences.

Local attractions

Natural mountain lakes, beautiful Salzburg and its classical concert programme.

GOLF FACILITIES

Best season for golf: April to October.

COURSES:	LENGTH	PAR	FEES
Schladming			
	5700m	72	Sch500
Weissenbach			
	5648m	70	Sch400-450
Bad Ischl			
	5890m	72	Sch500-600

Practice facilities; golf academy and three-hole training course; tournaments guests can play in.

Facilities key

110   300

HOTEL GEISLER

Hotel information

Judenstein 23
A - 6074, Rinn b.Innsbruck

Tel: +43 (0) 5223 78168
Fax: +43 (0) 5223 78168-220
Email: geisler@tirol.com

Accolades

★★★☆

Airport

Innsbruck: 20 mins, Munich: 1 hr 30 mins

Accommodation price guide

Accepted credit cards
AE DC MC V

Local attractions

City of Innsbruck; Swarovski Crystal Worlds at Wattens; Tyrolean Olympic mountains.

AMERICAN EXPRESS OFFER
For advance booking on American Express Card you receive a **room upgrade, subject to availability.**
Quote 'Great Golf Hotels offer' when you book.

S et on a magnificent sun-kissed plateau above the beautiful city of Innsbruck, with the awesome Tyrolean mountains as a picturesque backdrop, are the 27 delightful holes of the Hotel Geisler's Rinn golf course. Both keen experts and enthusiastic amateurs will discover an atmosphere here that turns their sport into a veritable passion.

Nature, peace, beauty, sporting challenge and the comfort of a deluxe four-star hotel all make for a superb golfing break. Inclusive golf packages are available on a variety of splendid Alpine courses. Also on offer is an exhilarating guided hiking and picnic tour up to the hotel's Alpine lodge, while, for shopping and sightseeing, the wonderful city of Innsbruck is just 12 kilometres away.

Meeting/business facilities

Two rooms, for up to 60 delegates; organisation office.

Recreational facilities

Leisure centre with herbal steambath, sauna, etc.; Henri Chenot cosmetic centre; tennis courts, hiking, skiing.

GOLF FACILITIES

Best season: April to October.

COURSES:	LENGTH	PAR	FEES
Rinn	5945m	71	Sch466
Lans	4657m	66	Sch466
Seefeld	5960m	72	Sch674

Driving range, chipping and putting green; tuition packages available.

Facilities key

30 60

HOTEL ST. PETER DE LUXE

Hotel information

Moeserer Strasse 53
6100 Seefeld
Tyrol

Tel: +43 (0) 5212 4555-0
Fax: +43 (0) 5212 4555-45
Email: info@mountains.at
Web: www.mountains.at

Accolades

★★★☆

Airport

Innsbruck: 25 mins
Munich: 1hr 30 mins

Accommodation price guide

€

Accepted credit cards
AE DC MC V

Local attractions

Seefeld Casino, historic Innsbruck, mountains and lakes.

B uilt in the style of a vast traditional Alpine chalet, the delightful Hotel St. Peter makes the most of its majestic Tyrolean setting. Family-run by Josef and Monika Tauber, the hotel features spacious and luxurious accommodations, a huge heated indoor pool, and ready access to the best of Austrian golf, being very close to the outstanding Seefeld-Wildmoos championship course.

The hotel's own golf professional is available for coaching – offering special courses for beginners – and house guests benefit from half-price rates at Seefeld's excellent new golf academy.

Hotel St. Peter offers outstanding Austrian cuisine served in an historic ambience, and guests have the good fortune to be a part of a legendary viniculture in authentic surroundings.

Meeting/business facilities

Two rooms, for up to 100 delegates.

Recreational facilities

Pool, sauna, steambath, solarium, sauna, whirlpool, fitness facilities; gardens, park; skiing, hiking, riding locally.

GOLF FACILITIES

Best season for golf: Summer.

COURSES:	LENGTH	PAR	FEES
Seefeld Wildmoos	6150m	72	Sch360-630
Innsbruck Lans	4660m	66	Sch520-640
Innsbruck Rinn	5960m	71	Sch520-640

Putting green, driving range, bunker, chipping green; 15 per cent discount of green fees at Seefeld for guests.

Facilities key

90 100

200

SWITZERLAND Mountain charm

Switzerland is not a huge golfing country, but what it lacks in terms of quantity is made up for by the quality of the spectacular courses that utilise the country's magnificent scenery. There are now nearly 70 courses in a range of settings from palm trees to glaciers. Summer is the time to play – for sheer exhilaration, playing high up in the mountains is a peerless experience.

The senior clubs include Engadine (the oldest), Crans-sur-Sierre, Geneva, Lausanne, Lucerne and Zurich. Land pressure and the difficulty and expense of building on mountainous terrain means development has not been as great as in other European countries.

Nevertheless, booming demand from golf travellers has led to a new crop of four- and five-star golf hotels, spread throughout Switzerland, which aim to recognise the needs of the golfer, and also to pamper.

NEW DEVELOPMENTS

- **The new Swiss Golf Pass is a magic opening to the leading golf courses and golf hotels. It includes vouchers for hotels and green fees. For info call +41 (0) 1 877 47 77.**
- **Swiss Golf Hotels organise competitions for guests, club members and partners.**
- **The Lucerne 'Golfpass' gives you a choice of five courses combined with a hotel booking.**

CLIMATE

There are great differences between the climate of the valleys and the higher mountains. The wind is a perennial problem, with the phenomenon known as the *föhn* bringing sudden, unexpected warm, dry winds.

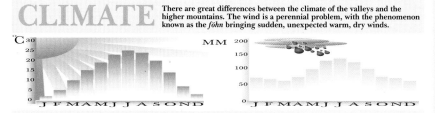

Sample point: Zürich

RECOMMENDED CAR HIRE — Hertz

UK: +44 (0) 870 848 4848
Germany: +49 (0) 180 533 3535
Website: www.hertz.com

Price guide

| Round of golf | Golf balls |
| Small beer | 4/5 star hotel room |

CONTACT

Switzerland Tourism, Bellariastrasse 38, CH-8027 Zurich, Switzerland
Tel: +41 (0) 1 877 4777   Fax: +41 (0) 1 881 4344

Switzerland is a colourful mix of different cultures and languages, all bound together by an almost obsessive sense of independence.

Long established as a prime winter sports destination, this country is now making great efforts to expand its appeal for Summer activities too. Along with walking and mountain biking, golf is a key part of the master plan.

GETTING THERE Switzerland has several major international airports: Geneva (for courses in the Jura and the Savoy Alps), Zürich and Basle (also serving Franche Comte and Germany's Black Forest). The country also networks with the French TGV system.

APRÈS GOLF There is plenty of sophisticated evening entertainment to be had and provision for family fun by day, with safe artificial beaches on many of the lakes. Swiss wines are often delicious, while the style of cuisine tends to follow the nature of the language spoken.

OFF THE COURSE Switzerland is a nature lover's paradise with its Alpine flora and fauna. In this stridently modern country, there's also a strong sense of history and many notable castles and mediaeval towns and cities.

NOT TO BE MISSED Elegant, fashionable Geneva with its lakeside setting and views across towards Mont Blanc, the highest mountain in Western Europe; ride one of the mountain railway routes; marvel at the majestic Matterhorn; take a boat cruise on Lake Lugano.

FACTS & FIGURES

- **The Swiss Open was orginally played at Engadin, and has made its home at Crans-sur-Sierre since 1939.**
- **At the last count the country had some 30,000 players.**
- **Club de Bonmont is worth a visit for the wonderful 18th Century château that forms the clubhouse.**
- **Golf de Basel has the distinction of being a Swiss club, though it is actually on French territory.**

Golf at 1400 metres – Lenzerheide-Valbella

Favourite fairways

1 CRANS-SUR-SIERRE

Stunning scenery with views over Mont Blanc and the snowy Valais Alps, complemented by fir woods, Alpine flowers and lakes. Crans has long been home to the Swiss Open which then became the European Masters. But it was reckoned to be a little too easy for the professionals and Seve Ballesteros and his design team gave it a two year face-lift. Said Seve: "We finally have a great course. It needs a lot of respect and strategy." The main problem is choice of club on the hilly gradients, which can make for a tiring round.
Par 72   Length 5785m
3953 Crans-sur-Sierre
Tel: +41 (0) 27 41 21 68 Fax: +41 (0) 27 41 95 68

2 GOLF CLUB DE GENÈVE

Designed by Robert Trent Jones, this is in a magnificent setting overlooking Lake Geneva. The many different tees and pin positions give players of all standards a chance, though it is a difficult course to score well on. The greens are huge so it provides an excellent test of pitching and putting skills.
Par 72   Length 6250m
70, Route de la Capite, CH-1223 Cologny
Tel: +41 (0) 22 707 48 00 Fax: +41 (0) 22 707 48 20

3 ENGADIN

North of St Moritz, this is the country's oldest and highest course, opened more than a century ago. Though perched at 2000 metres it is still reasonably flat with the pine trees and streams making it a fairly challenging course. The wind blowing from the Maloja pass can also be hazardous.
Par 72   Length 6080m
Engadin, 7505 Samedan
Tel: +41 (0) 81 852 52 26 Fax: +41 (0) 81 852 46 82

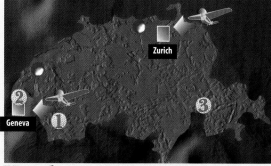

Hotels

- **Seehotel Kastenienbaum** Page 202
- **Club Bonmont Cheserex** Page 203

SEEHOTEL KASTANIENBAUM

Hotel information

CH - 6047 Kastanienbaum – Lucerne

Tel: +41 (0) 41 340 0340
Fax: +41 (0) 41 340 1015
Email: seehotel@kastanienbaum.ch
Web: www.kastanienbaum.ch

Accolades

☆☆☆☆   Member Swiss Golf Hotels

Airport

Zurich: 1 hr

Accommodation price guide

€

Accepted credit cards
AE MC V DC

Preferred tour operator

From UK
Swiss Travel
Service   Tel: +44 (0) 1992 456143
From Germany
DER   Tel: +49 (0) 69 9588 5502
From Switzerland
Alpine Classic
Hotels   Tel: +41 (0) 41 342 0642

Recreational facilities

Swimming pool, beach, own harbour on lake; KA2 'Wellness' club.

Meeting/business facilities

Four rooms, for up to 40 delegates.

Local attractions

City of Lucerne, lake of Lucerne; central Switzerland.

Picturesquely situated on the Horw Kastanienbaum Peninsula, just ten minutes by car from the heart of historic Lucerne, the Seehotel Kastanienbaum has its own harbour, a private beach, and supremely magnificent views across the lake to the mighty Alps.

This appealing venue features 42 pleasantly decorated and furnished guest rooms, two restaurants – one serving delicious fish dishes, the other Swiss specialities – and a welcoming bar, while guests also enjoy access to the Margot Kaz Wellness Club and Beauty Farm.

With play at its best from May right through to October, the six courses to be found within an easy half-hour drive of the hotel provide the opportunity to enjoy fine golf in the most spectacular of natural settings. Hotelier Olaf Reinhardt is himself an avid golf player and a full range of golf package programmes is on offer to his guests.

Access is easy, even by public transport, with buses from Lucerne city stopping right outside the door of the Seehotel, and many lake steamers calling at Kastanienbaum.

GOLF FACILITIES

Best season for golf: May to November.

COURSES:	LENGTH	PAR	FEES
Lucerne Dietschiberg	6082m	72	US$55
Sempachersee	6180m	72	US$50
Küssnacht	5397m	72	US$50
Holzhäusern	6037m	72	US$40
Schönenberg	5672m	72	US$55
Engelberg	2355m	36	US$30

Practice facilities, tuition available, tournaments for guests.

Facilities key

42   40

Golf à la carte in Switzerland!

Hotel Dolder Waldhaus ****
CH-8030 Zürich
Tel. +41-1-269 10 00
Fax +41-1-269 10 01

Suvretta House *****
7500 St.Moritz
Tel. +41-81-832 11 32
Fax +41-81-833 85 24

See & Park Hotel Feldbach***
CH-8266 Steckborn
Tel. +41-52-762 21 21
Fax +41-52-762 21 91

Hotel Margna ****
7515 Sils-Baselgia
Tel. +41-81-826 53 06
Fax +41-81-826 54 70

Le Montreux Palace *****
CH-1820 Montreux
Tel. +41-21-962 12 12
Fax +41-21-962 17 17

Solbad-Hotel Beatus ****
CH-3658 Merligen-Interlaken
Tel. +41-33-251 21 21
Fax +41-33-251 36 76

Bürgenstock Hotels & Resort *****
CH-6363 Bürgenstock-Luzern
Tel. +41-41-611 05 45
Fax +41-41-610 14 15

Hotel Origlio Country Club ****
CH-6945 Lugano
Tel. +41-91-945 46 46
Fax +41-91-945 10 31

Golfhotel Villa Magliasina ****
CH-6983 Magliaso-Lugano
Tel. +41-91-611 29 29
Fax +41-91-611 29 20

Esplanade Hotel Resort & Spa ****
CH-6648 Minusio-Locarno
Tel. +41-91-735 85 85
Fax +41-91-735 85 86

Sporthotel Signina ****
CH-7032 Laax
Tel. +41-81-927 90 00
Fax +41-81-927 90 01

Le Grand Chalet ****
CH-3780 Gstaad
Tel. +41-33-748 76 76
Fax +41-33-744 44 15

Relais & Châteaux Grand Hotel Park *****
CH-3780 Gstaad
Tel. +41-33-748 98 00
Fax +41-33-748 98 08

Wellness-Hotel Ermitage-Golf *****
CH-3778 Gstaad-Schönried
Tel. +41-33-744 27 27
Fax +41-33-748 60 67

GrandHotel Quellenhof *****
CH-7310 Bad Ragaz
Tel. 00 800 80 12 11 10
Tel. +41-81-303 30 30
Fax +41-81-303 30 33

Swiss Golf Passepartout.

The new Swiss Golf Pass is a magic opening to the leading golf courses and golf hotels of Switzerland. The two editions «Eagle» and «Albatros» include vouchers for lodging in swiss golf hotels and free green-fees.

Others swiss golf hotels: **Appenzell-Weissbad:** Hotel Hof Weissbad. **Arosa:** Arosa Kulm Hotel. **Ascona:** Park Hotel Delta, Relais & Châteaux Hotel Giardino, Hotel Casa Berno. **Davos:** Hotel Seehof, Golfhotel Waldhuus. **Engelberg:** Treff Hotel Regina Titlis. **Flims-Waldhaus:** Park Hotels Waldhaus. **Interlaken:** Victoria Jungfrau Grand Hotel& Spa. **Lenzerheide:** Hotel Schweizerhof. **Luzern:** Hotel Palace Luzern, Seehotel Kastanienbaum. **Orselina-Locarno:** Hotel Orselina. **Murten-Meyriez:** Le Vieux Manoir au Lac. **Pont-la-Ville:** Le Royal Golf Hôtel de la Gruyère. **St. Gallen:** Hotel Einstein. **Thun:** Hotel Seepark.

The Golf experience is not over at the 18th hole. Now our hotline is useful. And soon you will have the guide: swiss golf hotels 2000 in your hands. Get to know about the hotels in which golfers are specially taken care off. All the golf courses of Switzerland with information and distance tables. Tournament listings. **Just order one now and join the Swiss Golf Hotels Club!**

swiss golf hotels

Victor Zindel & Partner GmbH, 8302 Kloten, Fax +41-1-881 43 44, Phone Hotline +41-1-877 47 77.
E-mail: info@swissgolfhotels.ch – www.swissgolfhotels.ch

roduct of V&P

CHÂTEAU DE BONMONT

An easy drive away from Geneva airport and close to the Divonne Casino, the Château de Bonmont is set in a uniquely beautiful site. In its grounds, trees more than 100 years old surround a 12th Century Cistercian Abbey. The Bonmont is an 18th Century mansion containing eight guest rooms, including four suites, decorated with Regency, Louis XIII and Empire style furniture.

The terrace looks out over a magnificent private 18-hole course designed by the British architect Don Harradine. It is considered to be one of the finest golf courses in Switzerland.

Three tennis courts, riding stables, a heated swimming pool, a sauna and a sun lounge complete the Bonmont's superior sports facilities.

Meeting/business facilities

Four rooms, for up to 20 delegates.

Recreational facilities

Tennis, horse riding, sauna, indoor swimming pool, bikes available.

GOLF FACILITIES

Best season for golf: May to October.

COURSES:	LENGTH	PAR	FEES
Bonmont	5855m	71	SFr90
Divonne (Fr.)	6040m	72	E38
Domaine Imperial	6297m	72	SFr150

Pro-shop; practice facilities; 50% off green fees for hotel guests.

Facilities key

8   20

Ernie Els' Choice

Constellation
Chronograph.
OMEGA — Swiss made since 1848.

Omega, my choice

Ω OMEGA
The sign of excellence

ITALY A golfing renaissance

They say all roads lead to Rome. These days the tourists fan out from there to the entire peninsula, making it one of the world's foremost tourism destinations.

All that culture and history is the main draw of course – everyone wants to see St. Peter's, to visit the great galleries in Florence, to marvel at the Leaning Tower of Pisa, to enjoy the opera at Milan's La Scala, to take a gondola along Venice's canals and to, well, see Naples before they die.

There are natural delights too, from the misty plains of Lombardy to the rustic charms of hilly Tuscany; from the lofty heights of the country's Apennine spine to the spectacular Amalfi coast; from the beautiful lakes of the north to the southern wonders of Calabria – and those wondrous islands: Sardinia, Elba, Capri, Stromboli, Volcano, Sicily and the rest.

Italy is all about *la dolce vita* – good food and heady wines, cheering for Internazionale or Roma, debating politics over a hot, strong espresso, and savouring that round of golf against the backdrop of stunningly beautiful scenery.

GETTING THERE Milan, with its two major international airports (Malpensa and Linate), and Rome are well served destinations. There's also a web of well-placed regional airports putting all the golf within easy reach, even just for a long weekend.

APRÈS GOLF Families love Italy and Italy loves families. The country also boasts the one cuisine that all kids, of all ages, adore. From the polenta and rice of the north to the pasta and pizzas of the south, this is truly great food – and Italy has a surfeit of glorious wines to go with it. Even the smallest of towns will have at least one late-night bar and probably a passable disco too, while there's no shortage of museums, galleries, theatre, music and sport.

Rome's Trevi Fountain

OFF THE COURSE This is the land for all culture vultures, whether looking for that centuries-old architecture, stunning art galleries, Roman artefacts, world-class music festivals or such class spectacles as the annual horse racing around the streets of mediaeval Sienna.

NOT TO BE MISSED Shopping in Milan; a look at some at least of the works of Leonardo, Michelangelo, David and the other great masters; Rome's Coliseum, Spanish Steps and Trevi Fountain; Sardinia's outstanding beaches; Tarranto's great natural harbour.

FACTS & FIGURES

- The recent growth of the Italian game has been spectacular. Older courses have been upgraded, new ones opened and more are under construction.
- From 2,300 players in 1960, there are now 55,500. Courses have increased from 25 to 258, although some of these have less than nine holes.
- The oldest course is Golf Club Roma, established in 1903. The highest course is Golf Club del Cervino at 2050 metres, which means it is only playable in July and August.

Golf in the pines – Golf la Pineta, Como

To be fair, Italy has always had much more going for it than golf. After food, fashion, culture, the great legacy of painting, opera, sculpture and history, sport has taken a secondary role. Although the British introduced the game just after the turn of the century, it had only grown to seventeen courses by 1954 and with a mere 1200 players. But where Italy has been low on quantity, it makes up on quality. If the French see golf as an excuse to dress, the game in Italy centres around the clubhouse, and its restaurant.

The golfing visitor can look forward to two certainties – courses, often in dramatically beautiful settings, with room to play (especially midweek) and levels of clubhouse luxury and refinement unsurpassed anywhere, with a menu to match. Clubhouses are sometimes likened to palaces; in Italy they often are just that – *palazzi* – ornate historic mansions with golf attached.

The game has grown in popularity in recent years. There are now around 200 courses to play, some by famous designers, mostly in the northern half of the country. Almost all are members' clubs, rather than holiday resorts, located near the major cities rather than taking advantage of the warmer climate further south. Best times to visit are spring through autumn; some northern clubs even close mid-winter.

The Italian landscape ranges from snow-capped mountains through rich farmland to Mediterranean beach. There is golf to match – elegant, timeless, part of a total experience that will suit mature couples, art lovers, gourmands and the well-heeled.

NEW DEVELOPMENTS

- The number of courses in the country has doubled in the last nine years, with many more planned.
- With a nation only just embracing the game in numbers, there are (in addition to courses of nine, 18, 27 or 36 holes) a number of 'promotional courses' with three or four holes for beginners, as well as 44 driving ranges, many also with holes to play.
- A 'Green Pass' scheme allows golfers to buy a card giving a 20 per cent discount on green fees at participating clubs. Details from International Golf Consultants. Tel: +39 02 436 975, Fax: +39 02 481 3013.

Favourite fairways

① PEVERO

Robert Trent Jones has called it his masterpiece and who can argue? Here is fantasy made flesh – one of the most beautiful yet savage courses in the world. Ribbons of fairway wind past and over rocky Sardinian hills, with lakes, wild flowers and distant Corsica on the horizon. Off the fairway is a lost ball but the views are sensational.

Par 72   Length 6107m

07020 Porto Cervo, Costa Smeralda, Sassari, Sardinia
Tel: +39 0 789 96210/1   Fax: +39 0 789 96572

② OLGIATA

Although now nearly 30 years old, this 27-hole course, designed by CK Cotton in 1961, stands the test of time. Given room to play with, the result is a series of highly memorable holes, few straight, each demanding placement and good judgement. The World Cup and Eisenhower trophies have been held here; class tells.

West Course Par 72, Length 6347m

Largo Olgiata 15, 00123 Roma
Tel: +39 0 6 3088 9141   Fax: +39 0 6 3088 9968

③ BERGAMO

Set amongst wooded terrain in the Italian Alpine foothills, this is a beautiful setting for golf – richly green and blessed with a mild climate. Home to Costantino Rocca, the rolling slopes of this 27-hole club have a wealth of mature trees and are kept in excellent condition.

Red/Blue Course 5943 m, Blue/Yellow Course 6021m, both Par 72.

Via Longoni, 12-24030 Almenno S.Bartolomeo (Bergamo)
Tel: +39 0 35 640 028   Fax: + 39 0 35 643 066

④ VARESE

It is not often the clubhouse supercedes the course, especially since Varese dates from 1934. Here, however, you change and dine in a 12th Century Romanesque monastery, complete with bell tower and cloisters. Mature parkland with splendid trees, lovingly manicured and a delight to play – a pleasant contrast to many modern layouts and a journey in time.

Par 72   Length 6105m

Via Vittorio Veneto 32, 21020 Luvinate (Varese)
Tel: +39 0 332 229 302   Fax: +39 0 332 222 107

⑤ ADRIATIC CLUB CERVIA

Set close to the sea, this is a very pleasant parkland course, combining open links-style holes with a front nine running narrowly through a pinewood. Plenty of strategic water to avoid on the closing holes of a course designed by Marco Croze. Relaxed golf in a sylvan setting.

Par 72   Length 6246m

Via Jelenia Gora 6, 48016 Cervia/Milano Marittima, Ravenna
Tel: +39 0 544 992 786 Fax: +39 0 544 993 410

Hotels

Park Hotel Sienna & Villa Gori Golf Club	
	Page 208
Riva dei Tessali Golf Hotel	Page 209
Hotel Romazzino	Page 210
Hotel Cala di Volpe	Page 210
Hotel Pitrizza	Page 211
Hotel Cervo & Conference Centre	Page 211
Hotel Alleluja	Page 212
Hotel Cala del Porto	Page 212

RECOMMENDED CAR HIRE

UK: +44 (0) 870 848 4848
Germany: +49 (0) 180 533 3535
Website: www.hertz.com

CLIMATE

Italy's summers are usually gloriously hot while, because of the effects of mountains and sea, winters can be cold and foggy. Spring comes early, though, especially to Sicily, the South and Sardinia.

Sample point: Rome

Price guide   €

Round of golf	🏌🏌🏌	Golf balls	🏌🏌🏌🏌
Small beer	🏌🏌🏌	4/5 star hotel room	🏌🏌🏌

CONTACT

ENIT Italian State Tourist Board, Via Marghera 2, 00185, Rome
Tel: +39 06 49 711
Fax: +39 06 44 63379

PARK HOTEL SIENA

Hotel information

Via Marciano 18
53100 Siena

Tel: +39 0577 44803
Fax: +39 0577 49020
Email: reservation_phs@charminghotels.it
Web: www.thecharminghotels.com

Accolades

★★★☆

Airport

Florence: 1 hr

Accommodation price guide

Accepted credit cards
AE MC V DC

Preferred tour operator

From UK
The Charming
Hotels   Freefone 0800 917 6613
From Germany
The Charming
Hotels   Freefone 0800 180 8063
From USA
The Charming
Hotels   Toll free 1 888 770 0447

Perched majestically atop a rolling Sienese hill, a few minutes from picturesque Piazza del Campo and less than an hour from Florence, is the lovely Park Hotel Siena. With its public rooms graced by vaulted ceilings and carved stone fireplaces, this faithfully restored early 16th Century Tuscan villa takes guests back to an aristocratic past yet offers all the most modern comforts of an exclusive hotel.

Originally designed by the celebrated Renaissance architect Baldassarre Peruzzi, the villa retains all its historic significance.

The hotel's delightful Olivo restaurant features a lovely traditional veranda overlooking the historic city of Siena and serving the finest Tuscan and Italian specialities along with an excellent selection of wines, many of them from local vineyards. Before or after dinner, the welcoming Caminetto Bar provides an ideal place to relax.

It was respected American golf architect Jim Fazio who designed Siena's Villa Gori Golf Club, which occupies naturally rolling countryside adjacent to the Park Hotel Siena. Despite its relatively small scale, at 6 par 3, Villa Gori offers a valid and entertaining trial course for players aiming to perfect their short game. The club also has a practice net and driving range, a comfortable club house, tennis court and a large swimming pool.

Recreational facilities

Outdoor swimming pool in summer; tennis court, golf course; Italian garden.

Meeting/business facilities

Four rooms, for up to 160 delegates.

Local attractions

Historic Siena city centre; Chianti wine region, Brunello region.

GOLF FACILITIES

Best season for golf: April to October.

COURSES:	LENGTH	PAR	FEES
Villa Gori Golf Club	543m	18	E16-21
Castelfalfi	6298m	73	E35
Ugolino	5776m	72	E41
Le Pavoniere	6124m	72	E31-41
Poggio Dei Medici	6367m	73	E33-42

Putting green, pitching green, bunker, practice net.

Facilities key

69   160

RIVA DEI TESSALI GOLF HOTEL & RESIDENCE CLUB HOTEL

Hotel information

74011 Castellaneta
Taranto

Tel: +39 (0) 99 843 9251
Fax: +39 (0) 99 843 9255
Email: tessali@iol.it
Web: www.rivadeitessali.it

Accolades

✩✩✩✩ First category

Airport

Bari: 1 hr
Brindisi: 1hr
Hotel shuttle service to and from airports.

Accommodation price guide

Accepted credit cards
AE MC V DC

Recreational facilities

Private beach, windsurf school, pools, tennis courts; watersports, bicycle rides, gymnasium; piano bar, discotheque; four restaurants, car hire at the hotel.

Meeting/business facilities

One room, for up to 120 delegates; full banqueting service.

Local attractions

Metaponto and other archaeological sites located nearby.

Designed by the studio of well-known British golf architect John D. Harris in association with Marco Croze, the Riva dei Tessali venue is a championship golf course in the best tradition.

In an ideal climate for golf, the 18 holes are laid out among splendid pine woods, recalling in some parts the famous British links. With over six kilometres of draft and within a rifle shot of the magnificent Metaponto ruins, the course has improved year on year and now attracts important tournaments such as the Tessali Open, part of the European Challenge Tour. The first nine holes, together with holes 16 and 17, are the trickiest. Players of all levels will find Riva dei Tessali technically demanding and visually stimulating.

Perfectly complementing this sporting challenge, the adjacent Riva dei Tessali Golf Hotel provides 70 en-suite rooms, equipped with all modern amenities and high standards of luxury. A new and modern Residence on the golf course offers equal luxury.

The seaside location provides direct access to an idyllic private beach while there is some delightful countryside to explore along the shores of the Ionian Sea. Riva dei Tessali has four restaurants, two piano bars and a discotheque.

GOLF FACILITIES
Best season for golf: All year round.

COURSES:	LENGTH	PAR	FEES
Riva dei Tessali	5947m	71	E36

18 hole golf course, driving range, three hole pitching area, putting green, special offer golf packages, golf card; tuition with pro available, buggy hire.

Facilities key

70   170

HOTEL ROMAZZINO

A precious gem nestled between sparkling emerald green seas, bright jade lawns and fragrant gardens, the Hotel Romazzino is a true Mediterranean oasis of elegant tranquillity.

The whitewashed 93-room building slopes graciously down to a long, private beach. Guests can take in the exquisite panorama, along with fresh air and the soft sounds of lapping sea waters. A grand outdoor sea water pool gives onto the beach, where a host of water activities is on offer.

Rooms are decorated in casual Mediterranean style, with terraces overlooking sea and gardens. Service is attentive, and the hotel maintains the highest standards of cuisine and attention to detail in making every guest welcome.

Hotel information

07020 Porto Cervo
Sardinia

Tel: +39 0789 977 111
Fax: +39 0789 962 58
Web: www.luxurycollection.com/romazzino

Accolades

✩✩✩✩✩ Luxury Collection

Airport

Olbia Airport: 35 mins

Recreational and meeting/business facilities

As Hotel Cala di Volpe (below).

Accommodation price guide

€ 🪙🪙🪙🪙

Accepted credit cards
AE DC MC V

Local attractions

Tennis, riding, carting, mountain biking, fishing, scuba diving; shopping at Porto Cervo village.

GOLF FACILITIES
Best season for golf: All year round.

COURSES:	LENGTH	PAR	FEES
Pevero	5792m	72	tbc

Set between the Gulf of Pevero and the Bay of Cala di Volpe, the Robert Trent Jones-designed Pevero Golf Club is one of the best-loved courses in the world. Its 18 challenging holes wind through rocks and past attractive ponds, redolent with the heady scent of juniper, myrtle and arbutus.

Guests can visit the Costa Smeralda Golf Academy, which employs the latest computer graphics technology and skilful PGA professionals to help its attendees improve their game.

Facilities key

93 25

HOTEL CALA DI VOLPE

A tranquil heaven on Sardinia's Costa Smeralda – The Emerald Coast – the Hotel Cala Di Volpe is located in a distinctive setting surrounded by infinite stretches of shoreline and distant mountains. Built like an ancient village, with towers, terraces and varied roof peaks, this charming resort on the sea blends magnificently with its lush surroundings.

The luxury hotel commands incomparable views from the terraces of each of the 123 rooms, which overlook the Cala Di Volpe bay, the swimming pool or the lush gardens. The sunny rooms feature traditional furnishings with elegant appointments.

The exclusive hotel dining room and the barbecue restaurant are renowned for the quality of their gourmet Italian and international cuisine.

Hotel information

07020 Porto Cervo
Sardinia

Tel: +39 0789 976 111
Fax: +39 0789 976 617
Web: www.luxurycollection.com/caladivolpe

Accolades

✩✩✩✩✩ Luxury Collection

Airport

Olbia Airport: 35 mins

Accommodation price guide

€ 🪙🪙🪙🪙

Accepted credit cards
AE DC MC V

Local attractions

Boat rental, horse-riding, mini-golf, carting, mountain biking, fishing, snorkelling & scuba diving.

Meeting/business facilities

One room on site for up to 20 delegates; the Porto Cervo Conference Centre, a short distance away, caters for groups from 50 to 600 delegates.

Recreational facilities

Swimming pool, private beach, tennis, water-skiing, jet ski, mountain biking, fitness centre, five-a-side football; boat rental (excursions), fishing, snorkelling and scuba diving; horse riding, putting green.

GOLF FACILITIES
See Hotel Romazzino (above).

Facilities key

123 20

HOTEL PITRIZZA

The Hotel Pitrizza offers its guests the refined intimacy and privacy of a lovely ancestral island home in one of the world's most romantic places.

The hotel consists of a small group of villas scattered discreetly amongst rocks and flowers overlooking the beautiful shimmering waters of the bay of Liscia di Vacca.

Each of the 51 guest rooms has its own private terrace or patio, offering breathtaking views of the bay, of the private beach or of the swimming pool carved out of pink granite. Renowned for its superb international cuisine, the Hotel Pitrizza provides a picturesque setting for sparkling seaside lunches in the barbecue area, romantic dinners in the main restaurant or sunset cocktails on the terrace.

Hotel information

07020 Porto Cervo
Sardinia

Tel: +39 0789 930 111
Fax: +39 0789 930 611

Web: www.luxurycollection.com/hotelpitrizza

Accolades

✩✩✩✩✩ Luxury Collection

Airport

Olbia Airport: 45 mins

Accommodation price guide

Accepted credit cards
AE DC MC V

Local attractions

Boat rental, golf, tennis, horseback-riding, carting, fishing, snorkelling and scuba diving; from May to September superb seafood and fish specialities are served on the waterfront terrace.

Meeting/business facilities

One room, for up to 40 delegates; the Porto Cervo Conference Centre, a short distance away, caters for groups from 50 to 1000 delegates.

Recreational facilities

Swimming pool, private beach, water-skiing, wind surfing, fitness centre, health centre.

GOLF FACILITIES
See Hotel Romazzino (opposite).

Facilities key

51 40

HOTEL CERVO
& CONFERENCE CENTRE

When the Hotel Cervo was built in 1963, it was designed as an integral part of the village of Porto Cervo. Pink stones and Moorish patios define the hotel, which overlooks the famous piazzetta.

It is a place where magnificent landscapes enclose a host of the finest facilities and services – a luxury resort, state-of-the-art conference centre, selection of restaurants and bars, famous sporting club and a fleet of boats all add to the colour and glamour of this first-class resort facility.

The Cervo Hotel can accommodate meetings for up to 600 attendees and banquets for up to 1000 persons in purpose-built facilities inside the hotel, in the new conference centre, at the Tennis Club, and within the village of Porto Cervo itself.

Hotel information

07020 Porto Cervo
Sardinia

Tel: +39 0789 931 111
Fax: +39 0789 931 613

Web: www.sheraton.com/cervo

Accolades

✩✩✩✩✩ Sheraton Hotels & Resorts

Airport

Olbia Airport : 40 mins

Accommodation price guide

Accepted credit cards
AE DC MC V

Local attractions

Beaches, water-sports, carting, fishing, snorkelling and scuba diving; Designer boutiques and shopping arcade in Porto Cervo.

Meeting/business facilities

The Porto Cervo Conference Centre, with its 11 meeting rooms, caters for groups from 50 to 1000 delegates.

Recreational facilities

Swimming pool, private beach, tennis, squash, water-skiing, jet ski, mountain biking; health and beauty treatments at the spa, fitness centre, five-a-side football; boat rental (excursions), fishing, snorkelling and scuba diving; horse riding.

GOLF FACILITIES
See Hotel Romazzino (opposite).

Facilities key

108 600

HOTEL CALA DEL PORTO

The Hotel Cala del Porto, sister to the Hotel Alleluja, stands in a fairytale setting between emerald green pine trees and golden beach, on a winding coastline which inspired D'Annunzio to call the area Punta Ala. Viewed from the hotel terrace, the island of Elba – surrounded by a sea of deepest blue – seems close enough to touch.

The hotel's 42 rooms and suites are air-conditioned and supplied with every comfort, from satellite TV to linen sheets. From service to decor, this is the ideal place for guests who demand the very best. The hotel's three restaurants, on the beach, by the pool and indoors, all serve top quality international and regional cuisine, with an especially wide variety of seafood dishes on offer.

Meeting/business facilities

One room, for up to 50 delegates.

Recreational facilities

Swimming pool; watersports and sailing at beach, summer and weekends; piano bar.

GOLF FACILITIES

Best season for golf: April-May and September-October.

COURSES:	LENGTH	PAR	FEES
Punta Ala	6213m	72	US$40-65

Hotel information

58040
Punta Ala (Grosseto)

Tel: +39 0564 92 24 55
Fax: +39 0564 92 24 55

Accolades

★★★☆

Airport

Pisa: 1 hr, Rome/Florence: 2 hrs 30 mins

Accommodation price guide

€

Accepted credit cards
AE DC MC V

Local attractions

Isle of Elba; isle of Giglio; nearby Etruscan sites; trips to Florence, San Gimigniano and Uccellina Park.

 AMERICAN EXPRESS OFFER For advance booking on American Express Card you receive a **room upgrade** (subject to availability); bottle of Prosecco in room; free newspaper.

Facilities key

 42 50

HOTEL ALLELUJA

Surrounded by the natural beauty of the Maremma Grossetana, the Hotel Alleluja is in walking distance of a beach of fine white sand, with the Punta Ala Golf Club close by.

In a land rich in history and tradition, the hotel is built and furnished in typically Tuscan style, with an ambience of serenity and cordial good humour.

The 38 air-conditioned rooms and suites are well appointed, comfortable and welcoming, making you feel truly at home.

The hotel's restaurants, one indoors, one on the private beach and one in the beautiful garden, are all renowned for the excellence of their Tuscan and international cuisine. Bar, pool, tennis court and a large parking lot complete the services of the hotel.

For golf, meeting/business and recreational facilities, see Hotel Cala del Porto above.

Hotel information

58040 Punta Ala (Grosseto)

Tel: +39 0564 92 20 50
Fax: +39 0564 92 07 34
Email: allelujapuntaala@baglionihotels.com

Accolades

★★★☆

Airport

Pisa: 1 hr, Rome/Florence: 2 hrs 30 mins

Accommodation price guide

€

Accepted credit cards
AE DC MC V

Local attractions

Isle of Elba; isle of Giglio; nearby Etruscan sites; trips to Florence, San Gimigniano and Uccellina Park.

AMERICAN EXPRESS OFFER For advance booking on American Express Card you receive a **room upgrade** (subject to availability); bottle of Prosecco in room; free newspaper.

Facilities key

 38

LOUIS XIII, DRINK THE PAST
CELEBRATE THE FUTURE

A new Millennium is a once in a lifetime experience. To celebrate this exceptional moment in history, the house of Rémy Martin has released a commemorative edition of the most prestigious Cognac ever, Louis XIII, the King of Spirits. Savor this rarest of cognacs, composed of hundreds of the finest *eaux-de-vie*. Each has been preciously aged for between forty years and a century, making our finest Grande Champagne Cognac an unforgettable experience.

You can also celebrate the Millennium with the exceptional of the exceptional : the prestigious limited edition of 2000 Louis XIII decanters*, engraved and gilded with 24 carat gold. To leave your mark in time, acquire your own personalized decanter. For further information on this "Louis XIII Rendez-vous 2000" limited edition, call our Universal Free Phone Number : +800 13 00 2000

*by capacity of 70 cl/700 ml and 75 cl/750 ml, according to the regulations in force in the countries of commercialization.

RÉMY MARTIN

GRANDE CHAMPAGNE COGNAC

TURKEY Where East meets West

The land where the West and the Orient really do meet – look for the signs proclaiming "Welcome To Asia" as you cross the two impressive modern bridges spanning the Bosphorus in Istanbul – Turkey is full of intriguing surprises.

For starters, while there's a wealth of archaeological and cultural history, stretching back to the days of the Greek, Roman, Byzantine and Ottoman empires, it's a more modern, westernised country than you might expect. Secondly, it's clean, well ordered and the people are friendly and welcoming. And then there's the scenery, with a lot more greenery than you might expect.

Impressive mountain ranges run down to the Mediterranean coast where most of the golfing action is based.

GETTING THERE A huge and bustling city, Istanbul has daily connections with major cities in Europe, the Middle East, Asia and the USA, direct flights or convenient connections are available into Izmir, Antalya and Ankara. Traffic conditions in the big cities can be chaotic but the roads are surprisingly well engineered, even in the hinterland.

APRÈS GOLF Though the vast majority of Turks are Muslims, the country is a secular state. Evening entertainment ranges from Arabic belly-dancing to western opera.

Fruit and veg are of high quality, assuring tender salads to go with the good quality grilled meats and fish, often served as kebabs. Kick start your day with a strong black Turkish coffee and spend some time people watching.

OFF THE COURSE Sightseeing has to be a priority, with not only glorious countryside and fascinating cities, towns and villages to explore but a wealth of architectural sites to induce cultural overload in this epicentre of the ancient world.

NOT TO BE MISSED In Istanbul: the Topkapi Palace, Blue Mosque, Aya Sofia Museum, Dolmabahçe Palace. At the coast: wealth of Greek and Roman ruins; the site of the ancient city of Troy.

NEW DEVELOPMENTS

● **Golf is a fast-growing sport in Turkey and the country currently boasts five courses, of which four are located in the holiday region of Belek.**

Traditionally Turkey was a non-golfing destination, but all that has now changed and the game is set to become a central plank in the country's tourism strategy, especially during the cooler months of autumn, winter and spring.

Over the past three years, four superb new courses have opened within five miles of each other at Belek, a young resort on the south-east Mediterranean coast. This region is now known as the Turkish Riviera and offers excellent value whether you are seeking accommodation at a five-star hotel, dining out at a sophisticated restaurant or bartering for designer clothes at quality seconds prices.

As for golf, that costs a fraction of what you part with when you tee up in the Algarve or Southern Spain, and apart from benefiting from the obvious advantages of the latest golf contruction technology, the four courses at Belek are uncannily reminiscent of the finest Algarve venues. The greens are slick and true, and the trees similar in shape and maturity to those at, say, Vilamoura or Penina.

Turkey's other popular golf destination can be found near Istanbul, where Tony Jacklin designed the Klassis Golf & Country Club almost seven years ago. Istanbul is one of the world's most historical cities and the five-star ambience of the Klassis complex is suitably sybaritic. Last May, Klassis found itself in the shop window when Tommy Horton won the Beko Seniors Classic there.

Given the undeniable quality of Turkey's courses, Tommy certainly won't be the last British golfer to return with a smile on his face.

Hotels

- ● **Gloria Golf Hotel** — Page 216
- ○ **Klassis Golf Resort** — Page 217
- ◐ **Sheraton Voyager** — Page 218
- ● **Tatbeach Golf Hotel** — Page 219
- ● **Altis Golf Hotel** — Page 220
- ◐ **Merit Arcadia** — Page 220

RECOMMENDED CAR HIRE
UK: +44 (0) 870 848 4848
Germany: +49 (0) 180 533 3535
Website: www.hertz.com

The most up-to-date golf travel information is always at
www.golftravel4u.com

Favourite fairways

① NATIONAL GOLF CLUB

The best known and toughest of the Belek courses is the David Feherty-designed National Golf Club, which staged a European Seniors Tour event within a few months of opening in 1996. The National, which also has a 1547-metre nine-hole golf academy course and a 40-bay driving range, is built on gently sloping terrain and set amongst mature trees, with four natural water features.
Par 72   Length 6182m
Belek Turizm Merkezi, 07500 Serik, Antalya
Tel: +90 (0) 242 725 5400   Fax: +90 (0) 242 725 5399

② GLORIA GOLF RESORT

The Turkish Seniors Open switched last year to the nearby Gloria Golf Resort, which was designed by Frenchman Michel Gayon. The course winds its way through the ancient forest en-route to separating the sea from seven inland lakes while the centrepiece of the complex is a massive five-star hotel which can accommodate up to 850 people and provides access to the beach via a bridge over the Acisu River.
Par 76   Length 6288m
Acisu Mevkii, Mail Box 27, Belek, Serik, Antalya
Tel: +90 (0) 242 715 1520   Fax: +90 (0) 242 715 1525

③ NOBILIS GOLF CLUB

Across the road from Gloria Golf Resort is the Dave Thomas-designed course at the Nobilis Golf Club & Villas Resort Hotel, the newest and perhaps most visually attractive of the four Belek golf venues. The background views from several holes of the Taurus Mountains are worth the green fee alone while mature trees and gentle water hazards border green fairways and generously large greens.
Par 72   Length 5858m
Acisu Mevkii, Belek, Antalya
Tel: +90 (0) 242 715 1987   Fax: +90 (0) 242 715 1985

④ TAT GOLF INTERNATIONAL

The last though by no means least of the four Belek golf complexes is the Hawtree-designed Tat Beach International club, which has three nine-hole loops, each measuring in excess of 3000 metres, and several holes running enchantingly by the sea. The course offers many different challenges and gives the golfer the chance to play off lush fairways on to generous greens. The complex also boasts a large modern clubhouse.
Par 72   Length 6115m
Uckum Tepesi Mevkii, Mail Box 71, Belek, Antalya
Tel: +90 (0) 242 725 5303/4   Fax: +90 (0) 242 725 5299

⑤ KLASSIS GOLF & COUNTRY CLUB

The five-star Klassis Golf Resort, which is just a 45-minute drive from Istanbul Airport, was designed by Tony Jacklin and opened seven years ago. Last May, Klassis found itself in the shop window when Tommy Horton conquered the hilly but strikingly fertile layout to win the Beko Seniors Classic. Given the steepness of the climbs, as high as 60 metres in some cases, a golf cart is definitely recommended.
Par 72   Length 5850m
Sineklikoyu Mevkii, Silivri, Istanbul
Tel: +90 (0) 212 748 4600   Fax: +90 (0) 212 748 4643

CLIMATE   Turkey has a wide variety of weather conditions, from year-round snow on the Anatolian plateau, to hot arid summers in the interior. The coastal areas have high rainfall and warm winters.

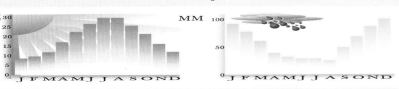

Sample point: Istanbul

Price guide €

| Round of golf | ●● | Golf balls | ●●● |
| Small beer | ●● | 4/5 star hotel room | ●●● |

CONTACT

Turkish Tourist Office, Ismetinonü Bulvari, No 5
Bahcelievler, Anchord Turkey
Tel: +90 (0) 312 212 8300
Fax: +90 (0) 312 212 8391

GLORIA GOLF RESORT

Hotel information

Acisu Mevkii
Belek Mail Box: 27
Serik
Antalya

Tel: +90 (0) 242 715 1520
Fax: +90 (0) 242 715 1525 / 715 1635 1635
Web: www.gloria.com.tr

Accolades

★★★★☆

Airport

Antalya International: 30 mins

Accommodation price guide

€

Accepted credit cards
AE DC MC V

Preferred tour operator

From UK
Alternative
Travel   Tel: +44 (0) 207 241 2687

From Germany
Singold Travel Tel: +49 (0) 89 358 0990

From Netherlands
Cretas Golf
Reizen   Tel: +31 (0) 104 129 265

Recreational facilities

Tennis court, squash, children's complex, gym, sauna, Turkish bath, massage, watersports.

Meeting/business facilities

10 rooms, for up to 600 delegates.

Local attractions

Historical sights, shopping, Antalya yacht harbour, Taurus mountains.

Host to the 1998 Beko Classic PGA European Seniors Tournament, the luxurious five-star Gloria Golf Resort has completed major improvements to its on-site championship golf course, ranging from the fairways being replanted from ray grass to Bermuda grass to the opening of a two storey 48-bay driving range and a 3500m² 18-hole miniature putting green.

With three other major courses within a 15-mile drive, a location giving spectacular views of the beautiful Taurus mountains and a superb Mediterranean beach on its southern edge, Gloria Golf Resort ranks among the world's best.

The hotel has 420 luxuriously appointed and air-conditioned rooms, including suites, junior suites and villas which are set among the gardens and pines overlooking the course.

Superb on-site sporting facilities include tennis, watersports, gymnasium, squash, fitness centre, massage, sauna and Turkish bath. There are several outdoor and two indoor swimming pools, a wonderful children's club and a luxury surround-sound cinema.

Guests can relax in the clubhouse or at three bars, while the four restaurants offer a seductive mix of culinary alternatives, including Turkish, Italian, seafood and international cuisine.

GOLF FACILITIES
Best season for golf: September to end of May.

COURSES:	LENGTH	PAR	FEES
Championship			
	6877m	72	US$60
Academy			
	265m	9	US$15

Driving range featuring lake and target greens, 18-bay two storey driving range, 18-hole putting green; three chipping greens; pitching green; tuition packages; tournaments arranged; golf pro shop.

Facilities key

420   600

KLASSIS RESORT HOTEL

Hotel information

34930 Silivri
Istanbul

Tel: +90 (0) 212 727 4050
Fax: +90 (0) 212 727 0417
Web: www.klassis.com.tr
Email: info@klassis.com.tr

Accolades

★★★★☆

Airport

Istanbul Atatürk: 45 mins

Accommodation price guide

Accepted credit cards
AE DC MC V

Preferred tour operator

From UK
Alternative
Travel   Tel: +44 (0) 207 92 33230
From Germany
Singold
Travel   Tel: +49 (0) 89 358 0990
From Holland
Cretas Golf
Reizen   Tel: +31 (0) 10 412 9265

Set just outside Istanbul, the historic capital of the old Ottoman Empire and where Europe meets Asia, the Klassis Resort Hotel features a wide range of leisure activities which make it the only complete leisure resort in the region.

Built on the seafront using a combination of Greco-Roman and Ottoman architectural styles, the hotel is pleasing to the senses, combining visual delights with comfortable rooms, most with views of the Marmara sea. There are three spacious restaurants, four bars, sea view terraces and sea front banquet areas plus matchless sporting and leisure facilities.

The en-suite rooms feature mini-bar, hairdryer, 19-channel TV, air-conditioning, direct dial phone and 24 hour room service. Each villa provides a living room, terrace and gardens.

Guests have full access to all the facilities at the Klassis Golf & Country Club, which is an exclusive golfing venue located 14 km from the hotel. The club meets all the requirements for international golf tournaments. The 5865-metre par 72 championship course was designed by Tony Jacklin to meet all European norms and standards.

Within the club's grounds is a superb equestrian centre and other activities and services that make Klassis Resort Hotel and the Klassis Golf and Country Club the perfect environment for a memorable visit to fascinating Turkey.

Recreational facilities

Watersports, tennis courts, two outdoor pools, one indoor pool, squash courts, ice rink (winter only), Institute Clarins beauty centre, hairdresser, night club, disco.

Meeting/business facilities

12 rooms, for up to 1500 delegates.

Local attractions

Istanbul with its famed attractions: Blue Mosque, Topkapi Palace, Santa Sophia mosque and covered markets and shopping malls.

GOLF FACILITIES
Best season for golf: All year round.

COURSES:	LENGTH	PAR	FEES
Championship Course			
	5865m	72	US$50
Academy Course			
	1000m	27	US$25

Driving range, putting green, chipping areas, lessons by head pro, buggies available; host to 1997 & 1998 PGA European Challenge Turkish Open,1999 PGA Beko Senior Open.

Facilities key

303   1500

SHERATON VOYAGER ANTALYA HOTEL

Hotel information

100 Yil Bulvari
07050 Antalya

Tel: +90 (0) 242 243 2432
Fax: +90 (0) 242 243 2462
Email:reservations_voyager@sheraton.com
Web: www.sheraton.com/voyager

Accolades

☆☆☆☆☆

Airport

Antalya: 20 mins

Accommodation price guide

€

Accepted credit cards
AE MC V DC

Preferred tour operator

From UK
Thomson
Travel   Tel: +44 (0) 0990 502 550
From Germany
Terramar   Web: www.terramar-reisen.de

Recreational facilities

Beautiful formal gardens, shopping arcade, coiffeur; health centre with indoor pool, sauna, hammam, Jacuzzi, fitness centre, aerobics and step lessons, squash, floodlit tennis courts (tuition available), outdoor pool, water sports; beach; golf, horse riding, rafting, diving, sailing, all available locally.

Meeting/business facilities

Seven small meeting rooms, one ballroom for up to 700 delegates.

Local attractions

Beaches; Dueden and Kursunlu waterfalls; wild water rafting on the Koprulu River; horseback riding at international standard ranches; water games at Aqualand; Antalya Museum, one of Turkey's best-perserved archeological collections; daily tours to ancient Lycian sites of Aspendos, Perge and Side; music and drama at Roman theatre in Aspendos during Summer season.

Framed by extensive gardens and a delightful pool area, the luxurious Sheraton Voyager Antalya Hotel provides all the sophistication of a modern city centre hotel, yet in a relaxed resort setting, with the blue Mediterranean and the picturesque Taurus Mountains as its backdrop.

Located on Konyaalti Beach, the Sheraton Voyager Antalya offers holidaymakers, conference delegates and business travellers alike the ultimate in luxury accommodation – featuring 395 elegantly designed rooms, all with balconies – and is conveniently located for the region's top quality golf courses.

Corporate golfing parties will find a choice of seven fully-equipped meeting rooms of various sizes, with the elegant Grand Ballroom capable of seating up to 700 people. Tee-times at four championship golf courses in Belek – just 30 minutes drive away – are bookable directly through the hotel while, closer to home, the beach is just three minutes walk and the city centre is just one kilometre distant.

Besides enjoying the hotel's own first-rate amenities, guests will find a wealth of leisure and cultural activities locally, from wild water rafting on the Koprulu River to daily tours of the ancient Lycian sites of Aspendos, Perge and Side.

GOLF FACILITIES
Best season for golf: All year round.

COURSES:	LENGTH	PAR	FEES
National	white/yellow		
	6222/5564m	72	US$55
Nobilis			
	6312m	72	US$50
Tatbeach			
	5504m	72	US$50
Gloria			
	6288m	72	US$60
Tee-times bookable through hotel.			

Facilities key

395   700

TATBEACH GOLF HOTEL

Hotel information

PO Box 01
07507
Belek Turizm Merkezi
Antalya

Tel: +90 242 725 4080
Fax: +90 242 725 4099/725 4100
Email: info@tatbeach.com
Web: www.tatbeach.com

Accolades

☆☆☆☆☆

Airport

Antalya: 25 mins

Accommodation price guide

Accepted credit cards
AE MC V

Preferred tour operator

From UK
Alternative
Travel   Tel: +44 (0) 20 7923 3230
From Germany
Öger Tours   Tel: + 49 (0) 4032001168
From Sweden
Golf World
Travel   Tel: +46 (0) 8661 7940

Situated in the popular Mediterranean resort of Belek, just 35 kilometres from Antalya International Airport and 45 kilometres from downtown Antalya, the attractive Tatbeach Golf Hotel sits on a magnificent seafront lot covered with pistachio pines and just by a lovely beach.

A mild sub-tropical climate year round makes this a great venue for golfing holidays, especially since there is a superb course, the first and only 27-hole championship course in Turkey, adjacent to the hotel, with three more first-class clubs within easy reach.

The hotel offers a range of double rooms, superior rooms, junior suites, standard suites and three honeymoon suites. All rooms are equipped with the most modern amenities, including TV with satellite programmes and video channel, air-conditioning and either a balcony or a patio, each with either a sea or garden view.

Tatbeach Golf Hotel has a popular main restaurant offering open buffet breakfast and dinner, *à la carte* lunches, pool bar, lobby bar, fitness bar, beer garden, disco bar and open-air disco.

Recreational facilities

Indoor and outdoor pools; six tennis courts (four floodlit); fitness centre: sauna, massage and whirlpool; watersports; mountain bike and quattro-cycle rental; in-hotel shops.

Meeting/business facilities

Three rooms, for up to 550 delegates.

Local attractions

Köprülü Canyon National Park; historic sites of Perge, Side, Aspendos, Termessos, Olympos, the sunken city of Kekova, and Myra, the birthplace of St. Nicholas; Antalya old city.

GOLF FACILITIES
Best season for golf: September to June.

COURSES:	LENGTH	PAR	FEES
Tat Golf International			
	9275m	3 x36	$55
National Golf Club			
	6089m	72	$55
Gloria Golf Club			
	6263m	72	$60
Nobilis Golf Club			
	5858m	72	$55

Special rate green fees are avialable to hotel guests.

Facilities key

 650 550

MERIT ARCADIA RESORT HOTEL

Hotel information

Iskele Mevkii
07506 Belek
Antalya

Tel: +90 (0) 242 715 1100
Fax: +90 (0) 242 715 1084
Email: meritarcadia@superonline.com

Accolades

✫✫✫✫✫

Airport

Antalya: 40 mins

Accommodation price guide

Accepted credit cards
AE MC V

Local attractions

Great beaches, sailing, seaside resorts and fishing towns, archaeological ruins.

AMERICAN EXPRESS OFFER
For advance booking on American Express Card you receive a **room upgrade, subject to availability.**

Belek is a new holiday town in Antalya, the hub of recreation, entertainment and culture tourism in Turkey. The great beaches, clear water, and nearby forests rich with fauna make this an ideal place for year-round recreation.

Merit Arcadia has become Belek's flagship resort. Its 473 luxuriously appointed rooms include 83 suites and junior suites and four grand suites, while three championship golf courses – Nobilis, the National and Tat Golf – lie within a ten-kilometre radius, providing an enviable choice of play.

The resort hotel features a superb sandy beach, various swimming pools, live entertainment, a full range of sports and leisure activities, and just about everything else a holidaymaker could wish for.

Meeting/business facilities

Three rooms, for up to 400 delegates.

Recreational facilities

Fitness centre; sauna, Turkish bath; mini football, archery; darts, pool table; cycling.

GOLF FACILITIES
Best season for golf: October to end of April.

COURSES:	LENGTH	PAR	FEES
Nobilis	6080m	72	US$50-60
National	6109m	72	US$50-60
Tat Golf	6190m	72	US$50-60

Facilities key

473   400

ALTIS GOLFHOTEL

Hotel information

Belek Turlem Mercezi
Belek
Antalya

Tel: +90 (0) 242 725 4242
Fax: +90 (0) 242 725 4234
Email: info@altis.com.tr
Web: www.altis.com.tr

Accolades

✫✫✫✫✫

Airport

Antalya: 20 mins

Accommodation price guide

Accepted credit cards
AE DC MC V

Local attractions

Beaches, seaside resorts and fishing towns, sailing cruises, ancient ruins.

Altis Golfhotel was purpose-designed to cater for all golfers – amateur and professional alike. The hotel is just minutes away from the National and Tat Beach golf clubs and within half an hour of the popular Nobilis course, with free transportation services provided for guests.

Traditional Turkish hospitality meet international standards to create an unbeatable combination. The hotel's 296 designer-decorated rooms and suites all feature air-conditioning, balconies, satellite TV, mini-bar and safe. There are additionally 20 villas located within the beautifully landscaped gardens.

At Altis Golfhotel, guests can enjoy a lavish buffet breakfast before setting out to conquer the golf course or enjoy the turquoise blue Mediterranean.

Meeting/business facilities

Five rooms, for up to 500 people.

Recreational facilities

Golf course; gardens.

GOLF FACILITIES
Best season for golf: October to May.

COURSES:	LENGTH	PAR	FEES
National	6109m	72	US$50-60
Tat Beach	6190m	72	US$50-60
Nobilis	6080m	72	US$50-60

On-site six-hole practice course.

Facilities key

315   500

Best of the rest
Where else to stay

For another 200 top class resorts that cater to the needs of golf travellers, look no further

AUSTRALIA
Burswood International
Resort Casino, Great Eastern
Highway, PO Box456,
Burswood, Perth 6100
Tel: +61 (0) 8936 27 777

Hyatt Regency Sanctuary
Cove, Manor Circle, Casey
Rd, Hope Island, Surfers
Paradise, Queensland 4212
Tel: +61 (0) 7553 01 234

Laguna Quays Resort,
Daydream Island,
Whitsundays, Daydream
Island, Queensland 4740
Tel: +61 (0) 2955 28 708

Radisson Resort Palm
Meadows, Palm Meadows
Drive, Palm Meadows, Gold
Coast, Queensland 4211
Tel: +61 (0) 7555 57 700

Royal Pines Resort, Ross St,
Ashmore, Surfers, Paradise,
Queensland 4213
Tel: +61 (0) 7559 71 111

Rydges Capricorn
International Resort, Level
2, 49 Market Street, Sydney
Tel: +61 (0) 2928 61 131

Rydges Capricorn
International Resort,
Farnborough Road, Yeppoon,
Queensland 4703
Tel: +61 (0) 2928 61 131

Sheraton Mirage Port
Douglas, Davidson Street,
Port Douglas, North
Queensland 4871
Tel: +61 (0) 7409 95 888

AUSTRIA
Domino Suites Hotel & CC,
Dominostrasse 1, 2483
Ebreichsdorf
Tel: +43 (0) 225 474 614

BELGIUM
Hotel La Reserve,
Elizabetlaan 160, 8300
Knokke-Heist
Tel: +32 (0) 50 603 706

The Montgomery, Avenue de
Tervuren 134, 1150 Brussels
Tel: +32 (0) 2 741 8500

BRAZIL
Hotel Do Frade & Golf
Resort, Rio de Janeiro
Tel: +55 (0) 21 259 7195

JAMAICA
Half Moon Golf, Tennis and
Beach Club, Rose Hall,
Montego Bay, Jamaica
Tel: +1 876 953 2211

COSTA RICA
Marriott Los Sueños Beach
& Golf Resort, Herradura
Tel: +506 298 00 33

Melia Playa Conchal Beach
& Golf Resort, Guanacaste,
Playa Conchal, Santa Cruz
Tel: +506 293 88 12

CZECH REPUBLIC
Grandhotel Pupp, Mirove
namesti 2, Karlovy Vary
36091
Tel: +420 (0)17 310 9111

DENMARK
Golf Hotel Viborg,
Randersvej 2, DK 8800,
Viborg
Tel: +45 (0) 86 61 02 22

DOMINICAN REPUBLIC
Bavaro Beach Resort,
Careterra Bavaro, Punta
Cana, Higuey
Tel: +1 809 971 469 417

ENGLAND
Carden Park Hotel, Golf &
Health Resort, Carden, Nr
Chester, Cheshire, CH3 9DQ
Tel: +44 (0) 1829 731 000

De Vere Slaley Hall, Slaley,
Hexham, Northumberland,
NE47 0BY
Tel: +44 (0) 1434 673 350

Marriott Breadsall Priory
Hotel, Moor Road, Morley,
Near Derby, Derbyshire,
DE7 6DL
Tel: +44 (0) 1332 832 235

Marriott Forest of Arden
Hotel, Maxstoke Lane,
Meriden, Warwickshire, CV7
2HR
Tel: +44 (0) 1676 522 335

Marriott Goodwood Park,
Goodwood, Chichester, West
Sussex, PO18 0QB
Tel: +44 (0) 1243 775 537

Marriott Hanbury Manor
Hotel, Ware, Hertfordshire,
SG12 0SD
Tel: +44 (0) 1920 487 722

Marriott Hollins Hall,
Hollins Hill, Baildon,
Shipley, West Yorkshire,
BD17 7QW
Tel: +44 (0) 1274 530 053

Marriott Manchester Hotel
and CC, Worsley Park,
Walkden Road, Worsley,
Manchester, M28 2QT
Tel: +44 (0) 161 799 6187

Marriott Meon Valley Hotel,
Golf & C.C., Sandy Lane,
Shedield, Southampton,
Hampshire, SO3 2HQ
Tel: +44 (0) 1329 833 455

Marriott Tudor Park Hotel,
Ashford Road, Bearsted,
Maidstone, Kent, ME14 4NQ
Tel: +44 (0) 1622 734 334

Mottram Hall Hotel,
Wilmslow Road, Mottram St
Andrew, Prestbury,
Cheshire, SK10 4QT
Tel: +44 (0) 1625 828 135

Nailcote Hall Hotel,
Nailcote Lane, Berkswell,
Warwickshire, CV7 7DE
Tel: +44 (0) 1203 466 174

Shrigley Hall Hotel & CC,
Pott Shrigley, Nr.
Macclesfield, Cheshire,
SK10 5SB
Tel: +44 (0) 1625 57 57 57

FRANCE
Château des Vigiers, 24240
Monestier
Tel: +33 (0) 5 53 61 50 31

Domaine & Golf de Belesbat,
Domaine de Belesbat, 91820
Boutigny sur Essone
Tel: +33 (0) 1 69 23 19 01

Domaine de Taulane, Route
Nationale 85, Le Logis du
Pin, 83840 La Martre
Tel: +33 (0) 4 93 60 33 23

Domaine Royal d'Evian, BP
8, Domaine du Royal Club
Evian, 74502 Evian Les
Bains, Cedex
Tel: +33 (0) 4 50 75 38 40

Golf de Sainte Maxime,
Route du Debarquement,
83120 Sainte-Maxime
Tel: +33 (0) 4 94 55 02 03

Golf Plaza Hôtel & Country
Club, PO Box 29, Golf de
Sainte-Maxime, 83120
Sainte-Maxime
Tel: +33 (0) 4 94 56 66 00

Gray d'Albion Hôtel, BP
295, 38, rue des Serbes,
06408 Cannes, Cedex
Tel: +33 (0) 4 93 99 26 10

Hôtel du Golf de Deauville,
38, Rue Jean Mermoz,
Lucien Barrière Hôtel &
Resor, 14800 Deauville
Tel: +33 (0) 2 31 14 24 01

Hôtel du Golf de la
Breteschel, 44780 Missillac
Tel: +33 (0) 2 40 66 99 47

Hôtel du Golf Le Saint
Denac, 44500 La Baule
Tel: +33 (0) 2 40 17 57 58

Hôtel Majestic, BP 163, 14,
La Croisette, 06407 Cannes
Tel: +33 (0) 4 93 38 97 90

Le Domaine d'Hardelot, 111,
Avenue FranÁois I, 62152
Hardelot
Tel: +33 (0) 3 21 83 29 71

Manoir Hôtel, BP 41,
Avenue du Golf, 62520 Le
Touquet
Tel: +33 (0) 3 21 06 28 29

Moulin de Vernègues, 13370
Mallemort de Provence
Tel: +33 (0) 4 90 59 15 90

Novotel Golf National, St-
Quentin en Yvelines, 1,
Avenue du Golf, 78114
Magny les Hameaux
Tel:+33 (0) 1 30 57 65 00

Le Méridien Saint Martin,
Anse Marcel, 97056 Saint
Martin, Antilles
Tel: +590 (0) 87 67 55

Le Méridien St. François, St.
François, BP 37, 97118
Guadeloupe, Antilles
Tel: +590 (0) 88 50 28

Le Méridien Trois Ilets, Fort
de France, BP 894, 97243
Martinique
Tel: +596 (0) 66 00 74

GERMANY
Die Wutzschleife, D-92444
Rotz-Hillstett/opf
Tel: +49 (0) 9976 180

Hotel Konig Ludwig, Am
Kurwald 2, D-94086 Bad
Griesbach
Tel: +49 (0) 85 32 7990

Jakobsberg Golfhotel &
Club, Im Tal der Loreley,
56154 Boppard-Rhen
Tel: +49 (0) 67 42 80 80

Kempinski Hotel Sporting
Club Berlin, Parkallee 1, D-
15526 Bad Saarow
Tel: +49 (0) 3 36 31 617 05

Margarethenhof Golf &
Country Club, Gut Steinberg,
Postfach 1101, D-83701
Gmund, am Tegernsee-
Marienstein
Tel: +49 (0) 8022 750 60

Maximillian Hotel, Kurallee
1, 94086 Bad Griesbach,
Bavaria
Tel: +49 (0) 8532 79 5502

Parkhotel Adler, D-79856
Hinterzarten
Tel: +49 (0) 7652 1270

Parkhotel Schlangenbad,
Hessisches Staatsbad, Land
Hessen, Rheingauer Strasse
47, D-65388 Schlangenbad
Tel: +49 (0) 6129 420

Romantik Hotel Altes
Gymnasium, Suderstrasse 6,
D-25813 Husum
Tel: +49 (0) 4841 83 30

Schloss Waldeck, D-34513
Waldeck, am Edersee
Tel: +49 (0) 5623 58 90

HUNGARY
Danubius Thermal & Sport
Hotel Buk, Szent Istvan Ter
11, Budapest 1051
Tel: +36 (0) 1374 72 38

INDONESIA
Hyatt Regency, Jendral
Desukirachmat 106-128,
Surabaya, 60271
Tel: +62 (0) 31 531 1234

Imperial Century Hotel, Blvd
Central-Sudirman 1300,
Lippo Karawaci, Tangerang,
15811
Tel: +62 (0) 21 546 0101

IRELAND
Ashford Castle, Cong, Co.
Mayo
Tel: +353 (0) 92 46 003

Galway Bay Golf & Country
Club Hotel, Oranmore, Co.
Galway
Tel: +353 (0) 91 790500

Kildare Hotel and Country
Club, Straffan, Co. Kildare
Tel: +353 (0) 1 601 7268

Kilkea Castle Hotel and Golf
Club, Castledermot, Co.
Kildare
Tel: +353 (0) 503 45156

Luttrellstown Castle Golf &
Country Club, Clonsilla, Co.
Dublin
Tel: +353 (0) 1 808 9903

Sheen Falls Lodge, Kenmare,
Kerry
Tel: +353 (0) 644 1600

Waterford Castle, The Island,
Ballinakill, Waterford
Tel: +353 (0) 51 878 203

Waterville House & Golf
Links, Ring of Kerry,
Waterville, Co. Kerry
Tel: +353 (0) 667 4102

ISRAEL
Dan Caesarea Hotel, PO Box
1120, Caesarea, Caesarea
Tel: +972 (0) 66 269 111

ITALY
Gallia Palace Hotel, Via delle
Sughere, 58040 Punta Ala,
Grosseto
Tel: +39 0564 92 0229

Grand Hotel Gardone
Riviera, Via Zanardeli 74,
25083 Gardone Riviera (BS)
Tel: +39 0365 22 695

Hotel des Bains, Lungomare
Marconi 17, 30126 Venezia
Lido
Tel: +39 041 526 0113

Hotel Splendido, Salita
Baratta 16, 16034 Portofino,
Genova
Tel: +39 0185 269 614

Il Castello di Carimate,
Piazza Castello 1, 22060
Carimate (Co)
Tel: +39 031 790 683

Is Molas Golf Hotel, Is
Molas, 09010 Pula, Sardinia
Tel: +39 070 924 1002

L'Hotel de la Ville, 20052
Monza
Tel: +39 039 36 76 47

La Meridiana, 17033
Garlenda
Tel: +39 0182 58 0150

Palazzo Arzaga Hotel Golf &
Saturnia Spa, 25080 Carzago
di Calvagese
Tel: +39 030 680 62 68

Royal Hotel, Corso
Imperatrice 80, 18038 San
Remo
Tel: +39 0184 661 445

Villa Condulmer & Villa
Braida, Via Zermanese 1, 31021
Zerman di Mogliano (TV)
Tel: +39 041 457 134

Villa San Michele, Via Doccia
4, 50014 Fiesole
Tel: +39 055 59 8734

JAPAN
Hotel Europe, 7-7 Huis ten
Bosch, Sasebo-shi, Nagasaki
Prefecture, 859-32
Tel: +81 (0) 956 58 1111

KENYA
Windsor Golf and Country
Club, PO Box 45587, Nairobi
Tel: +254 (0) 2 862 300

LUXEMBOURG
Sheraton Aerogolf Hôtel, PO
Box 1973, Route de Treves,
1019 Luxembourg
Tel: +352 (0) 340 217

MALAYSIA
Holiday Inn Crowne Plaza
Johor Bahru, Jalan Dato
Sulaiman Taman Century,
80990 Johor
Tel: +60 (0) 73 323 800

Hyatt Regency Saujana, 2km
off Sultan Abdul Aziz Shah,
Airport Highway, 47200
Subang, Selangor
Tel: +60 (0) 37 461 234

Merlin Inn Resort, Post Box
4, Tanah Rata 39007
Tel: +60 (0) 54 911 211

Nexus Golf Resort
Karambunai, P.O. Box 270,
88450 Menggatal, Sabah
Tel: +60 (0) 88 411 222

Pulai Springs Resort, 20km,
Jalan Pontian Lama, Pulai,
Johor, 81110
Tel: +60 (0) 75 212 121

The Mines Resort City, Lot A-
6-1, 6th Floor, Block A, Mines
Waterfront Business Park,
No. 3 Jalan Tasik, 43300 Seri
Kembangan, Selangor Darul
Ehsan
Tel: +60 (0) 39 436 633

The Pan Pacific Sutera Hotel,
1 Sutera Avenue, 88 100 Kota
Kinabalu, Sabah, Borneo
Tel: +60 (0) 88 318 888

MAURITIUS
Le Paradis, Case Noyale,
Lemorne
Tel: +230 (0) 450 5050

Le Touessrok, Trou d'Eau
Douce, Flacq
Tel: +230 (0) 419 2451

MEXICO
Acapulco Princess / Pierre
Marques Princess, Playa
Revolcadero, Acapulco,
Guerrero 39300
Tel: +52 (0) 74 69 10 38

Avandaro Golf & Spa Resort,
Colonia Polanco, Anatole
France, 139, 11550 Mexico
DF
Tel: +52 (0) 52 80 00 92

Caesar Park Beach & Golf
Resort, Ret. Lacandones Km
17, Cancun, Quintana Roo
77500
Tel: +52 (0) 98 81 80 82

Caribbean Village Golf &
Beach Club, Playa Del
Carmen, QR 77710
Tel: +52 (0) 98 73 10 47

Las Brisas, Carretera
Escenica #5255, Acapulco,
Guerrero 39868
Tel: +52 (0) 74 46 53 32

Marriott Casa Magna, 48300
Puerto Vallarta, Jal
Tel: +52 (0) 52 82 88 04

Palmilla Hotel & Golf Club,
Carretra Transpeninsular, San
Jose de Los Cabos, BCS 23
Tel: +52 (0) 11 44 51 00

Sierra Plaza Golf & Spa,
Marina Vallarta, 311
Pelicanos, Puerto Vallarta,
Jalisco 4835
Tel: +52 (0) 32 21 08 01

MONACO
Hôtel de Paris, Place du
Casino, MC 98000 Monte
Carlo
Tel: +377 (0) 92 16 38 51

MOROCCO
La Palmeraie Golf Palace, BP
1488, Les Jardins de la
Palmeraie, Marrakesh
Tel: +212 (0) 4 30 90 00

Royal Golf Hotel de Jadida,
Km 7, Route de Casablanca,
El Jadida
Tel: +212 (0) 3 353 473

NEW ZEALAND
Millbrook Resort, Malaghan
Road, Arrowtown, Private
Bag, Queenstown
Tel: +64 (0) 3 441 7000

NORTHERN IRELAND
Radisson Roe Park Hotel,
Roe Park, Limavady, Co.
Londonderry
Tel: +44 (0) 1504 722 222

PANAMA
Coronado Hotel & Resort,
Apartado 4381, Panama 5
Tel: +507 (0) 223 8513

PARAGUAY
Hotel Paraguayo Casino
Yacht & Golf Club, PO Box
1795, Lambare, Avenida del
Yacht ,11, Asuncion
Tel: +595 (0) 21 906 120

PORTUGAL
Caesar Park Penha Longa
Golf Resort, Estrada da Lagoa
Azul, 2710 Sintra
Tel: +351 (0) 21 924 90 07

Hotel Quinta do Lago, Quinta
do Lago, 8135
Almancil
Tel: +351 (0) 289 39 63 93

Le Meridien Dona Filipa,
Vale Do Lobo, 8136 Almancil,
Codex
Tel: +351 (0) 289 39 42 88

Le Meridien Penina Golf &
Resort, PO Box 146, 8502
Portimão Codex
Tel: +351 (0) 282 415 000

Reid's Hotel, Madeira,
Estrada Monumental, 139,
9000 Funchal
Tel: +351 (0) 291 717 164

The Sheraton Algarve Hotel
& Resort, PO Box 644, Praia
da Falesia, 8200 Albufeira
Tel: +351 (0) 289 500 122

PUERTO RICO
El Conquistador Resort &
CC, 1000 El Conquistador
Avenue, Las Croabas 00738
Tel: +1 787 860 3200

Hyatt Dorado Beach &
Cerromar Resort, Road 693,
Dorado Beach 00646
Tel: +1 787 796 89 75

RUSSIA
Le Meridien Moscow Country

Club, Park Hotel, Golf &
Resort, Nakhabino,
Krasnogorsky District,
Moscow Region 143430
Tel: +7 (0) 95 926 5911

SCOTLAND
Carnoustie Golf Course
Hotel, Carnoustie, Angus,
DD7 7JE
Tel: +44 (0) 1241 411 999

Gleneagles Hotel,
Auchterarder, Perthshire,
PH3 1NF
Tel: +44 (0) 1764 662 231

Marriott Dalmahoy Hotel,
Kirknewton, Nr Edinburgh,
EH27 8EB
Tel: +44 (0) 1313 331 845

Old Course Hotel, Old
Station Road, St Andrews,
Fife, KY16 9SP
Tel: +44 (0) 1334 474 371

The Roxburghe Hotel & Golf
Course, Kelso, Roxburgshire,
TD5 8JZ
Tel: +44 (0) 1573 450 331

Turnberry Hotel, Golf
Courses and Spa, Turnberry,
Airshire, KA24 9PB
Tel: +44 (0) 1655 331 000

SINGAPORE
The Beaufort Hotel &
Conference Centre, 2 Bukit
Manis Road, Sentosa, 099891
Tel: +65 (0) 275 0331

SLOVENIA
Grand Hotel Toplice, PO Box
41, 4260 Bled
Tel: +386 (0) 64 7910

SOUTH AFRICA
Champagne Sports Resort,
PO Box 763, Hill Crest, 3650
Tel: +27 (0) 31 765 7100

Erinvale Estate Hotel & GC,
1 Erinvale Avenue,
Sommerset West, Cape
Province 7130
Tel: +27 (0) 21 847 1160

Grande Roche Hotel,
Plantasie St, PO Box 6038,
Paarl, Western Cape 7622
Tel: +27 (0) 21 863 2727

Mount Edgecombe Golf
Lodge, P O Box 3311,
Randburg, 2125
Tel: +27 (0) 11 789 1661

Selbourne Country Lodge &
Golf Club, PO Box 2,
Pennington, 4148
Tel: +27 (0) 323 975 1133

Steenberg Country Hotel, P.O.
Box 32017,
Summerstrand, Port
Elizabeth, 6019
Tel: +27 (0) 41 583 5055

Sun City Hotel, PO Box 2,
Sun City, North West 0316
Tel: +27 (0) 146 521 000

SPAIN

Almenara Hotel & Health Club, Sotogrande San Roque, Cadiz
Tel: +34 956 790 046

Atalaya Park Golf Hotel, Ctra. Cadiz-Malaga, km. 165, 29688 Estepona
Tel: +34 95 288 90 02

Hotel Alfonso XIII, San Fernando 2, 41004 Sevilla
Tel: +34 95 421 60 33

Hotel Arts, Carrer de la Marina 19-21, 08005 Barcelona
Tel: +34 93 483 80 64

Hotel Maria Cristina, Paseo Republica Argentina 4, 20004 San Sebastian
Tel: +34 943 42 98 63

Hotel Mencey, Avda Dr. José Naveiras, 38, 38004 Santa Cruz de Tenerife
Tel: +34 922 28 00 17

Hotel Ritz, Plaza de la Lealtad 5, 28014 Madrid
Tel: +34 91 532 87 76

Montecastillo Hotel & Golf Resort, Apartado 56, Ctra. de Arcos, km. 9,5, 11406 Jerez de la Frontera
Tel: +34 95 615 12 15

Parador de Turismo El Saler, Avda. de los Pinares, 151, 46012 Valencia
Tel: +34 96 162 70 16

Parador Malaga Golf, Apdo 324, 29080 Malaga
Tel: +34 95 238 21 41

Suites Hotel at San Roque Club, Apdo. 127, The San Roque Club, 11360 San Roque
Tel: +34 956 61 30 12

Torrequebrada Hotel, Ctra. Cadiz-Malaga, km. 220, 29630 Benalmadena
Tel: +34 95 244 57 02

SWEDEN

Jaravallens Conference and Country Club, Box 214, 24602, Loddekopinge
Tel: +46 (0) 4677 7050

SWITZERLAND

Beau Rivage Palace, Chemin de Beau-Rivage, 1006 Lausanne Ouchy
Tel: +41 (0) 21 613 33 34

Burgenstock Hotel & Resort, 6363 Burgenstock
Tel: +41 (0) 41 610 14 15

Golf Hotel Rhodania, 3963 Crans Montana
Tel: +41 (0) 27 481 51 00

Grand Hotel Quellenhof, 7310 Bad Ragaz
Tel: +41 (0) 81 303 20 22

Hôtel des Bergues, 33 Quai des Bergues, 1201 Geneva
Tel: +41 (0) 22 732 1989

Park Hotel Delta, Via Delta 137, 6612 Ascona
Tel: +41 (0) 91 791 67 24

Suvretta House, St. Moritz
Tel: +41 (0) 81 833 85 24

Villa Magliasina Golf Hotel, Via Vedeggi, 6983 Magliaso-Lugano
Tel: +41 (0) 91 611 29 20

THAILAND

Dusit Laguna Resort, 284 Prabaramee Road, Patong, Kathu District, Phuket 83150
Tel: +66 (0) 76 340 501

Hotel Sofitel Central Hua Hin, 1 Damnernkasem Rd, Prachuabkirikhan, 77110
Tel: +66 (0) 32 512 038

Rose Garden Country Resort, 197/15 Sol Chokhai Jongiamroen, Rama III Rd, Yannawa, Bangkok 10200
Tel: +66 (0) 22 953 261

Royal Chiangmai Golf Resort, 169 Moo 5, Chiang Mai-Prao Rod, KM 26, Mae Fak, Sansai, Chiang Mai
Tel: +66 (0) 53 849 301

Thai Muang Beach Golf & Marine, Phangnga
Tel: +66 (0) 76 571 513

TUNISIA

Abou Nawas Diar el Andalous, Port El Kantaoui, BP 40, 4089 Sousse
Tel: +216 (0) 3 246 348

UAE

Jebel Ali Hotel, Jebel Ali, PO Box 9255, Dubai
Tel: +971 (0) 483 6000

Le Meridien Jumeira Beach Hotel, PO Box 24970, Dubai
Tel: +971 (0) 4399 5555

The Jumeirah Beach Hotel, PO Box 11416, Dubai
Tel: +971 (0) 448 0000

The Ritz-Carlton Dubai, PO Box 59, Dubai
Tel: +971 (0) 4399 4000

USA

Amelia Island Plantation, Highway A1A South, Amelia Island, Florida, 32034
Tel: +1 904 261 6161

Belleview Biltmore Resort, 25 Belleview Blvd, Clearwater 33756, Florida
Tel: +1 727 443 3701

Boca Raton Resort & Club, 501 East Camino Real, Boca Raton, Florida, 33432
Tel: +1 561 447 3000

Callaway Gardens Resort, PO Box 2000, Highway 27, Pine Mountain, Georgia, 31822
Tel: +1 706 663 2281

Château Elan Winery & Resort, 100 Rue Charlemagne, Braselton, 30517, Georgia
Tel: +1 770 932 0900

Doral Golf Resort & Spa, 4400 NW 87th Ave, Miami 33178, Florida
Tel: +1 305 591 6631

Grenelefe Golf & Tennis Resort, 3200 State Road 546, Grenelefe 33844, Florida
Tel: +1 941 421 5004

Grove Park Inn Resort, 290 Macon Avenue, Asheville, North Carolina, 28804
Tel: +1 828 252 2711

Hyatt Regency Hilton Head Resort, PO Box 6167, Hyatt Circle, Palmetto Dunes, Hilton Head Island, South Carolina, 29938
Tel: +1 843 785 1234

Jekyll Island Club Hotel, 371 Riverview Drive, Jekyll Island, Georgia, 315
Tel: +1 912 635 2600

Keswick Hall & Club, Ashley House Hotels, 701 Club Drive, Keswick, 22947, Virginia
Tel: +1 804 979 3440

Kiawah Island Resort, 12 Kiawah Beach Dr, Charleston, South Carolina, 29455
Tel: +1 843 768 2121

Main Street Inn, PO Box 23886, Hilton Head Island, South Carolina, 29925
Tel: +1 843 681 3001

Marriott at Sawgrass Resort, 1000 TPC Blvd, Ponte Verde Beach, Jacksonville 32082, Florida
Tel: +1 904 285 7777

Marriott Grand Vista Resort, 11501 International Drive, Orlando, Florida, 32821
Tel: +1 407 238 6800

Mission Inn Golf & Tennis Resort, 10400 Country Road 48, Howey-In-The-Hills, Florida, 34737
Tel: +1 352 324 3101

Naples Beach Hotel & Golf Club, 851 Gulf Shore Blvd, Naples, Florida, 33940
Tel: +1 941 261 2222

PGA National Resort & Spa, 400 Avenue of the Champions, Palm Beach Gardens, Florida, 33418
Tel: +1 561 627 2000

Pinehurst Resort, PO Box 4000, Pinehurst Village, North Carolina, 28374
Tel: +1 910 295 8477

Plantation Inn & Golf Resort, 9301 W Fort Island Tr, Crystal River, Florida, 34429
Tel: +1 352 795 4211

Renaissance Pine Isle Resort, 9000 Holiday Rd, Lake Lanier Island, Atlanta, Georgia
Tel: +1 770 945 8921

Renaissance Vinoy Resort, 501 Fifth Avenue NE, St. Petersburg, Florida, 33701
Tel: +1 727 894 1000

Saddlebrook Resort Tampa, 5700 Saddlebrook Way, Wesley Chapel, Tampa, Florida, 33543
Tel: +1 813 973 1111

Sea Palms Golf & Tennis Resort, 5445 Frederica Rd, St. Simon Island, Georgia, 31522
Tel: +1 912 638 3351

Seabrook Island Resort, 1002 Landfall Way, Seabrook Island, South Carolina, 29455
Tel: +1 843 768 1000

The American Club, Highland Drive, Kohler, Wisconsin, 53044
Tel: +1 920 457 4441

The Broadmoor, Colorado Springs, Colorado, 80901
Tel: +1 719 577 5777

The Cloister, Sea Island Company, P.O. Box 30351, Sea Island, Georgia, 31561
Tel: +1 912 638 3611

The Equinox, Historic Route 7Alk, Manchester Village, Vermont, 05254
Tel: +1 802 362 4700

The Greenbrier, White Sulphur Springs, West Virginia, 24986-2498
Tel: +1 304 536 1110

The Homestead 1766, P.O. Box 2000, Hot Springs, Virginia, 24445
Tel: +1 540 839 1766

The King and Prince Beach & Golf Resort, St. Simon Island, Georgia
Tel: +1 912 638 3635

The Registry Resort, 475 Seagate Drive, Naples, Florida, 33940
Tel: +1 941 597 3232

The Ritz-Carlton Naples, 280 Vanderbilt Beach Road, Naples, Florida, 33963
Tel: +1 941 598 3300

The Ritz-Carlton Amelia Island, 4750 Amelia Island Parkway, Amelia Island, Florida, 32034
Tel: +1 904 277 1100

The Westin Innisbrook Resort, PO Drawer 1088, Tarpon Springs, Florida, 34688
Tel: +1 727 942 2000

The Westin Resort, Port Royal, 2 Grasslawn Ave, Hilton Head Island, South Carolina, 29928
Tel: +1 843 681 4000

Wild Dunes, 5757 Palm Blvd, Isle of Palms, Charleston, South Carolina, 29451
Tel: +1 843 886 6000

Woodlake Golf & Country Club, 150 Woodlake Boulevard, Vass/Pinehurst, North Carolina, 28394
Tel: +1 910 245 4031

World Golf Village Resort Hotel, 21 World Golf Place, St Augustine, Florida, 32092
Tel: +1 904 940 8000

Ocean Edge Resort & Golf Club, 2907 Main Street, Brewster, MA 02631
Tel: +1 508 896 9000

Wild Dunes, 5757 Palm Blvd, Isle of Palms, Charleston, Sth Carolina, 29451
Tel: +1 843 886 6000

Woodlake Golf & Country Club, 150 Woodlake Boulevard, Vass/Pinehurst, North Carolina, 28394
Tel: +1 910 245 4031

World Golf Village Resort Hotel, 21 World Golf Place, St Augustine, Florida, 32092
Tel: +1 904 940 8000

Ocean Edge Resort & Golf Club, 2907 Main Street, Brewster, MA 02631
Tel: +1 508 896 9000

WALES

Celtic Manor, Coldra Woods, Newport, Gwent, NP44 3UW
Tel: +44 (0) 1633 410 250

Marriott St Pierre Hotel and Country Club, St Pierre Park, Chepstow, Gwent, NP6 6YA
Tel: +44 (0) 1291 625 261

St David's Park Hotel & Golf Club, St David's Park, Ewloe, Flintshire, CH5 3YB
Tel: +44 (0) 1244 520 800

ZIMBAWBE

Elephant Hills Inter-Continental Resort, PO Box 300, Victoria Falls
Tel: +263 (0) 13 47 939

Leopard Rock Hotel, PO Box 171, Mutare
Tel: +263 (0) 20 60 115

Best of the rest
Where else to play

Every year, our team of golf travel writers select their most 'favourite fairways' for each region.
This year, to give you even more choice, they've also given us their pick of the rest of the best

THE AMERICAS

ARIZONA
The Boulders Golf Course,
34631 N. Tom Darlington
Drive, Carefree 85377
Arizona
Tel: +1 602 488 9028
Par 72 6155m (North)
Par 71 6336m (South)

TPC of Scottsdale, 17020 N.
Hayden Drive, Scottsdale
85260 Arizona
Tel: +1 602 585 3939
Par 71   5946m

Kierland Golf Club, 15636
Clubgate Drive, Scottsdale
85254 Arizona
Tel: +1 480 922 9283
Par 72   6377m
(Ironwood to Acacia)
Par 72   6321m
(Acacia to Mesquite)
Par 72   6416m
(Mesquite to Ironwood)

Alta Mesa Country Club,
1460 North Alta Mesa Drive,
Mesa 85205 Arizona
Tel: +1 602 827 9411
Par 72   6079m

Gold Canyon Golf Club,
16100 South Kings Ranch
Road, Apache Junction
85219 Arizona
Tel: +1 602 982 9449
Par 71   5490m

The Raven Golf Club at
Sabino Springs, 9945 East
Snyder Road Tucson 85749
Arizona
Tel: +1 520 749 3636
Par 71   5452m

Desert Fairways Golf Club,
813 West Calle Rosa, Casa
Grande 85222 Arizona
Tel: +1 520 723 4418
Par 70   4363m

London Bridge Golf Club,
2400 Clubhouse Drive, Lake
Havasu 86403 Arizona
Tel: +1 520 855 2719
Par 70   5757m (West)
Par 70   5638m (East)

Francisco Grande Resort &
Golf Club, 26000 Gila Bend
Highway, Casa Grande
85222 Arizona
Tel: +1 520 426 9205
Par 72   6378m

Verde Santa Fe Golf Course,
1045 South Verde Santa Fe
Parkway, Cottonwood 86325
Arizona
Tel: +1 520 634 5454
Par 71   5410m

THE CARIBBEAN
Manchester Country Club,
Mandeville, Jamaica

Tel: +1 876 962 2403
Par 35   2619m (9 holes)

Castle Harbour Golf Club, 6
Paynters Road, Hamilton
Parish, Bermuda
Tel: +1 441 298 6959
Par 71   5888m

Carenage Bay Beach & Golf
Club, Canouan Island, St
Vincent, St Vincent &
Grenadines
Tel: +1 784 458 8000
Par 72   5760m

Breezes Golf & Beach
Resort, PO Box 58, Runaway
Bay, Jamaica
Tel: +1 876 973 4820
Par 72   6201m

Port Royal Golf Course, PO
Box SN 189, Southampton,
Bermuda
Tel: +1 441 234 0974
Par 71   5999m

Sandy Lane Golf Club, St
James, Barbados
Tel: +1 246 432 1311
Par 72   6225m

Sandals, Ocho Rios, Jamaica
Tel: +1 876 975 0119
Par 71   5801m

Belmont Golf & Country
Club, PO Box WK 251,
Warwick, Bermuda
Tel: +1 441 236 6400
Par 70   5275m

Pok Ta Pok Club de Golf,
Cancun, Quintana Roo,
Mexico
Tel: +1 529 883 0871
Par 72   6068m

FLORIDA
The Golf Club of Amelia
Island, Amelia Island, Fl
32034
Tel: +1 904 277 8015
Par 72   5567m

Naples Beach Hotel And
Golf Club, 851 Gulf Shore
Boulevard North, Naples, Fl
39102
Tel: +1 941 261 2222
Par 72   6073m

Grenelefe Golf and Tennis
Resort, 3200 SR 546, Haines
City, Fl 33844
Tel]: +1 941 422 7511
Par 72   6219m (East)

Saddlebrook Resort, 5700
Saddlebrook Way, Wesley
Chapel, Tampa, Fl 33543
Tel: +1 813 973 1111
Par 70   6002m

Innisbrook Hilton Resort,
36750 US 19 N, Palm
Harbor, Fl 34684
Tel: +1 813 942 2000
Par 71 6480m (Copperhead)

Admiral Lehigh Golf Resort,
225 East Joel Boulevard,
Lehigh Acres, Fl 33972
Tel: +1 941 369 2121
Par 73 5397m (Mirror Lakes)

Wyndham Resort And Spa,
250 Racquet Club Road, Fort
Lauderdale, Fl 33326
Tel: +1 954 389 3300
Par 72   5393m
(Green Monster)

Palm Coast Resort, 300
Clubhouse Drive, Palm
Coast, Fl 32127
Tel: +1 904 445 300
Par 72   5725m

Ridgewood Lakes, 200 Eagle
Ridge Drive, Davenport, Fl
33837
Tel: +1 941 533 9183
Par 72   5986m

SOUTH CAROLINA
Arthur Hills Signature
Course, Palmetto Dunes
Resort, Hilton Head Island,
SouthCarolina 29938
Tel: +1 843 785 1138
Par 72   6303m

Hilton Head National,
Highway 278, Hilton Head
Island, South Carolina
29925
Te:l +1 843 842 5900.
Par 72   6165m

Wild Dunes, 10,000 Palmetto
Drive, Isle of Palms, South
Carolina 29451
Tel: +1 843 886 2180
Par 72 6224m (Links)

True Blue Golf Club, 900
Blue Stem Drive, Pawleys
Island, South Carolina
29585
Tel: +1 843 235 0900
Par 72   6481m

Dunes Golf & Beach Club,
9000 N. Ocean Blvd, Myrtle
Beach, South Carolina 29572
Tel: +1 843 449 5914
Par 72   6625m

Myrtlewood Golf Club, 1500
48th Ave North Ext. Myrtle
Beach, South Carolina 29578
Tel: +1 843 449 5134
Par72   6148m (Palmetto)

Old Carolina Golf Course,
89 Old Carolina Drive,
Bluffton, South Carolina
29910
Tel: +1 843 785 6363
Par 72   6296m

Wild Wing, 1000 Wild Wing
Blvd, Conway, South
Carolina 29526
Tel: +1 843 347 9464
Par72   6599m (Avocet)

Long Bay Golf Club, 350
Foxtail Drive, Myrtle Beach,
South Carolina 29568

Tel: +1 843 399 2222
Par72   6504m

Shipyard Golf Club, 45
Shipyard Drive, Hilton Head
Island, South Carolina
29928
Tel: +1 843 681 1785
Par72   6324m

NORTH CAROLINA
The National Golf Club, 1
Royal Troon Drive, 28374
Tel: +1 910 295 4300
Par72   6512m (Pinehurst)

The Pit Golf Links, 410 Pit
Link Ln, 28370
Tel: +1 910 944 1600
Par71   6035m (Pinehurst)

Tanglewood Park,
Championship, Hwy. 158 W.,
Clemmons, 27012
Tel: +1 336 778 6320
Par72   6421m

High Hampton Inn &
Country Club, Hwy. 107 S.,
28717
Tel: +1 828 743 2411
Par71   5497m (Cashiers)

Legacy Golf Links, U.S.
Highway 15-501 South,
28314
Tel: +1 910 944 8825
Par72   6401m (Aberdeen)

New England
TPC at River Highlands,
Golf Club Road, Cromwell,
Connecticut 06416
Tel: +1 860 635 2211
Par70   6236m

Owl's Nest Golf Club, Owl
Street, PO Box 470,
Campton, New Hampshire
03223
Tel: +1 603 726 3076
Par72   5864m

Brattleboro Country Club,
Upper Dummerston Road,
Brattleboro, Vermont
Tel: +1 802 257 7380
Par71   5747m

Lyman Orchards Golf Club,
Junction Routes 147 & 157,
Middlefield, Connecticut
06455
Tel: +1 860 349 1793
Par 71   6035m
(Gary Player Signature)
Par 72   6411m
(Trent Jones Championship)

Mount Washington Course,
Route 302, Bretton Woods,
New Hampshire 03575
Tel: +1 603 278 1000
Par 71   5627m

Sun Valley Golf Course, 329
Summer Street, Rehoboth,
Massachussetts 02769
Tel: +1 508 336 8686
Par 71   5837m

Nonesuch River Golf Club,
304 Gorham Road,
Scarborough, Maine 04074
Tel: +1 207 883 0007
Par 70   5760m

Haystack Golf Club, 70
Spyglass Drive, Wilmington,
Vermont
Tel: +1 802 464 8301
Par 71   5988m

Bridgton Highlands Country
Club, RR Box 1065,
Highland Ridge Road,
Bridgton, Maine 04009
Tel: +1 207 647 3491
Par 72   5540m

Amherst Golf Club, 365
South Pleasant Street,
Amherst, Massachussetts
01002
Tel: +1 413 256 6894
Par 35 2793m (9-hole)

ASIA AND THE PACIFIC

AUSTRALIA
Lake Karriyup Country
Club, Summerton Road,
Calista 6167, Perth, Western
Australia
Tel: +61 (0) 8 447 5777
Par 72   6100m

INDONESIA & CHINA
Bali Golf & Country Club,
P.O. Box 12, Nusa Dua,
80361 Bali
Tel: +62 (0) 361 771 791
Par 72   6254m

Finna Golf & Country Club,
Jl. Raya Basari Prigen,
Pandaan 67157
Tel: +62 (0) 343 634 888
Par 72   6345m

Bumi Serpong Damai
Course, Jalan Bukit Golf 1,
Sektor VI & VII, Serpong,
Tangerang 15310
Tel: +62 (0) 21 537 0290
Fax: +62 (0) 21 537 02888
Par 72   6544m

Gunung Geulis Country
Club, Jl. Pasir Angin, Gadoz
Bogor
Tel: +62 (0) 251 241 500
Par 71   6085m (West)
Par 72   6056m (East)

Imperial Klub Golf, 2709 Jl.
Pulau Golf, Lippo Karawaci,
Tangerang 15811, Jawa Barat
Tel: +62 (0) 21 546 0120
Par 72   6316m

THAILAND
Navatanee Golf Club, 22
Moo 1, Sereeethai.
Kannayao, Bangkok 10230
Tel: +66 (0) 237 61 034-6

The Imperial Lake View
Hotel & Golf Club, 79 Moo
4, Hubgrapong-Pranburi Rd.,
Samphraya Cha-Am,
Petchburi 76120
Tel: +66 (0) 32 520 091
Par 72   6054m

The Rose Garden Golf Club,
53/1 Moo 4, Petchkasem
Highway Road, Sam Phran,
Nakhon Pathom 73110
Tel: +66 (0) 332 2769-71
Par 72   5884m

Blue Canyon Country Club,
165 Moo 1`, Thepkasattri
Road, Maikaw, Thalang,
Phuket 83140
Tel: +66 (0) 76 327 440-7
Par 72   5772m

The Majestic Creek Country
Club, 1645 Moo 4, Taptai,
Hua Hin, Prachuab Khiri
Khan 77110
Tel: +66 (0) 32 520 102-6
Par 72   5811m

MALAYSIA
Palm Resort Golf & Country
Club, Jalan Persiiaran Golf,
off Jalan Jumbo, 81250
Senai, Johor
Tel: +60 (0) 7599 6222
Par 72   6051m (Alamanda)

Awana Golf & Country Club,
Km 13 Genting Highlands,
69000 Genting Highlands,
Pahang
Tel: +60 (0) 3211 3015
Par 71   6064m

Desaru Golf & Country
Club, Tanjong Penawar,
81907 Kota Tinggi, Johor
Tel: +60 (0) 7822 1187
Par 72   6043m

Starhill Golf & Country
Club,
6.5km, Kg. Maju Jaya,
Kempas Lama, 81330
Sekudai, Johor Bahru, Johor
Tel: +60 (0) 7556 6325-6
Par 72   6249m (Bintang)
Par 72   6298m (Bukit)

Perangsang Templer Golf
Club, No.1 Jln. Ipoh-Rawang
Km.20, Rekreasi Templer,
1800 Rawang, Selangor
Tel: +60 (0) 3691 0022
Par 72   6227m

AFRICA AND THE MIDDLE EAST

INDIAN OCEAN
Trou aux Biches Village
Hotel Trou Aux Biches,
Mauritius
Tel: +230 (0) 265 6562

Paradis Hotel, Mauritius
Tel: +230 (0) 683 6773

Gymkhana Club Vacoas,
Mauritius
Tel: +230 (0) 696 1404

SOUTH AFRICA
San Lameer, PO Box 88,
Southbroom 4277
Tel: +27 (0) 39 313 5141
Par 72   5477m

Hans Merensky, PO Box 67,
Phalaborwa 1390
Tel: +27 (0) 15 781 3931
Par 72   6074m

Royal Cape, Ottery Road,
174 Wynberg, 7800 Cape
Tel: +27 (0) 21 761 6551
Par 72   6174m

Stellenbosch, PO Box 277,
Stellenbosch 7600
Tel: +27 (0) 21 880 0103
Par 74   6149m

Houghton, PO Box 87240,
Lower Houghton 2198
Tel: +27 (0) 11 728 7337
Par 72   6506m

Selbourne, PO Box 2,
Pennington 4182
Tel: +27 (0) 323 975 1133
Par 72   5443m

Wild Coast, PO Box 23, Port
Edward 4295
Tel: +27 (0) 39 305 9111
Par 71   5807m

Royal Johannesburg, PO Box
46017, Orange Grove,
Johannesburg 2119
Tel: +27 (0) 11 640 3021
Par 72   6660m (two courses)

Clovelly, PO Box 22364, Fish
Hoek, Cape Town 7975
Tel: +27 (0) 21 782 1118
Par 72   5857m

EUROPE

ENGLAND: NORTH & MIDLANDS
Kenilworth, Crewe Lane,
Kenilworth, Warwicks
Tel: +44 (0) 1926 854 296
Par 71   5864m

Leominster, Fort Bridge,
Leominster, Hereford,
HR6 OLE
Tel: +44 (0) 1568 612 863
Par 69   5513m

Branston Golf And Country
Club, Burton Road, Burton-
on-Trent, Staffs, DE14 3DP
Tel: +44 (0) 1283 512 211
Par 72   6078

Patshull Park Hotel Golf &
Country Club, Pattingham,
Wolverhampton, WV6 7HR
Tel: +44 (0) 1902 700 100
Par 72   5863m

Lincoln, Torksey, Lincoln,
Lincs, LN1 2EG
Tel: +44 (0) 1427 718 210
Par 71   5886m

Shaw Hill Hotel Golf &
Country Club, Preston Road,
Whittle-le-Woods, Nr
Chorley, Lancs, PR6 7PP
Tel: +44 (0) 1257 269 221
Par 73   5705m

Aldwark Manor, Aldwark,
Alne, York, YO6 5AE
Tel: +44 (0) 1347 838 533
Par 70   5642m

Pannal ,Folifoot Road,
Pannal, Harrogate, HG3 1ES
Tel: +44 (0) 1423 871 641
Par 72   6055m

Mount Oswald, Mount
Oswald Manor, South Road,
Durham, DH1 37Q.
Tel: +44 (0) 191 386 7527
Par 69   5578m

Malton And Norton, Welham
Park, Malton, N Yorks, YO17 9QE
Tel: +44 (0) 1653 692 959
Par 71   5903m

ENGLAND SOUTH & WALES
Royal Cromer, Cromer
Norfolk
Tel: +44 (0) 1263 512 884
Par 72   5950m

Royal Cinque Ports, Deal,
Kent
Tel: +44 (0) 1304 374 007
Par 72   6204m

Woburn Golf & Country
Club, Milton Keynes,
Buckinghamshire
Tel: +44 (0) 1908 370 756
Par 72   6376m (Dukes)

Ferndown, Dudsbury, Dorset
Tel: +44 (0) 1202 874 602
Par 71   6184m

Manor House, Castle Combe,
Wiltshire
Tel: +44 (0) 1249 782 982
Par 73   6340m

Little Aston, Sutton
Coldfield, West Midlands
Tel: +44 (0) 121 353 2942
Par 72   6099m

Notts Golf Club, Kirky in
Ashfield, Nottinghamshire
Tel:+44 (0)1623 753 225
Fax: +44 (0) 1623 753 655
Par 72   6428m

Tenby Golf Club, Tenby,
Pembrokeshire
Tel: +44 (0) 1834 844 447
Par 69   6224m

Denham Golf Club, Denham,
Buckinghamshire
Tel: +44 (0) 1895 835 777
Par 72   6880m

Frinton Golf Club, Frinton-
on-Sea, Essex
Tel: +44 (0) 1255 674 618
Par 71   5728m

FRANCE: SOUTH
Golf de Biarritz-Le Phare, 2
Avenue Edith Cavell, 64200
Biarritz
Tel: +33 (0) 55 90 37 180
Par 69   5059m

Makila Golf Cl;ub, Route de
Cambo-Biarritz, 64200
Bassussarry
Tel: +33 (0) 55 95 84 242
Par 72   5790m

Golf Club d'Hossegor,
Avenue du Golf, 40150
Hossegor
Tel: +33 (0) 55 84 35 699
Fax: +33 (0) 55 84 39 852
Par 71   5867m

Golf Country Club de
Cannes Mougins, 175 avenue
du Golf, 06250 Mougins
Tel: +33 (0) 49 37 57 913
Par 72   5889m

Golf de la Grande-Motte, BP
16, 34280 La Grande-Motte
Tel: +33 (0) 46 75 60 500
Par 72   5768m

FRANCE: NORTH
Golf du Touquet, Avenue de
Golf, 62520 Le Touquet
Tel: +33 (0) 32 10 62 800
Par 72   6330m (La Mer)

Golf National, 2 Avenue du
Golf, 78280 Guyancourt
Tel: +33 (0) 13 04 33 600
Par 72   6155m (Albatros)

Golf de la Baule, Domaine
de St. Denac, 44117 Saint-
Andre des Eaux
Tel: +33 (0) 24 06 04 618
Par 72   5769m (Rouge)

Golf de Royan, Maine
Gaudin, 17420 Saint-Palais
sur Mer
Tel: +33 (0) 54 62 31 624
Par 71   5970m

Golf International Les
Bordes, 41220 Saint-Laurent
Nouan
Tel: +33 (0) 25 48 77 213
Par 72   6023m

IRELAND NORTH & EAST
Narin & Portnoo, County
Donegal
Tel: +353 (0) 75 45107
Par 69   5322m

Bundoran, Co. Donegal
Tel: +353 (0) 72 413202
Par 69   5599m

Greenore, Co. Louth
Tel: +353 (0) 42 73212 /
73678
Par 71   6514m

Blacklion, Toam, Co. Cavan
Tel: +353 (0) 72 53024
Par 72   5614m

Delvin Castle, Clonyn, Co.
Westmeath
Tel: +353 (0) 44 64315 /
64733
Par 70   5800 m

Boyle, Co. Roscommon
Tel: +353 (0) 79 62594
Par 67   4868m

IRELAND SOUTH & WALES
Callan, Co. Kilkenny
Tel: +353 (0) 56 25136/25949
Par 72   5831m

Parknsilla, Co. Kerry
Tel: +353 (0) 64 45122
Par 70   5400m

Limerick Golf and Country
Club, Ballyneety, Co. Limerick
Tel: +353 (0) 61351 881
Par 72   6137m

Tralee, West Barrow, Co.
Kerry
Tel: +353 (0) 66 36379
Par 71   5939m

Wicklow, Dunbur Rd,
Wicklow
Tel: +353 (0) 404 67379
Par 71   5556m

Dungarvan,
Knocknagranagh, Co.
Waterford
Tel: +353 (0) 58 41605 /
43310
Par 72   5998m

ITALY
Circolo Golf Is Molas, P.O.
Box 49, 09010 Pula
(Cagliari), Sardinia
Tel: +39 070 924 1013/4
Par 72   6383m

Golf Club Punta Ala, Via del
Golf, 1-58040 Punta Ala
(Grosseto)
Tel: +39 0564 922 121
Par 72   6213m

Il Picciolo Golf Club, Via
Picciolo, 1-95012 Castiglione
di Sicilia

Tel: +39 0942 986 171
Par 72   5870m

Golf Club Monticello, Via
Volta, 4-22070 Cassina
Rizzardi (Como)
Tel: +39 031 928 055
Par 72   6028m

PORTUGAL ALGARVE
Palmares Golf, Meia Praia,
8600 Lagos
Tel: +351 282 762 961
Par 71   5614m

Golf Ria Formosa, Quinta do
Lago, 8135 Almansil
Tel: +351 289 390 700
Par 72   5804m

Penina Golf Club, P.O. Box
146 Penina, 8502 Portimao
Codex
Tel: +351 282 415 415
Par 73   5671m

Parque da Floresta, Vale do
Poco, Budens, 8650 Vila do
Bispo
Tel: +351 282 695 335
Par 72   5324m

Golf Pinheiros Altos, Quinta
do Lago, 8135 Almansil
Tel: +351 289 394 340
Par 72   5291m

Troia Golf Club, Apartado
106, 2902 Setubal Codex
Tel: +351 265 499 335/494
112
Par 72   5831m

Aroeira Golf Club, Herdade
de Aroeira, Fonte da Telha,
2825 Monte Caparica
Tel: +351 212 971 345
Par 72   5700m

Praia D'El Rey Country
Club, Vale de Janelas,
Apartado 2, 2510 Obidos
Tel: +351 262 905 005
Par 72   6056m

Belas Club de Campo,
Alamela do Aqueduto, 2745
Belas
Tel: +351 219 62 3536/37
Par 72   6065m

Golf Quinta da Marinha,
Casa 36, 2750 Cascais
Tel: +351 214 869 881/9
Par 71   5606m

SCOTLAND
Marriott Dalmahoy Hotel
and Country Club,
Kirknewton, Midlothian
EH27 8EB
Tel: +44 (0) 131 3358010
Par 72   6105m (East)

Brora Golf Club, Golf Road,
Brora KW9 6QS
Tel: +44 (0) 1408 621417
Par 69   5586m

Loch Lomond, Rossdhu
House, Luss by Alexandria,
Dunbartonshire G83 8NT
Tel: +44 (0) 1436 655555
Par 72   6455m

Royal Troon, Craigend Road,
Ayrshire KA 10 6EP
Tel: +44 (0) 1292 311555
Par 73   6473m

St Andrews, Fife KY16 9JA
Tel: +44 (0) 1334 466666
Par 72   6003m(Old)

Ballater, Victoria Road,
Aberdeenshire AB35 5QX
Tel: +44 (0) 13397 55567
Par 69   5588m

Tain, Chapel Road, Ross-
shire IV19 1PA
Tel: +44 (0)1862 892314
Par 70   5734m

Buchanan Castle, Drymen,
Glasgow G63 OHY
Tel: +44 (0) 1360 660307
Par 69   5540m

Machrie Hotel and Golf
Links, Port Ellen, Isle of
Islay, Argyll PA42 7AN
Tel: +44 (0) 1496 302310
Par 70   5693m

Southerness, Kirkbean,
Dumfries DG2 8AZ
Tel: +44 (0) 1387 880677
Par 72   6003m

SPAIN: ANDALUCIA &
MURCIA
Los Naranjos Golf Club,
Apartado 64, 29660 Nueva
Andalucia (Malaga)
Tel: +34 952 815 206
Par 72   6038m

La Cala Golf & Country
Club, La Cala de Mijas,
29647 Mijas Costa (Malaga)
Tel: +34 952 589 100
Par 73   5723m (North)
Par 71   5440m (South)

Almenara Golf club, Avenida
de Los Cotijos s/n, 11310
Sotogrande (Cadiz)
Tel: +34 956 790 111
Par 72   6188m

San Roque Club, Apartado
127, 11360 San Roque
(Cadiz)
Tel: +34 956 613 030
Par 72   6048m

Monte Mayor Golf Club,
Urb. Los Naranjos Country
Club, 29660 Marbella
(Malaga)
Tel: +34 952 113 088
Par 70   5354m

SPAIN: BALEARICS
Capdepera Golf Club, Roca
Viva Ctra. Arta - Cala Rajada
at km 3.5, E-07570 Arta,
Mallorca
Tel: +971 56 58 75
Par 72   5863m

Club de Golf Vall d1Or Ctra.
Porto Colom Cala d1Or at
km 8, E-07660 Cala d1Or,
Mallorca
Tel: +971 83 70 01
Par 71   5532m

Canyamel Golf Ctra. de las
Cuevas, Urb. Canyamel, E-
07589 Capdepera, Mallorca
Tel: +971 84 13 13
Par 73   5785m

Son Antem Academia de
Golf Ctra. de Palma -
Llucmajor at km 4, E-07620

Llucmajor, Mallorca
Tel: +971 66 11 24
Par 72   6002m

Golf Son Servera Urb. Costa
de los Pinos, E-07550 Son
Servera, Mallorca
Tel: +971 85 00 96
Par 72   5899m

Club Pollensa Ctra. de Palma
- Pollensa at km 49.3,
E07460 Pollensa, Mallorca
Tel: +971 53 32 16
Par 35   2534m

Club Son Vida Urb. Son
Vida, E-07013 Palma,
Mallorca
Tel: +971 79 12 10
Par 72   5651m

Pula Golf Ctra. Son Servera -
Capdepera at km 3, E-07559
Son Servera, Mallorca
Tel: +971 56 74 81
Par 71   5946m

Club de Golf Ibiza Ctra.
Santa Eulalia del Rio,
Apartado de Correos 1270,
E-07800 Ibiza
Tel: +971 19 61 18
Par 72   5818m

Club Son Parc Apartado de
Correos 634, Mahon,
Menorca
Tel: +971 35 90 59
Par 72   5529m

SPAIN: CATALONIA &
VALENCIA
Golf d'Aro, Apartado de
Correos 429, 17250 Playa de
Aro (Gerona)
Tel: +34 972 826 900
Par 72   6004m

Apartado de Correos 601,
17080 (Girona)
Tel: +34 972 171 641
Par 72   6058m

Caldes International Golf
Course, Cami Antic de
Caldes a Sta. Eulalia s/n,
Apdo. 200, 08140 Caldes de
Montbin
Tel: +34 93 865 3828
Par 72   5912m

Club de Golf Escorpion,
Ctra. Sn Antonio Benageber-
Betera, km.3, 46117 Betera
Tel: +34 96 160 1211
Par 72   6091m

Club de Campo del
Mediterraneo, Urbanizacion
La Coma, s/n, 12190 Borriol
Tel: +34 964 321 227
Par 72   6038m

SWITZERLAND
Golf Club Patriziale Ascona,
Via al Lido 81, 6612 Ascona
Tel: +41 (0) 91 791 21 32
Par 71   5948m

Bad Ragaz, CH 7310
Tel: +41 (0) 81 303 37 17
Par 70   5494m

Golf And Country Club
Blumisberg, CH 3184,
Wunnewil
Tel: +41 (0) 26 496 34 38
Par 73   5707m

Breitenloo, Untere Zaune 9,
CH 8001 Zurich
Tel: +41 (0) 1 836 40 80
Par 72   5750m

Golfpark Holzhausern, CH
6343 Rotkreuz
Tel: +41 (0) 41 799 70 10
Par 73   6050m

Golf De La Gruyere, La
Chateau, CH 1649 Pont-La-
Ville
Tel: +41 (0) 26 414 91 11
Fax: +41 (0) 26 414 92 20
Par 68   4740m

Interlaken, Postfach 110
Tel: +41 (0) 33 823 60 16
Par 72   5875m

Lugano, CH 6983 Magliaso
Tel: +41 (0) 91 606 15 57
Par 71   5775m

Luzern, Dietschiberg, CH
606 Luzern
Tel: +41 (0) 41 420 97 87
Par 72   5760m

Montreux, Route d'Evian,
CH 1860 Aigle
Tel: +41 (0) 24 466 46 16
Par 72   5828m

The Great Golf Hotel Guide

Published by Big Publishing Ltd.
22 Stephenson Way
London NW1 2HD
United Kingdom
Tel: +44 (0) 20 7383 2335
Fax: +44 (0) 20 7383 0357
Email: gghginfo@bigpublishing.com

Visit the world's leading golf web site at:
www.golftravel4u.com

PUBLISHER: Peter Gould
ASSOCIATE PUBLISHER: Richard Barnes
EDITORS: Trevor Parsons & Roger St. Pierre
ASSISTANT EDITOR: Gaynor Edwards
MEMBERSHIP SERVICES MANAGER: Joanna Fay
MEMBERSHIP SERVICES ASSISTANT: Joanne Easton
MEMBERSHIP DIRECTORS: Richard Barnes, Georgia Saxon, Maria Ortega Noguerol
ART DIRECTOR: Dominic Salmon
ART EDITOR: Andy Medlock
RESEARCH EDITOR: Charlie Parsons
PRODUCTION & CIRCULATION MANAGER: Lucy Martin
CONTRIBUTORS: Peter Burrington, Nigel Coombes, Jacque Delgarde, Michael
Gedye, Peter Jolly, Robert Klammer, Roger St. Pierre, Paul Trow,
ACCOUNTS: Iream Siddiqui & Duncan Hussey
ORIGINATION: Neon Graphics Ltd & Saffron Reprographics Ltd.
PRINTING & BINDING: Goodhead Print Ltd.
SPECIAL THANKS TO: Alain Chervaz, Bill Jones, David Russell

**Further copies of *The Great Golf Hotel Guide* are available from
bookshops or direct from the publishers (price £9.99,
including free post and packing). Write to: Book Sales, Great
Golf Hotel Guide, Big Publishing Ltd, 22 Stephenson Way,
London NW1 2HD or phone +44 (0) 20 7383 2335.**

PICTURE ACKNOWLEDGEMENTS
Photographs used to illustrate entries in The Great Golf Hotel have been supplied by the hotels and resorts concerned.
Pictures featured in the regional intros and general information pages of the Guide have been kindly supplied by
Michael Gedye, by Great Golf Hotels members and by the regional and national tourist boards of the countries
and regions covered and remain their copyright. We gratefully acknowledge the help of the appropriate regional
and national tourist boards for Austria, Australia, Barbados, North and South Carolina, Denmark, Dubai,
England, France, Florida, Germany, Greece, Indonesia, the Republic of Ireland, Northern Ireland, Israel, Italy,
Jamaica, Malaysia, Mauritius, Morocco, Portugal, Qatar, Spain, Sweden, Switzerland, Turkey, Scotland, South
Africa, Tunisia, Thailand and Wales.
The cover illustration by Kevin O'Brien was exclusively commissioned for *The Great Golf Hotel Guide*.